IET COMPUTING SERIES 40

E-learning Methodologies

Other volumes in this series:

E-learning Methodologies

Fundamentals, technologies and applications

Edited by
Mukta Goyal, Rajalakshmi Krishnamurthi and
Divakar Yadav

The Institution of Engineering and Technology

Published by The Institution of Engineering and Technology, London, United Kingdom

The Institution of Engineering and Technology is registered as a Charity in England & Wales (no. 211014) and Scotland (no. SC038698).

© The Institution of Engineering and Technology 2021

First published 2021

The Institution of Engineering and Technology
Michael Faraday House
Six Hills Way, Stevenage
Herts, SG1 2AY, United Kingdom

www.theiet.org

British Library Cataloguing in Publication Data
A catalogue record for this product is available from the British Library

ISBN 978-1-83953-120-0 (hardback)
ISBN 978-1-83953-121-7 (PDF)

Typeset in India by MPS Limited
Printed in the UK by CPI Group (UK) Ltd, Croydon

Contents

About the editors

Mukta Goyal is an Assistant Professor in the Department of Computer Science and Engineering, Jaypee Institute of Information Technology, Noida, India. She attained her doctorate in the domain of Soft Computing from Jaypee Institute of Information Technology, Noida. She has over 20 years of teaching experience at both undergraduate and postgraduate levels. Mukta has organized special sessions in conferences and is in the program committee of various conferences of repute. She has many national and international research publications to her credit. She is an active researcher in the field of soft computing, e-learning, e-governance, blockchain, and machine learning. She has guided various M.Tech. theses, more than 100 B.Tech. projects. Presently, she is guiding three Ph.D. scholars.

Rajalakshmi Krishnamurthi is currently working as an Assistant Professor (Senior Grade) in the Department of Computer Science and Engineering at Jaypee Institute of Information Technology, Noida, India. She is a senior member of IEEE, a professional member of ACM, SIAM, and CSI. She is currently serving as a treasurer, Delhi ACM-W chapter. She has over 17 years of teaching experience both at undergraduate and postgraduate levels. She has more than 50 research publications in various reputed international journals, book chapters, and international conferences. She is serving as a guest editor in Springer Nature. Her research interest includes Internet of Things, cloud computing, mobile computing, and e-learning. She has introduced and developed several courses at B.Tech and M.Tech levels. She has refereed in reputed journals like IEEE, IoT, wireless networks, peer-to-peer Springer. She has been a technical program member in several international conferences. Currently, she is supervising two Ph.D. scholars and one Ph.D. completed. She has supervised more than 14 M.Tech theses and 100 B.Tech major projects.

Divakar Yadav is currently working as an Associate Professor in the Department of Computer Science and Engineering at National Institute of Technology, Hamirpur (HP), India. Prior to joining this institute, he had worked at Madan Mohan Malaviya University of Technology, Gorakhpur (UP), India as an Associate Professor and Jaypee Institute of Information Technology, Noida, India as an Assistant as well as an Associate Professor. He did his undergraduate degree (B.Tech) in Computer Science and Engineering in 1999 from IET, Lucknow, postgraduate degree (M.Tech) in Information Technology in 2005 from Indian Institute of Information Technology, Allahabad and Ph.D. in Computer Science and Engineering in 2010 from Jaypee Institute of Information Technology, Noida. He also worked as a post-doctoral fellow at the University of Carlos III, Madrid, Spain between 2011 and 2012. He supervised four Ph.D. theses, 22 M.Tech dissertations, and many undergraduate projects. He also published more than 85 research articles in reputed international journals and conference proceedings. His area of research includes information retrieval and machine learning. He is a senior member of IEEE.

Preface

E-learning is the twenty-first century learning where learning materials are shared on an e-learning platform for learners using various e-learning technologies and techniques. The novel COVID-19 pandemic all over the world has also given a new direction of the teaching–learning process. Unlike wars, recession, natural calamities, it has affected everyone in a different manner. The education sector becomes very uncertain about the learning of participants during this COVID-19 period. COVID-19 urges to move the education sector to e-learning systems for the teaching–learning process. Thus, the necessity of e-learning systems requires smart systems that are more student-centric learning rather than lecture and note-taking. The aim is to provide readers with current research results of the smart e-learning environment in terms of pedagogies, techniques, and technologies.

The book is organized into three parts:

Part I: Introduction and pedagogies of e-learning systems with intelligent techniques

The first part, which includes four chapters, is focused on the introduction of e-learning system and pedagogies of e-learning systems with intelligent techniques. The second part that has discussed the technologies assisted in the e-learning system consists of seven chapters. Finally, the last section illustrates the two case studies in the current scenario. Lastly, the book has concluded the research work that has been done so far in the e-learning scenario and future prospects.

First, this book starts with the edited author's chapter Introduction that discussed how classroom teaching evolves to smart learning. The chapter also explores that the latest technologies such as IoT, cloud, mobile learning, big data, augmented reality (AR) can be used to enhance the e-learning platforms. This chapter highlighted the research gaps in current e-learning systems.

The chapter "Goal-oriented adaptive e-learning" introduces a different approach by captivating the continuous improvement of learners as per their learning goals to refine their learning paths after every level covered in the course. The chapter considers the fact that a learner's ability to grasp learning material is neither a predetermined factor nor can it be computed uniformly for all learners. Rather, a learner progresses to hone her grasping capability continuously. An e-learning system should integrate these features to evaluate such enhancements in the context of learners' predefined goals.

The chapter "Predicting student's behavioral engagement in microlearning using learning analytics model" discusses the student's behavioral engagement in microlearning. The study in this chapter aims to predict the student's behavioral engagement in microlearning using the developed learning analytics model. Prediction results using neural network model and logistic regression model are compared to choose the best prediction method. The findings in this chapter are important for future learning analytics research toward predicting student's behavioral engagement in the microlearning environment as these techniques had not been implemented widely.

The chapter "Student performance prediction for adaptive e-learning system" explores the learner's learning style, personality, and knowledge level to classify his/her performance accordingly. An intuitionistic fuzzy genetic algorithm is used to aggregate the performance of the e-learner whereas *K*NN classification algorithm is used to classify the learners. The result shows 78% accuracy to classify the learner according to learning style, personality level, and knowledge level.

Part II: Technologies in e-learning

The chapter "Artificial intelligence in e-learning" discusses a deeper examination and appreciation of AI and machine learning as e-Learning. It is presented to understand the experiential learning, access to extensive educational resources, online tutoring, academic connectivity, advanced grading, and measurement, creating a comprehensive curriculum, crowdsourced learning, smart learning software. Authors also discuss the cutting-edge competition in the market, and job-losses in every sector, education/skilling oneself, which is the need of the hour. Getting educated in a brick-mortar setup is far-fetched when an individual has their current on-going engagement, be it job/studies. Hence, the need for online education would play a key role.

The chapter "Mobile learning as the future of e-learning" discusses mobile learning as an e-learning tool. E-learning plays a crucial role in the growth of an adult and thus the future of a nation in today's age of information and communication technology. In traditional learning, a successful teacher cannot teach at multiple locations in a single moment. E-learning neutralizes this drawback of modern learning and becomes a very effective tool for the individual's intellectual development and helps one to create an intelligent society. Among the various new trends in e-learning, mobile learning is the big revolutionary measure and has lots of scopes and potential to transform India's educational system.

The chapter "Smart e-learning transition using big data: perspectives and opportunities" discusses the transition of information such as emotions of the people when they are interacting with the computers into a smart e-learning. It also discusses how users will interact with the content by using headphones ON. While interacting with the content, their emotions can be captured by the facial recognition system to bring real classroom learning into the existing e-learning system. The online learning platforms generate massive learner behavioral data and educational data. Transforming these data into information and knowledge for educational decision-making, teaching optimization, and academic improvement is the service of big data in e-learning. The authors also discuss the issues for effective analysis and utilization of the data to improve the quality of e-learning. The chapter also provides an overview of the big data techniques such as prediction, clustering, relationship mining, structure discovery, and various tools used for big data analytics in e-learning.

The chapter "E-learning using big data and cloud computing" provides an enriched learning experience, including interactive features to challenge the user's depth of understanding and level of preservation. The chapter provides insight into the drawbacks of the conventional e-learning model, e-learning using the technology of cloud computing, and big data. It also shows how big data and cloud computing are integrated to provide support for e-learning. Moreover, it uncovers some of the case studies in e-learning industries and concludes with challenges.

The chapter "E-learning through virtual laboratory environment: developing of IoT workshop course based on Node-RED" discusses the growth and opportunities in the field of the IoT. Further, it discusses the requirement and adaptation of IoT to various application systems, such as smart city, smart grid, smart healthcare system, smart transportation, to enhance the smartness of such systems. The chapter discusses the need for preparing engineering graduates to face this demand for IoT technology. The chapter presents the requirements of offering IoT courses, Node-RED that is a programming environment, course contents delivered, learning outcomes, course assessments, projects, and results achieved through this course by students.

The chapter "Mnemonics in e-learning using augmented reality" discusses the concern of e-learning systems to motivate the participants and reduce the isolation. Advancement of information communication technology (ICT) has the potential to adapt the technology in education that influences students and motivates them to learn and participate while learning. The student should not feel isolated during the learning process by using the online learning method. AR application has the ability to involve participants in a realistic word. E-learning using the AR tool allows students to be more attentive and effective in learning processes. AR-/virtual reality-based system can set milestone to reduce knowledge loss.

The chapter "E-learning tools and smart campus: boon or bane during COVID-19" discusses the sudden spread of novel coronavirus COVID-19 across the world, an aspect of the education system. The authors discuss the e-learning tools due to the quick closure of universities and schools for public health safety during the COVID-19 pandemic. These tools have become a catalyst for searching innovative solutions within a short span of time. To overcome this new and challenging situation, e-learning tools have become the new educational policy and practice for virtual classrooms. It also presents an analysis of various e-learning tools for synchronous and asynchronous learning. It also focuses on the various health issues arising due to the excessive exposure of everyone to screens with the growing usage of online learning.

Part III: Case studies

The chapter "Bioinformatics algorithms: course, teaching pedagogy and assessment" discusses the case study for presenting various modes of in-class lecture delivery, student–instructor interaction, and topic discussion. The aim of using numerous forms of teaching–learning pedagogy is for justifying and achieving the learning outcomes of the course. The chapter also discusses the concept development and exploration, course-related material design and development, and evaluation and analysis. The measurement framework is developed based on the following criteria of intuitive capability levels, in-class response, topic understanding (based on student's informal and formal feedback), and marks-based evaluations. This inherently incorporates certain evaluation practices followed in this course. This chapter also illustrates the possibility of life cycle analysis in teaching the course of bioinformatics algorithms. Having a high cohesion with bioinformatics, the course helps in offering computational solutions to sustainability-related issues. Further, based on NBA requirements, the course outcomes are also measured as per the given directives.

The chapter "Active learning in E-learning: a case study to teach elliptic curve cryptosystem, its fast computational algorithms and authentication protocols for resource constraint RFID-sensor integrated mobile devices" discusses the implementation of interactive active learning processes in UPES. An interactive active learning process is applied to the network security course having an elliptic curve cryptography module in all of its units. The active learning process involves students to approach their preferred way of learning rather than a passive classroom teaching–learning methodology. After applying the active learning process over teaching and evaluation of discussed contents, it has been observed that the proposed active learning process is much better than traditional learning and shows improvements in all evaluations. Both short- and long-term evaluations are performed to study the impact of the proposed active learning process. Results show that the proposed approach is comparatively much better in all scenarios.

Part I

Introduction and pedagogies of e-learning systems with intelligent techniques

Chapter 1

Introduction

Mukta Goyal[1], Rajalakshmi Krishnamurthi[1] and Divakar Yadav[2]

The recent advancement in technology and networking capabilities impacts the education industry on a greater perspective globally. The education institutes need enhancement to meet the growing demand for new digital and interactive learning strategies. It is observed that there is an increasing demand for digitized lifelong learning methods contrary to specialized university degrees. The contemporary learners expect the education system to provide a sophisticated learning environment, with dynamic learning content, which enables students to learn anytime and anywhere across the globe. The basic step that must be implemented by any government is the equitable education in which remote areas of the society get schooling facility and learning opportunities. E-learning can help society in an effective manner due to healthy relationships among staff and knowledge distribution among users.

There are many issues in e-learning such as advantages, disadvantages, challenges, and critical success factors. These issues have been grouped according to the stakeholders of e-learning, where the stakeholder is anyone who is a constituent of an organization, e.g., learners, instructors, course designers, employers, educational institutes, accreditation bodies Improvement in the quality of education is one of the issues of sustainable development goals. To fulfill the goal of sustainable development, UNESCO has designed Education for All (EFA) Movement. The EFA movement can work well through e-learning that transfers knowledge to a large area of the society [1].

Success factors of e-learning are different in a context, e.g., in developing countries, in which the main focus is on learners and their instructors while some of the hindrances are the accessibility of infrastructure, availability of resources, etc. In developed countries, the main focus is on the quality of information as well as lifelong learning [2,3]. This chapter explores the different methodologies and techniques that help one to upgrade the e-learning system.

[1]Department of Computer Science and Engineering, Jaypee Institute of Information Technology, Noida, India
[2]Department of Computer Science and Engineering, National Institute of Technology, Hamirpur, India

This e-learning facility enhances the learning ability of individuals without any constraints on age, time, and boundaries of the learners. E-learning describes the virtual classroom learning environment where the web-based learning tools along with the Internet facilitate the learners. Learning management system (LMS) is a well-known popular platform of e-learning.

The web-based learning tool enables tutors to record lectures, design content of course, download learning materials, upload assignments, and submissions, student feedback systems, learner registration, learner development tracking, and identify the learning gaps. However, e-learning is not to be perceived as a substitution of traditional class teaching-learning methodology. E-learning is generally classified into the following three ways:

- *Partial classroom learning*: In this type of learning, the traditional class environment is provided as an infrastructural utility of learners, and then remaining involves a remote learning facility.
- *Distance learning (remote classroom learning)*: It is a fully remote learning method with constraints to spatial and temporal entities.
- *Smart distance learning (anytime anywhere)*: The concept of teaching and learning methodology under this classification is further classified into different categories such as asynchronous and synchronous learning, blended learning, distance learning, or Classroom 2.0 and smart learning. The next section explains the different methodologies used in the e-learning scenario in detail.

1.1   Asynchronous learning and synchronous learning

In asynchronous learning, learners can learn whenever they want. Both the learner and teacher work in offline mode. The mode of asynchronous learning is e-mail, web, and discussion forums for a learner. Learners access the learning material anytime, anywhere, whereas the teacher can post the learning material and assignments. The drawback of asynchronous learning is that it does not motivate the learner as he/she can study at their own pace. The student may feel isolated and demotivated.

Real-time learning through online chat and videoconferencing is to be known as synchronous e-learning. It allows teachers and students to interact with each other then and there itself during the learning session. The advantage of synchronous learning is that students can ask queries and doubts during the class session, which reduces the isolation of the students. Due to the binding of time to attend a specific lecture schedule, asynchronous and synchronous learning have been measured as cognitive participation and personal participation, respectively. Cognitive participation increases reflection and ability to process information, whereas personal participation reflects increased motivation [4].

Synchronous e-learning can be seen from different perspectives such as the student's perspective, lecturer perspective, and administrative perspective [5]. From a student's perspective, students are required to have live sessions with the facilities such as software installation, correct audio level, up-to-date machine, and network specifications. Students must ensure that there is enough interaction between the teacher and student, in which the student should not feel fatigued during a session of 55 min as there is enough face-to-face content. The teacher perspective reflects that the lecturing content should be more interactive and understandable, so that students do not get bored and lost in the slide content. Teachers should be well trained in speaking level with no big pause. Online learning, for better outcomes, recommended two consecutive lectures for a better presentation that supports each other without pauses. Administrative concern realizes that the technical staff must be well trained, and universities or individuals must have licensed software that should be updated timely, and the network speed must be continuously upgraded at a reasonable cost.

The success factor in any learning system depends on the successful delivery of content, effective use of the system, and positive impacts on learners. Earlier research was more focused on the technological issues but as the technology evolves, the focus has been shifted to attitude and interaction of learners as well as their instructors to the success of e-learning. Thus the measure of success of the e-learning system was defined by technology acceptance model (TAM). The TAM is used in asynchronous e-learning system to train people in high tech companies for the new technologies, products, and services [6]. These instruments are based on the features such as software reliability, content validity, criterion-related validity, convergent validity, discriminant validity, and nomological validity that reveal the learner satisfaction for asynchronous learning [7]. The impact of synchronous and asynchronous learning reveals that asynchronous learning is beneficial for second language learners but suggests a blend of both for an ideal environment [8].

Synchronous learning enhances collaborative learning, student-centered instructions, multimodal content representation, and a variety of learning activities, psychologically safe environment, timely and constructive feedback, and teacher control over group interaction [9]. The learning styles instrument also plays a role to detect the nature of the learner whether he is asynchronous or synchronous. In regard to this, inventory learning style tools such as Kolb's Learning Styles Inventory is used to identify that synchronous e-learners preferred assimilating and diverging styles, whereas asynchronous e-learners preferred assimilating and converging styles [10]. Student traits and knowledge acquisition skills are beneficial for online synchronous learning. Synchronous learning embarked with motivation and enhanced knowledge acquisition skills and traits [11]. The synchronous virtual classroom can be used in many ways. The teacher can discuss the learning material which he delivers in an asynchronous manner. The session can be conducted in an online–offline manner in better dialog delivery. Findings reveal that the virtual classroom can promote interactivity, develop community, and teach students at different locations [12].

1.2   Blended learning, distance learning, and Classroom 2.0

Blended learning embedded the face-to-face classroom with the technologies, activities, and events. Blended learning follows two main models of learning: (i) program flow model, (ii) core and spoke model. The program flow model acts as traditional training where the learning activities are organized in a sequential manner, whereas the core and spoke model supplements the materials to strengthen the main course [13].

Innovative blended learning combines the strategy of an online discussion with critical thinking, reflection, articulating with in-class oral discussion, and off-class online discussions. These in-class online discussions may promote cognitive thinking skills and in-depth processing. Limitations of time become the hurdle of posting and implementing online discussion for face-to-face classroom learning. The impact of participation on in-class online discussion is that everyone in the class participates and is expressive to their ideas. Moreover, learners judge their peers by their knowledge of other factors such as socioeconomic [14]. The strength of face-to-face instruction is that audience gets easily connected and an idea can be exchanged spontaneously, whereas in computer-mediated instructions, students are flexible to participate in the discussion according to their time and place. Learners get more time to work out their ideas and provide claims more thoughtfully [15]. First-generation of e-learning programs realize that it often gives an error of long sequences of "page-turner" content and point-and-click quizzes. This may lead to insufficient to engage learners for successful learning and performance. The next phase of e-learning where blended learning models are used to combine various delivery modes indicates that it not only offers more choices but also it is more effective [16]. Blended learning or online learning requires new equipment, online resources, and additional support learning materials, increases enrolment, student satisfaction, and lowered the dropout rates. Here the students are free to choose their preferred method either in the asynchronous mode (lecture capture) or synchronous mode (on-campus or live broadcasted lecture). Interaction between professors and students takes place through ICT mediums such as live web chat, online live tutorials, face-to-face lectures, or online discussion forums [17]. Group work is also one of the techniques that can be implemented for successful blended learning. Their perception of analysis of images can be asked through interviews and questionnaires [18].

The success of distance education programs depends upon the perception of tutors, coordinators, learners, office staff, and others toward the quality of support services. The success of the distance learning program also depends upon the registration procedures, quality of course materials, access to instructors, clarity of syllabi, and course objectives. It is required for the timely delivery of the study materials. The quality of the instructional method and access to Internet services are also important [19]. Distance education helps the student to understand the content if using multimedia techniques [20].

Classroom 2.0 is recognized as a new technology in which students use a computer with Internet access and an interactive whiteboard in a classroom. The activities mostly used in Classroom 2.0 are group exercises, keynote addresses, collective analysis from the Internet videos or newspaper and presentation of papers and materials used on the work, and so on. The issues related to classroom teaching are more time to prepare lectures, Internet connection problems, software failures, and problems with students' computers [21]. Some of the new technologies such as podcasts, e-portfolio, and RSS/XML can be used as Classroom 2.0. These are also known as Web 2.0 strategies in the classroom. Research shows that students prefer classes with new technology and techniques that focus on real-world tasks and examples. It has its own advantages and disadvantages. These technologies are being integrated into developing research blogs, forming recruitment groups on social networking sites by faculty. The disadvantage of this technology is that students must not take an entertainment tool versus an information tool [22].

1.2.1 E-learning

E-learning is an aggregation of all kinds of learning that use the computer for medial support of the learning process. Lee, Hsieh, and Hsu [23] defined e-learning as *"An information system that can integrate a wide variety of instructional material (via audio, video, and text mediums) conveyed through e-mail, live chat sessions, online discussions, forums, quizzes, and assignments."* In fact, the e-learning definition has been updated as the definition of web evolved from Web 0 to Web 4.0. At the initial stage of the web, i.e., during the web of version-0, e-learning was based on the Internet where anyone can just read from the Web. After the evolution of the next generation of web, i.e., with Web 2.0 and Web 3.0, real-time interaction and connected intelligence were allowed. Finally, with Web 4.0, the direct interaction of the human brain, as well as machine, is possible. From the earlier discussion, finally, e-learning can be defined as the transfer of knowledge and skills through intelligently designed course materials with the help of an electronic media like the Internet, Web 4.0, intranets, and extranets [24].

E-learning helps society in an effective way because it has many advantages, in terms of healthy relationships among staff, knowledge distribution, and students' satisfaction [25]. In addition, education quality can also be improved through the access to online learning resources of global standards [26]. In e-learning, there is an interaction among teachers, students, and online facilities. This is the twenty-first century learning where a teacher uploads all the required learning materials such as e-books, video lectures, assignments, quizzes, question bank with or without solutions, and animations onto e-learning platform, from where students can access them [27]. This is indeed in a need of devices such as laptop, smartphone, and PDA with a high-speed Internet connection [28]. Learners can significantly increase their knowledge by adopting e-learning concept through the massive open online courses (MOOCs) that will grow continuously in countries that have a large population [29]. In addition, several learning outcomes for students can also be increased. People who are familiar with this technology will access e-learning very easily [30].

The motive of e-learning educational program is to design such pedagogical approaches that help every type of learner. Each learner has its own unique style of learning. There are some instruments that measure the learning style of a learner. Felder–Solomon is one instrumental tool among them which is very popular to detect the learning style of the learner. Currently most of the e-learning systems are using Felder–Silverman learning style tool to detect the learning style of the learner. Though e-learning systems provide greater flexibility to select the learning material according to their performance need, learners realize the need of face-to-face interaction among their peers [31].

Adaptive learning has a lot of potential as it provides personalized information and learning materials for learners of various fields and areas [32]. The adaptive e-learning systems are now an ingrained vehicle of modern education. It accommodates an extensive range of learners with varied backgrounds who register with their specific learning aims. The main challenge in this situation is to generate adaptive learning paths so that learners can achieve their goals most successfully. Previous works used static features such as learners' level of knowledge, browsing preferences, grasping ability, and learning styles to determine personalized learning materials.

1.2.2   Smart e-learning

From personalized learning to smart learning, the components of e-learning technique require customized delivery techniques in terms of learning materials and e-teaching according to a learner profile. The idea of smart learning environment is developed from personalized learning environment. With the evolution of technology enhancement, smart learning concept has come into a realization. Researchers have suggested smart learning as a combination of modern technologies and data analytic techniques. The objective of smart learning is to embed the intelligent techniques and emerging technologies to the instructional design theories as well as cognition theories into an e-learning environment [33]. Smart learning is the mixture of intelligent technologies such as Internet of Things (IoT), cloud computing data analytic techniques, and smart devices such as ubiquitous computing, artificial intelligence (AI), and wearable technology such as glasses, backpacks, or clothes. These technologies are dependent on each other as IoT and most wearable devices require big data to generalize personal information [34]. Smart analytic data techniques require intelligent techniques such as machine learning techniques, data mining, and evolutionary techniques help one to classify the learner to categorize the learner information and provide the learning material accordingly. A smart learning environment requires smart pedagogy based on learner's behavioral, social environment so that the learner classification and feedback in the smart learning environment behave correctly [35,36]. Designing a smart learning environment requires e-learning system with goal and objectives, engagement of learners, cost effective, adaptions, flexible enough to access anywhere, anytime, and reflectiveness where the learner can learn from their mistakes [37]. Figure 1.1 shows the smart e-learning environment.

Different researchers have suggested different techniques to recommend a personalized path to the learners. Most of the authors have suggested that whenever learners enter into an e-learning system, a quiz would be conducted based on the prerequisite concepts of the subject that learner wants to learn. The suitable learning

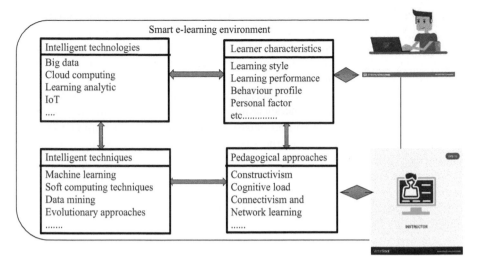

Figure 1.1   Smart e-learning environment

material may be provided to the learner according to their performance [38] using the technologies such as IoT and cloud computing, and techniques such as data mining, machine learning, and deep learning. Development of cloud computing provides support for smart e-learning system through social networking sites [39]. Deep learning model based on the learning style, cognitive style, and sentiment analysis for smart e-learning systems identifies the learning style based on the Felder Silverman Learning Style. The input variables are content chosen forum interaction etc. [40]. Learners' sentimental analysis can be analyzed on the basis of opinion, emotions, feeling, attitude, or thought on the comments and posts. Cognitive level is defined through five levels that are ritual engagement, retreatism, authentic engagement, strategic engagement, and rebellion. Smart learning techniques experiment not only for theory courses, but they also explore these techniques for laboratory courses. Using AI and ML techniques [41], the smart learning analysis can be done for video-based learning. The exploratory features of video-based learning are type of content, practices and pedagogies of video learning, assessment functionalities for video learning, and expected results and outcomes [42]. The next section discusses the different frameworks of e-learning.

1.3   Different frameworks of smart e-learning

1.3.1   AI in e-learning

AI techniques can be used in an e-learning system to assess the knowledge of the user, evaluation techniques, and analysis of the performance of the learner. It may also be used as the system process control, supervision, and automation. An intelligent e-learning system can provide a communication between speech and NLP for external users to identify speech recognition, word and sentence recognition, sentence meaning analysis, and user reaction assessment. A hybrid neural network can be used to recognize natural language sentence [43]. AI develops a learning environment to provide skills to employers, capital to investor, and customer to supplier [44]. It enables human to engage more in innovation and creative thinking by reducing the task of processing and analyzing data.

AI helps one to develop the customized learning interface and digital curriculum by using various mediums such as audio, video, and online assistant. Intelligent tutoring systems provide the content to learn according to learners' knowledge. Virtual assistants such as robot, 3D gaming, and computers are used to create realistic virtual characters and interactions. A smart analytic is required to monitor the progress of students. AI makes a classroom for all those who speak different languages or who are disabled. A teacher can apply AI to personalize the content according to the performance of the learner. AI technique is used to determine the learning style of the students considering multiple learning models and to suggest the appropriate learning model for a student according to the environment [45]. AI can be integrated with adaptive e-learning systems in which techniques can be used to explain the answers so that learner can find out their own mistakes instead of showing the correct answer to the learner. It also provides the learning materials in different languages without translating them [46]. AI techniques such as soft computing techniques and shallow text processing are used to monitor asynchronous discussions group that helps teacher to guide learners accordingly. It also helps teachers to make assignments and answers queries of students through virtual teaching assistant. AI uses machine learning and data mining techniques to personalize the learning material to the student accordingly [47]. AI has the ability to develop human reasoning and decision-making process that reduces the uncertainty in learner's mind [48]. Figure 1.2 shows the framework of AI in an e-learning scenario. Different modules of AI such as intelligent tutoring system, smart learning content, AI collaboration with teachers, content analysis, and access to the user are shown in Figure 1.2.

1.3.2   *Mobile learning*

Authors in [49] identified the problems associated with conventional methods of English language learning such as (i) lack of inspiration in learners; (ii) inability to identify the objective of study in literature—no relevant literature or reports; (iii) lack of understanding the language, difficulties with limited vocabulary stock; (iv) lack of learning equipment, language software, evaluation tools, and techniques; (v) lack of unified teaching techniques and curriculum; and (vi) lack of quality of teaching. Authors in [50] proposed adaptive triggering for mobile learning (m-learning)-based course content for working skilled professionals. The authors identified the demerits associated with traditional MOOCS such as web browsers-dependent content delivery, restricted mobility to user through laptop or desktop workstations, and more time-consuming while carrying out specific tasks such as programming or report writing. In this chapter, pervasive context aware-based

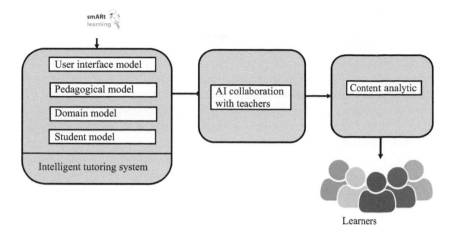

Figure 1.2   Framework of AI in e-learning

m-learning is incorporated. The objective of m-learning is to incorporate learning process anytime and anywhere through mobile devices. This objective requires learning course contents to be customized as per the mobile screen size and various interactive input and output device techniques.

Recent trends of the m-learning platforms are integrated with Internet and cloud computing platforms. In [51], authors presented that the objectives of cloud-based m-learning were to enhance the user experience, computing capability, and accuracy. To achieve these objectives, it requires performance enhancement of load balancing in cloud computing for an m-learning application. For this purpose, the authors utilized dominant firefly algorithm as load balancing strategy for cloud. Here, the cloud servers are considered as dominant fireflies, while the mobile application running on cloud as submissive fireflies. The dynamic request and response between cloud application and the available resources on cloud servers are estimated based on firefly strategy where the requests for the dominant cloud servers are balanced. Two sets of m-learning test cases, namely, simple query and hard query, are studied. The authors presented that QoS metrics are improved due to this proposed method. Authors in [49] surveyed the existing literature for analyzing the effect of gaining English language knowledge through m-learning. Some of the research questions that the authors answered in their work are (i) to survey on various work done toward the mobile-based English language learning; (ii) to elaborate the merits and demerits using mobile for English language learners; and (iii) to measure the user effectiveness toward the usage of mobile-based learning of English language. In this, various blended applications of mobile toward learning process through non-gaming mode, gaming mode, tools, and media were presented. The non-gaming mode includes learning of English language skills such as vocabulary, listening, speaking, reading, and writing. The gaming mode includes various mobile games that enhance the English language skills such as scramble, crosswords, puzzles, and word matching games. The tools for English language skills include the usage of mobile devices for selective skill enhancing such as reading tool, language writing tools, language translation tools, and grammar correction tools. The authors also addressed the m-learning through media for English language skill capable of connecting other devices such as television, video on demand, webinars, and online streaming.

The m-learning benefits the learners with aspects such as mobility, portability, seamless connectivity, effective peer interactions, context sensitive learning strategy, cost effective, feasible learning environment, and easy installation of m-learning applications. In recent years, the use of mobile phones is widespread across the world, enables the learning process in both formal and informal ways. In addition, through m-learning process, the learning materials are enjoyable through innovative graphical user interfaces and attractive teaching presentations. The feedback of teaching learning process is also associated for the improvisation of both teachers' and learners' ability.

1.3.3   Cloud-based learning

The modern e-learning models depend on Internet technology. However, the e-learning model lacks the necessary enhanced support in terms of computation capacity, storage capability, and interoperability. The developing, deploying, and maintenance of e-learning system within the campus infrastructure involves huge capital cost, low gain of profit return, skilled professionals, local data center power managements, and several deployment problems. As an efficient solution, the remote cloud computing platforms provide enhanced support for e-learning systems and learning application development. The cloud computing technology provides an enhancement of e-learning through various services such as (i) software-as-a-service (SaaS), (ii) platform-as-a-service (PaaS), and (iii) infrastructure-as-a-service (IaaS) [52]. Any e-learning system can utilize these different cloud services through either private or public remote cloud systems. Thus, the cloud computing-based e-learning systems are efficient and feasible in terms of investments and maintenance. Figure 1.3 illustrates the major difference in architecture of the traditional e-learning and the cloud-based e-learning systems.

Here, the SaaS provides the cloud-based software as service interconnected through Internet; thus the client's need of software installation and availability can be addressed. This mechanism of remote software platform avoids the investment and maintenance at client's system. The different cloud computing services required by any systems involve (i) design of computing strategy, (ii) analysis of specific system requirements, (iii) development of necessary application interfaces, and (iv) implementation of application that meets the time and computation cost of the end user needs [53]. The major services that can be offered through software include remote system interconnection through Internet for accessing the resources and managing the various activities on the cloud. Software installation and updates are remotely performed by cloud management system and transparent to the end users. Hence, cloud-based e-learning enables the instructors and students to the available remote resources efficiently without any problem.

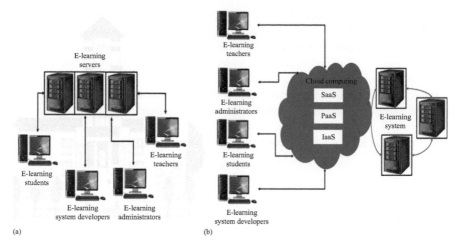

Figure 1.3   (a) Traditional versus (b) cloud computing-based e-learning system

Authors in [54] presented various e-learning services that are offered by the cloud platforms. These include communication, e-mail, messaging, blogging, collaborative editing services, on-demand collaboration, video call conferencing, audio call conferencing, shared desktops, shared whiteboards, quiz, various assessment techniques, assignment submission, grading, group activity storage, individual content storage, newsfeed, feedback, polling, surveys, and glossary. The authors mainly discussed about two major cloud service providers, namely, Google and Microsoft. In addition, authors in [53] discussed some more openly available types of cloud computing-based e-learning management systems such as WizIQ, Docebo, Litmos, and TalentLMS.

Authors in [55] addressed the major advantages of using e-learning based on cloud in terms of tutors, learners, and entire institution. Some of the major impacts are (i) scalability of user participation; (ii) less time and reduced cost of maintenance; (iii) modular-based e-learning approach; and (iv) equal and positive interaction between learners, teachers as well as various educational institutions involved. Authors in [56] addressed the major issues with cloud computing and e-learning as (i) security, (ii) privacy, (ii) reliability, (iv) reliability, (v) legal issues, (vi) compliance, and (vii) open standards. The security concern targets on the data storage in a remote system where the trust and data access methods are unknown and transparent to the ordinary users. The privacy targets on the possibility of data attack, leaking of critical information, and misuse of remotely stored user data. The cloud computing relies on remote access through Internet, which intern involves performance factors such as available bandwidth, downtimes, and server slowdowns [57]. Legal issues of cloud computing-based e-learning involve the safety precautions and user confidentiality through legislative methods. It also concerns about the choice of freedom to users about their own data storage and retaining user's own copies of data. Generally, the cloud service providers offer application program interfaces that are specific to the service. These services are not inter-operable and involve complex key exchanges between the providers and users. Hence, there is requirement for a consensus of open cloud computing platforms such as open cloud consortium. The compliance involves the regulations on data storage and access by the cloud data centers through standardized audit and reporting trails by cloud service providers. This includes the customers to be aware of the compliance standards and to enable them to comply with these regulations.

1.3.4   Big data in e-learning

The e-learning through ICT generates a huge volume of data that need analysis and knowledge generation based on variety of measurable e-learning data. In turn, the big data-based data analytics and data mining on education data lead to the enhancement of entire education process such as strategy for learning and tutoring, impact assessment of e-learning, outcome-based approach, and customization of learner centric training. Over recent years, by an intervention of big data in e-learning, the quality and efficiency of e-learning mechanisms are improved tre-mendously. The e-learning factors in the context of big data such as volume, velocity, variety, variability, complexity, and veracity are shown in Figure 1.4.

Volume includes the huge amount of educational data that are generated by the education systems such as schools, universities, institutions, and training centers. These raw educational data are collected from the different sources and are stored in big data systems for extracting useful insight about the education information.

Velocity includes the real-time data generation at different temporal and spatial relationships. The stakeholders of education system, including learners, tutors, management, administration, and service providers, handle different types of data at different instances, rate of time, and at different locations. These velocity factors play vital roles in critical decision-making of overall educational process such as assessment, goal achievement, and learning resources quality.

Variety includes the wide spectrum of education information such as formats of learning resources, size and storage capacity requirement, phase of information, plan for education process, student portfolio, and learning styles. This phenomenon of variety in e-learning big data allows one to perform classification, correlation, and grouping of e-learning information data.

Veracity includes processing of the raw data gathered from different educa-tional sources. The data processing involves noise detection, missing data impu-tation, and outlier and anomaly detections. The data processing depends on the temporal and spatial relationship of data and trustworthiness of education data for critical decision-making in the educational process.

Variability includes the validity of storage data, tracking of educational information, updating of data on the storage and remote systems. The performance of variability is essential to be measured to handle inconsistencies across dis-tributed big database centers that are containing the educational information.

Complexity includes the heterogeneous information sources for educational purpose. Hence, the data processing, analyzing, and managing such varied

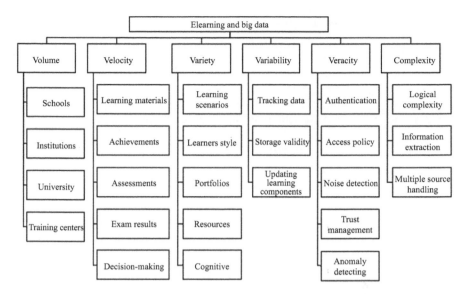

Figure 1.4   Big data concepts in e-learning

information are essential for collective decision-making across different educational institution and systems.

Authors in [58] focused on big data analytics toward the e-learning systems where the objective is to optimize the learning process by obtaining insight about the knowledge information for the tutors and the learners. The data analysis methodology for educational information involves two-step processes, namely, big data and data mining. The big data handle the storage of voluminous heterogeneous data from different educational sources. The data mining process involves useful knowledge discovery from the raw educational data. The common techniques used are prediction, clustering, relationship identification, and data visualization of the e-learning data. Authors in [59] target on (i) a distributed system of storage space by integrating cloud computing and big data, and (ii) data analysis on online real-time education system. Here, the role of Hadoop Distributed File systems along with various other cloud computing-based ecosystems such as Apache Spark, Apache Fume, Apache Hive, and Apache Sqoop are discussed. Also, authors in [60] proposed multilayer big data-based e-learning management systems that include big data acquisition from education systems and knowledge discovery, big data based data presentation, big data modeling, big data processing, and data visualization. Authors in [61] presented a practical case study on blended e-learning environment to evaluate the effective use of big data technology on voluminous data from different collaborative tools. Author claims that the analytical study provides clear and optimized outlook of designed e-learning resources for tutors and learners.

1.3.5   IoT framework of e-learning

The IoT-based e-learning framework leverages on e-learning methodology through emerging technologies such as big data, cloud computing, data analytics and AI. This IoT-based e-learning provides a platform for learning community with knowledge enrichment possibility at anytime, anywhere. Further, this platform incorporates the knowledge sharing irrespective of any age through enhanced technique for data gathering, developing course contents, accessibility of contents, and pedagogy for learners and awareness of knowledge. The entities of this IoT-based e-learning framework include learners, teachers, authoritative, business vendors, agents, virtual institutions, and community group with focused objectives. Each entity projects autonomous functionality; however, together it is able to meet the learners' objectives in a collective way. For instance, the teacher plays a vital role in content design, delivers, and evaluates mechanism; however, the teacher is part of large organization that carries out IoT-based e-learning system. In this, the profiles and requirements of the learner are considered as inputs to the system; in turn, this enhanced system provides probable collaboration, prospects, recommendations, and opportunities to the interested learners.

Authors in [62] presented the Intelligent Space as an enhanced IoT-based modular education process. The proposed system was developed using open cloud software platform such as Amazon web services, Microsoft Azure, and IBM Bluemix. Next, the IoT sensors, such as temperature, loudness, light intensity detector, and air monitoring were used. The motion and movement of the students were tracked using a depth camera Kinect, a digital camera, and ultrasound sensors. The sensor data were generated and collected. The initial analyses were carried out at the fog computing infrastructure. The data are migrated to cloud for providing deep insight about the sensor data and then using machine learning models' critical decision such as localization, navigation, and path planning of the tutor robots. Further complex operations such as the human–computer interaction and the students' gait and movement prediction were carried out. Authors in [63] proposed IoT-based enhancement of online mode learning and tutoring process. The IoT sensors were used to collect information such that educational LMS could make critical decisions. Here, different data mining and data analysis algorithms were used on the centralized data storage of IoT sensor data. The operations like noise reduction, sorting, fusion, feature extraction, and feature analysis were performed. The final data were presented for visualization at different levels of education management system.

Teaching IoT and virtual IoT laboratories, science, technology, engineering, and mathematics, education involves traditional methods of laboratory infrastructures. Generally, the laboratory sessions are prescheduled, and it has limitation of space, time. Further, the limited time of practice will not meet the need of mixed learner's ability. It is to note that slow learners may need more time to cope with the concepts and need more effort to complete the target assignments satisfactorily. Similarly, learners may need to practice extra tasks apart from those already assigned by the teachers. In this way, the laboratory space constraint lacks to facilitate the learner's ability. On the other hand, more of the time the laboratory equipment are underused due to lack of proper usable time. In fact, this traditional laboratory setup is cost inefficient and most of the time facilities and resources are underused.

As a solution to this, the practical sessions based on Internet provide favorable environment for geographically far away learners for the IoT course. In this case, the contents are provided to distance learners through networking of computers across different places, classrooms, and universities. This platform provides wide scope for learners to participate in practical sessions. In this line, cyber physical systems play a vital role in enhancing the practical-based skill honing as learners are involved in community-based learning environment. The popular example of virtual laboratory is the digital twins.

The basic cyber physical system based e-learning framework consists of four main components, namely, (i) remote client systems, (ii) Internet, (iii) workstations performing experiments, and (iv) security and privacy mechanism as depicted in Figure 1.5. The remote clients from distance geographical locations access the learning contents and perform experimental through Internet from the cyber physical system of laboratory. The cyber physical systems are the physical location of the computing workstations where real experimentations are performed by teachers and research collaboration. In turn, the cyber physical systems are an autonomous local area network that consists of several workstations, servers, and database. The cyber physical systems provide security and privacy through firewall. The Internet bridges the remote client machines with the cyber physical systems to meet the objectives of anytime and anywhere learning environment.

1.3.6 Augmented reality in learning

Augmented reality (AR) and gamification techniques play a big role in engaging the learning while learning the subject. AR creates a real-world environment to augment

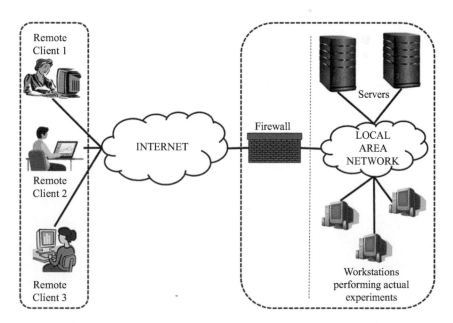

Figure 1.5 Basic framework of cyber physical systems of e-learning

the physical view by sensory inputs of computer. Advanced computer techniques of AR such as computer vision, object recognition help one to visualize the real-world environment very interactive and manageable. The content of the curriculum can be designed using the text, graphics, video, and audio into a learner's real environment. Learners can correlate the simulation of various events generated by AR tools. It allows learners to remember and understand the subject in a better way. Remote collaboration is also possible if needed, and instructor and learner can interact in this environment. Some of the researchers have developed a content of science for K-12 education to deliver the content for comprehensive understanding to the subject [64–66]. The combination of adaptive learning, AR, and gamification techniques shows the positive impact of learning in MOOC around the world as it was being noted that dropout rate was increasing [67]. The common application of AR can be seen in mobile phones to navigate the nearby area. Some of the authors have used the AR and virtual reality (VR) applications in engineering design, production technology, and maintenance engineering. Applications, such as path planning for an industrial robot can be designed. The use of AR in higher education may reduce the cost of AR tools as the hardware may be used in laboratories [68]. This may enhance the adaptation of AR/VR technology to the age of Industry 4.0. AR can be explored in the product design process. In product design process, prototype making and testing are the two key elements. AR techniques have been used to find design solutions at various stages [69].

Animation is a better way to address the special need of the children with intellectual disabilities to learn and imitate. AR plays an important role there as it brings a virtual object into real world. The properties of AR such as display, tracking, and interaction do not keep special need children away from their familiar environments and improve their interacting abilities. In addition to this, AR helps us to provide individual knowledge from them [70]. Figure 1.6 shows how AR application helps one to learn the "what to do to keep safe from the novel COVID-19."

Q   What to do if a person is sneezing?
A   Give him a mask.
Q   What should you do when you see a crowded place?
A   Wear a mask or leave that place.
Q   I wore that mask for a day. What should I do now?
A   Throw that mask.
Q   What should I do before eating lunch?
A   Wash hands.

Table 1.1 summarizes the advantages and disadvantages of different frameworks of e-learning.

Figure 1.6   Augmented reality application in e-learning

Table 1.1 Advantages and disadvantages of different frameworks of e-learning

S. no.	Frameworks of e-learning	Device required	Examples	Advantages	Disadvantages
1	AI	Chatbots, optimized search engines	Duolingo, Carnegie Learning's MATHia, Massive Open Online Courses, Upside LMS, KEA	Personalized content, monitored progress of the learner, assisted learning through chatbots, provide adaptive learning	Learners may have technology addiction, high cost of power
2	Mobile	Smartphone, PDA, Tablets	Android, iPhone, Blackberry, Windows	Anytime anywhere accessibility to users, mobility, low cost of maintenance	Hardware and software up gradation, small screen, limited contents can be displayed on the mobile screen
3	Cloud	Personal computers, workstations, Internet, cloud access	Amazon web services, Microsoft Azure, Google Cloud, IBM Bluemix	Low cost of installation and maintenance, different stakeholders, anytime, anywhere e-learning possible, device and platform independent	Remote storage systems, latency, data confidentiality and storage access, security and privacy
4	Big data	Workstations, distributed systems with huge storage space and computing capability	Hadoop, Apache Spark, Apache Hive, Apache Fume, Apache Sqoop, NoSQL databases, Mongo DB	Deep insight into the learners' learning style, teaching style, assessment, data visualization, data mining through efficient machine learning models	Voluminous e-learning data, complex data processing, time inefficient for real-time data analysis
5	IoT	Sensors, actuators, computing devices	Arduino, Raspberry Pi along with software platforms like Node-RED, IBM Things Work	Smart e-learning, monitoring of learners and tutors, blended learning	Security and privacy, compliance, open standards, resource constraint IoT devices
6	Augmented reality [1–3]	Head-mounted display, handheld display, spatial displays	Mobile AR English learning, softwaremedien.welten, AR Human Body System, CONNECT,3 Desktop AR Applications and HUMAN Library, Games: AR GreeNET and Basic GreeNET [3]	Better understanding of content, increased motivation, long-term memory retention, better collaboration, learner easy to remember	Ineffective classroom integration, usability, difficulties, performance difference

1.4   Gaps in existing frameworks

Most work has been done from the perspective of the learners. E-teaching also plays an important role in the perspective of the teachers. The content developed by the teachers in an online setting should be adapted by the learner. A well-designed training and sufficient knowledge of the digital equipment should be required for efficient online teaching or blended teaching. In classroom teaching, teachers are solely responsible to develop the course content [12], whereas in online teaching, it is required to develop the content in a collaborative manner. E-teaching is a pre-requisite component to enhance the process of teaching and learning in the e-learning system [71].

Motivation is one of the important factors of interactive e-learning systems to improve the performance of the learner. Smart pedagogies and multimedia strategies might improve the motivation of the learner in the teaching and learning process of e-learning. This does not necessarily mean that the advancement of technology improves the learning outcome of any course. Instructors should take feedback from the students from time to time about the enhancement of the quality of teaching and learning. It is the most influential factor in the delivery of learning content. A poor Internet connection and bandwidth sometimes disrupt the interest and motivation of the learner [72].

Time is also an important consideration to improve and understanding the teaching and learning process. Some of the issues analyzed are the time conceptualization, inclusion of time explicative model, introduced in a research process, and so on [73].

1.5   Conclusion

E-learning in the twenty-first century is a learning platform where learning materials are shared for learners using smart e-learning applications. Different technologies and techniques are used to handle the teaching activities and assist the student to learn the content in an effective manner. In the last few years, the field of education gets MOOCs that is an excellent innovation of the e-learning concept used in largely populated countries from which learners can increase their knowledge. One of the main advantages of e-learning is that the learners get the chance to attend lectures of excellent professors of their fields. E-learning can be made successful with the help of a positive attitude and inter-action between learners and instructors. This book explores the different technologies and techniques of e-learning systems that may handle the retention and satisfaction of learners with socioeconomic well-equipped systems. It also explores the methods and techniques toward the e-learning system for the quality of the curriculum, flexibility of the course, course usefulness, and ease of use of the system.

References

[1] Majid NA and Fuada S. E-learning for society: A great potential to implement education for all (EFA) movement in Indonesia. International Journal of Mobile Technology. 2020;14:250–8.

[2] Bhuasiri W, Xaymoungkhoun O, Zo H, Rho JJ, and Ciganek AP. Critical success factors for e-learning in developing countries: A comparative analysis between ICT experts and faculty. Computers & Education. 2012;58 (2):843–55.

[3] Mohammadi H. Investigating users' perspectives on e-learning: An integration of TAM and IS success model. Computers in Human Behavior. 2015;45:359–74.

[4] Hrastinsky S. Asynchronous and synchronous e-learning. Educause. 2008;31 (4):51–5.

[5] Redmond JA, Parkinson A, Mullally A, and Dolan D. Synchronous e-learning: Three perspectives. In: Innovations in E-learning, Instruction Technology, Assessment, and Engineering Education 2007 (pp. 175–80). Springer, Dordrecht.

[6] Ong CS, Lai JY, and Wang YS. Factors affecting engineers' acceptance of asynchronous e-learning systems in high-tech companies. Information & Management. 2004;41(6):795–804.

[7] Wang YS. Assessment of learner satisfaction with asynchronous electronic learning systems. Information & Management. 2003;41(1):75–86.

[8] Perveen A. Synchronous and asynchronous e-language learning: A case study of virtual university of Pakistan. Open Praxis. 2016;8(1):21–39.

[9] Racheva V. Social aspects of synchronous virtual learning environments. InAIP Conference Proceedings 2018 Dec 10 (Vol. 2048, No. 1, p. 020032). AIP Publishing LLC.

[10] Shahabadi MM and Uplane M. Synchronous and asynchronous e-learning styles and academic performance of e-learners. Procedia—Social and Behavioral Sciences. 2015;176(20):129–38.

[11] Politis D and Politis JD. The relationship between an online synchronous learning environment and knowledge acquisition skills and traits: The blackboard collaborate experience. Electronic Journal of e-Learning. 2016;14(3):204–22.

[12] Martin F and Parker MA. Use of synchronous virtual classrooms: Why, who, and how. MERLOT Journal of Online Learning and Teaching. 2014;10 (2):192–210.

[13] Ghirardini B. E-learning methodologies: A guide for designing and developing e-learning courses. Food and Agriculture Organization of the United Nations, Rome; 2011.

[14] Chen W and Looi CK. Incorporating online discussion in face to face classroom learning: A new blended learning approach. Australasian Journal of Educational Technology. 2007;23(3).

[15] Graham CR. Chapter One: Blended learning systems. In: The Handbook of Blended Learning: Global Perspectives, Local Designs 2006 (pp. 3–21). San Francisco, CA: Pfeiffer.

[16] Singh H. Building effective blended learning programs. Educational Technology. 2003;43(6):51–4.

[17] Martínez PJ, Aguilar FJ, and Ortiz M. Transitioning from face-to-face to blended and full online learning engineering master's program. IEEE Transactions on Education. 2019;63(1):2–9.

[18] Ellis RA. Students' approaches to groupwork in a blended course, associations with perceptions of the online environment and academic achievement – When is learning engaged? Education and Information Technologies. 2016;21(5):1095–112.

[19] Messo IN. Students' perception on the quality of open and distance learning programmes in Tanzania. Huria: Journal of the Open University of Tanzania. 2014;18(1):119–34.

[20] Kutluk FA and Gulmez M. A research about distance education students' satisfaction with education quality at an accounting program. Procedia— Social and Behavioral Sciences. 2012;46:2733–7.

[21] Coscollola MD and Graells PM. Classroom 2.0 experiences and building on the use of ICT in Teaching. Comunicar. Media Education Research Journal. 2011;19(2).

[22] Rhoades E, Friedel C, and Irani T. Classroom 2.0: Student's feelings on new technology in the classroom. NACTA Journal. 2008;52:32–8.

[23] Lee YH, Hsieh YC, and Hsu CN. Adding innovation diffusion theory to the technology acceptance model: Supporting employees' intentions to use e-learning systems. Journal of Educational Technology & Society. 2011;14(4):124–37.

[24] Choudhury S and Pattnaik S. Emerging themes in e-learning: A review from the stakeholders' perspective. Computers & Education. 2020;144:103657.

[25] Abd El Aziz R and Abd El Halim H. Assessing criteria that matter to students' satisfaction in private higher education. International Journal of Advanced Information Technology. 2018;8(4/5):1–14.

[26] El Gamal S and Abd El Aziz R. The perception of students' regarding e-learning implementation in Egyptian universities. In: The Fifth International Conference on Digital Society, eL&mL 2011.

[27] Kattoua T, Al-Lozi M, and Alrowwad AA. A review of literature on E-learning systems in higher education. International Journal of Business Management & Economic Research. 2016;7(5):754–62.

[28] Alenezi AM and Shahi KK. Interactive e-learning through second life with blackboard technology. Procedia—Social and Behavioral Sciences. 2015;176:891–7.

[29] Purnomo W. Penerapan massive open online course (MOOC) berbasis Moodle sebagai learning management system (LMS). In: Simposium Nasional Pengembang Teknologi Pembelajaran 2016.

[30] Ismail ME, Utami P, Ismail IM, Hamzah N, and Harun H. Development of massive open online course (MOOC) based on ADDIE model for catering courses. Jurnal Pendidikan Vokasi. 2018;8(2):184–92.

[31] Goyal M, Yadav D, and Sood M. Decision making for e-learners based on learning style, personality, and knowledge level. In: 2018 5th IEEE Uttar Pradesh Section International Conference on Electrical, Electronics and Computer Engineering (UPCON) 2018 Nov 2 (pp. 1–5). IEEE.

[32] Goyal M. Intuitionistic Fuzzy Modeling of ELearners. 2016; http://hdl.handle.net/10603/125714

[33] Gamalel-Din SA. Smart e-learning: A greater perspective; from the fourth to the fifth generation e-learning. Egyptian Informatics Journal. 2010;11(1):39–48.

[34] Temdee P. Smart learning environment: Paradigm shift for online learning. In: Multi Agent Systems-Strategies and Applications 2020 Apr 22. IntechOpen.

[35] Zhu ZT, Yu MH, and Riezebos P. A research framework of smart education. Smart Learning Environments. 2016;3(1):4.

[36] Spector JM. Conceptualizing the emerging field of smart learning environments. Smart Learning Environments. 2014;1(1):2.

[37] Soonthornphisaj N, Rojsattarat E, and Yim-Ngam S. Smart e-learning using recommender system. In: International Conference on Intelligent Computing 2006 Aug 16 (pp. 518–23). Springer, Berlin, Heidelberg.

[38] Veeramanickam MR and Radhika N. A smart e-learning system for social networking. International Journal of Electrical & Computer Engineering (2088-8708). 2014;4(3).

[39] Chanaa A and El Faddouli NE. Deep learning for a smart e-learning system. In: Proceedings of the 2nd International Conference on Smart Digital Environment 2018 Oct 18 (pp. 197–202).

[40] Gros B. The design of smart educational environments. Smart Learning Environments. 2016;3(1):15.

[41] Munawar S, Toor SK, Aslam M, and Hamid M. Move to smart learning environment: Exploratory research of challenges in computer laboratory and design intelligent virtual laboratory for eLearning Technology. EURASIA Journal of Mathematics, Science and Technology Education. 2018;14(5):1645–62.

[42] Giannakos MN, Sampson DG, and Kidziński Ł. Introduction to smart learning analytics: Foundations and developments in video-based learning. Smart Learning Environments. 2016;3(1):1–9.

[43] Kacalak W and Majewski M. E-learning systems with artificial intelligence in engineering. In: International Conference on Intelligent Computing 2009 Sep 16 (pp. 918–27). Springer, Berlin, Heidelberg.

[44] https://www.gc-solutions.net/resources/articles/the-future-of-responsive-elearning-with-artificial-intelligence.html. [Accessed on May 6, 2020]

[45] Bajaj R and Sharma V. Smart education with artificial intelligence based determination of learning styles. Procedia Computer Science. 2018;132:834–42.

[46]   Adamu S and Awwalu J. The Role of Artificial Intelligence (AI) in Adaptive eLearning System (AES) Content Formation: Risks and Opportunities Involved. arXiv preprint arXiv:1903.00934. 2019 Mar 3.

[47]   Pedro F, Subosa M, Rivas A, and Valverde P. Artificial intelligence in education: Challenges and opportunities for sustainable development. Working Papers on Education Policy. UNESCO, Education Sector, The Global Education 2030. 2019.

[48]   Colchester K, Hagras H, Alghazzawi D, and Aldabbagh G. A survey of artificial intelligence techniques employed for adaptive educational systems within e-learning platforms. Journal of Artificial Intelligence and Soft Computing Research. 2017;7(1):47–64.

[49]   Elaish MM, Shuib L, Ghani NA, and Yadegaridehkordi E. Mobile English language learning (MELL): A literature review. Educational Review. 2019;71(2):257–76.

[50]   Kljun M, Pucihar KČ, and Solina F. Persuasive technologies in m-learning for training professionals: How to keep learners engaged with adaptive triggering. IEEE Transactions on Learning Technologies. 2018;12(3):370–83.

[51]   Sekaran K, Khan MS, Patan R, Gandomi AH, Krishna PV, and Kallam S. Improving the response time of m-learning and cloud computing environments using a dominant firefly approach. IEEE Access. 2019;7:30203–30212.

[52]   Mircea M and Andreescu AI. Using cloud computing in higher education: A strategy to improve agility in the current financial crisis. Communications of the IBIMA. 2011;2011:1–15.

[53]   Aldheleai HF, Bokhari MU, and Alammari A. Overview of cloud-based learning management system. International Journal of Computer Applications. 2017;162(11).

[54]   Sclater N. eLearning in the cloud. International Journal of Virtual and Personal Learning Environments (IJVPLE). 2010;1(1):10–9.

[55]   Bosamia M and Patel A. An overview of cloud computing for e-learning with its key benefits. International Journal of Information Sciences and Techniques (IJIST). 2016;6:1–10.

[56]   kasi Viswanath MD, Kusuma S, and Gupta SK. Cloud computing issues and benefits modern education. Global Journal of Computer Science and Technology. 2012;12.

[57]   Al Tayeb A, Alghatani K, El-Seoud S, and El-Sofany H. The impact of cloud computing technologies in e-learning. International Journal of Emerging Technologies in Learning (iJET). 2013;8.

[58]   Secades VA and Arranz O. Big data & eLearning: A binomial to the future of the knowledge society. IJIMAI. 2016;3(6):29–33.

[59]   Dahdouh K, Dakkak A, and Oughdir L. Big data: A distributed storage and processing for online learning systems. International Journal of Computational Intelligence Studies. 2019;8(3):192–205.

[60]   Abdelouarit KA, Sbihi B, and Aknin N. Big-learn: Towards a tool based on Big Data to improve research in an e-learning environment. International Journal of Advanced Computer Science and Applications. 2015;6(10):59–63.

[61] García OA and Secades VA. Big data & learning analytics: A potential way to optimize elearning technological tools. In: International Association for Development of the Information Society. 2013 Jul.

[62] Vaščák J, Kajáti E, and Zolotová I. Concept of intelligent space in education of IoT applications in robotics. In: 2018 16th International Conference on Emerging eLearning Technologies and Applications (ICETA) 2018 Nov 15 (pp. 629–34). IEEE.

[63] Njeru AM, Omar MS, Yi S, Paracha S, and Wannous M. Using IoT technology to improve online education through data mining. In: 2017 International Conference on Applied System Innovation (ICASI) 2017 May 13 (pp. 515–8). IEEE.

[64] Eleftheria CA, Charikleia P, Iason CG, Athanasios T, and Dimitrios T. An innovative augmented reality educational platform using Gamification to enhance lifelong learning and cultural education. In: IISA 2013 Jul 10 (pp. 1–5). IEEE.

[65] Dutta K. Augmented Reality for E-Learning. Available on line at https://www.researchgate.net/.../304078112_Augmented_Reality_for_E-Learning. Retrieved on. 2018:13–7.

[66] Santos ME, Chen A, Taketomi T, Yamamoto G, Miyazaki J, and Kato H. Augmented reality learning experiences: Survey of prototype design and evaluation. IEEE Transactions on Learning Technologies. 2013;7(1):38–56.

[67] Chauhan J, Taneja S, and Goel A. Enhancing MOOC with augmented reality, adaptive learning and gamification. In2015 IEEE 3rd International Conference on MOOCs, Innovation and Technology in Education (MITE) 2015 Oct 1 (pp. 348–53). IEEE.

[68] Çolak O and Yünlü AP. A review on augmented reality and virtual reality in engineering education. Journal of Educational and Instructional Studies in the World. 2018;8(1).

[69] Lai YC. Is augmented reality a new paradigm in design education when educational subsidy decreases? InDS 88: Proceedings of the 19th International Conference on Engineering and Product Design Education (E&PDE17), Building Community: Design Education for a Sustainable Future, Oslo, Norway, 2017 Sep 7 & 8 (pp. 549–54).

[70] Azuma RT. A survey of augmented reality. Presence: Teleoperators & Virtual Environments. 1997;6(4):355–85.

[71] Guri-Rosenblit S. E-teaching in higher education: An essential prerequisite for e-learning. Journal of New Approaches in Educational Research. 2018;7(2):93–97.

[72] Abou El-Seoud M, Taj-Eddin I, Seddiek N, El-Khouly M, and Nosseir A. E-learning and students' motivation: A research study on the effect of e-learning on higher education. International Journal of Emerging Technologies in Learning (iJET). 2014;9(4):20–6.

[73] Barbera E and Clarà M. Time in e-learning research: A qualitative review of the empirical consideration of time in research into e-learning. ISRN Education. 2012;2012.

Chapter 2

Goal-oriented adaptive e-learning

Sushma Hans[1] and Shelly Sachdeva[1]

Adaptive learning has a lot of potential as it provides personalized information and learning material for learners of various fields and areas. The adaptive e-learning systems are now an ingrained vehicle of modern education. It accommodates an extensive range of learners with varied backgrounds who register with their specific learning objectives. The main challenge in the current situation is to produce adaptive learning paths so that learners can attain their goals successfully. Previous works used static features such as learners' level of knowledge, browsing preferences, grasping ability, and learning styles to determine personalized learning materials.

This chapter introduces a different approach by captivating the continuous improvement of learners as per their learning goals, to refine their learning paths after every level covered in the course. The authors consider the fact that a learner's ability to grasp learning material is neither a pre-determined factor nor it can be computed homogeneously for all learners. Rather, a learner progresses non-stop to hone her grasping capability. An e-learning system should integrate these features to evaluate such enhancements, in the context of learners' pre-defined goals.

Key contributions of the current chapter are as follows:

1. All aspects of a student's learning in a course are matched with its pre-specified learning goal (LG). We put in a revolutionary concept of customized evaluation which is planned and assessed in the sense of its own LG for each learner. In addition, the system actively selects for each student learning materials, and experiences that are more important to the achievement of their desired LG.
2. We propose and develop the goal-oriented adaptive e-learning system (GOALS) which actively leverages the benefits of continuous learner improvement.
3. At each point of the learning process, we use the meta-heuristic ant colony optimization (ACO) to dynamically generate a new optimized future learning sub-path. As per the LG of the learner, ACO maximizes the breadth of learning as well as coverage of subjects in a course with minimal complexity under defined time constraints.

[1]Department of Computer Engineering, National Institute of Technology Delhi, Delhi, India

2.1   Introduction

The utilization of e-learning in the current teaching system has developed extensively. Now, the learners and teachers do not need to be present simultaneously at a specific location. The learning paths may be tailored as per an individual's learning capability, without place and time constraint. Attractive attributes such as simulations, multimedia presentations, personalized tests, and navigational support are integrated to aid effectual learning [1–4]. Adaptive e-learning refers to an e-learning paradigm that modifies the content of a course built on the results and feedback obtained from the individual learner. Faculty member's excellence can be measured based on not just finding out whether a student is correct or not, but to identify why he/she is incorrect and what all measures should be taken to improve student's understanding.

A key initiative to be discussed is to create custom-made learning pathways for all learners based on their educational goals and constraints to fully understand the viewpoint of adaptive learning in e-learning aids. Present literature faucet the static learning features of learners like their learning styles, previous knowledge level, learning ability, and browsing activities to provide adaptive learning materials [2–4]. Previous works have mainly neglected the fact that there are progressive enhancements in the grasping ability of a learner as she proceeds in the course. Furthermore, in an e-learning scenario, each learner enrolls with her own specific learning goals in mind. For example, a learner with research as his / her learning target should be able to explore current novelties and fetch in fresh thoughts while another learner whose objective is to clear an interview should aim to completely cover basic concepts.

Comparing with preceding e-learning techniques, it has been realized that a learner's learning capacity is not a homogeneous factor that increases or decreases at the same pace for all learners. Rather, a learner continuously evolves to sharpen her learning capabilities. An e-learning system should integrate a method to evaluate such enhancements, in the framework of their pre-decided learning goals. This chapter introduces a novel idea of adapting learning material based on learners' learning goals.

We organize further sections of this chapter in the following manner. Section 2.2 gives the literature survey in the field of adaptive e-learning. Section 2.3 explains the complete architecture of the goal-oriented adaptive e-learning system (GOALS). Section 2.4 presents the experimental results. Section 2.5 summarizes the chapter. Section 2.6 gives the future scope of the work.

2.2   Literature survey

An adaptive e-learning system takes into account all the characteristics of personalized learning and uses a sophisticated, data-driven approach that continuously keeps track of learners' changing behavior or evaluates their performance during learning sessions at regular intervals, compares their data with their initial knowledge levels and targeted knowledge levels, and adapts the learning path automatically.

Building up an adaptive e-learning system requires a thorough observation. The system should provide real-time support to increase learners' engagement and motivation in learning. Adaptation provides better learners' satisfaction. Researchers have shown keen interest in adaptive learning for almost a decade now. They implement some implicit or explicit mechanisms to capture learners' feedback and change the system accordingly for further suggestions. Now, we describe briefly some of the important contributions in the adaptive e-learning field that are categorized based on the features used in bringing adaptivity in these systems.

The authors in [1] suggest a two-step method to create an adaptive learning route called ACO-Map. Initially, the system computes a similarity key utilizing k-means clustering based on learners' knowledge in various concepts. Secondly, it implements ACO in combination with a concept map to generate a learning path for every group of learners. This method lacks due to the cold start problem, as it requires a good amount of database of similar users to make clusters in the first step. The technique does not take into account each learner's complete personalization and provides group adaptation because all learners are matched to the centroid cluster, i.e., the average learning features of a group. Also, the cluster-oriented mapping used here allows only one category to be associated with a learner.

In [2], the authors put forward a scheme to arrange the learning topics in a hierarchical order, in the form of text, power-point slides, and a quiz given as lecture material. Their approach initially determines the background knowledge and learning style of a learner through a series of questions. Such information is used to help set their goals as part of the organized course. With this approach, it stays constant during the course until the knowledge level is determined for a learner. The authors in [5] suggest an adaptive system that utilizes the genetic algorithm (GA) to generate a learning path for each learner. The system starts with determining the weight of each linguistic term in courseware using term frequency function. Later, it uses these weights to determine the ordering of concepts using the cosine measure. Lastly, it determines incorrect courseware concepts for each learner and generates a learning path among the incorrect concepts starting from the concept with the lowest difficulty level.

The authors in [6] perform a two-step process to bring personalization and adaptation in a learner's learning process. These processes work on the student's domain model that shows her area of learning and student's model that stores the learner's exact knowledge and goals. In the first step, the system personalizes learning material as well as filters tags and comments on various learning objects (LOs) based on learner's knowledge. Later on, it tracks learners' behavior while learning and use it to adapt to learning material.

The authors in [7] develop an intelligent adaptive system that utilizes Bayesian Networks (BN) as an inference engine to guide a student's learning process. The system contains two modules (1) input module updates the BN based on feedback or information collected from each student and (2) output module provides adaptive guidance to students, which includes navigational support through online course material, prerequisite recommendations for problem-solving, and generating appropriate learning sequences while learning a concept.

The authors in [8] initialize students' model by determining their knowledge level through a pre-test for each topic. The pre-test contains a set of multiple-choice questions, which defines a knowledge level of a topic. The system provides learning material to each learner based on his/her pre-test results. Afterward, it keeps a track of student's information while learning the lessons and doing activities. The system updates student's knowledge level after each concept learned based on the test scores and uses it in the adaptation process to deliver suitable course content to the students.

The authors in [9] start the adaptive process by determining learner's background knowledge using two sets of well-selected tests. The system generates these tests using a personalized rule-based reasoning technique exploiting questions repository and learner and domain modules. Additionally, it records the most recent three sessions of the learning procedure of each learner to determine their learning styles and dynamically adapt learning material to fit their actual needs.

Although learners' prior knowledge level and difficulty level of educational content are good factors for choosing appropriate learning material, researchers prove the significance of taking personal preferences and learning habits into account. Learning styles indicate a way students perceive and process learning content; therefore, the authors consider it a vital factor among various personal features [10,11].

Tseng *et al.* propose a novel approach that uses two sources of information for accounting personalization, namely individual styles of learning that include their sequential thinking skills, discriminatory skills, analytical skills, and spatial skills and learning habits that include learning performance, concentration, and learning achievement [12]. They offer an interactive tutoring platform that helps teachers create web-based courses and provide students with relevant learning material to improve their learning performance.

Researchers in the e-learning area realize the impact of the learner's learning ability on her learning process. Therefore, they emphasize that the e-learning system should adapt based on learners' learning abilities. They believe that this feature can promote learners' learning performances and save them from disorientation.

The authors in [13] propose a personalized e-learning scheme that considers the difficulty of course content and learner's learning ability to determine a personalized learning path. They utilize maximum likelihood estimation to calculate the learner's ability more precisely based on the learner's explicit feedback. Moreover, they use item characteristic function to model course materials and employ a collaborative voting technique for adjusting its difficulty. The system utilizes these updated information to recommend appropriate learning material to learners, thereby facilitating effective learning.

E-learning systems lack adaptive and personalized assessment. Ahmad Baylari and Montazer, G.A. develop a personalized multi-agent e-learning system that estimates learner's learning ability using item response theory (IRT). The system provides adaptive tests after every level based on learners' new learning abilities [14]. Also, the system uses artificial neural networks to diagnose learners' weak points and recommending appropriate learning material to all learners.

The authors in [15] propose an adaptive and personalized e-learning system (APeLS) that adapts the learning content as well as the learning process for learners to improve the quality of learning. APeLS self-adjusts and self-organizes the learning content and paths to change as per learners' abilities, interests, and behavior. Here, they unite educational theories with their technique to find students' learning results. The system starts with identifying an ideal learning curve through database mining to calculate a learner's potential accomplishment. Later on, APeLS adjusts each learner's learning curve to match with the ideal learning curve referred to and generates appropriate learning material.

The author in [16] proposes a personalized mobile English vocabulary learning system that can aptly recommend English news articles based on learners' reading capabilities [16]. The system utilizes fuzzy IRT to evaluate the learner's reading ability based on her feedback. Also, the system automatically discovers the unfamiliar vocabularies of the individual learner for enhancing their reading abilities and vocabulary learning.

The authors in [17] implement a self-regulated learning-assisted scheme in the proposed personalized system to encourage spontaneous and self-regulated learning abilities of learners. The self-directed learning-assisted mechanisms effectively assist learners in self-examining and self-evaluating their learning objectives and performances during the learning process.

The authors in [18] present an ontology-based approach to design an e-learning decision support system (DSS) that includes various adaptive features. Initially, the proposed approach utilizes the information collected during the registration process to identify the learner's characteristics. The DSS also updates the learner's model based on the result of activities and tests and the learner's ability to make use in the adaptation process. The updated learner model is utilized to spawn diverse learning paths for individual users.

Concept map presents learning order of concepts that makes relationships between concepts more systematic and organized. Researchers utilize concept maps to determine students' misconceptions in their learning process. The work in [19] uses a fuzzy association rule mining algorithm to determine all prerequisite relationships between concepts and form a concept map. The system determines learner's familiarity with each concept. Based on her familiarity score for each concept and using the concept map, it determines those concepts that are learning barriers for that learner and suggests learning material accordingly.

The authors in [20] utilize GA and case-based reasoning (CBR) techniques for personalized curriculum sequencing. Whenever a learner fails in a unit, the system recommends a personalized sequence of curriculum generated based on GA. Thus, learners can revise the same concepts through different sequencing and learning materials in corrective activities. CBR provides formative assessment (after each unit) and summative assessment (after several units) for each individual.

Researchers work on various other learners' features such as their learning contexts, emotions, preferences, and learning object features. The work in [21] proposes adaptive e-learning and context-aware method that supports ubiquitous learning log system. This approach aims to help learners by using information that they have logged in the past in some particular contexts (location, time, and their learning activity) and learners' learning habits. The system aids learners to capture their learning logs, reuse the required knowledge at the correct time and place.

The work in [22] puts forward a self-adaptive framework of learning objects based on learner's learning contexts. Learning contexts include learner's personal information and her digital environments such as access devices and networks. The system generates different versions of LOs dynamically based on these contexts.

The authors in [23] explore the emotions that evolve during a learning process and propose an e-learning system that distinguishes and respond properly to each learner's emotional changes. The learning model considers eight basic learning emotions: satisfaction, interest, hopefulness, engagement, confusion, frustration, boredom, and disappointment. The authors work on these emotions to improve learning experiences. The system utilizes BN to form relations between various emotional states and their contributory variables.

The authors in [24] propose a new intelligent algorithm that uses association rules mining and collaborative filtering to mine a variety of categories of interesting teaching resources and recommend few teaching resources, respectively. The major drawback of this approach is that the solution recommends only teaching resources and hence is incomplete as it lacks recommendation and adaptation in the learning path.

We find that a majority of existing adaptive e-learning systems use learners' features such as their learning styles, preferences, interests, and knowledge levels. All these features are indirect parameters that only give information about learners, but not about their abilities to take up a course that ultimately helps them in enhancing their knowledge. Some systems take explicit feedback from learners or utilize learners' learning logs to update any change in learners' learning styles or their knowledge level [5,6]. The systems that provide adaptation based on learner's knowledge level suffers from the lacunae that they put them in the low, medium, and high category [8]. This information is not exact and enough to judge and guide students.

Only a few adaptive systems utilize a learner's updated learning ability after each level for suggesting appropriate learning material [14,17,18]. The major drawback of these systems is that they consider learning ability as general. They compute it based on a learner's performance and difficulty of learning material. However, different learners have different types of abilities that may or may not help them in achieving their learning goals. Therefore, the system should be capable enough to judge and guide students accordingly. Moreover, these systems categorize LOs of a concept based on their difficulty level only. Although the difficulty is an important parameter, the system should categorize learning material on some other significant parameters that correspond to the knowledge of a course from various perspectives and learning goals.

2.2.1   State-of-the-art

Table 2.1 presents the state-of-the-art that helps in insights gained and some research gaps in recent literature.

Table 2.1 Insights gained and research gaps in the literature

Research paper	Publishing details	Content incorporated	Research gaps
Personalized E-learning with Adaptive Recommender System [25]	International Journal of Learning and Teaching, 2016	• It uses ACO to provide a personalized e-learning path. • It focuses on the pheromone deposition along a particular path which further helps in determining the most optimum path.	• Involving the heuristic factor can yield a better result.
Research on Personalized E-Learning Based on Decision Tree and RETE Algorithm [26]	International Conference on Computer Systems, Electronics and Control (ICCSEC), Dalian, 2017	• It prescribes using decision trees to classify the learners. • RETE algorithm is used to provide a production rule engine which further helps in diagnosing and helping learners.	• It gives more weightage to the behavior and learning experience of other users compared to the learner himself.
Personalized E-learning Model: A Systematic Literature Review [27]	International Conference on Information Management and Technology (ICIM-Tech), Yogyakarta, 2017	• The interaction of students is introduced globally. • Best techniques and learning algorithms were obtained based on previous research data.	• It does not include many factors of personalized e-learning such as feeling, cultural background, student environment, etc.
Modified Ant Colony Optimization with pheromone mutation for traveling salesman problem [28]	14th International Conference on Electrical Engineering/Electronics, Computer, Telecommunications and Information Technology (ECTI-CON), Phuket, 2017	• ACO has been improved based on the mutation of pheromone when an ant is caught in a local optimum. • It is tested on 22 paths in the traveling salesman problem.	• It increases the number of evaluation calls to a large extent.
A Personalized Group-Based Recommendation Approach for Web Search in E-Learning [29]	IEEE Access, 2018	• Augmentation of web search is done with a personalized recommendation of web search based on the learning style and behavior of students. • It improves performance as well as the satisfaction of students.	• Social identities of students are not taken into account. • It allows just 100 queries per day which is quite low.

(Continues)

Table 2.1 *(Continued)*

Research paper	Publishing details	Content incorporated	Research gaps
A Personalized E-Learning Services Recommendation Algorithm Based on User Learning Ability [30]	IEEE 19th International Conference on Advanced Learning Technologies (ICALT), Maceió, Brazil, 2019.	• It uses user information data and user learning behavior to design a similarity matrix while asymmetric similarity is designed based on the learning ability of the user. • These are used for recommending paths to the user.	• The correlation between user learning timing issues and knowledge is not taken into account by this algorithm.
An adaptable and personalized E-learning system applied to computer science Programmes design [31]	Education and Information Technology, 2019	• Various learning sources are extracted based on the learner's model having the background, learning style, and needs of the user.	• Predictive evaluation lacks accuracy. • Multimedia sources are not taken into account in this for learning.
Rule-based Adaptive User Interface for Adaptive E-learning System [32]	Education and Information Technology, 2019	• The natural language-processing technique is then used to utilize these extracted resources for path generation. • The adaptive user interface is based on learners' learning styles to adapt to learning material. • Learning path developed using concept map mechanism.	• Addresses learners in groups based on their learning styles. • No individual feature has been taken into account for adaptation.
Real-time personalization and recommendation in Adaptive Learning Management System [33]	Journal of Ambient Intelligent Human Computing, 2020	• Personalization based on learners' educational and behavioral skills. • Naïve Bayes classifier to classify learners based on their skills.	• Manual formation of a questionnaire to determine learners' skills.
Integrating an Intelligent Tutoring System into an Adaptive E-Learning Process [34]	Recent Advances in Mathematics and Technology, 2020	• Integrate artificial intelligence into e-learning systems to adapt learning material based on their learning styles and earning behavior.	• Worked on only learning styles and learning behavior features but not on direct performance parameters like their learning ability.
Approach Based on Artificial Neural Network to Improve Personalization in Adaptive E-Learning Systems [35]	Embedded Systems and Artificial Intelligence, 2020	• Utilize artificial neural networks to personalize learning material based on learners' knowledge background.	• The approach still needs to be tested in a real scenario.

2.3 Goal-oriented adaptive e-learning system

This chapter introduces an innovative idea of designing an e-learning framework in which all facets of a student's participation with a course are aligned together with her pre-specified learning goal. Each student undergoes a personalized assessment that is designed and evaluated in the context of her own LG. GOALS works for generating an adaptive learning path for each learner based on his/her initial learning ability and motive behind learning a course that is termed as LG. Figure 2.1 gives the complete model of GOALS. GOALS dynamically leverage the advantages of consistent improvements attained by a learner using a new metric, the goal-oriented dynamic learning ability. Through each step of the learning process, the system utilizes the meta-heuristic ACO to create a new optimized potential learning sub-path.

As a learner registers for a course with a specific learning goal, the system performs a personalized assessment of the learner based on his/her LG. This assessment is considered as a learner's initial learning ability (represented by γ) that gives an insight into the learner's knowledge of the course as per the required LG. The system stores the initial learning ability and registered learning goal of the learner into the database. After this process, the system checks whether the database contains some previous learner's records having the same LG and learning ability. If the record exists, the system provides the path saved for that user to the current learner without passing this information to the adaptive learning path generation using the ACO module. If there is no existing data, then GOALS passes the current learning ability and LG to the ACO module. The ACO module uses this information along with the database to generate a personalized learning path from the current node to the final node in the course graph. ACO generates the best optimum forward path. This process keeps on repeating until the learner completes the course.

The complete working of GOALS is explained in the following sub-sections. Section 2.3.1 introduces the goal-oriented course graph implemented by the system

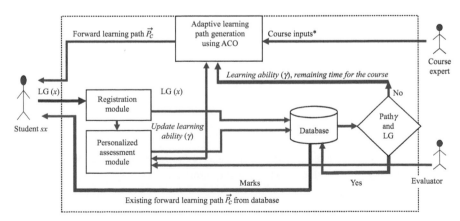

Figure 2.1   Goal-oriented adaptive e-learning system

to structure the course as per learner's LG. Section 2.3.2 explains the working of the registration module. Section 2.3.3 elucidates the personalized assessment module. Section 2.3.4 explains the ACO-based adaptive learning path generation with its objective and constraints. Section 2.3.5 explains the role of the database in GOALS.

2.3.1   Goal-oriented course graph structure

The goal-oriented course structure is the idea of designing a course in which each concept is explained through various perspectives as per the requirement of different learners depending on their goals for taking up the course. Suppose, we want to create an e-course for data structures (DS) subject. Learners can have various objectives to learn this course. For example, a prospective learner for a course on DS can register for any one of the following learning goals:

1.   Preparing for a final-semester B.Tech course exam
2.   Getting set for a job interview
3.   Starting a project, designing, and implementing new data structures
4.   Concentrating on academic aspects for teaching purposes
5.   To improve its understanding by learning about new data structures

Here, the authors of the course might be teachers, practitioners, or researchers that may contribute their views on the identical concept. Each author explains various concepts according to their knowledge and experience. For instance, a teacher explains its perspective about the concept 'Queues' using theory and examples as needed for end-semester examination goals whereas a researcher may explain the concept of queues using research papers explaining the new type of queues that help organize data in various research areas. Various perspectives at a level in the course graph represent the contribution of these authors. Figure 2.2 shows a representative course graph (CG) structure. The CG structure consists of varied components and a database as described below.

2.3.1.1   CG components

Here, we explain briefly the CG and its components.

Levels: As we all have experienced reading through a book and feel cozier with that system of organizing courses into chapters. Each chapter concisely explains a concept with different hypotheses and illustrations. This association ensures that we have covered all the topics related to that course. We adopt the same structure and organize a course in a sequence of nL levels from $Level_1 \ldots \ldots Level_{nL}$ where each level represents a specific concept.

Each of the concepts contributes distinctively towards the learning of the course. For instance, the concept of arrays and pointers has more contribution when contrasted with built-in data types in the C language course. Experts finalize the value of the Maximum Learning Success MLS_j accomplished by the student if she had learned the concept at level j.

Perspectives: Each new student who wants to take up a course has a predecided LG. Therefore, our entire organization of the course is focused on the

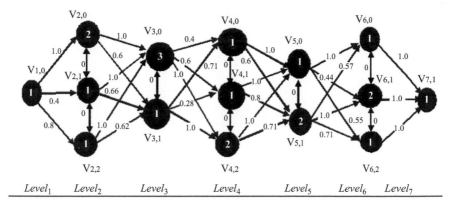

Figure 2.2   Course graph structure

learner's LG. Various experts such as practitioners, researchers, or instructors can add their perspectives on the same concept having different contributions for various LGs. Multiple vertices $\{v_{j,k}\}$ at the level j characterize the perspectives of the jth concept. Here, k signifies various perspectives at the jth level.

Learning objects: Each concept can be explained using a set of Learning Objects (LOs) which are different modules of educational material. Suppose, the concept of pointers in C can be explained starting with theory and following up by diagrams, examples, presentation for additional information. Each concept j has a fixed number nLO_j of LOs in which first LO is mandatory and all others are optional. We have not shown LOs in the CG graph to maintain clarity.

Node weight: Weight of a node $t_{j,k}$ symbolizes the aggregate time that a learner can spend on the kth perspective of concept j. This assigned time is segregated among all its LOs based on their priority towards the learner's LG. The mandatory LO and their priorities are decided by the course experts for each level.

Edge weight: A weight $DL_{j,k,k'}$ along the edge ($v_{j,k} \rightarrow v_{j+1,k'}$) signifies the level of difficulty in moving from perspective k at level j to a perspective k' at the following level $j+1$. We keep zero-edge weight for the perspectives of the same level to encourage students to pick more perspectives of a level to upgrade their learning.

2.3.1.2   Database

As learner's LG is the center point of this scheme, course experts maintain a database associated with the LG specific course graph. The database consists of various tables as explained below.

Perspective goal contribution table (PGCT): Different authors based on their experience and perception can include various perspectives of a concept. For example, a teacher explains the ACO algorithm through simple steps from a book followed by an example, whereas a researcher explains the same with the help of a research paper with its implementation. Therefore, experts decide the contribution of these perspectives accordingly towards various LGs. Table 2.2 shows the sample PGCT implemented by GOALS.

Table 2.2 Perspective goal contribution table

Learning Goal	Level$_1$	Level$_2$			Level$_3$		Level$_4$			Level$_5$		Level$_6$			Level$_7$
	$V_{1,0}$	$V_{2,0}$	$V_{2,1}$	$V_{2,2}$	$V_{3,0}$	$V_{3,1}$	$V_{4,0}$	$V_{4,1}$	$V_{4,2}$	$V_{5,0}$	$V_{5,1}$	$V_{6,0}$	$V_{6,1}$	$V_{6,2}$	$V_{7,0}$
LG$_0$	1.0	0.60	0.15	0.25	0.80	0.20	0.19	0.20	0.61	0.90	0.10	0.11	0.29	0.60	1.00
LG$_1$	1.0	0.30	0.17	0.53	0.35	0.65	0.29	0.56	0.15	0.65	0.35	0.29	0.56	0.15	1.00
LG$_2$	1.0	0.16	0.54	0.30	0.68	0.32	0.56	0.22	0.22	0.38	0.62	0.56	0.3	0.22	1.00

Learning object priority table (LOPT): Each perspective is explained by a set of LOs, but not all these LOs are equally significant for all the learners with different LGs. For example, an LO that explains ACO through MATLAB® implementation is good enough for a student with research as LG but not valued for a B. Tech student who wants to prepare for an interview and just wants an overview of ACO. So, the system maintains a LOPT database to store the relevance of LOs for various LGs. Table 2.3 shows the sample LOPT table with a different number of learning objects at different levels.

Table 2.3 Learning object priority table

	$Level_1$	$Level_2$	$Level_3$	$Level_4$	$Level_5$	$Level_6$	$Level_7$
Learning Aim	LO_0 LO_1 LO_2	LO_0 LO_1	LO_0 LO_1 LO_2	LO_0 LO_1	LO_0 LO_1 LO_2	LO_0 LO_1	LO_0 LO_1

Question relevance table (QRT): As the system assess a student after every level to work out the change in her mental ability from the previous level, this assessment is sensitive to the learner's LG. The assessment sheet contains questions associated with all learning goals but each question is assigned a weight that corresponds to its importance for a learning goal. Whenever an active learner takes an assessment, he/she is going to be assessed based on his/her LG. We incorporate a personalized examination scheme (PES) for this purpose that evaluates each question based on its relevance for her LG. QRT_j stores the relative importance of every question in the examination held at level j towards various LGs.

2.3.2 Registration module

This module registers every new learner who wants to learn the course with his/her learning goal. It passes this information to the personalized assessment module (PAM) for determining the learner's initial knowledge of the course. It also saves the learner's registered LG in the database.

2.3.3 Personalized assessment module

When a student enrolls for a course, the system keeps track of the learner's dynamic learning ability (DLA) after every level to recommend him/her the appropriate learning material according to DLA. To measure DLA, PAM examines each level covered by the student s_x as she progresses in the course. The system calculates the performance $P_j(x)$ of s_x at level j by taking a weighted average of the marks achieved by her as given below.

$$P_j(x) = \frac{\sum_{i=1}^{N_q} QRT_j[LG(x)][i] * M_j[i](x)}{\sum_{i=1}^{N_q} QRT_j[LG(x)][i]} \tag{2.1}$$

Where *Nq* gives the total number of questions in the examination. QRT table furnishes the importance of the question relative to different learning goals *LG(x)*. $M_j[i](x)$ gives the marks obtained by the candidate learner *x*.

2.3.3.1   Dynamic learning ability

The weight of each question is given in the *QRT* database. Her new learning ability $\gamma_j(x)$ at level *j* is a weighted blend of performance $P_j(x)$ of that level and previous level $\gamma_{j-1}(x)$ as shown below:

$$\gamma_j(x) = \gamma_{j-1}(x) \times \Omega + P_j(x) \times (1 - \Omega) \tag{2.2}$$

Where $0 \le j \le nL\text{-}1$ and $0 \le \gamma_j(x) \le 1$.

The system determines the overall learning achieved by taking the generated learning path as cumulative learning achieved by taking each perspective added to the path.

2.3.3.2   Dynamic learning success

The dynamic learning success $DLS_{j,k}(x)$ of student s_x after learning the kth perspective of level *j* is given by:

$$DLS_{j,k}(x) = MLS_j\left(1 - e^{-\gamma_j(x)t_{j,k}(x)}\right) \tag{2.3}$$

$DLS_{j,k}(x)$ is a mapping of a student's dynamic learning ability $\gamma_j(x)$ and the time spent $t_{j,k}$ in learning the perspective $v_{j,k}$. To evaluate the future learning paths of a learner who has just finished learning level *c*, we utilize her latest ability $\gamma_c(x)$ to calculate $[DLS_{j,k}(x)]_{\gamma c}$ at subsequent levels.

2.3.4   *ACO-based learning path generation*

At each level, the ACO sub-system begins its search with the aid of ants for the best forward learning path. Each ant utilizes the learner's updated learning ability $\gamma_c(x)$ and dynamic learning success to compute the best learning path. The best learning path comprises of the following objectives and constraints:

2.3.4.1   Objectives

GOALS tries to offer the most contributed perspectives at each level towards the learner's LG as well as deepen the knowledge of concepts by offering more perspectives that she can take within the time limit. The objectives utilized to determine an optimized dynamic learning path are given below:

Coverage factor: Assume student s_x has completed the course till level *c*. The coverage factor (CF) for student s_x is calculated by taking cumulative DLS of the first perspective chosen at every level along the forward path $\tilde{P}_c$ from *c* till the end of the course using (2.4):

$$CF(\tilde{P}_c, x) = \sum_{k \in \tilde{P}_c, j=c}^{nL} \left[DLS_{j,k}(x)\right]_{\gamma_c} \times PGCT_j[LG(x)][k] \tag{2.4}$$

The system can maximize the CF if it suggests a concept learning by first giving the most contributed perspective towards LG.

Depth factor: The depth factor (DF) measures the depth of learning of s_x by learning various perspectives of a concept probably in the order of their contribution towards LG as shown in below equation.

$$DF_j(\tilde{P}_c, x) = \frac{\sum_{k \in \tilde{P}_c} [DLS_{j,k}(x)]_{\gamma_c} \times PGCT_j[LG(x)][k]}{\sum_{k=1}^{nP(j)} PGCT_j[LG(x)][k]} \qquad (2.5)$$

The cumulative DF for the forward path $\tilde{P}_c$ is calculated as:

$$CDF_c(\tilde{P}_c, x) = \sum_{j=c}^{nL} DF_j(\tilde{P}_c, x) \qquad (2.6)$$

Cumulative difficulty level: This factor measures the difficulty of the forward path $\tilde{P}_c$. Cumulative difficulty level (CDL) is computed by adding the weights of the edges along the path. Thus:

$$CDL_c(\tilde{P}_c) = \sum_{j=c}^{nL} \sum_{k \in \tilde{P}_c} DL\left(v_{j,k} \rightarrow v_{j+1,k'}\right) \qquad (2.7)$$

Path-value: Adding up all the above parameters give us the path-value (PV) of the candidate path that represents the overall fitness of the generated solution is presented below:

$$PV_c(\tilde{P}_c, x) = w_1 \times CF(\tilde{P}_c, x) + w_2 \times CDF_c(\tilde{P}_c, x) - w_3 \times CDL_c(\tilde{P}_c) \qquad (2.8)$$

w_1, w_2, and w_3 are the pre-determined weights to decide the importance of the three coverage factors CF_c, CDF_c, and CDL_c, respectively.

2.3.4.2 Time constraint

As the course has some pre-defined time limit T_{max}. Suppose, the time spent by a learner s_x to learn the course till level c be $T_c(x)$. The system should check that the time taken by the generated path should not exceed the remaining time for the course. Thus,

$$\sum_{j=c..nL-1} \sum_{k \in \tilde{P}_c} t_{j,k}(x) \leq T_{max} - T_c(x) \qquad (2.9)$$

2.3.4.3 Ant colony optimization

All ants spot their routes by building guided evolution from one node to another node. After this, it deposits a definite amount of pheromone on its selected traversal path, which represents its fitness as per the required solution. This process keeps on repeating for ensuing nodes until all the assigned ants in the current population turn up at the final destination. Figure 2.3 shows a complete ACO workflow while finding the best learning path. The following sub-sections show the various steps followed in the workflow.

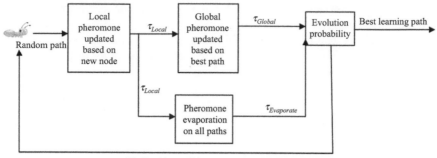

Figure 2.3   Ant colony optimization working

1. **Pheromone updation:** All paths are loaded with a constant initial pheromone level, which is incrementally modified by a population of ant-agents afterward. Assume $\tau_{u \to v}^{old}$ be the quantity of pheromone value of edge (u, v) at a specified time. When an ant makes a move from node u to node v while generating a learning path, the pheromone value is locally revised as follows:

$$\tau_{u \to v}^{new} = \begin{cases} \tau_{u \to v}^{old} + \in \times \delta & \textit{If } DL_{u \to v} = 0 \\ \tau_{u \to v}^{old} + \in \times \left([DLS_v(x)]_{\gamma_u} \right)^{\phi} & \textit{Otherwise} \end{cases} \qquad (2.10)$$

The δ is a positive constant factor that facilitates an even shift between various perspectives on the same level. Remember that the amount of pheromone increases in direct proportion to the expected value of DLS, for perspectives at dissimilar levels. The parameter φ shows the strength of the DLS factor in increasing the pheromone level.

The ant, which determines the subsequent node that gives the most effective learning PV among all its competitor ants increases the pheromone values globally. Let best represents that node. Then,

$$\tau_{u \to v}^{new} = \tau_{u \to v}^{new} + \psi \times PV_{best}(x) \qquad (2.11)$$

where ψ is the factor that represents the impact of the PV factor in incrementing the pheromone level.

2. **Transition probability:** As per the balanced fitness heuristic, the probability of an ant jumping from node u to node v is in direct proportion to the pheromone level that is accumulated on edge (u,v). Let $\{W\}$ be the set of all nodes that are directly accessible from u. Then,

$$prob_{u \to v} = \frac{\tau_{u \to v}^{new}}{\displaystyle\sum_{x \in \{W\}} \tau_{u \to x}^{new}} \qquad (2.12)$$

3. **Pheromone evaporation:** After one set of ants have carried ahead their hunt in iteration *i*, the next generation of ants tracks suit in iteration *i*+1. The accrued pheromone levels over numerous generations on various nodes diminish slowly that reinstates the outdated information by recently gained experience. Assume μ represents the pheromone evaporation rate.

$$\tau_{u \to v}(i+1) = \begin{cases} \tau_{u \to v}(i) \times (1-\mu) & \textit{If}\, \tau_{u \to v}(i) \times (1-\mu) \geq \in \\ \in & \textit{Otherwise} \end{cases} \quad (2.13)$$

4. **Convergence:** Successive generations of ants continue scanning the search space until the pheromone levels reach a stable state. The aim is to search out a learning path with the highest value while ensuring that the time constraint is met. The ant finds the learning path that maximizes $PV_c\left(\tilde{P}_c, x\right)$ convergence. The system returns this route as the optimal forward learning path from the current level to the ultimate level of the course.

The ACO-generated optimal learning path includes all the concepts, perspectives, and learning objects that are truly beneficial for the learner to achieve their desired LG. The learner responds by learning from the current node or topic, the primary node of the recommended forward learning path. The system continues to repeat the iterative evolution driven by ACO from one node to the next until it achieves its learning goal.

ACO seeks to constantly adjust the changing learning ability of the learner. The fitness of a learning path, i.e., PV, is optimized by maximizing factors related to coverage and depth and minimizing difficulty level. There is, however, a tradeoff involved, as studying paths with greater scope and complexity is inherently difficult. ACO takes this point off by reducing the level of difficulty for weak learners and increasing it for those learners who affirm consistent progress. Consequently, if a hitherto weak learner subsequently increases in performance, then the system recommends her with more difficult learning paths, which may be difficult but may have broader coverage and greater depth of the course topics. When her learning ability declines, then as per her learning goal, ACO recommends an easier learning path with appropriate perspectives and LOs. In all cases, the system attempts to optimize the PV.

2.3.5 *Persistence into database and self-learning*

A new user registers by providing the learning goal and taking a quiz. Based on the marks obtained in the quiz, the initial learning ability of the student is determined and this information about the student is stored in the database, which will later be retrieved by PAM. The database is used for storage and retrieval of marks obtained by the user in a quiz after the completion of each level. The above-retrieved information may be used in updating the learning ability. The database may help the recommender system to give accurate and timely decisions. Thus, the system will enhance the capability of self-learning.

2.4   Experimental results

We implemented the GOALS using Python 2.7.3 in its IDE named IDLE on the Intel Core i5 processor with windows 10. Table 2.4 describes the constants used by the system with their values.

Table 2.4   Input parameters

S. No.	Constant/threshold	Symbol	Value
1.	Maximum time for course completion	T_{max}	35
2.	Weight to decide the relative importance of past and current performances	Ω	0.8
3.	Weight for coverage: *CF*	w_1	6
4.	Weight for depth: *CDF*	w_2	3
5.	Weight for path difficulty: *CDL*	w_3	2.5
6.	Initial pheromone level	$\in$	0.1
7.	Evaporation rate	μ	0.3
8.	Parameter to control the impact of Pheromone factor	α	0.8
9.	Balancing factor for pheromone factor	δ	10
10.	Controlling the impact of DLS in local pheromone update	φ	1.5
11.	Controlling the impact of DLS in global pheromone update	Ψ	T_{max}

2.4.1   *Data preparation*

Learning patterns: We simulated the following learning patterns:

1. **Linear improvement pattern:** The candidate student S_1 starts with $\gamma_{initial} = 0.20$ and subsequently, her dynamic learning ability improves by 20% for each level she covers compared to the previous level.
2. **Late improvement pattern:** Sometimes, a student may start with high initial learning ability, but then suffers low performance when the system prescribes difficult learning paths based on her initial potential. To simulate this scenario, we consider a student S2 starts with $\gamma_{initial} = 0.5$. Her dynamic learning ability decreases by 20% after *Level₁*, *Level₂*, and *Level₃.* The system then rectifies the path by suggesting less difficult perspectives. The student responds with an improvement of 20% at *Level₄* and retains this rate of improvement at subsequent levels.

2.4.2   *Evolution of learning path with regular improvement*

Table 2.5 displays the forward learning paths produced after each level. It shows the values of *CF, CDF, CDL, CPV,* and time utilized for the initial and the final learning path.

2.4.2.1   Static learning path

Firstly, the learner begins her studies with the initial learning ability $\gamma_{initial} = 0.2$. At this point, the best learning path for her is the static path produced by the module

Table 2.5 Learning paths generated after each level for S_1 and path attributes

Current node	γ	Forward path(Level, {succession of perspectives taken at particular level})(taken nodes marked bold)	Values for forward paths CF	CDF	CDL	CPV	Time
ϕ	0.20	$(1, 0) \to (2, \{1, 0\}) \to (3, 1) \to (4, 1) \to (5, 1) \to (6, \{0, 2\}) \to (7, 0)$	1.79	1.95	3.65	7.46	29.4
$v_{1,0}$	0.24	$(2, \{1, 0\}) \to (3, 1) \to (4, 2) \to (5, 0) \to (6, \{2, 0\}) \to (7, 0)$					
$v_{2,0}$	0.288	$(3, \{1, 0\}) \to (4, \{1, 2\}) \to (5, 0) \to (6, 2) \to (7, 0)$					
$v_{3,0}$	0.345	$(4, \{0, 2\}) \to (5, 0) \to (6, 2) \to (7, 0)$					
$v_{4,2}$	0.415	$(5, 0) \to (6, \{1, 2\}) \to (7, 0)$					
$v_{5,0}$	0.498	$(6, \{1, 2\}) \to (7,0)$					
$v_{6,2}$	0.597	$(7, 0)$					
FINAL PATH		$(1, 0) \to (2, \{1, 0\}) \to (3, \{1, 0\}) \to (4, \{0, 2\}) \to (5, 0) \to (6, \{1, 2\}) \to (7, 0)$ Values for the Final Path	3.25	3.71	3.84	21.03	30.3

for generating the learning path. Referring to Figure 2.2, we can observe that the ACO sub-system gives preference to edges with fewer difficulty levels. This shows that, despite the less initial learning ability of the learner, the system charts an easy path with high cumulative PV.

2.4.2.2   Dynamic learning paths

Subsequently, the student learning ability enhances with $\gamma_1 = 0.24$ at $Level_1$. The system identifies this fact and is working to refine its learning according to its new capability. The findings show the below outcomes:

1. ***More perspectives:*** The static learning path (first row of Table 2.5) suggested only one perspective, i.e., $v_{3,1}$ at $Level_3$ and $v_{4,1}$ at $Level_4$ whereas the final path in the last row includes two perspectives at $Level_3$ and $Level_4$. This clearly shows the system is attempting to improve the learning depth.
2. ***Perspectives with a high contribution towards LG(x):*** The static learning path focuses on low difficulty edges as compared to higher contributing nodes, as it assumes students at the same level throughout the course. We show this by an example. The static learning path ignored higher contributing perspectives $v_{3,0}$ at $Level_3$ and $v_{4,2}$ at $Level_4$ whereas the dynamic learning path focuses on perspectives with a higher contribution towards LG_0. This can be cross-checked from the *PGCT* database given in Table 2.2. We verified that all higher contributing perspectives are included in the dynamic learning path shown in the last row.
3. ***Increase in path difficulty:*** Comparing the static learning path with the complete (last row) dynamic learning path, we find that the overall *CDL* complexity increases from 3.65 to 3.84. This suggests that the system is prodding the initially weaker students to explore more complex transitions while they learn.
4. ***Boost in path value:*** We conducted this experiment with three initially weak students having $\gamma_{initial}$ equal to 0.30, 0.40, and 0.50, and found that the *CPV* in each case doubled on average as opposed to their respective static paths. We also tested two moderate students with $\gamma_{initial}$ equal to 0.5 and 0.7 and obtained an average 50% improvement in *CPV* relative to their static learning paths.
5. ***Time constraint fulfilled:*** Since the course has a tight deadline of 35-time units, it has been able to fulfill the full adaptive learning path. The adaptive learning path scheme also improves time usage as compared to the static learning path scheme. We can verify the same from the last column of Table 2.5.

2.4.3   Evolution of learning path with late improvement

This experiment is conducted to demonstrate the difference in learning paths in the case of a student who initially does not perform well but then slowly improves her performance in the course. Having confidence in her ability, assume learner S_2 will register with a fairly high $\gamma_{initial} = 0.50$ and learning goal as LG_0. However, as she continues with the course, she finds it difficult to cope with it and her γ decreases by 20% of its previous value after $Level_1$, $Level_2$, and $Level_3$. Table 2.6 shows the created forward paths and the values for the different path attributes.

Table 2.6 Learning paths generated after each level for S_2 and path attributes

Start node	Γ	Forward path(Level, {Succession of perspectives taken at particular level})	Values for forward paths				
			CF	CDF	CDL	CPV	Time
ϕ	0.50	(1, 0)→ (2, {0, 2}) → (3, 0) → (4, 0) → (5, 0) → (6, {1, 2}) → (7, 0)	2.87	3.33	4.84	15.11	28.8
$v_{1,0}$	0.40	(2, 0) → (3, {1, 0}) → (4, {2, 0}) → (5, 0) → (6, {1, 0}) → (7, 0)					
$v_{2,0}$	0.32	(3, 0) → (4, { 1, 2}) → (5, 1) → (6, {2, 1}) → (7, 0)					
$v_{3,0}$	0.256	(4, {0, 2, 1}) → (5, {1, 0}) → (6, 2) → (7, 0)					
$v_{4,1}$	0.307	(5, {1, 0}) → (6, {2, 0}) → (7, 0)					
$v_{5,0}$	0.369	(6,{1, 2}) → (7, 0)					
$v_{6,2}$	0.442	(7, 0)					
FINAL PATH		(1, 0) → (2, 0) → (3, 0) → (4, {0, 2, 1}) → (5, {1, 0}) → (6, {1, 2}) → (7, 0)	Overall values for the final path				
			3.16	3.44	4.64	17.68	32.8

2.4.3.1   Static learning path

Because S_2 is an above-average student, the system gives more priority to higher contributing perspectives that include making transitions on edges with high difficulty levels.

2.4.3.2   Dynamic learning paths

When the learner learns the $Level_1$ concept, they reduce their performance, and at $Level_1$ γ_1 decrease to 0.40. Still, S_2 has comparable high dynamic learning ability, it gives preference to the nodes with a higher contribution towards LG_0. Still, the student does not show any improvement and γ_2 decreases to 0.32 and γ_3 become 0.256. Therefore, it selects only those perspectives in each level transition that can be accessed with lesser difficulty-level edges. For example, with reference to Figure 2.2, we perceive that from node $v_{3,0}$, it goes to the next-level perspective $v_{4,0}$ with $DL_{3,0,0} = 0.4$ instead of choosing upper contributing perspective $v_{4,2}$ with $DL_{3,0,2} = 1.0$. Thus, the system selects perspectives based on its capacity and does not consider changes in coverage and depth. After the learner shows some progress after $Level_3$, the focus on generating the learning path moves to paths with a high degree of coverage and depth.

The experimental findings indicate that as learners progress when learning the course, the system provides them with the choices for more challenging learning paths, with a greater focus on increasing the learning path coverage and depth. Nevertheless, if they degrade in performance, the system searches for fewer difficulty-level perspectives and reduces path complexity by removing some less important perspectives from adaptive learning paths determined based on their LGs.

2.5   Conclusion

The chapter presents an innovative learning-goal-oriented e-learning scheme. After each level is covered by the learner, the system dynamically adapts his learning path based on his pre-determined objectives and personalized performance assessment. GOALS aims to bring about a substantial change in the different values of the learning path for learners with evolving learning abilities. Precisely the GOALS framework:

1. Tries to provide as many perspectives as possible of a concept to expand the learning depth of that topic within the time limit allotted for the course;
2. Often provides perspectives that lead to a greater contribution to the common learning goal of the learners, so that learners need to know about each topic relevant to their learning goal;
3. Discovers challenging transition paths for learning to search for better and more perspectives as a learner improves his learning ability, and
4. Follows the time limit for completion of the specified course.

2.6 Future scope

Goal-oriented adaptive e-learning has a very promising future. This approach not only focuses on learner's attributes but also their goal for learning a course. In today's scenario where COVID-19 has put everything in lockdown, all schools and colleges have started their online classes. This situation has put a lot of pressure on teachers as well as on kids, as it is very difficult to manage kids in live sessions and fruitfully utilize all time. Our developed adaptive system can relieve the pressure from kids as they can attend the session as per their time requirements. Teachers can also be helped, as they need not record sessions or present live sessions but only have to update the system with the learning material, keeping in mind the level of each topic to be taught and using different learning objects so that kids can learn a topic in many ways as per their understanding. The same system can be utilized for multiple classes as we can explain a topic in multiple ways and with increased details using various perspectives. Also, even if a student is of the lower grade but wants to gain some extra knowledge of some topic, they can choose perspectives designed for the higher classes.

References

[1] Kardan AA, Ebrahim MA, and Imani MB. A new personalized learning path generation method: Aco-map. Indian Journal of Scientific Research. 2014;5 (1):17–24.
[2] Al Saiyd NA, and Al-Sayed IA. A generic model of student-based adaptive intelligent web-based learning environment. In Proceedings of the World Congress on Engineering 2013 (Vol. 2, pp. 781–786).
[3] Riad B, Ali S, Mourad H, and Hamid S. An adaptive learning based on ant colony and collaborative filtering. In Proceedings of the World Congress on Engineering 2012 (Vol. 2, pp. 851–855).
[4] Basuki A. Personalized learning path of a web-based learning system. International Journal of Computer Applications. 2012;53(7).
[5] Hong CM, Chen CM, and Chang MH. Personalized learning path generation approach for web-based learning. In 4th WSEAS International Conference on E-ACTIVITIES, Miami, Florida, USA 2005 Nov 17 (pp. 62–68).
[6] Šimko M, Barla M, and Bieliková M. ALEF: A framework for adaptive web-based learning 2.0. In IFIP International Conference on Key Competencies in the Knowledge Society 2010 Sep 20 (pp. 367–378). Springer, Berlin, Heidelberg.
[7] Tsolis D, Stamou S, Christia P, et al. An adaptive and personalized open source e-learning platform. Procedia-Social and Behavioral Sciences. 2010;9:38–43.
[8] Esichaikul V, Lamnoi S, and Bechter C. Student modelling in adaptive e-learning systems. Knowledge Management & E-Learning: An International Journal. 2011;3(3):342–55.

[9]   Al Saiyd NA, and Al-Sayed IA. A generic model of student-based adaptive intelligent web-based learning environment. In Proceedings of the World Congress on Engineering 2013 (Vol. 2, pp. 781–786).

[10] Hsu CK, Hwang GJ, and Chang CK. Development of a reading material recommendation system based on a knowledge engineering approach. Computers & Education. 2010;55(1):76–83.

[11] Papanikolaou KA, Grigoriadou M, Magoulas GD, and Kornilakis H. Towards new forms of knowledge communication: The adaptive dimension of a web-based learning environment. Computers & Education. 2002;39 (4):333–60.

[12] Tseng JC, Chu HC, Hwang GJ, and Tsai CC. Development of an adaptive learning system with two sources of personalization information. Computers & Education. 2008;51(2):776–86.

[13] Chen CM, and Duh LJ. Personalized web-based tutoring system based on fuzzy item response theory. Expert Systems with Applications. 2008;34 (4):2298–315.

[14] Baylari A, and Montazer GA. Design a personalized e-learning system based on item response theory and artificial neural network approach. Expert Systems with Applications. 2009;36(4):8013–21.

[15] Liu HI, and Yang MN. QoL guaranteed adaptation and personalization in E-learning systems. IEEE Transactions on Education. 2005;48(4):676–87.

[16] Chen CM, Hsu SH, Li YL, and Peng CJ. Personalized intelligent m-learning system for supporting effective English learning. In 2006 IEEE International Conference on Systems, Man and Cybernetics 2006 Oct 8 (Vol. 6, pp. 4898–4903). IEEE.

[17] Chen CM. Personalized E-learning system with self-regulated learning assisted mechanisms for promoting learning performance. Expert Systems with Applications. 2009;36(5):8816–29.

[18] Yarandi M, Jahankhani H, and Tawil AR. An adaptive e-learning decision support system. In 2012 15th International Conference on Interactive Collaborative Learning (ICL) 2012 Sep 26 (pp. 1–5). IEEE.

[19] Hung CL, and Hung YW. A practical approach for constructing an adaptive tutoring model based on concept map. In 2009 IEEE International Conference on Virtual Environments, Human-Computer Interfaces and Measurements Systems 2009 May 11 (pp. 298–303). IEEE.

[20] Huang MJ, Huang HS, and Chen MY. Constructing a personalized e-learning system based on genetic algorithm and case-based reasoning approach. Expert Systems with Applications. 2007;33(3):551–64.

[21] Li M, Ogata H, Hou B, Uosaki N, and Yano Y. Personalization in context-aware ubiquitous learning-log system. In 2012 IEEE Seventh International Conference on Wireless, Mobile and Ubiquitous Technology in Education 2012 Mar 27 (pp. 41–48). IEEE.

[22] Jiuxin C, Bo M, and Junzhou L. The self-adaptive framework of learning object based on context. In 2008 International Conference on Computer Science and Software Engineering 2008 Dec 12 (Vol. 5, pp. 941–944). IEEE.

[23] Shen L, Wang M, and Shen R. Affective e-learning: Using "emotional" data to improve learning in pervasive learning environment. Journal of Educational Technology & Society. 2009;12(2):176–89.

[24] Gong M. Personalized e-learning system by using intelligent algorithm. In First International Workshop on Knowledge Discovery and Data Mining (WKDD 2008) 2008 Jan 23 (pp. 400–401). IEEE.

[25] Bourkoukou O, El Bachari E, and El Adnani M. A personalized e-learning based on recommender system. International Journal of Learning and Teaching. 2016;2(2):99–103.

[26] Zhou TF, Pan YQ, and Huang LR. Research on personalized E-learning based on decision tree and RETE algorithm. In 2017 International Conference on Computer Systems, Electronics and Control (ICCSEC) 2017 Dec 25 (pp. 1392–1396). IEEE.

[27] Jando E, Hidayanto AN, Prabowo H, and Warnars HL. Personalized E-learning model: A systematic literature review. In 2017 International Conference on Information Management and Technology (ICIMTech) 2017 Nov 15 (pp. 238–243). IEEE.

[28] Ratanavilisagul C. Modified ant colony optimization with pheromone mutation for travelling salesman problem. In 2017 14th International Conference on Electrical Engineering/Electronics, Computer, Telecommunications and Information Technology (ECTI-CON) 2017 Jun 27 (pp. 411–414). IEEE.

[29] Rahman MM, and Abdullah NA. A personalized group-based recommendation approach for web search in e-learning. IEEE Access. 2018;6:34166–78.

[30] He H, Zhu Z, Guo Q, and Huang X. A personalized E-learning services recommendation algorithm based on user learning ability. In 2019 IEEE 19th International Conference on Advanced Learning Technologies (ICALT) 2019 Jul 15 (Vol. 2161, pp. 318–320). IEEE.

[31] Aeiad E, and Meziane F. An adaptable and personalised e-learning system applied to computer science Programmes design. Education and Information Technologies. 2019;24(2):1485–509.

[32] Kolekar SV, Pai RM, and MM MP. Rule based adaptive user interface for adaptive e-learning system. Education and Information Technologies. 2019;24(1):613–41.

[33] Jagadeesan S, and Subbiah J. Real-time personalization and recommendation in adaptive learning management system. Journal of Ambient Intelligence and Humanized Computing. 2020:1–1.

[34]   Hibbi FZ, and Abdoun O. Integrating an intelligent tutoring system into an adaptive e-learning process. In Recent Advances in Mathematics and Technology 2020 (pp. 141–150). Birkhäuser, Cham.

[35]   Azzi I, Jeghal A, Radouane A, Yahyaouy A, and Tairi H. Approach based on artificial neural network to improve personalization in adaptive e-learning systems. In Embedded Systems and Artificial Intelligence 2020 (pp. 463–474). Springer, Singapore.

Chapter 3

Predicting students' behavioural engagement in microlearning using learning analytics model

*Wan Mohd Amir Fazamin Wan Hamzah[1],
Mohd Hafiz Yusoff[1], Ismahafezi Ismail[1] and
Norkhatimah Ismail[2]*

3.1 Introduction

Today, the use of mobile and cloud computing as well as technology has influenced the e-learning development in many organizations [1]. The student-centred learning trend is one of the e-learning service factors in universities and schools that have been improved with added values. Now, students can access the e-learning platform on a cloud server with their mobile devices. Several ways and practices in e-learning today include learning management systems (LMS), blended learning, microlearning, mobile learning, open learning, self-learning, and virtual learning [2].

Microlearning refers to the micro perspective in learning contact, education, and exercise [3]. This practice is widely used in the e-learning domain and other fields related to the new paradigm of the learning process in the microenvironment. Microlearning relates to smaller learning units and short-term learning activity. It is more on push technology through push media, which reduces the cognitive burden on students. Microlearning has been considered as a very flexible, efficient, relaxed, and effective way of learning [2]. Gabrielli, Kimani, and Catarci [4] listed technology and content usability factors as among the essential requirements for a microlearning experience. Technology enables the most intuitive and natural interaction among different people from different levels of expertise.

In terms of education, student engagement refers to self-participation and interaction with learning materials, activities, and communities [5]. Meanwhile, e-learning involves students' interaction with computer systems and applications [6]. Student engagement is one of the key indicators of a successful implementation of e-learning [7]. Traditionally, the questionnaire method was used to measure and evaluate students' engagement in e-learning. Today, there is a growing interest in

[1]School of Information Technology, Faculty of Informatics and Computing, Universiti Sultan Zainal Abidin, Terengganu, Malaysia
[2]Panitia Pengajian Am, SMK Bukit Tunggal, Terengganu, Malaysia

e-learning data analysis based on log files. Several previous studies analysed log files to predict student engagement and motivation in using e-learning applications [8–13]. Those studies were carried out based on the educational data mining technique, which is widely used in analysing the various patterns of online learning behaviour and predicting learning outcomes. Another popular technique that uses a similar approach but with different focus is learning analytics (LA).

LA is a field of study that comes from various learning-related areas. The studies on LA combined several existing techniques such as academic analytics, action research, educational data mining, recruitment system and personal adaptive learning. LA is generically related to all terms describing the field of technology-enhanced learning (TEL) that focus on development method for analysing and tracking the patterns of data collected from educational settings and utilize them to support learning experience [14–19]. Numerous LA studies have been carried out on students' behaviour in e-learning. Those studies included learning environment based on basic settings in universities/colleges, schools, and informal settings. However, LA study on predicting students' behavioural engagement in microlearning is yet to be widely conducted. The data-access method used in the previous studies was unable to track and record students' behaviour in microlearning. The learning data recorded for the studies were related to student's data in attempting the applications, accessing learning content, time durations, and login frequency [8–13]. Studies on the methods used for predicting students' behavioural engagement in microlearning application did not expand well.

Conducting a study to predict the student behavioural engagement in microlearning is significant to overcome the problems associated with students' behavioural engagement. After the prediction results are obtained, the proposed solutions will be given, followed by finding the best solution, signals, and alerts, guiding and evaluating as well as design improvements [20–22]. Thus, this study was conducted to develop a LA model in predicting students' behavioural engagement in microlearning. The results of this study are expected to help teachers, lecturers, or developers of microlearning applications in taking actions based on the findings obtained.

3.2   LA studies

According to Nistor, Derntl, and Klamma [23], an analytical study on learning is carried out based on three basic settings; universities/colleges, schools, and informal settings. The study involves four areas of LA study, namely knowledge domain modelling, information visualization, trend analysis and prediction, as well as personalization and adaptation. Analytical study on learning in universities/colleges is mostly done using analytics tools of learning designed and developed to analyse the students. There are also universities like the University of Maryland, Baltimore County (UMBC), that used built-in analytics tools in their LMS. Table 3.1 shows the analytics studies conducted at universities/colleges. Universities/colleges also use LA data to help their students in gaining better

Table 3.1   Learning analytics studies at universities/colleges

Researcher	Learning analytics study
[22]	*Predictive models to provide meaningful feedback to students.* This research used learner analytics by applying Course Signals to challenging courses, which showed a great promise concerning the success of first and second-year students as well as their overall retention to the university. The continued use of Course Signals as a means of helping instructors provided detailed feedback to their students and assisted them in their academic endeavours ultimately, which is highly warranted.
[24]	*The exploratory study of two language learnings in MOOCs.* This exploration described drop-outs as among the causes of the decrease in the forum activity. This pattern was also present when researchers considered only students who passed the course as well as in other non-MOOCs experiments.
[25]	*A study on profiling and supporting learners to access Open Educational Resources (OERs) in microlearning context.* The researchers used conceptual maps to illustrate what is found by the educational data mining (EDM) and learning analytics (LA) study. This research aimed to bridge the gap between the promise of online open learning (OL) and OL's current limitations by leveraging the concept of microlearning to maximise its advantages by offering learners a better learning experience.
[26]	*Analysing students' behaviour for developing their writing skills using LMS data and how it impacts the course design.* The study's purpose was to demonstrate what instructors can learn about students' behaviours and learning design on their success for a particular outcome. This study was particularly important for the instructors as there is a need for new ways of understanding what is happening within the courses. The researchers continue to try to close the achievement gap in education. Many students tend to avoid writing assignments; nevertheless, the study failed to address the motivation, factors, and reasons students decided not to complete their assignments.
[29]	*Understanding students' learning behaviour when interacting with the tools of Technology Enhanced Learning (TEL).* The research explained a comprehensive experiment designed with the participation of 120 students. Comparison between interaction data to the learning outcomes was performed, which led to the discovery of common patterns and cross-correlations between variables for profiling students learning activities and attitudes. This was also achieved through the experiment, observations, interviews, and demographic questionnaires to acquire the learners' background, motivation, and feedback.
[30]	*Grouping to improve the educational process mining while optimising performance and modelling abilities gained at the same time.* The researchers proposed using clustering to improve educational process mining and simultaneously optimise the performance/fitness and comprehensibility/size of the model obtained. In particular, the comprehensibility of a model is the core goal in education due to the transferral of basic knowledge it entails. Forming graphs, models, or visual representation is very useful for monitoring the learning process and providing feedback; one of our future goals being to do it in real-time.

(Continues)

Table 3.1   (Continued)

Researcher	Learning analytics study
[31]	*Providing an understanding of various data-related sources in learning, analysing data from their understanding of practices at the faculty/departments and issuing reports that summarise the key points, and give action recommendations.* This research explained that the data wrangler process is not uniform. It utilises the individual strengths of the data wranglers and key stakeholders in the faculties. This is as wanted in capacity-building training; the process must start from people's existing expertise. If capacity building is required, this expertise will be lacking. The issues of data quality discovered through the data wrangler process showed the value of the sense-making activity.
[32]	*Utilising the arrangement of artefact spaces to provide visualisations that generate summary data of idea distribution.* This research used purely computational techniques to make sense of the dynamic creation of artefacts and interactions that lack the flexibility to work on multi-modal representations. By leveraging a user-interaction driven method of concept classification, the summary level information has been generated on idea distribution, allowing teachers to adjust their teaching in real-time. The study concluded that including students as part of the sense-making process has a two-fold benefit.
[33]	*Exploring the use of student video annotation tools when two different teaching approaches are used.* The research results indicated that students in the course with graded self-reflections adopt more linguistic and psychological related processes compared to the course with non-graded self-reflections. Generally, the effect size of the graded reflections was lower for students who took both courses in parallel. Consistent with previous research, the research identified that students were inclined to make the majority of their self-reflection annotations early in the video timeline.
[34]	*Methods for identifying patterns and tracking students' evolution over time.* The analysis of the Design of Interactive Teaching and Learning Systems course using the identifying patterns and tracking student evolution over time method has provided some useful insights concerning the patterns of resource usage of the students. From tracing the bipartite student-resource clusters overtime during the lecture period, it was seen that majority of the students behave similarly. They access the lecture slides assigned to the topic and the wiki articles written by other students every week.
[35]	*Determining expectations with optimal expectation of course options for all engineering students.* This study comprised developing a course recommendation system and better-supporting students through their chosen source of study by balancing that against the wealth of knowledge that the institution has at its disposal regarding those course selections. Students obtaining a lot of information about successful characteristics may raise ethical questions such as replicating gender, ethnicity, or socioeconomic differences in choosing courses.

(Continues)

Table 3.1   (*Continued*)

Researcher	Learning analytics study
[36]	*Measuring the level of attention based on the coordination of students' actions.* This research explained the observations on student-to-student influence and measurements. Researchers showed parallel findings with previous theories and formulated a new concept for measuring the level of attention based on synchronization of student actions. Observations by researchers indicated that students with lower levels of attention are slower to react then focused students, a phenomenon we named "sleepers' lag".
[37]	*Evaluating the level of consent between students and instructors in assessing individual brief reports.* Researchers examined the kids who assessed the reports solely based on their look. Analysis results showed a strong agreement between grades assigned by students and instructors and little agreement between grades by students and kids. These results were obtained from a well-defined evaluation scenario and a large number of reviewers for a single report.
[38]	*Analysts to consider the transition of grammatical elements.* This research described the use of an analyser to identify the sequence of concepts inside the Computer Science and Information Technologies proposal drafts. The goal of the research was to aid students in improving their drafting. Researchers proposed four methods integrated into an analyser, which was designed considering the transitions of grammar constituents (subject and object) in the parts of Problem Statement, Justification and Conclusions.
[39]	*Progress visualisation approach combining open-ended student modelling prospects and social visualisations.* This research introduced a combination of open learning models and social visualisation in social progress visualisation. A classroom evaluation indicated that this combination may be beneficial in engaging students, guiding them to suitable content and enabling faster content access.
[40]	*An upper/bottom-up analytics approach that uses data to inform decision-makers at universities.* This research explained the top-down approach utilising information on programs, modalities and college implementation of web initiatives. Meanwhile, the bottom-up approach continuously monitors the outcomes attributable to distributed learning, including student ratings and student success. The combination of top-down and bottom-up approach turned into a powerful means for using large existing university datasets to provide significant insights that can be instrumental in strategic planning.
[41]	*Supporting students and interventions.* This research described a new, analytics-driven approach to support students in large introductory physics courses. Researchers have assembled data for more than 49,000 students at the University of Michigan. They merge an extensive portrait of background and preparation with details of progress through the course and outcome. This information allowed researchers to construct models predicting students' performance with a dispersion of half a letter grade.

(Continues)

Table 3.1   (Continued)

Researcher	Learning analytics study
[42]	*Tracking performance and predicting students' success.* The research focused on investigating the measurement, collection, analysis, and reporting of data as predictors of students' success and drivers of departmental process and program curriculum. The research examined what has been done to endorse students, whether or not they are effective, and if not, why, and what educators can do. The research also examined how the obtained data can be used to create new metrics and inform a continuous cycle of improvement.
[43]	*Improving data visualization of student learning experiences.* The research aim was to create a visual representation of the continuity of care exposed to students during a longitudinal placement as part of a medical degree. This research explained a case study of the process of refining a visualisation of students' learning experience data. In this case, the aim was to develop a visual representation of the continuity of care exposed to students during a longitudinal position as part of a medical degree. The visualisation process refinement was outlined along with the lessons learned along the way.

performance in the courses they are in. "Understanding the behaviour", "anticipate", and "intervention" are some of the main purposes of analytics study by educational institutions. Meanwhile, "tracking the progress and achievement of students" is one of the analytics objectives of the learning done. There have been on-the-ground analytics studies carried out involving the use of massive open online course (MOOC) platforms [24]. Based on the studies conducted, two of them involved a microlearning environment. The studies were about profiling and supporting the learners to access open educational resources (OERs) in the microlearning context [25] and analysing students' behaviour in developing their writing skills using LMS data and how it impacts the design of the course [26].

Studies on LA in school included the engagement of mobile learning and web-based e-learning including intelligent tutoring system (ITS) and LMS. Table 3.2 presents the LA studies conducted at schools, which were done for understanding the behaviour, proposing intervention, as well as tracking the progress and performance of students. Besides, there was also a study carried out to evaluate and model students' behaviour. A study with an automated assessment tool for microlearning [27] has been conducted in the microlearning environment. LA study of informal learning settings by Niemann and Wolpers [28] was not formally involved in the online learning portal. It introduced usage-based techniques for grouping the learning resources accessed on online learning portals. The approach used was solely based on the use of learning resources and did not consider their content or relationship between users and resources. An assessment has been made on the

Table 3.2   Learning analytics studies at schools

Researcher	Learning analytics study
[27]	*Automated assessment tool for microlearning. This tool is used for recording and analysing educational data.* The researchers explained about a tool called the Functional Understanding Navigator! (FUN! Tool). They used this tool for different research projects, which allowed the organization of workflow process from start to finish, recording of log data of all analyses and a platform to share analyses with others through GitHub. This research extended and improved existing work in educational data mining and LA.
[44]	*The features of a teaching program are matched by students' interests and experience.* This research explored the associations of aggregate preference "honouring" with learner performance, which defined a notion of "strong" learner interest area preferences and found that honouring such preferences has a small negative association with performance. Despite that, learners with merely particular choices either interest area preferences or setting names of friends/classmates and those who express strong preferences inclined to perform in ways that are associated with better learning compared to learners who do not express such preferences.
[45]	*LA for manipulative-based fractional intervention programmes.* This research described a portion of the design research process used to develop the type of LA that needs to meet researchers' long-term goals, which also highlighted the importance of collecting qualitative data about student users. The qualitative interviews conducted with seven individual students captured valuable information about the process used by students to solve fraction problems with manipulatives that were unable to be captured previously.
[46]	*Identifying the sequence of "characteristic stay behaviours" and related student body postures as well as estimating the location of three dimensions of student interest.* Researchers considered a method to systematically integrate heterogeneous factors of real-world learning: learners' internal situations, their external situations and the learning field. After that, they proposed a method for formatively assessing the situation of real-world learning. The method enabled the identification of the sequence of characteristic stay behaviour and the associated body postures of a learner to estimate the 3D location of his/her interest. The method also allowed the estimation of not only the learning topic that a learner is currently examining in a field but also the prospective topics that he/she should learn.
[47]	*Behavioural assessment and student modelling on the autism spectrum.* This research showed a different scenario of mobile learning application and specifically, its use and applicability regarding the evaluation and modelling of behaviour, inside the classroom, of special educational needs, and specifically, for students with problems regarding behaviour and language. dmTEA is a software technology that permits the evaluation of autist spectrum. There are 12 learning activities adapted to interact with the mobile device for a specific context, which aims to work with disorders to solve them gradually by modelling behaviour while allowing students to acquire the necessary knowledge and competences.

(Continues)

Table 3.2   (Continued)

Researcher	Learning analytics study
[48]	*Approach to support task sequencing in ITS customization by compromising recognition to features obtained from student input.* The research was aimed at supporting the sequencer to gain information source namely speech input from the interaction of students with the tutoring system. The proposed approach extracted features from students' speech data and applied an automatic affect recognition method to that features. The output of the affect recognition method determined whether or not the last task was too easy, too challenging or appropriate for the students. Therefore, as stated by Vygotsky's theory, the next step should not be too easy or too hard for the students to neither bore nor frustrate him.
[49]	*Analytics in a mathematical error environment.* The researchers showed how to utilize an online mathematics homework system where students simply provided their final answers to exercises given. Through data mining techniques, researchers were able to ascribe a particular type of mechanical error or misconception to 60%–75% of the incorrect responses made by students on the subset of problems analysed. As such, researchers illustrated the methods for extracting this data to discover knowledge components embedded in an exercise, expose item bias and reveal students' cognitive states.

results of the grouping obtained, which were then used to improve the recommended system.

3.3   Methods

A LA model in predicting students' behavioural engagement in microlearning was developed based on the Long and Siemens LA model [20,50], which has the appropriate components for the present model. In addition, many researchers have used this model as a reference in the field of LA and in other related areas [51–54]. Figure 3.1 illustrates the LA model for this study, which consisted of five main components, namely:

1. Data collection.
2. Data storage.
3. Data cleaning and filtering.
4. Analyse and predict outcomes of engagement.
5. Action.

The first three components of the LA model included the process of data collection, storing and cleaning, as well as filtering data. The fourth component was the process of analysing and predicting the outcomes from the students' behavioural engagement. The findings from analysed and predicted components were used for the fifth component, which was action.

-Intervention
-Finding the best solution
-Signal and warning
-Guiding and assessing
-Design improvement

Data tracking from the
microlearning application

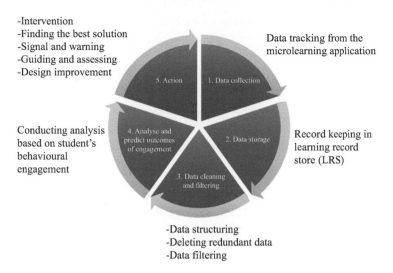

Conducting analysis
based on student's
behavioural
engagement

Record keeping in
learning record
store (LRS)

-Data structuring
-Deleting redundant data
-Data filtering

*Figure 3.1   LA model in predicting students' behavioural engagement in
microlearning*

E-learning authoring software that complied with the Tin Can application pro-gramming interface (API) specification was used in developing microlearning application to track learning data [55]. Articulate Storyline 2 was used in this study to create the microlearning application, the software that is able to produce Flash and Hypertext Markup Language revision 5 (HTML5) file formats. The microlearning application developed was a sub-topic of General Studies subjects for pre-university students. The specification allowed the data to be captured in the form of action statements on student activities. The microlearning application was placed on the website and integrated with the social networking application canvas. Since students usually access microlearning applications through websites or social networks using a computer or smartphone, the collection of learning data was identified by matching the username and e-mail entered by the students before starting the application.

Based on the previous LA studies, some have been carried out with a small sample size; the smallest number involved was two samples [47], while the largest data collection reached ten to one hundred thousand students' involvement [24,31]. However, in determining the sample size for quantitative studies, most researchers generally referred to the sample size determination method by Krejcie and Morgan [56] and Cohen [57]. Sample size determination can also be done based on the method by Roscoe [58], which suggests the following rules of thumb in deter-mining sample size:

1. The sample size higher than 30 and less than 500 is ideal for most studies.
2. The minimum sample size for each category is 30 (if the sample of a study consists of sub-samples such as male/female or junior/senior).

3. In multivariate studies (including multiple regression analysis), the sample size should be at least ten times or more, depending on the total number of variables in a study.
4. For pure experimental studies conducted using tight experimental control like matched pairs, the possible sample size must at least as small as 10 to 20.

Therefore, the sample size for this study was referred to as the rules of thumb for multivariate study [58] where the sample size should be ten times or more based on the number of variables in the study. Seventy-one students as the sample for this study chosen from a population of 83 students aged 19 years old from one pre-university programme in Malaysia. All students have the experience of using microlearning application in e-learning. The total sample consisted of 26 male students and 45 female students who have been using microlearning applications for one month. The recorded learning data from student activities involved more than 500 statements on students' behaviour. This statement was used to analyse the students' behavioural engagement. The learning data were stored centrally in the Learning Record Store (LRS) comprising the verbs "attempted", "experienced", "answered", "completed", "passed", and "failed". Table 3.3 illustrates the description of the learning data. LRS can store data from multiple microlearning applications at the same time. The learning data were tracked by the students' behaviour when using microlearning applications in the form of text or Tin Can statements. The Tin Can statements format file was generated by the JavaScript notation (JSON).

The next process involved cleaning and filtering the collected learning data. In this process, unstructured data were restructured before cleaning and filtering procedures. This process required the use of Structural Query Language (SQL) from LRS. Cleaning involved removing overlapping learning data that have the same identification to avoid similar data from being analysed more than once. The learning data were then filtered and classified based on the categories namely "attempted", "experienced", "answered", "completed", "passed", and "failed".

Table 3.3   Description of learning data

Learning data	Description
"Attempted"	Notifies the LRS that a microlearning application has begun.
"Experienced"	Shows the content that has been viewed.
"Answered"	Denotes that a question has been answered.
"Completed"	Used when a course or objective has been completed, and the completion is based on the number of contents viewed.
"Passed"	Notifies the LRS that a microlearning application has been completed with a passing score.
"Failed"	Notifies the LMS that a microlearning application has been completed with a failing score.

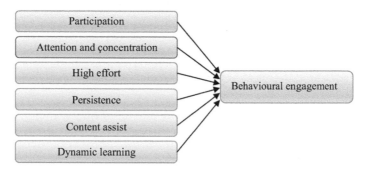

Figure 3.2   Relationship of the independent and dependent variables

Then, all the collected data were mapped with the right variables used in this study. Independent variables were "participation", "attention and concentration", "high effort", "persistence", "content assist", and "dynamic learning" while the dependent variable was behavioural engagement. Figure 3.2 shows the relationship between independent and dependent variables to predict the students' behaviour in microlearning.

Detailed explanation for each variable in this study is as followed:

–   "Participation" was defined as the students' behaviour in engaging themselves during learning activities. Therefore, "participation" will affect students' behavioural engagement in using microlearning application. It is relevant to predict that the students who show participation will use the app again after their first attempt.
–   "Attention and concentration" was defined as the students' desire or behaviour in exploring the learning content. Therefore, "attention and concentration" will affect students' behavioural engagement in using microlearning applications. It is relevant to predict that the students who show attention and concentration will explore the content of the microlearning application.
–   "High effort" was defined as the behaviour of the students who work hard to learn something. Therefore, "high effort" will affect students' behavioural engagement in using microlearning application. It is relevant to predict that the students who show high effort will use the app repeatedly.
–   "Persistence" was defined as continuous students' behaviour in facing difficulties, barriers, and failures in learning. Therefore, "persistence" will affect students' behavioural engagement in using microlearning application. It is relevant to predict that the students who show persistency will continuously use the app to get a better grade.
–   "Content assist" was defined as the interaction of students' behaviour with learning content during the learning session. Therefore, "content assist" will affect the students' behavioural engagement to use the microlearning application. It is relevant to predict that the students who show content assistance will continuously interact with learning content during the learning session.

Table 3.4   Mapped learning data to variables

Variables	Learning data	Measurement	Role
Participation	"Attempted"	Flag	Input
Attention and concentration	"Experienced"	Flag	Input
High effort	"Attempted"	Continuous	Input
Persistence	"Attempted" "Experienced" "Answered"	Flag	Input
Content assist	"Attempted" "Experienced" "Answered" "Passed" "Failed"	Continuous	Input
Dynamic learning	"Experienced"	Flag	Input
Behavioural engagement	"Attempted" "Experienced" "Answered" "Passed" "Failed"	Flag	Output

-   "Dynamic learning" was defined as the behaviour of the students who are doing non-sequent learning activities. Therefore, "dynamic learning" will affect the students' behavioural engagement to use the microlearning application. It is relevant to predict that the students who show dynamic learning will do non-sequent learning activities in using microlearning application.
-   "Behavioural engagement" was defined as the behaviour of the students who try and experience the microlearning application and turn in their full score.

Table 3.4 displays the learning data mapped to behavioural engagement variables. "Attempted", "experienced", "answered", "completed", "passed", and "failed" were the variables involved. Data measurement was divided into two; "flag" and "continuous". "Flag" measured the learning data classified based on students' behaviour either "yes" or "no", whereas "continuous" measured the learning data on students' behaviour frequency. The independent variables were the input, while the dependent variable was the output.

The method used in analysing students' behavioural prediction in microlearning was by comparing the results of the analysis between neural network (NN) and logistic regression (LR) models by SPSS Modeler software. The models were chosen due to their suitability to the learning data obtained. Moreover, previous studies have shown that these models are proven and often used for predictive studies [59–63]. NN and LR are among the supervised learning algorithms in machine learning [64]. Meanwhile, classification algorithms and regression techniques are used in supervised learning to develop predictive models [65]. The analysis for NN model involved nodes and nugget models as shown in Figure 3.3. Nodes used in this analysis were statistic file node, data audit node, statistic node,

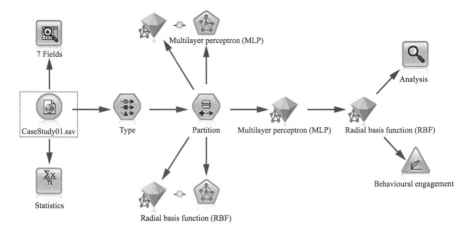

Figure 3.3   Analysis with NN model

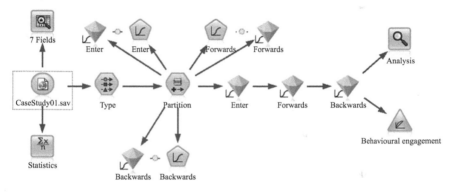

Figure 3.4   Analysis with LR model

type node, partition node, neural net node, analysis node, and evaluation node. Two neural net nodes used in two NN models were multilayer perceptron neural network (MLPNN) and radial basis function neural network (RBFNN). Nugget model for MLPNN and RBFNN represented the outcome of NN model operation. Analysis node provided the output for NN model, which consisted of accuracy value for training and testing. Meanwhile, the evaluation node displayed the gain chart that shows training and testing percentile. If there were any unbalanced data, balance node would be used to balance the data.

Analysis with the LR model involved the use of nodes and nugget models as shown in Figure 3.4. Statistic file node, data audit node, statistic node, type node, partition node, logistic node, analysis node, and evaluation node were used in this analysis. Three logistic nodes were used for three methods of the LR model. The "enter", "backwards", and "forwards" nugget models represented the outcomes from LR model operation. The output from the analysis node LR model consisted of accuracy value for training and testing. The evaluation node displayed the gain chart that shows the percentile for training and testing. Meanwhile, the use of balance node in the model was to balance the data.

Comparative analysis was carried out to choose the best model in predicting students' behavioural engagement using microlearning application based on low error value, high-accuracy value, sensitivity, and specificity. The accuracy value was identified from the analysis node. Meanwhile, accuracy value (correct positive ratio) and specificity (correct negative value) were calculated based on the confusion matric.

The proposed actions suggested for the students and microlearning applications were based on the results of prediction analysis on the students' behavioural engagement by depending on the less important variables to predict their behavioural engagement. These suggested actions were intervention, finding the best solutions, signals and warnings, guiding and assisting, as well as design improvement [20–22]. Processes in the LA model will continuously repeat if the interventions or design improvement carried out require the students' behavioural engagement prediction analysis to be analysed again.

3.4   Results

3.4.1   Analysis of using NN

In selecting the best method to predict the students' behavioural engagement analysis in microlearning, two analyses were performed at intervals of 10% and 5% to obtain data-apportion value with a high-accuracy value. The first analysis was carried out using apportion values of 80% training and 20% testing, 70% training and 30% testing, 60% training and 40% testing, and 50% training and 50% testing. The data-apportion values were used to find the highest accuracy of training value. The optimum data-apportion values for training and testing were obtained from the trial and error method and relied on the existing data that can be used in the network equally. Based on Table 3.5, the highest accuracy of apportion values for the first analysis using MLPNN model was at 80% training and 20% testing, whereas the RBFNN model was at 60% training and 40% testing of data-apportion values.

Table 3.5   Apportion values in first analysis using the NN

Apportion value	Accuracy value (%)	
	MLPNN model	RBFNN model
80% training 20% testing	67.92	66.04
70% training 30% testing	66.67	64.71
60% training 40% testing	66.67	69.05
50% training 50% testing	64.86	64.86

Table 3.6   Apportion values in second analysis using the NN

Apportion value	Accuracy value (%)	
	MLPNN model	**RBFNN model**
90% training 10% testing	69.49	67.80
85% training 15% testing	69.09	67.27
80% training 20% testing	67.92	66.04
75% training 25% testing	66.67	64.71
70% training 30% testing	66.67	64.71
65% training 35% testing	68.09	68.09
60% training 40% testing	66.67	69.05
55% training 45% testing	66.67	66.67
50% training 50% testing	64.86	64.86

Table 3.7   Determination of optimum NN model structure

Model in NN	Numbers of neuron in hidden layer	Accuracy value (%)	Training value (%)
MLPNN	1	79.70	69.49
RBFNN	4	73.80	69.05

To obtain more accurate data-apportion values, the second analysis was carried out by breaking down the data values started with 50% training and 50% testing until 90% training and 10% testing as shown in Table 3.6. The interval size of the apportioning values used was 5% compared to 10% when the first analysis was carried out. Based on the finding of the second analysis, training values in the analysis using MLPNN model showed the highest accuracy at data-apportion values of 90% training and 10% testing compared to those of the RBFNN model, which were at data-apportion values of 60% training and 40% testing.

An optimum NN model structure was determined by adding the numbers of neurons in the hidden layer followed by an analysis conducted based on its numbers. The training process in the developed NN model was allowed to keep on going until it stopped. Table 3.7 shows that the MLPNN model was at data-apportion values of 90% training and 10% testing, which was considered as the best model since it gave the highest accuracy value through the small numbers of neurons in the hidden layer. The model also showed the highest training value. Based on the comparison below, the MLPNN model was chosen in predicting the students' behavioural engagement.

3.4.2   Analysis using LR

As in the analysis of the NN model, there were two analyses performed at intervals of 10% and 5% to obtain the data-apportion values with a high-accuracy value. The first analysis was carried out using data-apportion values of 80% training and 20% testing, 70% training and 30% testing, 60% training and 40% testing, and lastly

Table 3.8   Training values in the first analysis using LR

Apportion value	Accuracy value (%)		
	LR "enter" method	LR "forwards" method	LR "backwards" method
80% training 20% testing	64.15	52.83	66.04
70% training 30% testing	64.71	52.94	66.67
60% training 40% testing	64.29	57.14	64.29
50% training 50% testing	64.86	51.35	64.86

Table 3.9   Training values in the second analysis using LR

Apportion value	Accuracy value (%)		
	LR "enter" method	LR "forwards" method	LR "backwards" method
90% training 10% testing	66.10	55.93	67.80
85% training 15% testing	65.45	54.55	67.27
80% training 20% testing	64.15	52.83	66.04
75% training 25% testing	64.71	52.94	66.67
70% training 30% testing	64.71	52.94	66.67
65% training 35% testing	63.83	55.32	65.96
60% training 40% testing	64.29	57.14	64.29
55% training 45% testing	66.67	53.85	66.67
50% training 50% testing	64.86	51.35	64.86

50% training and 50% testing. According to Table 3.8, the highest accuracy was obtained using the LR model for "enter" method at data-apportion values of 50% training and 50% testing, "forwards" method at data-apportion values of 60% training and 40% testing, and lastly "backwards" method at data-apportion values of 70% training and 30% testing.

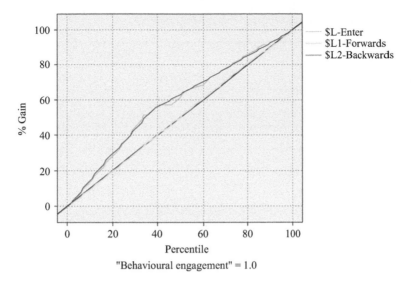

Figure 3.5   Analysis with LR model

For a more accurate data-apportion value, the second analysis was carried out using data-apportion values of 50% training and 50% testing until 90% training and 10% testing as shown in Table 3.9. The interval size of data apportions value was at 5% compared to 10% in the first analysis. Findings in the second analysis showed that training values had the highest accuracy when using LR model for "enter" method with the data-apportion values at 55% training and 45% testing, "forwards" method with 60% training and 40% testing and lastly "backwards" method at 90% training and 10% testing.

Students' behavioural engagement prediction model was determined using the best LR model made by comparing the training values with the highest accuracy for three methods; "enter", "forwards", and "backwards". The comparison showed that "backwards" method had the highest accuracy value of 67.80 at data apportion with the values of 90% training and 10% testing. Comparison was done using a Gain Chart as shown in Figure 3.5. Based on the chart, there was a slight advantage for "backwards" method at a percentile of 10 to 30 compared to "enter" and "forwards" methods. Therefore, the LR "backwards" method was chosen as it displayed the highest value in predicting students' behavioural engagement.

3.5   Comparison analysis using NN and LR

MLPNN and LR "backwards" method were tested for model validity. Confusion matrix was used in counting the sensitivity (actual positive ratio) and specificity (actual negative ratio) values. Prediction model with low error value, high accuracy, sensitivity, and specificity was selected. Table 3.10 shows the confusion

Table 3.10   Confusion matrix for MLPNN

		Prediction	
		Yes	**No**
Actual	Yes	2	2
	No	1	7

Table 3.11   Confusion matrix for LR "backwards" method

		Prediction	
		Yes	**No**
Actual	Yes	2	2
	No	2	6

Table 3.12   Error value, accuracy, sensitivity, and specificity for MLPNN and LR "backwards" method

Prediction method	Accuracy (%)	Sensitivity (%)	Specificity (%)	Error value (%)
MLPNN model	75.00	66.67	77.78	25.00
LR "backwards" method	66.67	50.00	75.00	33.33

matrix of MLPNN model. Meanwhile, Table 3.11 illustrates the confusion matrix of LR "backwards" method.

Table 3.12 shows the comparison of the error value, accuracy, sensitivity, and specificity between MLPNN and LR "backwards" method. A model with a high percentage of accuracy, sensitivity, specificity value, and low error value represents a good result. The findings indicated that MLPNN model was the best prediction model as it gave the highest accuracy, sensitivity, and specificity values. The model also had low error value of 25.00% compared to LR "backwards" method with error value of 33.33%. Figure 3.6 shows that MLPNN had higher confidence value in predicting students' behavioural engagement compared to the second model.

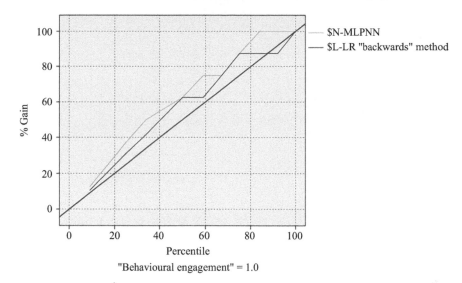

Figure 3.6   Gain chart of prediction analysis between MLPNN and LR "backwards" method

After determining the best model to predict students' behavioural engagement, prediction analysis on students' behavioural engagement in microlearning was carried out using the MLPNN model. The result from the analysis demonstrated the importance of predictors by showing the most important variables until the least important ones in predicting students' behavioural engagement in microlearning. The most important predictor was "persistence" with the value of 0.27, followed by "high effort" (0.19), "content assist" (0.16), "participation" (0.15), "dynamic learning" (0.13), and the least important predictor was "attention and concentration" with the value of 0.09. The most important predictor showed a strong influence in predicting students' behavioural engagement in microlearning. Thus, appropriate actions and microlearning applications were carried out to ensure the continuous behavioural engagement of students in learning.

Several actions were suggested for students and microlearning application based on the results of the analysis. Important variables can predict students' behavioural engagement. Three variables were identified as the most important predictors, which were "persistence", "high effort", and "content assist". Therefore, the best practices suggested for these students were finding the best solution, signal and warning, as well as guiding and assessing. The proposed actions for microlearning application were intervention and design improvement. Table 3.13 presents the details of the proposed actions for students and microlearning application.

Table 3.13 *Proposed actions for students and microlearning application*

Variables	Actions				
	Intervention	Finding the best solution	Signal and warning	Guiding and assessing	Design improvement
Persistence	Use attractive and motivational feedback display.	Interview with students who did not use a microlearning application to get a better result.	Explain to students about the benefits of striving for success.	Guide and assess the students for the right way of learning.	Design an attractive and motivational feedback display to boost students' interest.
High effort	Use a web-hosting server with high availability.	Conduct interview sessions with students who did not use microlearning application at different period.	Always monitor students who did not use microlearning application continuously at a different period.	Give a chance for students to use microlearning application during their free time at school.	Design a learning application that is easy to reach and require a short time to download.
Content assist	Prepare an easy-access link for students to interact with the learning content during learning session.	Interview sessions with students who did not have any interaction with learning content during the learning session.	Encourage the students to interact with learning content during learning session.	Guide the students on how to interact with learning content during the learning session.	Design an easy access link to ease students' interaction with learning content during the learning session.

3.6   Conclusion

Comparison for predicting students' behavioural engagement analysis in this study showed that NN model had the highest accuracy, sensitivity, and specificity compared to LR model. The results proved that NN model was the best model compared to LR model in predicting students' behavioural engagement in microlearning. The findings of this study supported those of the previous ones proving the NN model as the best prediction model compared to the LR model [59,60,62,63,66]. The findings in predicting students' behavioural engagement analysis with NN model showed three important variables namely persistence, high effort, and content assist. The next actions were suggested for the students and microlearning application based on the importance of each variable or predictor. Among the proposed actions were intervention, finding the best solution, signal and warning, guiding and assessing, as well as design improvement.

In conclusion, this study had successfully developed a LA model for predicting students' behavioural engagement in microlearning. This model is significant to predict students' behaviour and identify important predictors related to students' actions in microlearning. In addition, this study has solved the problems of the prediction method used in the previous studies that were unable to track and record students' behaviour in microlearning. The processes of assessing learning data from microlearning application and learning data storage in the learning record store were some of the processes involved in this LA model. The model had explained the variables used in this study and analysis methods for learning data in predicting students' behaviour.

3.7   Future scope

There were also significant limitations in this study as it focused only on a subtopic subject and a small sample size. Further study in the future may involve many subtopics and a large number of samples to provide more precise findings. The future study will also include predictions of emotional and cognitive engagement in microlearning.

References

[1]   Tsai CW, and Chiang YC. Research trends in problem-based learning (PBL) research in e-learning and online education environments: A review of publications in SSCI-indexed journals from 2004 to 2012. British Journal of Educational Technology. 2013;44(6): E185–90.

[2]   Yang HH. New world, new learning: Trends and issues of e-learning. Procedia-Social and Behavioral Sciences. 2013;77:429–42.

[3]   Hug T, Lindner M, and Bruck PA. Microlearning: Emerging concepts, practices and technologies after e-learning. Proceedings of Microlearning. 2005;5(3).

[4]   Gabrielli S, Kimani S, and Catarci T. The design of microlearning experiences: A research agenda. In Microlearning: Emerging Concepts, Practices and Technologies after E-Learning: Proceedings of Microlearning Conference 2005: Learning & Working in New Media (pp. 45–53). Innsbruck, Áustria: Innsbruck University Press.

[5]   Meece JL, Blumenfeld PC, and Hoyle RH. Students' goal orientations and cognitive engagement in classroom activities. Journal of Educational Psychology. 1988;80(4):514.

[6]   O'Brien HL, and Toms EG. The development and evaluation of a survey to measure user engagement. Journal of the American Society for Information Science and Technology. 2010;61(1):50–69.

[7]   Charles MT, Bustard D, and Black M. Game inspired tool support for e-learning processes. Electronic Journal of e-Learning. 2009;7(2):101–10.

[8]   Beck JE. Using response times to model student disengagement. In Proceedings of the ITS2004 Workshop on Social and Emotional Intelligence in Learning Environments 2004 Aug (Vol. 20).

[9]   Cocea M, and Weibelzahl S. Cross-system validation of engagement prediction from log files. In European Conference on Technology Enhanced Learning 2007 Sep 17 (pp. 14–25). Springer, Berlin, Heidelberg.

[10] Cocea M, and Weibelzahl S. Log file analysis for disengagement detection in e-Learning environments. User Modeling and User-Adapted Interaction. 2009;19(4):341–85.

[11] Hershkovitz A, and Nachmias R. Learning about online learning processes and students' motivation through web usage mining. Interdisciplinary Journal of E-Learning and Learning Objects. 2009;5(1):197–214.

[12] Ramaha NT, and Ismail WM. Assessment of learner's motivation in web based e-learning. International Journal of Scientific & Engineering research. 2012;3(8):1–5.

[13] Shukor NA, Tasir Z, Van der Meijden H, and Harun J. A predictive model to evaluate students' cognitive engagement in online learning. Procedia-Social and Behavioral Sciences. 2014;116:4844–53.

[14] Ferguson R. The state of learning analytics in 2012: A review and future challenges. Knowledge Media Institute, Technical Report KMI-2012–01. 2012 Mar.

[15] Greller W, and Drachsler H. Translating learning into numbers: A generic framework for learning analytics. Journal of Educational Technology & Society. 2012;15(3):42–57.

[16] Cristobal R, and Sebastian V. Data mining in education. Wiley Interdisciplinary Reviews: Data Mining and Knowledge Discovery. 2013;3 (1):12–27.

[17] Verbert K, Manouselis N, Drachsler H, and Duval E. Dataset-driven research to support learning and knowledge analytics. Journal of Educational Technology & Society. 2012;15(3):133–48.

[18] Wilson A, Watson C, Thompson TL, Drew V, and Doyle S. Learning analytics: Challenges and limitations. Teaching in Higher Education. 2017;22 (8):991–1007.

[19] Wong BT, Li KC, and Choi SP. Trends in learning analytics practices: a review of higher education institutions. Interactive Technology and Smart Education. 2018 Jun 18.

[20] Siemens G. Learning analytics: The emergence of a discipline. American Behavioral Scientist. 2013;57(10):1380–400.

[21] Pardo A. Designing learning analytics experiences. In Learning Analytics 2014 (pp. 15–38). Springer, New York, NY.

[22] Arnold KE, and Pistilli MD. Course signals at Purdue: Using learning analytics to increase student success. In Proceedings of the 2nd International Conference on Learning Analytics and Knowledge 2012 Apr 29 (pp. 267–270).

[23] Nistor N, Derntl M, and Klamma R. Learning analytics: Trends and issues of the empirical research of the years 2011–2014. In Design for Teaching and Learning in a Networked World 2015 (pp. 453–459). Springer, Cham.

[24] Santos JL, Klerkx J, Duval E, Gago D, and Rodríguez L. Success, activity and drop-outs in MOOCs an exploratory study on the UNED COMA courses. In Proceedings of the Fourth International Conference on Learning Analytics and Knowledge 2014 Mar 24 (pp. 98–102).

[25] Sun G, Cui T, Beydoun G, Shen J, and Chen S. Profiling and supporting adaptive micro learning on open education resources. In 2016 International Conference on Advanced Cloud and Big Data (CBD) 2016 Aug 13 (pp. 158–163). IEEE.

[26] Zucker DM. How to do case study research. School of nursing faculty publication series. 2009 Aug 1:2.

[27] Martin T, Brasiel S, Jeong S, Close K, Lawanto K, and Janisciewcz P. Macro data for micro learning: Developing the FUN! Tool for automated assessment of learning. In Proceedings of the Third (2016) ACM Conference on Learning@ Scale 2016 Apr 25 (pp. 233–236).

[28] Niemann K, and Wolpers M. Usage-based clustering of learning resources to improve recommendations. In European Conference on Technology Enhanced Learning 2014 Sep 16 (pp. 317–330). Springer, Cham.

[29] Vahdat M, Oneto L, Ghio A, et al. A learning analytics methodology to profile students behavior and explore interactions with a digital electronics simulator. In European Conference on Technology Enhanced Learning 2014 Sep 16 (pp. 596–597). Springer, Cham.

[30] Bogarín A, Romero C, Cerezo R, and Sánchez-Santillán M. Clustering for improving educational process mining. In Proceedings of the Fourth International Conference on Learning Analytics and Knowledge 2014 Mar 24 (pp. 11–15).

[31] Clow D. Data wranglers: Human interpreters to help close the feedback loop. In Proceedings of the Fourth International Conference on Learning Analytics and Knowledge 2014 Mar 24 (pp. 49–53).

[32] Coopey E, Shapiro RB, and Danahy E. Collaborative spatial classification. In Proceedings of the Fourth International Conference on Learning Analytics and Knowledge 2014 Mar 24 (pp. 138–142).

[33] Gašević D, Mirriahi N, and Dawson S. Analytics of the effects of video use and instruction to support reflective learning. In Proceedings of the Fourth International Conference on Learning Analytics and Knowledge 2014 Mar 24 (pp. 123–132).

[34] Hecking T, Ziebarth S, and Hoppe HU. Analysis of dynamic resource access patterns in a blended learning course. In Proceedings of the Fourth International Conference on Learning Analytics and Knowledge 2014 Mar 24 (pp. 173–182).

[35] Nam S, Lonn S, Brown T, Davis CS, and Koch D. Customized course advising: Investigating engineering student success with incoming profiles and patterns of concurrent course enrollment. In Proceedings of the Fourth International Conference on Learning Analytics and Knowledge 2014 Mar 24 (pp. 16–25).

[36] Raca M, Tormey R, and Dillenbourg P. Sleepers' lag-study on motion and attention. In Proceedings of the Fourth International Conference on Learning Analytics and Knowledge 2014 Mar 24 (pp. 36–43).

[37] Vozniuk A, Holzer A, and Gillet D. Peer assessment based on ratings in a social media course. In Proceedings of the Fourth International Conference on Learning Analytics and Knowledge 2014 Mar 24 (pp. 133–137).

[38] González-López S, and López-López A. Analysis of concept sequencing in student drafts. In European Conference on Technology Enhanced Learning 2014 Sep 16 (pp. 422–427). Springer, Cham.

[39] Loboda TD, Guerra J, Hosseini R, and Brusilovsky P. Mastery grids: An open source social educational progress visualization. In European Conference on Technology Enhanced Learning 2014 Sep 16 (pp. 235–248). Springer, Cham.

[40] Dziuban C, Moskal P, Cavanagh T, and Watts A. Analytics that inform the university: Using data you already have. Journal of Asynchronous Learning Networks. 2012;16(3):21–38.

[41] McKay T, Miller K, and Tritz J. What to do with actionable intelligence: E2Coach as an intervention engine. In Proceedings of the 2nd International Conference on Learning Analytics and Knowledge 2012 Apr 29 (pp. 88–91).

[42] Mattingly KD, Rice MC, and Berge ZL. Learning analytics as a tool for closing the assessment loop in higher education. Knowledge Management & E-Learning: An International Journal. 2012;4(3):236–47.

[43] Olmos MM, and Corrin L. Learning analytics: A case study of the process of design of visualizations. Journal of Asynchronous Learning Networks. 2012;16(3):39–49.

[44] Fancsali SE, and Ritter S. Context personalization, preferences, and performance in an intelligent tutoring system for middle school mathematics. In Proceedings of the Fourth International Conference on Learning Analytics and Knowledge 2014 Mar 24 (pp. 73–77).

[45] Mendiburo M, Sulcer B, and Hasselbring T. Interaction design for improved analytics. In Proceedings of the Fourth International Conference on Learning Analytics and Knowledge 2014 Mar 24 (pp. 78–82).

[46] Okada M, and Tada M. Formative assessment method of real-world learning by integrating heterogeneous elements of behavior, knowledge, and the environment. In Proceedings of the Fourth International Conference on Learning Analytics and Knowledge 2014 Mar 24 (pp. 1–10).

[47] Cabielles-Hernández D, Pérez-Pérez JR, Paule-Ruiz M, Álvarez-García VM, and Fernández-Fernández S. dmTEA: Mobile learning to aid in the diagnosis of autism spectrum disorders. In European Conference on Technology Enhanced Learning 2014 Sep 16 (pp. 29–41). Springer, Cham.

[48] Janning R, Schatten C, and Schmidt-Thieme L. Feature analysis for affect recognition supporting task sequencing in adaptive intelligent tutoring systems. In European Conference on Technology Enhanced Learning 2014 Sep 16 (pp. 179–192). Springer, Cham.

[49] McTavish TS, and Larusson JA. Labeling mathematical errors to reveal cognitive states. In European Conference on Technology Enhanced Learning 2014 Sep 16 (pp. 446–451). Springer, Cham.

[50] Siemens G, and Long P. Penetrating the fog: Analytics in learning and education. EDUCAUSE review. 2011;46(5):30.

[51] Daniel B. Big Data and analytics in higher education: Opportunities and challenges. British Journal of Educational Technology. 2015;46(5):904–20.

[52] Dietz-Uhler B, and Hurn JE. Using learning analytics to predict (and improve) student success: A faculty perspective. Journal of Interactive Online Learning. 2013;12(1):17–26.

[53] Ferguson R. Learning analytics: Drivers, developments and challenges. International Journal of Technology Enhanced Learning. 2012;4(5–6):304–17.

[54] Wamba SF, Akter S, Edwards A, Chopin G, and Gnanzou D. How 'big data'can make big impact: Findings from a systematic review and a longitudinal case study. International Journal of Production Economics. 2015;165:234–46.

[55] Maciołek P, and Dobrowolski G. Cluo: Web-scale text mining system for open source intelligence purposes. Computer Science. 2013;14(1):45–62.

[56] Krejcie RV, and Morgan DW. Determining sample size for research activities. Educational and Psychological Measurement. 1970;30(3):607–10.

[57] Cohen J. A power primer. Psychological Bulletin. 1992;112(1):155.

[58] Roscoe JT. Fundamental research statistics for the behavioral sciences [by] John T. Roscoe. 1975.

[59] Safiar NB. Model regresi logistik dan rangkaian neural. Doctoral dissertation, Terengganu: Universiti Malaysia Terengganu.

[60] Faradmal J, Soltanian AR, Roshanaei G, Khodabakhshi R, and Kasaeian A. Comparison of the performance of log-logistic regression and artificial neural networks for predicting breast cancer relapse. Asian Pacific Journal of Cancer Prevention. 2014;15(14):5883–8.

[61] Schumacher P, Olinsky A, Quinn J, and Smith R. A comparison of logistic regression, neural networks, and classification trees predicting success of actuarial students. Journal of Education for Business. 2010;85(5):258–63.

[62] Prasad R, Pandey A, Singh KP *et al.* Retrieval of spinach crop parameters by microwave remote sensing with back propagation artificial neural networks: A comparison of different transfer functions. Advances in Space Research. 2012;50:363–70.

[63] Refenes AN, Zapranis A, and Francis G. Stock performance modeling using neural networks: A comparative study with regression models. Neural Networks. 1994;7(2):375–88.

[64] Talabis M, McPherson R, Miyamoto I, and Martin J. Information security analytics: Finding security insights, patterns, and anomalies in big data. Syngress; 2014 Nov 25.

[65] Shobha G, and Rangaswamy S. Computational analysis and understanding of natural languages: Principles, methods and applications. Chapter 8: Machine Learning, Elsevier; 2018 Aug 27.

[66] Schumacher P, Olinsky A, Quinn J, and Smith R. A comparison of 1 logisticregression, neural networks, and classification trees predicting success of actuarial students. Journal of Education for Business. 2010;85(5):258–63.

Chapter 4

Student performance prediction for adaptive e-learning systems

Mukta Goyal[1], Divakar Yadav[2] and Mehak Sood[3]

4.1 Introduction

The development of new technologies can empower learners at all stages of their lives to learn more effectively, efficiently and comfortably. Today learners use smart devices to access everything, ranging from e-commerce to e-education. E-learning education is one of the domains that have gained much attention in recent times and is a concept that encompasses learning in the digital age. The rapid growth of e-learning systems has changed current learning behavior and tries to present a new framework for the learners. It greatly enhances and improves learning practices online. However, it also poses difficulties in terms of the vast variety of content and resources. A learner using the e-learning system to gain knowledge may get diverted because of the available resources and the indecision to pursue the right kind of material. Speaking of the right kind of material, there is no perfect resource or best material out of all as every user will have a different approach toward learning. Thus, an adaptive e-learning system that can provide the right kind of learning material based on the way a user can learn is a necessity.

Every learner should be provided with personalized learning materials in order to improve the e-learning system. Learners use educational web applications targeted at learning that corresponds to their knowledge expectations. Hence, it is of utmost importance to develop a system that can automatically adapt to learners' styles of learning, knowledge levels and personality. It is evident that learning and education differ greatly between learners due to their different preferences, needs and approaches to learning. A learner may prefer learning through the written notes, while others may prefer learning through the lecture videos.

The content each learner needs may also be of a different kind. Some might need specific examples and real-life situations while others might be able to grasp

[1]Department of Computer Science Engineering and IT, Jaypee Institute of Information Technology, Noida, India
[2]Department of Computer Science and IT, National Institute of Technology, Hamirpur, India
[3]Department of Management Information System, The University of Arizona, Tucson, United States

the content through the generalized description. Therefore, it is very important to accommodate the different styles of learners and the previous knowledge level they hold through learning environments that they prefer and find more efficient. We aim to evaluate the learning styles, personality factors and the knowledge level of each individual in order to provide them with the right material that suits them and helps them learn at their own pace.

This chapter discusses the classification of learners based on the learner model for e-learners. E-learning platforms have become common and approachable for a vast set of audiences. The COVID-19 pandemic in 2020 has triggered the application of these online learning platforms. The number of e-learning platforms has been increasing rapidly to fulfill the requirement. But the availability of these large numbers of educational storehouses makes it confusing and difficult for a learner to choose the content that would be appropriate for him/her. The amount of content available online results in a loss of interest and confusion among the learners. Whenever a person starts to learn a skill, the educational material that has just been dumped into the platform makes it difficult for him/her to know where to start. Every person is unique in his/her own way. Some learners prefer to use video content to grasp a new skill, whereas some learners prefer reading materials over visual content for learning. There is no right or wrong way to learn. It solely depends on the learner's personality and his/her learning style. This chapter tries to estimate the three factors consisting of learner's personality, learning style and knowledge level in order to recommend the content that is best suited to the learner. An ensemble approach to solving this problem has been used, which utilizes a genetic algorithm and KNN to find the content appropriate for the learner.

This chapter is organized as follows: Section 4.2 describes the literature survey, whereas Section 4.3 describes the methodology. Section 4.4 discusses the experimental results.

4.2   Literature survey

This section discusses techniques to predict the performance of the e-learner based on the learner profile using different soft computing techniques.

4.2.1   Learner profile

The learner profile of the e-learner can be measured between a number of factors such as learner grouping, rating and learning paths [1,2]. These specific demands and requirements have been considered in an e-learning system to improve the "educational aspects" for the learners. Learning style also plays an important role in learning for e-learners. Learning styles are being used to determine what kind of learner a student is. Researchers used the standardized Felder–Silverman learning style model (FSLSM) that has four pairs of dimensions [3–6]. A learner could be active or reflective, sensing or intuitive, visual or verbal and sequential or global. Here, each dimension reflects the thinking and the way of learning of a learner. These four pairs determine the overall learning style of a learner. More accurate representation is determined using this method as it not only implements the characteristics but also the values of different dimensions.

Personal and social factors also impact the performance of the learner [7]. The factors such as usage of learning materials, course information and academic data have also been considered for classification [8]. Some researchers have used knowledge of the concept as the performance of a learner from time to time [3]. A framework for adaptive e-learning depends on the learner's personality, his/her current knowledge of the topic, competence and style, which are used. Crowdsourcing, collaborative filtering (CF), content-based (CB) filtering and recommender systems help one to achieve an adaptive and personalized e-learning experience [9]. The research shows that some demographic social factors such as family background, gender, financial standing and personal motivation, affect the performance of a learner. These factors also need to be considered while developing a recommendation system.

4.2.2 Soft computing techniques

Data mining techniques [7,8,10] have proven that a correlation exists between the leaner's personality, demographic social factors and their academic achievements. A study in which the students' performances were calculated after each semester using different machine learning and data mining algorithms. Different decision trees were implemented and evaluated. These results were then compared with the actual grades of the students. The decision tree approaches, including CART, CHAID, ID3 and C4.5, were implemented where CART gave an accuracy of 40% that was considerably higher than the accuracy of CHAID (34.07%), C4.5 (35.19%) and ID3 (33.33%). It was observed that the classes created in the CART confusion matrix were not fully independent of each other. The results that should have been in a particular class were included in their nearest similar upper or lower class. For example, very good and good can have the same characteristics, and at times, the objects were unable to differentiate between these two classes. It becomes difficult to assign a particular class to a particular object. Other researchers used the student's academic history to classify and predict future student performance. The naïve theorem was used for the classification of the student information. Three basic steps were utilized to achieve the results that included the collection of academic data of the college students, transformation and cleaning of this data and then the application of naïve Bayes algorithm predicting the student performance in the future. The students of all categories can boost their performance and do well in their studies. Also, lecturers can help their students in a better way. Students who require special attention can be spotted by the teachers, which will eventually improve results and reduce the failure ratio. The lecturer and student can also take adequate actions for the upcoming semester or test [5,11].

A hybrid recommender system called relational CF is used, which is based on relational distance computation approaches [1]. A decision tree approach is used to predict the academic achievement of the learner. CHAID decision tree was utilized to build an SPSS predictive program [12].

The idea is to determine the learning style of the learner in visual (verbal), visual (nonverbal), auditory and kinesthetic dimensions and then use a crowd-sourcing system to make a personalized system for each learner. Further, a recommendation system is implemented in order to predict user preferences. The data used for predictions is collected and refined using CF, CB filtering, knowledge-based filtering and a hybrid approach. This approach has considered the competence behavior of a learner after learning a course, and the learners can also provide feedback through crowdsourcing. The competence behavior of a learner after learning a course can also provide feedback through crowdsourcing.

Web mining techniques, namely, association rule mining have been used for the construction of recommendation systems based on learner grouping, rating and learning paths [2,13]. This specific demands and requirements have been considered in an e-learning system to improve the "educational aspects" for the learners. The association rule has an antecedent (left-hand side) and a consequent (right-hand side). Example: I1, I2, ..., In ⇒ Iα, Iβ, ..., Iγ. First, candidate sets of length k are constructed. From the frequent itemsets of smaller length, a candidate set of itemsets of length $k + 1$ is constructed iteratively until further candidate itemsets are constructed. The automatic recommendation system for each learner can help one to improve the e-learning in a huge way. It is true that similar learners share the same kind of knowledge and follow the course; therefore, they can be recommended what the other similar learners are learning. On the other hand, the difference in every learner's knowledge and competence level is not considered. Each learner must be assessed individually and be provided with the right material [2].

Learning activities and the learner's profile could present them in a hier-archical tree structure. The precedence order and the learner's profile may provide unclear and uncertain data; hence, the concept of fuzzy tree matching is used. The learning sequence of the learner helps one to determine the precedence relations, and the CB filtering or CF is used to design the recommendation systems. The hybrid approach takes advantage of a knowledge-based and CF-based approach. It considers both the collaborative-based and semantic similarities of the learners, and then a recommender system is proposed, which is based on learning activities and learners' profiles [14,15].

Learner's knowledge is also one of the aspects that represent the knowl-edge level of the learner. Based on the knowledge level, an intuitionistic approach has been used to assess the knowledge level of the learner. Researchers suggest the knowledge level of the student is assessed by first taking a multiple-choice questionnaire on the basis of the topic selected by the learner and then evaluating his/her responses to get an insight of the knowl-edge level of the learner. Various rules have been used for updating the knowledge level of the learner over time [16,17]. A genetic algorithm is used to classify the learner accordingly [17].

It is also being discussed that learner's personality and his/her learning style impact academic achievement. The author argues that different learners have different thought processes that change their learning style as well as their academic achievement. They discuss the five personality traits and also their direct dependence on the academic performance of the learner individually. These traits depend on the learner's personality and how he/she perceives different things. Thus, it is very important to consider the personality traits of the learner while forming an e-learning system [18]. Features such as agreeableness, conscientiousness, neuroticism and extraversion also play an important role in the learner's behavior. There are different researches that also prove that there is a correlation between academic dishonesty and their personality [18].

There are some researches that used artificial neural networks to predict students' performance. These researches utilized various factors, including educational background and other social factors to predict the learner's performance. This model achieved an accuracy of 70% [19]. Researchers have ontologies assisted with student data to personalize the e-learning environment [4]. After identifying the learner's weakness they suggest the appropriate learning module. It is being identified that the support vector machine has the highest accuracy among the data mining algorithm [20].

The sustainability of an e-learning system is required on both individual and social levels [21]. E-learning has certainly provided comfort to the learners as they can access the learning materials any time and from anywhere. On the contrary, the vast availability of the learning materials poses some problems for the learners and in order to minimize this problem, many have done the research to provide an adaptive system that would judge the learner on some basis and recommend what he should learn and also provide the resources for the same. Thus, this is required to model the e-learner to predict learning content. This chapter discusses the learner model using the learning style, personality factors and knowledge level of the learner as a learner profile.

4.3 Methodology

The huge corpus of learning materials available decreases the motivation to learn through the e-learning platform. Assessing and predicting the class of the learner requires an assessment of the complete learner profile, including his personality, knowledge level and learning style. This would help us to recommend some learning materials that would be solely catered to one's needs. The problem then gets broken down into three tasks: the collection of the learner's data, data transformation using different models and selection of intuitionistic algorithms that would output membership and nonmembership values. The membership and nonmembership values can then be used to predict a learning track. The FSLSM and openness, conscientiousness, extraversion, agreeableness, neuroticism (OCEAN) tests are used for finding personality traits. Figure 4.1 shows the assessment model used.

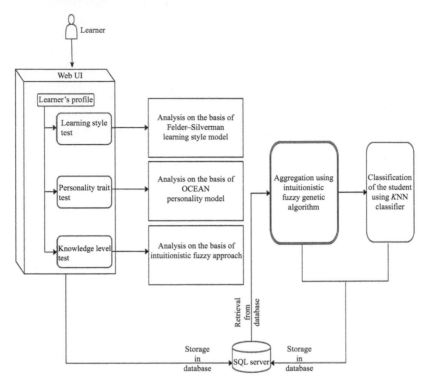

Figure 4.1   Architecture of learner assessment based on a learner profile

Here, the learner profile is the combination of learning style, personality test and knowledge level of the learner. Figure 4.1 shows the following steps:

- The learner must be authenticated and authorized before filling the three questionnaires to begin his learning and three classes to which he would belong should be evaluated only after all the three forms are filled.
- The intuitionistic fuzzy approach has to be used to calculate the score of every form to determine the aggregated values.
- The working of the back end such as genetic algorithm and *K*NN classifier should give the desired result.
- A learner should be assigned a class according to his/her results in the three questionnaires. Before explaining each module in detail, the next section describes the conversion of a numeric score into an intuitionistic fuzzy score.

4.3.1   Conversion of numeric to intuitionistic fuzzy value

Data has been collected in numeric value. The data has to be converted to intuitionistic fuzzy value. The intuitionistic fuzzy value consists of membership and nonmembership value. The following equation is being used to convert the numeric value. Here, μ(mu) represents the membership value, whereas v (nu) represents the nonmembership value. The hesitant degree is represented as *Pi*.

$$\mu = 1 - v - \pi \tag{4.1}$$

$$v = \frac{1 - \frac{x}{y}}{1 + 0.02 \times \frac{x}{y}} \tag{4.2}$$

$$\pi = \frac{1 - \frac{x}{y} - \left(1 - \frac{x}{y}\right)}{1 + 0.02 \times \frac{x}{y}} \tag{4.3}$$

After finding the values of nu (v) and mu (μ) for every learner, the aggregation of nu (v) and mu (μ) was then used to calculate the membership and nonmembership values.

$$\text{Membership value} : \mu = 1 - \prod_{i=1}^{n} (1 - \mu_i)^{w_i} \tag{4.4}$$

$$\text{Nonmembership value} : v = \prod_{i=1}^{n} (v_i)^{w_i} \tag{4.5}$$

These equations are being used to calculate the aggregate score of attributes of learner profile.

4.3.2   Learning style model

The FSLSM can be analyzed and the styles can be distributed in four dimensions. The first dimension differentiates between active and reflective learning styles, the second distinguishes between sensing and intuitive learning styles, the third is the visual–verbal dimension, and the fourth is sequential learning vs global learning. The questionnaire consists of 44 questions spread into each dimension. Each dimension consists of 11 questions. Active and reflective learning styles discuss how you prefer to process information. Sensing and intuitive are how you prefer to perceive information. How to present information is represented by visual and verbal, whereas sequential learning and global learning represent how you prefer to organize and progress toward understanding information. The scores for each of these dimensions are calculated according to the questions that determine these styles as follows:

Active (1) and reflective (0)—1, 17, 25, 29, 5, 9, 13, 21, 33, 37, 41
Sensing (1) and intuitive (0)—2, 14, 22, 26, 30, 34, 6, 10, 18, 38, 42
Visual (1) and verbal (0)—3, 7, 15, 19, 27, 35, 3, 7, 11, 23, 31, 39, 43
Sequential (1) and global (0)—4, 8, 12, 16, 28, 40, 24, 32, 20, 36, 44

The number of answers is correct in each dimension were recorded accordingly. These numeric values have been converted into an intuitionistic fuzzy value using (4.1)–(4.3). It is being converted to membership value represented as μ and nonmembership value v for each dimension. The aggregate score of the learning style of a student is calculated by using (4.4) and (4.5). Figure 4.4 shows the learning style questionnaire, whereas Figure 4.5 shows the response of the questionnaire of a learner. The next section describes the personality model of the learner.

4.3.3 Personality model

The OCEAN personality model represents openness to experience (O), conscientiousness (C), extraversion (E), agreeableness (A) and neuroticism (N). The questionnaire of the personality traits is measured from a scale of 1–5 representing the strength of the answer. All these personality traits are determined through the answers of the learner where each trait is described by the questions as follows:

$$E = 20 + (1) \underline{\quad} - (6) \underline{\quad} + (11) \underline{\quad} - (16) \underline{\quad} + (21) \underline{\quad} - (26)$$
$$\underline{\quad} + (31) \underline{\quad} - (36) \underline{\quad} + (41) \underline{\quad} - (46) \underline{\quad} = \underline{\quad}$$
$$A = 14 - (2) \underline{\quad} + (7) \underline{\quad} - (12) \underline{\quad} + (17) \underline{\quad} - (22) \underline{\quad} + (27)$$
$$\underline{\quad} - (32) \underline{\quad} + (37) \underline{\quad} + (42) \underline{\quad} + (47) \underline{\quad} = \underline{\quad}$$
$$C = 14 + (3) \underline{\quad} - (8) \underline{\quad} + (13) \underline{\quad} - (18) \underline{\quad} + (23) \underline{\quad} - (28)$$
$$\underline{\quad} + (33) \underline{\quad} - (38) \underline{\quad} + (43) \underline{\quad} + (48) \underline{\quad} = \underline{\quad}$$
$$N = 38 - (4) \underline{\quad} + (9) \underline{\quad} - (14) \underline{\quad} + (19) \underline{\quad} - (24) \underline{\quad} - (29)$$
$$\underline{\quad} - (34) \underline{\quad} - (39) \underline{\quad} - (44) \underline{\quad} - (49) \underline{\quad} = \underline{\quad}$$
$$O = 8 + (5) \underline{\quad} - (10) \underline{\quad} + (15) \underline{\quad} - (20) \underline{\quad} + (25) \underline{\quad} - (30)$$
$$\underline{\quad} + (35) \underline{\quad} + (40) \underline{\quad} + (45) \underline{\quad} + (50) \underline{\quad} = \underline{\quad}$$

After calculating the score of the questionnaire, these values are converted into an intuitionistic fuzzy score by using (4.1), (4.2) and (4.3). The aggregated score is calculated by using (4.4) and (4.5). Figure 4.2 shows the questionnaire of the personality model, whereas Figure 4.4 shows the response of the learner based on the personality test. Figure 4.6 shows the aggregate result of the learning style.

4.3.4 Assessment of knowledge level

The current understanding of the topic for a learner also plays an equally important role for the learner in determining the learning material. This skill level is called the knowledge level of the learner for a particular topic. This knowledge level is calculated using a fuzzy approach for each learner.

An objective questionnaire is being presented to the students based on the previous concept to measure the knowledge of a learner. The learner assigns a percentage of correctness to each option in the survey. The sum of the correct answer and incorrect answers should be less than or equal to 100. The value of μ_i and v_i is calculated as follows:

$$\mu_i = \frac{C_i}{100} \tag{4.6}$$

$$v_i = \frac{W_i}{100} \tag{4.7}$$

$$Score = (\mu_i, v_i) \tag{4.8}$$

Step 1: Get $(\mu i, vi)$: $i = 1$ to 3 from the learning, personality using equation (4.1), (4.2), (4.3).

Step 2: Aggregate the learning style intuitionistic fuzzy value of each question, personality and knowledge level intuitionistic fuzzy value of each question for a particular student using (4.4), (4.5).

Step 3: Apply genetic algorithm

(i): for $j = 0$ to n (choose an initial random population for μ and v of individuals)

(ii): for $i = 0$ to m (evaluate the fitness (F(x)) for μ of each individual)

(iii): for $i = 0$ to m (evaluate the fitness (F(y)) for v of each individual)

Calculate the fitness function using following equation for each student

$$f(x) = 1 - \prod_{i=1}^{n}(1 - \mu_i)^{w_i} \qquad --- (4.9)$$

$$f(y) = \prod_{i=1}^{n}(v_i)^{w_i} \qquad --- (4.10)$$

REPEAT

(iv): Select parents for individual randomly and mate them.

(v): Generate new individual using random crossover.

(vi): Apply mutations and generate the new chromosome.

(vii): Evaluate the fitness of new individuals.

(viii): Select the most suitable individual.

UNTIL

(viiii): Generations specified

Step 4: Calculate the Euclidian distance:

$$E(d) = \sqrt{(x - \mu)^2 + (x - v)^2} \qquad ----- (4.11)$$

(i): Generate the data points for classifier.

(ii): Use (μ, v) to calculate the Euclidian distance $E(d)$ with every data point.

(iii): Check for nearest k points.

(iv): Give the class according to most nearest elements to the student.

Figure 4.2   Algorithm for classification of learner

where c_i represents the value given to the correct answers, whereas the w_i represents the sum of the values given to the incorrect answers. The score of each question is defined as (4.8). The knowledge level can be aggregated using (4.4) and (4.5). Figure 4.6 shows the aggregate result of the personality test. Figure 4.7 shows the knowledge assessment form.

4.3.5   Intuitionistic fuzzy optimization algorithm and KNN classifier

The genetic algorithm is an optimization algorithm that is adaptive and self-learning. It exploits the benefit of choosing the fittest value-based similar to Charles Darwin's theory of evolution. The genetic algorithm provided us with an aggregated membership (μ) and nonmembership (v) values that were obtained from surveys and questionnaires.

Experimental results of a learner profile based on personality traits, the learning style of the learner and his knowledge level using intuitionistic fuzzy genetic KNN classifier are explained in the next section.

The *K*NN classifier maps the membership and nonmembership values obtained after the aggregation from the genetic algorithm to the nearest class specified. We made five classes to which the learners get assigned, including very low, low, medium, high and very high.

4.4   Experimental results

E-learning platforms have become common and approachable for a vast set of audiences. The COVID-19 pandemic in 2020 triggered the application of these online learning platforms. The application of these algorithms to assess the personality traits, knowledge level and learning style of the learner and then to recommend the best fitting educational track for the learner has been implemented in the web application. We get all the data required from the learner through three forms that are available on the website that is then used to predict the learning material and track suitable for the learner.

All these and the idea to provide the topics of a course in regard to all the prerequisites need to be implemented through a website. The implementation of providing the basic UI to the users has been done by creating an interactive home page using HTML and CSS in the ASP.NET Framework. The home page gives the basic view and information of the whole system along with the tabs to other pages. Figure 4.3 shows the home page of the e-learning screen.

The e-learning system provides the three tests to detect the personality traits, knowledge level and learning level of a learner. These tests are available on the home page that has a link to all the forms. The user simply logs in and takes the three tests and all the data acquired from these tests that predict the learning material suited for him/her on the website. Figure 4.4 shows the sample questionnaire of the learning style assessment test and personality test. The FSLSM was used to evaluate the learning style, and the OCEAN model was used to evaluate the

Figure 4.3   Home page screen test

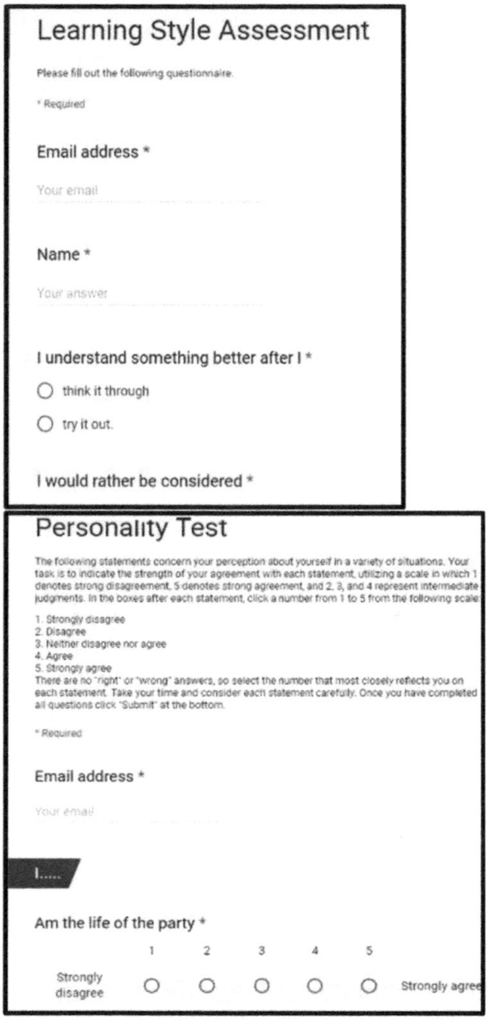

Figure 4.4   Learning style and personality test assessment

personality traits of the learner. The responses obtained from the learner were recorded and saved to a database. The ensemble model was then used to determine the aggregated membership (μ) and nonmembership (ν) values of both the personality assessment and the learning style assessment. On filling the forms, the data from each user is saved in a database that is accessed by the model to predict the learning material. Figure 4.5 shows the learning style responses. Figure 4.6 shows the personality trait responses. These responses help one to detect the learning style and personality type of the learner which do not change that much over time. These tests can be asked to be taken at regular intervals of 1 year, and the data can be

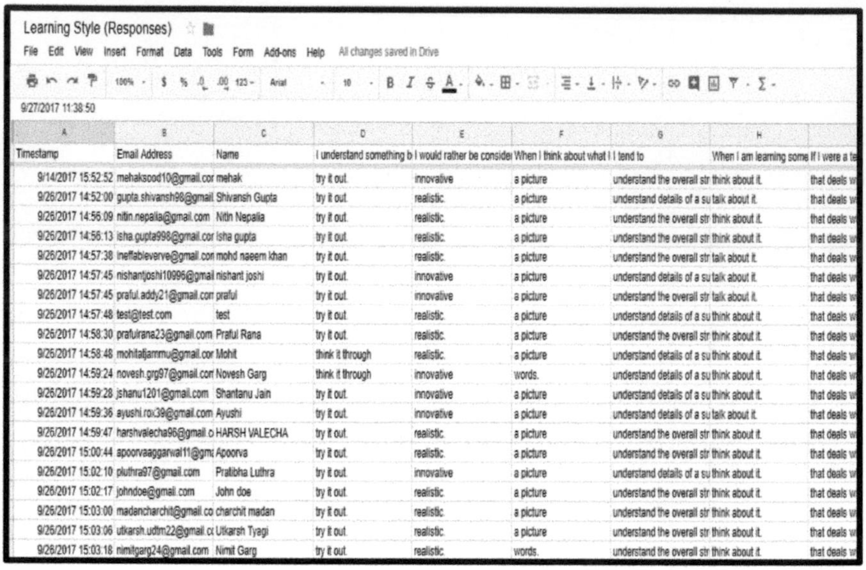

Learning Style (Responses)

File Edit View Insert Format Data Tools Form Add-ons Help All changes saved in Drive

9/27/2017 11:38:50

Timestamp	Email Address	Name	I understand something b	I would rather be conside	When I think about what I	I tend to	When I am learning some	If I were a te
9/14/2017 15:52:52	mehaksood10@gmail.cor	mehak	try it out.	innovative	a picture	understand the overall str	think about it.	that deals w
9/26/2017 14:52:00	gupta.shivansh98@gmail.	Shivansh Gupta	try it out.	realistic.	a picture	understand details of a su	talk about it.	that deals w
9/26/2017 14:56:09	nitin.nepalia@gmail.com	Nitin Nepalia	try it out.	realistic.	a picture	understand the overall str	think about it.	that deals w
9/26/2017 14:56:13	isha.gupta998@gmail.cor	Isha gupta	try it out.	realistic.	a picture	understand the overall str	think about it.	that deals w
9/26/2017 14:57:38	ineffableverve@gmail.con	mohd naeem khan	try it out.	realistic.	a picture	understand the overall str	talk about it.	that deals w
9/26/2017 14:57:45	nishantjoshi10996@gmail	nishant joshi	try it out.	innovative	a picture	understand details of a su	talk about it.	that deals w
9/26/2017 14:57:45	praful.addy21@gmail.con	praful	try it out.	innovative	a picture	understand the overall str	talk about it.	that deals w
9/26/2017 14:57:48	test@test.com	test	try it out.	realistic.	a picture	understand details of a su	think about it.	that deals w
9/26/2017 14:58:30	prafulrana23@gmail.com	Praful Rana	try it out.	realistic.	a picture	understand the overall str	think about it.	that deals w
9/26/2017 14:58:48	mohitatjammu@gmail.cor	Mohit	think it through	realistic.	a picture	understand details of a su	think about it.	that deals w
9/26/2017 14:59:24	novesh.grg97@gmail.con	Novesh Garg	think it through	innovative	words.	understand details of a su	think about it.	that deals w
9/26/2017 14:59:28	jshanu1201@gmail.com	Shantanu Jain	try it out.	innovative	a picture	understand details of a su	think about it.	that deals w
9/26/2017 14:59:36	ayushi.rox39@gmail.com	Ayushi	try it out.	innovative	a picture	understand details of a su	talk about it.	that deals w
9/26/2017 14:59:47	harshvalecha96@gmail.o	HARSH VALECHA	try it out.	realistic.	a picture	understand the overall str	think about it.	that deals w
9/26/2017 15:00:44	apoorvaaggarwal11@gm	Apoorva	try it out.	realistic.	a picture	understand the overall str	think about it.	that deals w
9/26/2017 15:02:10	pluthra97@gmail.com	Pratibha Luthra	try it out.	innovative	a picture	understand details of a su	think about it.	that deals w
9/26/2017 15:02:17	johndoe@gmail.com	John doe	try it out.	realistic.	a picture	understand the overall str	think about it.	that deals w
9/26/2017 15:03:00	madancharchit@gmail.co	charchit madan	try it out.	realistic.	a picture	understand the overall str	think about it.	that deals w
9/26/2017 15:03:06	utkarsh.udtm22@gmail.cc	Utkarsh Tyagi	try it out.	realistic.	a picture	understand the overall str	think about it.	that deals w
9/26/2017 15:03:18	nimitgarg24@gmail.com	Nimit Garg	try it out.	realistic.	words.	understand the overall str	think about it.	that deals w

Figure 4.5 Learning style responses

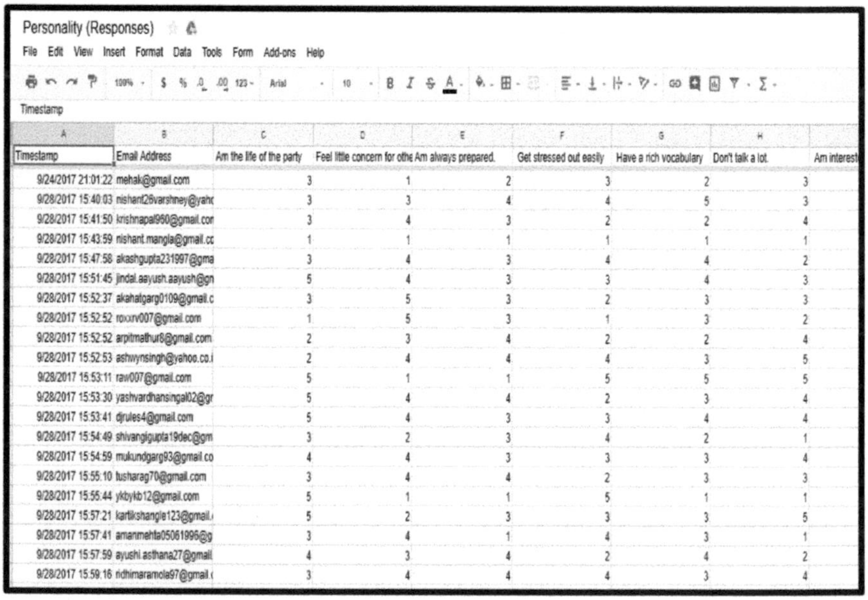

Personality (Responses)

File Edit View Insert Format Data Tools Form Add-ons Help

Timestamp

Timestamp	Email Address	Am the life of the party	Feel little concern for othe	Am always prepared.	Get stressed out easily	Have a rich vocabulary	Don't talk a lot.	Am interest
9/24/2017 21:01:22	mehak@gmail.com	3	1	2	3	2	3	
9/28/2017 15:40:03	nishant26varshney@yahc	3	3	4	4	5	3	
9/28/2017 15:41:50	krishnapal960@gmail.cor	3	4	3	2	2	4	
9/28/2017 15:43:59	nishant.mangla@gmail.cc	1	1	1	1	1	1	
9/28/2017 15:47:58	akashgupta231997@gma	3	4	3	4	4	2	
9/28/2017 15:51:45	jindal.aayush.aayush@gn	5	4	3	3	4	3	
9/28/2017 15:52:37	akahatgarg0109@gmail.c	3	5	3	2	3	3	
9/28/2017 15:52:52	roxxrv007@gmail.com	1	5	3	1	3	2	
9/28/2017 15:52:52	arpitmathur8@gmail.com	2	3	4	2	2	4	
9/28/2017 15:52:53	ashwynsingh@yahoo.co.i	2	4	4	4	3	5	
9/28/2017 15:53:11	raw007@gmail.com	5	1	1	5	5	5	
9/28/2017 15:53:30	yashvardhansingal02@gr	5	4	4	2	3	4	
9/28/2017 15:53:41	djrules4@gmail.com	5	4	3	3	4	4	
9/28/2017 15:54:49	shivangigupta19dec@gm	3	2	3	4	2	1	
9/28/2017 15:54:59	mukundgarg93@gmail.co	4	4	3	3	3	4	
9/28/2017 15:55:10	tusharag70@gmail.com	3	4	4	2	3	3	
9/28/2017 15:55:44	ykbykb12@gmail.com	5	1	1	5	1	1	
9/28/2017 15:57:21	kartikshangle123@gmail.(	5	2	3	3	3	5	
9/28/2017 15:57:41	amanmehta05061996@g	3	4	1	4	3	1	
9/28/2017 15:57:59	ayushi.asthana27@gmail.	4	3	4	2	4	2	
9/28/2017 15:59:16	ridhimaramola97@gmail.(	3	4	4	4	3	4	

Figure 4.6 Personality trait responses

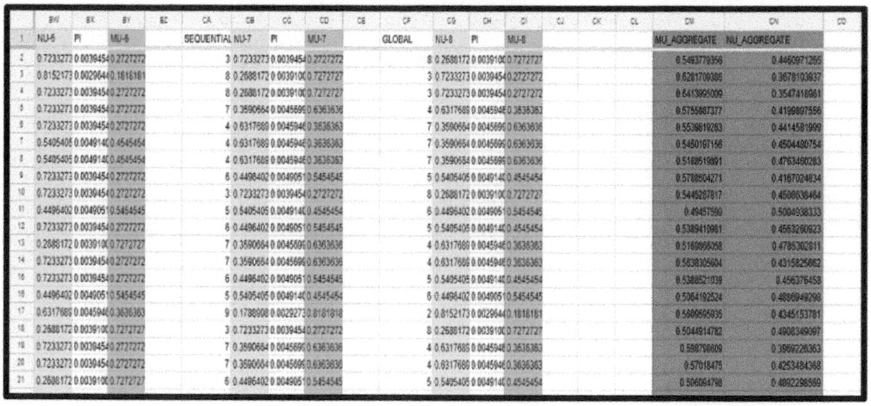

Figure 4.7 Learning style sheet after aggregation

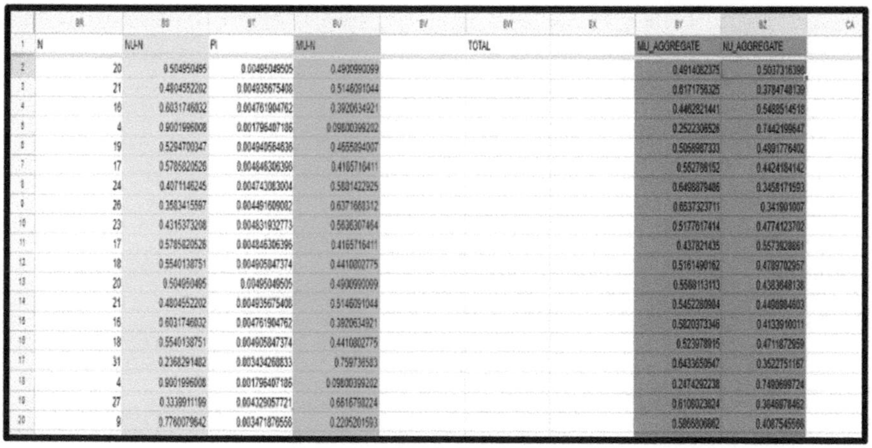

Figure 4.8 Personality sheet after aggregation

updated in the database. The personality is a factor that helps one to reveal the way a learner approaches to study or acquires a skill.

Figure 4.7 shows the snapshot of the learning style sheet of the learner after aggregation. The figure shows the sequential and global learning style of learners. Their numeric values along with the conversion of μ (membership), ν (non-membership values) and π (hesitant) values are shown in Figure 4.7. A column with the brick color is shown as aggregate of membership and nonmembership values of each dimension.

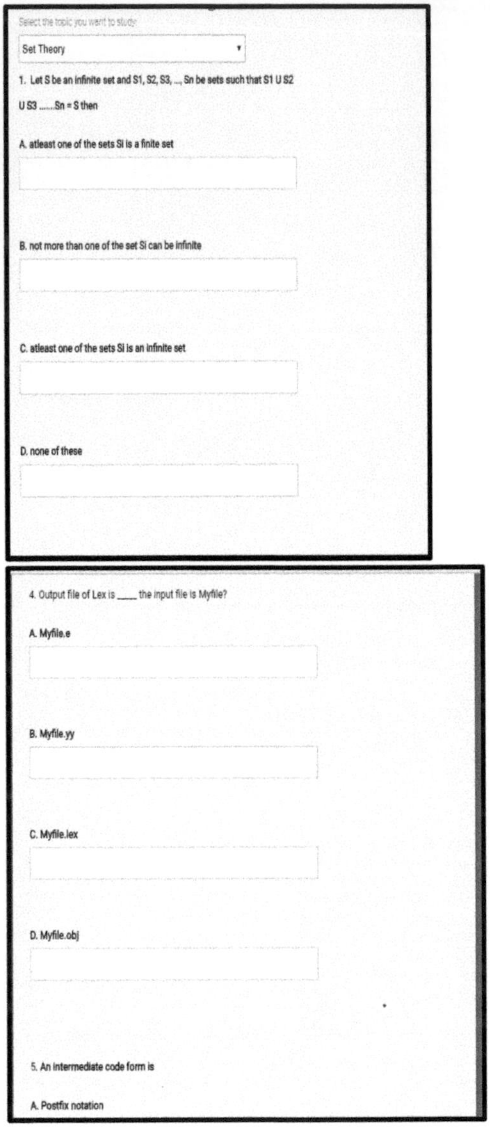
Select the topic you want to study

Set Theory

1. Let S be an infinite set and S1, S2, S3, ..., Sn be sets such that S1 U S2 U S3 ......Sn = S then

A. atleast one of the sets Si is a finite set

B. not more than one of the set Si can be infinite

C. atleast one of the sets Si is an infinite set

D. none of these

4. Output file of Lex is ____ the input file is Myfile?

A. Myfile.e

B. Myfile.yy

C. Myfile.lex

D. Myfile.obj

5. An intermediate code form is

A. Postfix notation

Figure 4.9 Knowledge level assessment form

Figure 4.8 shows the first column as the numeric score of each learner. The next column shows the membership and nonmembership value. The last column shows the aggregation value in each dimension.

Figure 4.9 shows the form of the knowledge assessment for a learner. All the answers from these were recorded and the specified formulas in the earlier

Table 4.1   Confusion matrix for defined classes

Classes	Low	Low–medium	Medium	Medium–high	High
Very low	TP_{low}	$E_{low-lowmed}$	$E_{low-med}$	$E_{low-medhigh}$	$E_{low-high}$
Low	$E_{lowmed-low}$	$TP_{low-med}$	$E_{lowmed-med}$	$E_{lowmed-medhigh}$	$E_{lowmed-high}$
Medium	$E_{med-low}$	$E_{med-lowmed}$	TP_{med}	$E_{med-medhigh}$	$E_{med-high}$
High	$E_{medhigh-low}$	$E_{medhigh-lowmed}$	$E_{medhigh-med}$	$TP_{med-high}$	$E_{medhigh-high}$
Very high	$E_{high-low}$	$E_{high-lowmed}$	$E_{high-med}$	$E_{high-medhigh}$	TP_{high}

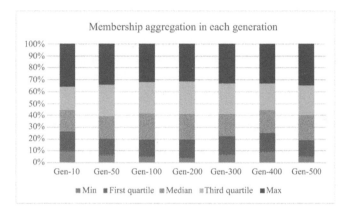

Figure 4.10   Aggregation of membership value in each generation

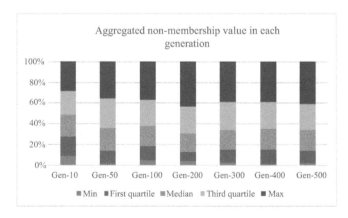

Figure 4.11   Aggregation of nonmembership value in each generation

proposed algorithm were used to determine the membership and nonmembership values for the user for the topic he/she wanted to learn. But unlike the personality and learning style, the knowledge level of a student changes when he/she learns

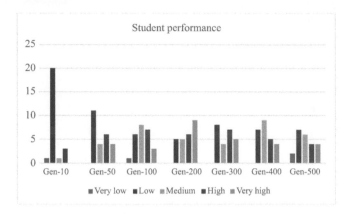

Figure 4.12   Student performance in each generation

Table 4.2   Defined class for Generation-10

For Generation-10			
Student no	**Aggregated membership value**	**Aggregated nonmembership value**	**Class**
1	0.340013769	0.630509955	2
2	0.299505449	0.405554058	2
3	0.342715947	0.545692661	2
4	0.36236969	0.427087522	2
5	0.312887698	0.615162986	2
6	0.507368347	0.492631653	4
7	0.359681628	0.619222293	2
8	0.416155891	0.552292069	2
9	0.356183096	0.643816904	2
10	0.341469641	0.574408524	2
11	0.601941185	0.38721887	4
12	0.393226364	0.603193205	2
13	0.361057022	0.539741278	2
14	0.359543773	0.637011124	2
15	0.399002258	0.59743289	2
16	0.589790744	0.399482296	4
17	0.394472577	0.602026409	2
18	0.300306092	0.375501342	2
19	0.475923734	0.520816897	2
20	0.332227203	0.664851304	2
21	0.464854057	0.531606538	2
22	0.202447179	0.768842311	1
23	0.373594889	0.622707397	2
24	0.396329432	0.600057164	2
25	0.738959704	0.261040296	3
26	0.398320792	0.598155792	2

Table 4.3   Defined class for Generation-50

	For Generation-50		
Student no	Aggregated membership value	Aggregated nonmembership value	Class
1	0.335376859	0.557154212	2
2	0.80918738	0.19081262	5
3	0.392834331	0.517838018	2
4	0.177803658	0.444785552	2
5	0.617119873	0.224462853	3
6	0.582923796	0.27687531	3
7	0.621280982	0.378719018	4
8	0.502351351	0.370731481	4
9	0.784033039	0.215966961	4
10	0.355347821	0.425545792	2
11	0.476720491	0.523279509	2
12	0.338888312	0.658025752	2
13	0.750380708	0.249619292	3
14	0.600167125	0.399832875	4
15	0.850565234	0.149434766	5
16	0.723049132	0.276950868	3
17	0.475539153	0.521204349	2
18	0.853847473	0.146152527	5
19	0.581631546	0.418368454	4
20	0.968995352	0.031004648	5
21	0.879984328	0.120015672	5
22	0.360249809	0.540098131	2
23	0.33403687	0.612616073	2
24	0.407415637	0.588947557	2
25	0.395549576	0.600523247	2
26	0.398242796	0.598328149	2

new concepts. Also, he/she may forget the topics he/she learned and thus the knowledge level of the student must be adaptive.

Genetic algorithm was utilized to aggregate the membership and non-membership values of the leaner from the three assessment tests. The genetic algorithm is an optimization algorithm that is adaptive and self-learning. It exploits the benefit of choosing the fittest value similar to Charles Darwin's theory of evolution. The genetic algorithm provided us with an aggregated membership (μ) and nonmembership (ν) values that were obtained from surveys and questionnaires. It consists of two main functions: mutation function and a fitness function. The values with better fitness scores are selected to produce an offspring.

Table 4.4   Defined class for Generation-100

For Generation-100			
Student no	Aggregated membership value	Aggregated nonmembership value	Class
1	0.771461782	0.228538218	4
2	0.248575701	0.36475289	2
3	0.156238588	0.687393649	1
4	0.372175101	0.627824899	2
5	0.711199324	0.288800676	3
6	0.298357709	0.08736682	3
7	0.653808955	0.346191045	3
8	0.70631694	0.29368306	3
9	0.369027039	0.584588737	2
10	0.250170859	0.200684019	3
11	0.727222373	0.272777627	3
12	0.380656442	0.615871431	2
13	0.684694662	0.315305338	3
14	0.566870506	0.234324355	3
15	0.638176048	0.361823952	4
16	0.416439383	0.420280673	2
17	0.867609464	0.132390536	5
18	0.817236559	0.182763441	5
19	0.555810063	0.444189937	4
20	0.780740257	0.219259743	4
21	0.573172167	0.426827833	4
22	0.613434745	0.386565255	4
23	0.615303258	0.384696742	4
24	0.775726199	0.224273801	4
25	0.400697765	0.595843814	2
26	0.889928686	0.110071314	5

The *K*NN classifier then maps the membership and nonmembership values obtained after the aggregation from the genetic algorithm to the nearest class specified. The distance between each class and data point is determined and the one with the least distance is selected. We have five classes to which the learners get assigned, including very low, low, medium, high and very high. These classes have been assigned 1, 2, 3, 4 and 5, respectively. Tables 4.2–4.8 show the aggregated membership (μ) and nonmembership (ν) values corresponding to the class.

A confusion matrix was used to compare the actual results with the values predicted through the ensemble model. The confusion matrix was calculated for the test data based on the results obtained from *K*NN. Such a matrix was generated by generating a 5×5 matrix that represented the values as shown in Table 4.1.

Table 4.5   Defined class for Generation-200

For Generation-200			
Student no	**Aggregated membership value**	**Aggregated nonmembership value**	**Class**
1	0.375559853	0.393225756	2
2	0.762034334	0.223711332	4
3	0.696144188	0.303855812	3
4	0.869218428	0.130781572	5
5	0.786387377	0.213612623	4
6	0.826927147	0.170501347	5
7	0.549319282	0.450680718	4
8	0.729172736	0.270827264	3
9	0.616170409	0.383829591	4
10	0.937065962	0.062934038	5
11	0.306531893	0.693468107	2
12	0.660503469	0.339496531	3
13	0.827646557	0.150947071	5
14	0.580699453	0.419300547	4
15	0.734480087	0.08246302	5
16	0.589936794	0.410063206	4
17	0.484236892	0.067809337	3
18	0.885363487	0.114636513	5
19	0.321285052	0.414571673	2
20	0.221777084	0.519096262	2
21	0.859311135	0.140688865	5
22	0.516347926	0.302484664	4
23	0.445542801	0.105549094	3
24	0.823574276	0.176425724	5
25	0.430115349	0.569884651	2
26	0.128595643	0.335849916	2

True positive—number of classes true according to prediction and true according to actual.

True negative—number of classes true according to prediction and false according to actual.

False positive—number of classes false according to prediction and true according to actual.

False negative—number of classes false according to prediction and false according to actual.

Here E represents error values that can be calculated as false-positive rate, false-negative rate and true-negative rate.

Table 4.6   Defined class for Generation-300

For Generation-300			
Student no	Aggregated membership value	Aggregated nonmembership value	Class
1	0.640779051	0.264290457	3
2	0.3071422	0.515405652	2
3	0.83829857	0.16170143	5
4	0.867504539	0.132495461	5
5	0.423871634	0.576128366	2
6	0.21092368	0.407632553	2
7	0.490590462	0.509409538	2
8	0.685766453	0.314233547	3
9	0.952145687	0.047854313	5
10	0.562198335	0.437801665	4
11	0.507897203	0.492102797	4
12	0.326321132	0.572794353	2
13	0.791227186	0.208772814	5
14	0.573965528	0.394708399	4
15	0.249808729	0.301127347	2
16	0.476543729	0.319735998	4
17	0.850126853	0.149873147	5
18	0.904169231	0.095830769	5
19	0.372951853	0.627048147	2
20	0.805767824	0.194232176	5
21	0.453846247	0.110460123	3
22	0.52778583	0.240740493	3
23	0.476400816	0.198531702	3
24	0.255940164	0.290465171	2
25	0.587828521	0.412171479	4
26	0.586334666	0.413665334	4

Tables 4.2–4.8 show the aggregated values of the membership and non-membership values using genetic algorithm as shown. The last column shows the classes corresponding to the membership and nonmembership values. Figures 4.9 and 4.10 show the aggregation values of each generation corresponding to membership and nonmembership values.

Figure 4.10 shows that 35% students have scored above 70, whereas it is varying in other generations as we increase the generation. Finally, Generation-500 also shows the same result.

Figure 4.11 shows the aggregation of the nonmembership value corresponding to the membership value. Figures 4.10 and 4.11 show the consistency of an algorithm in

Table 4.7 Defined class for Generation-400

For Generation-400			
Student no	Aggregated membership value	Aggregated nonmembership value	Class
1	0.613253845	0.386746155	4
2	0.780981462	0.210155435	4
3	0.449940861	0.550059139	2
4	0.405691986	0.392567818	2
5	0.635961829	0.364038171	4
6	0.635665738	0.364334262	4
7	0.556637335	0.238493896	3
8	0.464706263	0.354593942	4
9	0.66787209	0.33212791	3
10	0.976166071	0.023833929	5
11	0.679058629	0.266836705	3
12	0.557718331	0.063002216	3
13	0.674894551	0.325105449	3
14	0.824790543	0.175209457	5
15	0.837382448	0.094090015	5
16	0.702486309	0.26886952	3
17	0.273226849	0.603005562	2
18	0.494590854	0.505409146	2
19	0.305795008	0.251430639	3
20	0.469565847	0.388625493	4
21	0.33346128	0.66653872	2
22	0.592134824	0.12614396	3
23	0.470017238	0.326955502	4
24	0.529013492	0.446832529	3
25	0.475627079	0.467326013	2
26	0.502201502	0.497798498	2

each generation. As we increase the generation, it does not affect the results. Figure 4.12 shows the performance in each generation. In Generation-10, it shows that the student performance was in low category, whereas in Generation-50, the number of students was in low category, which is 11. Generation-10 does not classify the performance of the student who has performed very well or in another way whose performance is very high. Each generation has classified the high-performance learner between 4 and 5, whereas only Generation-200 has classified nine students as high performer. If we consider the average number of students who have performed well in other generations between 4 and 6, it measures the correctness of the algorithm. Likewise, we can consider the performance of other students in each category of the students and concluded the performance of the algorithm. The overall accuracy is given as follows:

$$Accuracy = \frac{sum\ of\ all\ TPs}{sum\ of\ all\ values} = \frac{39}{50} = 0.78$$

Table 4.8   Defined class for Generation-500

For Generation-500			
Student no	Aggregated membership value	Aggregated nonmembership value	Class
1	0.35490173	0.64509827	2
2	0.623292631	0.37670737	4
3	0.757904817	0.24209518	4
4	0.932252732	0.06774727	5
5	0.90696699	0.09303301	5
6	0.395522691	0.60447731	2
7	0.470861931	0.24221756	4
8	0.800237506	0.19976249	5
9	0.535108476	0.39994642	4
10	0.452953224	0.54704678	2
11	0.292757616	0.42978781	2
12	0.625439464	0.37456054	4
13	0.569861603	0.21881047	3
14	0.488709355	0.18185418	3
15	0.86105703	0.13894297	5
16	0.658115673	0.19159557	3
17	0.190515392	0.41992862	2
18	0.652611394	0.34738861	3
19	0.222653063	0.69263108	1
20	0.193927157	0.29017943	2
21	0.617766839	0.38223316	4
22	0.171818858	0.66254901	1
23	0.454932601	0.03814559	3
24	0.665014039	0.33498596	3
25	0.138903586	0.53148343	2
26	0.83524272	0.16475728	5

The accuracy in each generation is measured between 70% and 81%. It concluded the performance of the algorithm for aggregation and classification.

4.5   Future work

Future work can be suggested that after classifying the learner according to their assessment level performance, they can be suggested learning materials according to their performance. Learners who have classified as very low and low levels can be suggested learning materials with examples. The learner who would be categorized as a medium learner could be suggested the learning material along with analytical questions. Learners who have performed very well in assessment could be given the design problem to solve it.

Different assessment factors can be included to measure the performance of the learner. Evolutionary algorithms can be used to suggest a learning material.

4.6   Conclusion

The existing systems decide the knowledge level of a learner and define among the categories as low, medium and high that further provide the study materials to the learner without deciding if that kind of materials is right for the learner or not. The e-learning environment has a wide scope of improvement, in which a recommender system could be added that would predict a learner on his/her learning style, personality style and knowledge level of the topic chosen by the learner and give the most suited learning material. Something that would immensely improve a learner could be provided and in turn could help one to grow the e-learning environment by a major margin. The results are accurate at lower values of generation but fail or provide inaccurate results at large values. The chapter would evaluate a learner on the basis of his/her learning style and personality. Although these two styles would not be enough to determine what kind of class a learner should belong to and in turn provide him/her with the most suited materials. The topic he/she would choose to learn will also help along with the knowledge-level questionnaire. These three forms and their results for every student will be evaluated through the intuitionistic fuzzy genetic algorithm and KNN classifier to get a particular class for every learner. The future work could be enhanced to provide the learners with the most suited materials according to the class to which he/she would belong. Also, a new technique can be introduced to provide a better result and improve the algorithm. It would also include updating of the knowledge level by taking into consideration the change in the values for prerequisites.

References

[1]   Zhang W. Relational distance-based collaborative filtering for e-learning. In 2008 International Symposium on Computational Intelligence and Design 2008 Oct 17 (Vol. 2, pp. 354–357). IEEE.

[2]   Zaíane OR. Building a recommender agent for e-learning systems. In International Conference on Computers in Education, 2002. Proceedings 2002 Dec 3 (pp. 55–59). IEEE.

[3]   Goyal M, Yadav D, and Tripathi A. An intuitionistic fuzzy approach to classify the user based on an assessment of the learner's knowledge level in e-learning decision-making. JIPS. 2017;13(1):57–67.

[4]   Abdullah M, Daffa WH, Bashmail RM, Alzahrani M, and Sadik M. The impact of learning styles on learner's performance in E-learning environment. International Journal of Advanced Computer Science and Applications. 2015;6(9):24–31.

[5]   Khribi MK, Jemni M, and Nasraoui O. Automatic recommendations for e-learning personalization based on web usage mining techniques and information retrieval. In 2008 Eighth IEEE International Conference on Advanced Learning Technologies 2008 Jul 1 (pp. 241–245). IEEE.

[6]   Truong HM. Integrating learning styles and adaptive e-learning system: current developments, problems and opportunities. Computers in Human Behavior. 2016;55:1185–1193.

[7]   Saa AA. Educational data mining & students' performance prediction. International Journal of Advanced Computer Science and Applications. 2016;7(5):212–220.

[8]   Anoopkumar M and Rahman AM. A review on data mining techniques and factors used in educational data mining to predict student amelioration. In 2016 International Conference on Data Mining and Advanced Computing (SAPIENCE) 2016 Mar 16 (pp. 122–133). IEEE.

[9]   Faisal MH, AlAmeeri AW, and Alsumait AA. An adaptive e-learning framework: crowdsourcing approach. In Proceedings of the 17th International Conference on Information Integration and Web-based Applications & Services 2015 Dec 11 (pp. 1–5).

[10] Berkani L, Nouali O, and Chikh A. A recommendation-based approach for communities of practice of E-learning. In ICWIT 2012 (pp. 270–275).

[11] Devasia T, Vinushree TP, and Hegde V. Prediction of students performance using educational data mining. In 2016 International Conference on Data Mining and Advanced Computing (SAPIENCE) 2016 Mar 16 (pp. 91–95). IEEE.

[12] Kolo KD, Adepoju SA, and Alhassan JK. A decision tree approach for predicting students academic performance. International Journal of Education and Management Engineering. 2015;5(5):12.

[13] Sun J and Xie Y. Notice of retraction: a recommender system based on web data mining for personalized E-learning. In 2009 International Conference on Information Engineering and Computer Science 2009 Dec 19 (pp. 1–4). IEEE.

[14] Poorni G, Balaji K, and DeepthiNivetha C. A personalized e-learning recommender system using the concept of fuzzy tree matching. International Journal of Advanced Research in Computer Engineering and Technology. 2015;4(11).

[15] Zaïane OR. Building a recommender agent for e-learning systems. In International Conference on Computers in Education, 2002. Proceedings 2002 Dec 3 (pp. 55–59). IEEE.

[16] Arslan A and Kaya M. Determination of fuzzy logic membership functions using genetic algorithms. Fuzzy Sets and Systems. 2001;118(2):297–306.

[17] Graf S, Viola SR, Leo T, and Kinshuk. In-depth analysis of the Felder-Silverman learning style dimensions. Journal of Research on Technology in Education. 2007;40(1):79–93.

[18]   Komarraju M, Karau SJ, Schmeck RR, and Avdic A. The Big Five person-
       ality traits, learning styles, and academic achievement. Personality and
       Individual Differences. 2011;51(4):472–477.
[19]   Ibrahim Z and Rusli D. Predicting students' academic performance: com-
       paring artificial neural network, decision tree and linear regression. In 21st
       Annual SAS Malaysia Forum 2007 Sep 5.
[20]   Lu J. A personalized e-learning material recommender system. In
       International Conference on Information Technology and Applications 2004.
       Macquarie Scientific Publishing.
[21]   Alharthi AD, Spichkova M, and Hamilton M. Sustainability requirements for
       eLearning systems: a systematic literature review and analysis. Requirements
       Engineering. 2019;24(4):523–543.

Part II

Technologies in e-learning

Chapter 5

AI in e-learning

Mudita Sinha[1], Leena N. Fukey[1] and Ashutosh Sinha[2]

Artificial intelligence (AI) aims to imitate the human mind through technology. This means that it is an attempt to recreate human intelligence through machines. Machines can be programmed to perform, think and act like humans using AI. AI is the simulation of human intelligence in machines. The term may also be applied to any machine that exhibits traits associated with a human mind such as learning and problem solving.

AI is becoming an essential component in most industries, and with growing technological advancements, it is becoming a more prominent element in all industries. The applications that use AI are varying and go from computers playing chess to self-driving cars. Like other technologies, it is essential that the AI must be tailor-made to fit the varying needs of different organizations. The right fit for one organization might not be so for another; therefore, meaningful automation is need of the hour.

However, with most advancements, there are also a few risks associated with AI as security, and data storage is one of the important factors to be considered. AI often uses sensitive data, which is important to ensure security systems and prevent data breaches as these are becoming to pose serious threats to organizations.

Key contribution of this chapter is as follows:

1. discussion on the incorporation of AI in e-learning to make it more efficient,
2. AI in academic connectivity and
3. improving accessibility for e-learning by AI.

5.1 Artificial intelligence in India

India by its sheer size and diverse markets is the perfect test ground for global enterprises. Intellectual property (IP) is an area that concerns the AI innovators; there is a need to address this to take advantage of the AI Tsunami. The unique nature of AI solution development demands renewed efforts by the government

[1]CHRIST (Deemed to be University), Bengaluru, India
[2]Robonomics AI India Pvt Ltd, Bengaluru, India

authorities in strengthening the IP regime. Applying stringent and narrowly focused patent laws to AI applications is a challenge. The development of the model needs varied data and is one such example. To tackle issues, a suggestion is to establish IP facilitation centers. They will serve as a bridge between practitioners and AI developers, and training of relevant IP granting authorities, judiciary and tribunals are mandatory to facilitate a smooth transition of AI development.

It is predicted that agriculture, healthcare and education are the top industry sectors for AI applications. The top AI applications include automation of business processes, chatbots, natural language processing (NLP) and image recognition. The early 1990s saw the information technology (IT) and ITeS services sector blossom in India and a big economic boom. National Institution for Transforming India Aayogis is leading the national program on AI research. This approach is similar to US government programs where Google, Oracle, Microsoft and Amazon are trying to serve cloud computing and machine learning (ML) needs. The next few years may lead to similar dynamics in India. The government's policy for digitization and AI initiatives is going to help in overall development. Private firms will aim to win sizeable contracts—adding to the pool of funds, this will help one to develop new technologies and also boost AI and data science-related startups.

5.2   Artificial intelligence in education

In education, the use of computers is seen for over 22 years. In the initial years of development, it was mainly used for training and instruction to learn using computers. It was only partly effective in helping learners. The main difference is that the learner's aptitude is not considered.

Also, personalized attention from a human tutor or mentor for a student is missing. This was the trigger for research in the field of intelligent tutoring systems (ITSs). It offers considerable flexibility in the presentation of materials and a greater ability to respond to idiosyncratic learner needs. These systems achieve their "intelligence" by representing pedagogical decisions about how to teach as well as information about the learner. It allows for greater flexibility since it permits for altering the system's interactions with the student. ITSs are seen to add tremendous value and have helped one to elevate students' performance and motivation.

5.3   AI in e-learning

Today, e-learning is widely used for reaching desired educational outcomes under different educational conditions [1–7]. E-learning is making education available to people with or without any restriction for updating themselves. With the advancement of technologies, there arc too many ways to go for e-learning [8]. "AI" is a branch of computer science. The term "AI" was used for the first time in a 1956 conference that aimed at using computers to simulate human intelligence.

Making computers to expand its intelligence saw the application at game playing and proving the mathematical theorem. The need for the option to Search and having sound logic became the basis of the initial AI systems. E-learning tools and techniques saw AI and its applications playing an important role to impart intelligence into it. For more than the last two decades, apart from several other aspects of the Internet, it is applied successfully to achieve better communication, resource sharing and deeper collaboration, enhance and promote active learning and increasing the effectiveness of distance learning [9].

The use of computers and interactive learning is called adaptive learning. It is a modern education method. Focus is on the key points in the topics where students displayed a lack of understanding, which is reflected in their answer sheets. Training based on the strength of the learner's learning approach helps one to decide the intensity of teaching and strategy to be used [10]. Teo and Huang [11] studied a key variable "perceived ease of use (PEU) and how it influences the acceptance of the technology. The study showed that it did not have a significant influence on users" attitudes to technology. This was attributed to the teachers as they were conscientious and focused on the idea that the use of technology will enhance the effectiveness and efficiency of teaching.

Test developers faced challenges in constructing questions of good quality. The automatic question generation (AQG) technique was found to be a solution to these challenges. Sources are used via the algorithm to construct questions; these could be in a structured manner—example knowledge base or it could be unstructured like a simple plain text. AQG could reduce costs and educators can spend more time on instructions in the teaching process.

They can also use it for adaptive testing that ultimately helps in improvising the student learning knowledge as well as the needs. It has a control on the question's quality and difficulty as well as characteristics and cognitive level with good quality test and with a particular requirement.

Like all of the service sectors, the education sector is also influenced by AI. Its impact is very impressive and already seen and felt on the quality of services and time factor offered by the university, and it has also a great impact on the structure and workforce as the supercomputer can provide excellent quick feedback independent of the time. Machine (M) learning (L) is an artificial field. AI solutions are either dependent on the program or have an inbuilt structure to learn patterns and have a good maturity to arrive at fairly accurate predictions [12]. AI helps one to solve problems that challenge most human beings. AI has the intelligence for assessing, analyzing, adding and improving based on the program or real-time data, which is a great advantage.

5.4 Analysis and data

E-learning is constantly evolving, and the emergence of AI can be very beneficial for the sector. AI will make e-learning more personalized and effective as it has the capacity of analyzing big data and predicting patterns for the end-user.

Learners have various ways and pace to learn. Engaging the fast learners and at the same time adopting it for the slower ones is a major challenge in online learning. University teachers have in general a medium level of technological competence. With a somewhat lower level of information on the educational utilization of ICTs, which they fundamentally utilize for information transmission as opposed to content creation, by and large through Moodle-like tools. "While the current assessment of instructive strategies demonstrates that one-on-one guidance from a human mentor prompts preferred comprehension over either study hall or online exercises" [13]. "Simulated intelligence gives the students adequate chances to take an interest in changed learning conditions" not accessible to the e-learning industry scarcely any years prior. Other than upgrading the course content and customizing it as the course advances for every understudy, AI-empowered learning management system (LMS) can likewise deal with the monotonous routine assignments such as reviewing of understudies, on-boarding of understudies, giving beginning guidelines. Along these lines the educators can invest more energy in things that issue the most, for example, making new courses and in any event, learning new things themselves.

Considering the recent problem being faced by the e-learning sector is their insufficiency to store data. Due to the nature of information, it will only increase in size over time and certainly, for this, there must be a scalable, flexible analytics tool, thus AI [14].

5.5 Emphasis on the area that needs improvement in e-learning

E-learning research on the office space has progressed tremendously over the last decades. Various subjects on e-learning in workplace settings have increased, showing the staggering, dynamic and multidisciplinary nature of the field. Innovation offers numerous creative highlights that can be utilized to make guidance for additional students. E-learning is an upheaval that is right now climbing the graph chart. Instead of replacing the customary study pattern of education, e-learning fills in as an integral system for long-lasting and remote learning. Individuals get to experience the interactive media and instructional substance on the Internet that is prepared by specialists of the respective field. The focus of many studies has been on the evaluation of e-learning programs in workplace settings. E-learning program reviews have dealt with the issues of its effectiveness, return on investment and completion rates.

Opportunities to apply the theoretical knowledge acquired have coupled with personal recognition in order to support intrinsic feelings of satisfaction with e-learning. A sense of equity or fairness is also important. Students must feel that the amount of work required by the course was appropriate. There was internal consistency between objectives, content and tests and that there was no favoritism in grading. The majority of research on web-based learning focuses on its effectiveness compared with traditional classroom learning. The effectiveness is normally assessed by post-course questionnaires completed by students, direct observations of online activities, interviews with selected students and comparisons of test/course grades or other objective measures of performance [15]. In the absence of objective measures, higher education providers must rely on the students' perceptions of quality to identify the strengths and weaknesses of educational programs and to conceive appropriate improvement strategies. The cohesion is computed in several ways to highlight isolated people, active subgroups and various roles of the members in the group communication structure. The method allows the display of global properties both at the individual level and at the group level, as well as to efficiently assist the virtual tutor in following the collaboration patterns within the group [16].

Understanding a student's experience in a right manner is a challenge for practicing teachers. Identification and implementation of the most appropriate measurement tools are key to gain a better understanding of the quality issues. Since the objective measures are not in place, the higher education providers have to depend on the student's perceptions of quality to zero on the strengths and weaknesses of designed programs and to plan appropriate strategies for improvement. To highlight isolated people, active subgroups and various roles of the members in the group communication structure, the cohesion is computed in various ways. It displays global properties both at the level of individual and at the group. This assists the online tutor in understanding the collaboration patterns within the group [16].

5.6   Creating comprehensive curriculum

A written plan that guides the design of student's goals for learning and development (L&D), the experiences student will have to achieve those goals, and the way in which adults, both staff and families, will support student's learning to achieve education success is termed a comprehensive curriculum. Good design has to be more than just a resource guide; it must detail ideas and activities to do with students in classrooms or homes.

Elements such as goals and objectives, experiences for learning varied domains, connection to standards, plans for teachers, measures of student's learning, diversity, inclusivity have to be covered in a comprehensive curriculum. When looking at the service that students use on a daily basis, the results have shown that the most commonly used services are e-mail (79%), social networks (78%), browsing videos and pictures (66%), IM/chat (64%) and the use of wikis (46%). Therefore, the idea to implement such tools in the active learning process has emerged. The goal was to motivate students to create meaningful knowledge by using Web 2.0 visualization tools, such as Mindomo or Gliffy. To achieve this goal, assignment was created in which students needed to summarize theoretical knowledge covered by the course content and visualize it by developing a graphical model. The emphasis was on making connections and expressing all possible types of relationships [17].

"Curriculum has become focused on student giving an opportunity to create, continuously learn, ask questions, provide better feedback, identifying with the playing roles and social dimension, practice new tools and the most important bringing new ideas to e-learning process."

As more and more people start using the web for most of their various needs, there is constant improvement in the available technology. The demand for global business knowledge transfer has led to the development of new training modalities: online, collaborative learning and blended learning. Highest flexibility and a deeper understanding of the basic concepts can be achieved by adopting blending learning methods. Innovation in training is to encourage learning motives and outcomes. This is due to the use of online technology and media. POOL2Business is based on skills acquisition rather than enforced learning. Learning is integrated into real-life situations wherein the learners can acquire the skills. It gives them a chance to develop skills through a collaborative approach in projects. Combining knowledge and practice becomes a means of learning [18]. Learning objects are normally the discrete, self-contained units of instructional materials—assembled and reassembled around specific learning objectives. They are then used to build larger educational materials such as lessons, modules or complete courses as per a specific curriculum. Instructional design and pedagogical principles are used to produce learning objects and instructional materials by the content creator. Content management includes all the administrative functions needed to make e-learning content available to learners. Examples like portals, repositories, digital libraries, LMSs, search engines and e-Portfolios need content management that includes administrative functions (e.g. storing, indexing and cataloging).

Models used to design the curriculum are designed to give teachers a map. The model's aim is to allow the teacher to consistently follow the planned method to complete independently instruction-ready materials for their students. While the market is full of various types of curriculum models customized to fit any particular situation, they typically fall into three categories: classroom orientation, product orientation and system orientation. Classroom orientation models are designed to enhance their students' learning and classroom teachers. It is built in such a way that it can be applied by teachers at different levels, such as K-12, vocational school, college and university.

An educational plan advancement group is prescribed to bring both topic and instructive techniques skill to the task. Updates and changes, considering criticism from these gatherings, must be finished before altering starts. Proficient altering will guarantee legitimate language utilization, meaningfulness, suitable stream and consistency. The proficient structure and format of the educational program, frequently with the editorial manager and architect cooperating, will guarantee both exactness and an expert look. When planned, the item is printed or potentially posted on the web. When posting on the web, it is essential to incorporate openness highlights during the structure stage. When the educational plan is made commonly accessible, it ought to be assessed now and again to guarantee that it is off incentive to the clients and stays current [19].

5.7   Immersive learning

Regular learning is highly dependent on the interaction and exchange of information via dialogs between tutors and students. Text-based knowledge transfer has been the major basis for engagements with learners. Combining the text with voice and creating a virtual feeling of "presence" naturally allows for more complex social interactions. With the virtual world, the tutor has the freedom to design learning experiences and plays the role that encourages learner empowerment due to a higher level of interactions [20]. Involvement can be described as a subjective impression in which one is participating in a comprehensive, realistic experience. Actionable, symbolic and sensory factors can also be used as design elements to create an environment in which users believe that they are "inside" in this setting. Such immersive digital interfaces have been shown to be valuable tools to promote learning and engagement, as well as for the transfer from an in-classroom setting to a setting in a real-world scenario.

To reach a higher variety of learners, immersive learning creates an environment that involves all our five senses, with emphasis on vision, sound and touch. This replaces the dependency on print, video and audio that were the main tools for traditional learning. Focus is to rely on mixed reality, i.e. the merging of real world and virtual world to create a new environment to have a coexistence and interaction of physical and digital objects. In 1994, Paul Milgram defined that mixed reality can be viewed as existing on a spectrum, the virtually continuum. Immersive technology engages students in virtual environments both individually and in collaboration. They assimilate academic knowledge, learn problem solving, adapt critical thinking, enhance technical and creative skills to immersive experiences [21].

Where time is perceived to pass extremely fast and the aim of learning is to genuinely engage and be totally absorbed in an activity is immersive experiences [22]. For effective learning, total immersion in the activity has been shown to be encouraging and amazing and is considered as a cognitive state. IT worldwide has immensely influenced student learning process, approach and expectation. Learning methods and associated pedagogical models are influenced by IT.

One directional teacher-to-student has evolved and now it is dynamic IT-supported and elaborate learning environments. Creating various scenarios by educators enables learners to see and understand the material in a deeper interactive way. Learning objectives can be met and demonstrated by the learners. Conforming to the global standards of the content is possible. This gives the possibility to measure the learner's performance. Parameters like thresholds for learning a new language are well known and acceptable world over.

Legal education demands professional learning experiences. This is possible by embedding real-world scenarios in the content. The instructors can assist and give feedback that builds the confidence of the students [21]. Immersive learning has the possibility to offer fast acquisition and a good amount of retention of learning materials. For any course, the success factor is the right content delivery for every learner that must align with the learning outcomes. Immersive technologies are inclusive of methods adopted within a pedagogical classroom setting. However, they must remain supplementary to in-person academic programs, thereby allowing the scope of human relations and interactions. The ultimate aim is to guide the experience of social–emotional learning [23].

Immersive learning has the following technology used:

- Gesture recognition.
- Ease of use by employing speech interfaces.
- 3-D interactivity between the learner and the material for virtual reality.
- 2-D and 3-D objects with augmented reality.
- Head-mounted displays (wearable devices) show virtual worlds helping learn by seeing and doing.

5.8   Intelligent tutoring systems

Computer programs designed to implement methods of AI features for helping teachers understand better as to what they are teaching, to whom they are teaching and selection of best pedagogical tools are called ITS (as shown in Figure 5.1). Intelligent behavior of humans when depicted by a computer program or a machine is termed AI; the same way ITS attempt to replicate the intelligent behavior which can be termed "good teaching" that can try to understand students better and select the best teaching methods for improved teaching. The major pillars of such kind of technology to be brought into practice are advanced computer technology, intellectual psychology and academic research. These areas put together can pave a path for successful implementation of an ITS. The traversing area of these pillars is referred to as cognitive science, which forms the base of ITS for advancing teaching methodologies. "Intelligent tutors" are the new buzz word in computer-

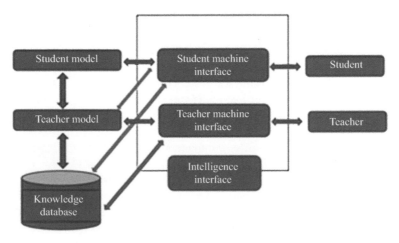

Figure 5.1   Intelligent tutoring system

assisted teaching, which incorporates a correct blend of AI into the normal computer-aided teaching to go an extra mile for upgrading technology-based teaching [24]. A regular computer base teaching evolves into a modified ITS by administering following three features—first and for most the important feature is subject knowledge or domain knowledge has to be fed into the computer so that it can draw the information at the time of decision-making; the second feature has to be an estimation capacity of understanding the learning pace of the student as it varies from individual to individual; and the third important aspect is a selection of correct pedagogical tool so the smart tutor can disperse the knowledge intelligently to the students. Therefore, the foundation of ITS largely depends on the collection of domain knowledge and problem-solving capabilities at a given point in time.

Smart machines have been discussed for centuries it started by an invention of the first calculator in the seventeenth century by Blaise Pascal called Pascal's calculator which could execute, mathematical functions. Leibniz, a great mathematician and philosopher, envisaged the smart machines skilled with reasoning and logic execution competencies which can be used for dispute settlements. Future application of computer development is based on all these early studies. In 1924 Sidney Pressey created a mechanical teaching device at Ohio State University used to facilitate students without a human teacher, instigated the notion of intelligent machine. This intelligent machine had a close resemblance to the typewriter with lots of keys on it and a window that reflected questions for students. In this machine user data input facility was also preset that gave instant feedback on the entered query of the user. The late 1970s and early 1980s witnessed the revolution of microcomputers that revived the computer-aided instructions and kick-started ITS progress. The resources required to own a computer were reduced to a great extent by the introduction of personal computers like Apple 2, Commodore PET and TRS-80 and by 1981 most of the schools in the United States started using computers. LISPITS a program implementing ITS base practically was a key breakthrough to ITS research. It indicated a good growth in student performance. It was developed and introduced in 1982 for teaching LISP programming language to students.

A lot of the learning techniques used in today's teaching environment inculcate shallow learning: memorizing things and replicating the same during exams. To put these concepts into practice, one needs deeper learning. Several types of research have proved that when you take a demanding test that requires reasoning, reading a book or listening to a lecture in preparation is similar to doing nothing, until and unless you have an interactive learning environment that can provide deeper learning. That is where ITSs come into the picture.

ITSs comprise four basic components as per the consensus of different researchers: the user interface model, student model, tutoring model and lastly domain model [12,19].

Power consumption is quite high in installing robot teachers, which is not possible for all institutions to bear with as they operate on different levels. The expenses of operation institutions will increase in such cases and power being nonrenewable resources must be consumed wisely. AI algorithms used by educational programs are not influenced by the repetition of work and will be constant day in and day out so the repletion of tasks will not affect the efficiency of the system. Technology addiction is one of the major disadvantages that can be generated by AI. Dependency on the machine makes the everyday task more efficient but on the other hand generated technology-addicted adults. Though AI can improve the overall learning experience but too much dependency on the same for grading and teaching may lead to education lapses that can harm the learners rather than helping. AI will bring more effectiveness of the teaching pedagogy that will in turn reduce the demand of human educators in the industry creating redundancy. Teachers when replaced by robots will generate a lack of personal engagement. Robots may be overloaded with knowledge but human educators are called "knowledge packs," who provide personal assistance, influence students and lead by example.

ITS (shown in Figure 5.2) and other related new technologies for education and training get hindered by two very important aspects: (a) the cost involved and consumption of electricity; (b) best employment of computers based on the practical and theoretical. Costs of computer are drastically decreasing every month but increasing power consumption directly changes the knowledge of consumer and application of technology.

The qualitative difference in computing possibilities can be created by desktop computers with 100 million instructions per second. Major domains such as home economics, calculus computer science, art, history and medicine are at the figure tips due to the software available. A foreign language can be translated, any information can be retrieved, the sales trend can be judged, and the list continues. Embedded "assistants" within the software will be available for 24/7 support to the learners.

Society is at the brink of all of this. Although the timeframe for such exciting developments is unclear, we do know that the work that has been carried out so far is merely a start of upcoming sudden influx that makes it crucial that we draw our lines when it comes to usage of most technology.

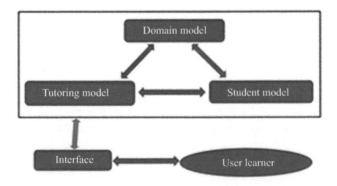

Figure 5.2   Component of intelligent tutoring system

5.9   Virtual facilitators and learning environment

Internet is used to transmit data and transfer knowledge related to the education field between various interested parties, namely teacher to student, organization to employee. This opens up a platform for a virtual learning environment (VLE) via an online system.

In recent years, online learning has evolved in VLEs. Most online education systems also follow a conventional homogeneous learning model of a common collection of learning materials for all participants, although they have varying backgrounds, learning styles and cognitive capacities. A lack of versatility in a homogeneous model may be one explanation of why VLEs have not been as successful as anticipated in supporting certain online education programs. Through applying the constructivist theory of learning, each individual learner has developed their own method of understanding and using learning materials, based on their skill and style of learning. It means that a VLE should tailor learning materials to suit the individual cognitive skill and style of each learner. Such a VLE should help learners learn more about the learning process online and feel pleased with that.

The recent work in the area of ITSs forms a major part of VLE science. With the growth of computing capabilities, more researchers have concentrated on VLEs to provide tailor-made learning content, instruction and instant interaction for individual learners through the use of smart agent technology.

A multi-agent network is a group of autonomous agents working together to solve problems that are beyond individual agents' capabilities. They offer a new and suitable way to build complex systems, especially in open and dynamic environments. ITSs are smart learning systems the components of which embody the values of the particular point of view that they focus on the essence of that knowledge (the domain model), the learning model and the teaching model.

Through the constructivist point of view, however, intelligent systems can have a learning environment to suit the needs of the individual learner. This form of ITS is adaptive, resulting in a customized personal virtual learning environment (PVLE) that supports e-learning by understanding the learning stage of an online learner and offering tailor-made guidance, including customized learning materials, testing and instant interactions. Literature indicates that instructional strategies that suit the learning style of an individual are more successful for learning, and a computer-based education system with a customizing aspect may be superior to a non-personalized one. The lack of research into the processes of personalization applied by intelligent agents needs to be held in mind. This requires Internet access or a computer-based program.

- Distance learning programs leading to a degree
- Courses leading to a professional certification
- Videos for instructions
- Lectures using video or audio media
- Online articles and books

- Audio recordings
- Webinars
- Online classes

Businesses and organizations use a VLE to share with the employee a hand-book, booklet of instructions on the use of new tools, customized training for sales or customer service, induction of a new entrant. VLE offers benefits as follows:

- Tracking and assessment: various techniques can be used to design the tracking and have a meaningful assessment.
- Seamless delivery: Leaners (employee or student) will access the study material. Changes are communicated to all at the same time; uniformity exists.
- Time management: New learners joining the group need not wait; the VLE offers the training program immediately.
- Financial advantages: Payment is done to develop the curriculum, once developed (in virtual learning platforms), can be used repeatedly.
- Communication and connection: Communication is using forums and message boards, experienced learners can comment, mentor and advice new learners.
- Flexibility: Learners and facilitators—both can decide on the timing they want independently for their activities.

There are a few challenges in the VLE. Dwindling attention spans is a challenge—there is a tendency to multitask while the learners are on their computers or some other tool resulting in multiple tabs being opened. It could lead to wandering into reading new articles or playing a video that transforms into background noise while simultaneously completing another project. The next challenge is to prevent loss of focus in the content-some learners want clarity in real time and can feel confused when they cannot ask a teacher. Others might require more hands-on, visual or auditory guidance than those posted on their website by the facilitators. First comes frustration with the use of technology, while many educational areas use technology, and learners are well versed in its use. One may still be in a field that does not need such technical expertise; in these situations, facilitators may have learners who feel they have too challenging tasks ahead of them: training and understanding the software virtual learning setting. A virtual learning experience may not be the most efficient way to teach someone a complex piece of machinery to construct or use. This also does not provide the face-to-face experience, which may restrict opportunities for brainstorming or discussion of team-building and role-playing activities.

5.10   Content analytics

Content analytics is the act of applying business intelligence (BI) and business analytics practices to digital content. Just like in business studies or analytical fields, there is a growing trend for using a technique based on the analysis of data in order to arrive on improved decisions [25]. Content analytics software uses natural language queries, trend analysis and predictive analytics to uncover patterns and trends across a company's unstructured content. Data is now analyzed and applied in increasingly diverse ways. Analytics can be applied to educational resources, which is in use for administrative, teaching and learning activities. Paradata gives details on how the learning resources are used, by whom and in what context. Analytics looks at developing actionable insights through problem definition, use of statistical tools and models.

Applying analytics to learning involves the collection and measurement of student's data and to analyze so that the learning experience is refined and is made more effective for the student. Moodle or Desire2Learn that is an LMS, collects a lot of data, including time spent resource-wise, frequency of posting, login numbers. This data is similar to the data Google Analytics or Piwikpicks from website visits. SNAPP, a new generation of tools, uses this data to analyze degrees of connectivity, social networks and peripheral learners.

The idea of three stages of theoretical learning is being put into practice. Macro-level allows for the exchange of data through various organizations. For a number of purposes such as benchmarking, it can be used. Meso-level operates at an institutional level. This provides insights focused upon approaches to BI. Micro-level is for individual learners who help process-level data monitoring and interpretation. Stanford University's Lytics Lab (Lytics, n.d.) is a recent example of programs designed to investigate the use of data from massive open online courses (MOOC) and social networks; it performs randomized study trials of courses offered by MOOCs; Coursera. Analytics is used to classify possible "threshold concepts" that thousands of students taking multiple-choice question tests may be exposed to. Opportunities are waiting to be established and may identify wider patterns of interaction within learner subpopulations.

Paradata created as learning resources are shared, used, reused, adapted, contextualized, preferred and tweeted multiple times. Often part data is intentionally created by users, e.g. likes and reviews, and others are automatically generated as a result of the tool being used, e.g. hits and download statistics. Paradata can be used as a basic level for tracking how users communicate with learning services through displaying, uploading, posting, enjoying, commenting and tagging. Paradata can also be used in the context of decentralized content delivery networks, such as learning and registry, to document complex aggregations of activities linked to a single resource. For example, social studies lecturers from February 2018 to January 2019, Economics and Management used this tool nine times for postgraduate teaching activities. The structure helps one to make your teaching more effective, as it provides teachers with data that you can use to make actionable decisions and also provides alternative suggestions. The analytics tool provides recommendations on various educational resources and methods to use on the basis of the student data to make a greater effect on students. The prescriptive assessment, focused on student success, offers insights into student comprehension and innovative instructional strategies for schools and teachers. Learning analytics uses techniques from various fields such as computer technology, sociology, psychology, mathematics, ML and data mining to analyze data obtained from the administration and services of education, teaching and learning. Learning analytics can create applications that directly affect existing practices in education.

5.11   Paving new pathways in the coming decade: AI and e-learning

Use e-learning to meet educational goals means linking individuals, technologies and services.

Students, teachers, service providers and organizations, professional associations and boards of education are all stakeholders in this process and we need to link them—the people.

Learning practices focused on pedagogical frameworks (e.g. collaborative and/ or interactive learning, and knowledge-building communities) and instructional techniques (e.g. facilitation problem solving, role-playing, contextualizing instruction), which correlates to programs.

The technology works for promoting content (curing, accessing and producing it), connectivity and collaboration [26].

Based on the learning needs of an individual student, the customized curriculum and learning objectives can be created; this sets the foundation for personalized learning. To assess student's learning style and preexisting knowledge and to deliver customized support and instruction is the job of ITSs. Knowing the student, i.e. his educational background, is the first step of personalized learning that begins. Further, with the help of AI, it creates a custom experience. These steps would undo the standardization of education for all students. AI can solve this problem in an effective manner when the students are confused about certain concepts. The confusion may be due to certain gaps in educational materials that the teachers may not be aware of.

Learning is not just confined to classrooms but in businesses as well. Neural networks are a series of algorithms that mimic the operations of a human brain to recognize relationships between vast amounts of data. Gamification is the next big thing when it comes to e-learning, and AI plays a critical role in planning tactical games for e-learning materials. The intention of appropriately and efficiently adding gamification to e-learning programs for learners will encourage and fascinate the educators to teach with a gaming setup.

A computer-assisted language learning (CALL) is an interactive e-learning environment that enables language skills to be developed in specific content. As CALL, an interactive e-learning system that allows language skills to be developed in different contexts. It is referred to as an integrated e-learning environment when a web-based system performs language learning tasks using work environments such as web browsers or e-mail to clients. Accessibility must be maintained on different channels and on cell phones and tablets.

Aiding computers to make cognitive decisions using AI is an important addition to CALL NLP that forms the technical basis for developing such a learning system and is of great interest to most linguists. Applying NLP technology, or utilizing AI technologies in CALL in a wider context, has also been called smart CALL.

NLP interacts between computers and natural human languages, particularly how to program computers to process and analyze large amounts of natural language data. For creating improvement in the educational system is definitely proving to be an effective approach. Implementing NLP involves initiating the process of learning through natural acquisition in the educational systems.

It provides a solution in a variety of different fields associated with the social and cultural context of language learning and is an effective approach for teachers, students, authors and educators in aiding for writing, analysis and assessment procedures. NLP can greatly improve today's computer-mediated teaching and learning activities, especially in languages other than English, where the adopted LMSs often do not even support the basic functionality of language-oriented object search and retrieval.

5.12   Improving accessibility for e-learning by AI

Advances in AI have become more prominent for the past 7–8 years and its import goes beyond automation, changing the production of assembling, offering and connecting better approaches to introduce e-learning and execution of support. Accessibility is about more than language, however. Microsoft's seeing AI application is one of the numerous devices to join AI advances—normal language preparing, visual handling, picture acknowledgment and optical character acknowledgment—to help outwardly impeded clients in translating their surroundings. Virtual assistants that react to voice directions give comfort to all clients; however for individuals with restricted mobility, they can be a distinct advantage. Voice-actuated aides, for example, savvy speakers, enable individuals to look through the web, get to data, play music or webcasts or generally interface without utilizing their hands. People whose mobility impairments make composing texts inconceivably grow their capability to produce content as these aids "adapt" more tasks. The manners in which they can build access to e-learning and execution support—AI will keep on expanding. Savvy speakers' developing collection of abilities is situated to some degree on AI innovations like characteristic language handling and AI.

Eye-tracking is getting more traction in VR as headset developers such as FOVE and HTC Vive work to integrate it into their consumer products. Contemplating an individual's look reveals to you what they are focusing on gives significant data to advertisers. In a virtual situation, eye following can build the sentiment of drenching or "nearness"; utilized in multiplayer VR games, it can improve the social correspondence among the players' symbols. The utility of eye following stretches out the possibility to improve games or even assemble information about students or players. Knowing where a student is glancing on VR-based preparation offers numerous chances to target substance and questions and likewise it improves availability. Eye-tracking can give triggers to prompt captions that disclose the sounds to students who cannot hear them. Medium blogger Lucas Rizzotto says that eye-following in VR is a serious deal since it enables clients to cooperate with content legitimately, without a controller. For students who cannot utilize a mouse or pointer or effectively contact explicit territories of the screen, eye following enables them to associate.

5.13   Artificial intelligence in personalized learning

Personalized learning can be defined as the diverse variety of instruction programs, learning experiences, didactic approaches and support strategies intended to address the unique and individual learning needs, interests and aspirations of individual learners. E-learning is defined as representing web-based delivery of personalized, interactive, immersive learning content, assisting practitioners with experts, building information communities and linking learners. It has become the most searched for the method of learning that is both convenient and effective. AI has a number of benefits in education: business, academic and social. AI aims to make the education of high quality available to everyone and allows students to learn at their own speed. Some of the best benefits of e-learning are to encourage students to learn at their own speed and to discover new materials emerging from simple searches. Students are able to discuss subjects in-depth and test their skills in challenging situations, instead of using the e-learning from an AI mentor to use basic right or wrong responses. AI-driven solutions can answer learners' questions, recommend resources and create personalized curriculums and grade assignments apart from teaching. Personalized learning is a great idea, but the success of its implementation depends on the incorporated methodology of teaching.

5.14   Cuts costs for students, eases burden on teachers

The fastest-growing method of education delivery from recent years has been distance education. Distance education refers to instruction that occurs when there is a difference in time, location, or both. There are a variety of distance education delivery systems: correspondence, broadcast, teleconferencing, computers and digital technologies, and the Internet and World Wide Web. Availability of technology and computer is one of the main reasons for thrust in the shift from classroom teaching to online. The 1980s saw a promising number of faculty deploying technologies to augment classroom instruction. This was the time when dramatic changes have occurred in college teaching. However, today's teaching is beyond just using it as a supplement instruction. Progress of the distance-learning programs and tremendous acceptability coupled with excellent delivery systems have fuelled and redefined the way higher education faculty experiences teaching.

There exist two perspectives while discussing the online learning plethora: one the student perspective and the other, the instructor/facilitator/teacher's perspective. Another reason for the increase in the online learning scope is the cost-effectiveness to the student. An architecture course from the IE University, Segovia, Spain has been offered at Coursera, an online learning platform to students across the world at INR 3,000 only. For a student who would want to pursue the same from a face-to-face traditional learning setup at the location would cost a ton higher than the fees offered at Coursera. Alongside this benefit, online learning for a student is convenient, accessible and flexible. While one of the largest ones (measured by the number of enrolled students) has 180,000, and one of the smallest ones has 20,000 students, according to a study done [27], just to give the feeling of enrolment spread. The transition of students or public users enrolling in thousands of different courses shows a vast number of students enrolling, as opposed to a face-to-face university course that never reaches these numbers of students, nor does the instructor see such a large number of students in their career time.

The faculty workload comparison between prior regular classroom teachings with online teaching has been studied. One definition used in all types of technology employed is that of a facilitator. Online course development needs higher effort and time; this is indicated by the comparison done for an experienced regular classroom teacher and experienced instructor for a new online course. The advantage is the delivery, and continuation for the larger number of audiences is so much lesser compared to classroom teaching sessions. Production, delivery time and commitment may rely somewhat upon the instructor's institutional support and experience.

The four main themes in the studies centered on preparation, design and distribution of online instructions are time, commitment, help and compensation.

In comparison with traditional teaching, online courses need more development and design time for instructors. Online teaching planning and design require extensive training, and here the organization is essential to the effective functioning of computer-mediated instructional activities. Experiences of the teacher indicate that they invest a lot of time in planning and training, and it begins long before the actual class begins; however, during recurrence, online teaching experiences spend less time preparing for distance courses taught in the same environment. Training is no longer a traditional form of teaching with the staff member being the only specialist in the new days of online education. Knowledge has become a continuously updated practice shared by the online learning community, and experience is a major stakeholder in the collaborative effort between the learners and the teacher. Because every step of online teaching might encounter a complex scenario that needs to be resolved, the teaching is now a constant and constructive process. From learner-centered environments, teaching and learning have forged a partnership. Education is a vast field, and online learning has a lot to offer for everyone to gain; the key is to be efficient while getting to it.

5.15   Artificial intelligence in academic connectivity

AI plays a huge role in the upcoming education system throughout the world. E-learning courses are developing at a very rapid rate. The learning experience is a challenge, however, as the machine is only the mechanical tool that conveys the information, and is therefore viewed by the user as a highly restricted one-way communication mechanism. Self-regulated learning [28] assists students in improving their learning habits. To improve the learning incentive of students and to develop practical skills, problem-based learning is considered one of the most suitable solutions [29]. The possibility of the use of AI within the classroom has been placed to relaxation with the aid of the creation of a chain of AI tools in colleges.

Opinions are varied and so are the commitments for AI applications in education systems. The use of extraordinary packages in recent times shows the effect of AI on the classroom teaching; to assist college students, teachers and others have applied a series of smart content materials, intelligent tutoring structures in a much greater custom-designed method. With the smart tutoring system and apps, the college students can study at their own space and pace. Depending on the students' performance could you bring can be customized.

There are apps for students who wish to study a completely new course. These apps basically convert textbooks materials into simplified form, into a manual. Since the machine intelligence is growing at a rapid pace, the future seems to be brighter than ever. There are certain drawbacks to AI when applied in education. The machine intelligence in education may not teach social skills and how to maintain human connections. Transformation and new technology always comes at a cost. In some countries, there could be a problem with Internet connectivity, of the speed. Like any new technology, "AI" will have cost implications. However, as the technology progresses, the cost will go down. It may not substitute teachers completely, since building human connection and social abilities improvement in students is not yet possible via AI. Nevertheless, it will make the tutor's job far more interesting and enriching.

5.16   Artificial intelligence in crowd service learning

Before going to the involvement of AI in crowd service-learning, let us understand what crowd service-learning is; crowd service-learning revolves around the concept of using the views and argument of a crowd to improve customer service, in other terms, it is a customer helping another customer. While there are many learning content systems, i.e. online learning platforms, the collaborative, community-based creation of rich e-learning content, it is still not sufficiently well supported. After the introduction of an AI-based one-to-one personalized learning system as well as a cloud learning system (learning through distant videos), the general paradigm of unstructured and text-only online learning system has changed a lot. While the concept of learning through VLE based on virtual reality and augmented reality is still in its initial stage, the VLE can be means of enhancing, motivating and stimulating learners' understanding of certain events, especially those for which the traditional idea of instructional learning has proven inappropriate or difficult. Open-source code, crowdsourcing and sharing economy have clicked the interest of all sectors and have resulted in harnessing talent pools from all locations. It has shown remarkable influence and progress beyond the earlier proven structure; this has inspired many researchers and developers in the field of AI and human–computer interaction to tap into the problems in crowd leaning structure and improvise it and make it even more useful for data collection and analysis. Other than just helping the learning community, this can also help IT, developers, to program the applications better with the help of crowdsourcing, i.e. learning through opinion and discussion. Crowd Service allows the company to capitalize on the talent within their business ecosystem and makes it easy to adjust their workforce to current demands immediately. With a large available skilled workforce, it offers flexibility if there is a need to accept new business and clients. By creating a Talent pool, from employees, subsidiaries, partners and customers, the company will always find the right person with the right expertise for the job. A successful example of a crowd service-based learning app is BYJU's. Byju has released a learning app that will take the company up to 35 million downloads, with 2.7 million annual users paying $150–$200 each. Their clients pay for animation, simulation and video lessons for students in grades 4–12 and students studying for competitive entrance exams in Indian colleges. The teaching methods of this organization stemmed from the tutoring sessions conducted offline by CEO Raveendran himself. Now the company is focusing on providing a more personalized learning experience. Apart from all this, there are still some challenges regarding the use of crowdsourcing although online crowds have the potential to shape innovation education. They can also be inconsistent and undereducated and can be biased; due to this, there is still a need for a proper quality control system to ensure that the content is more relatable and organized. From this, we can conclude that despite crowd service-learning being advantageous, there are still some major drawbacks that need further research and development to overcome these difficulties.

5.17 How to improve registration and completion of e-learning courses by using AI

AI has complex computer science, mathematics and programming to make any operation easy and more accurate, because of which AI has been used in various fields. One of the important fields in which AI has a major part is e-learning, an example might be a chatbot or quiz program that "decides" which question to ask a learner based on the learner's previous responses, and so on adding questions in areas where the learner had more incorrect responses or skipping to a higher level when the learner consistently enters correct responses. Another common use is in answering simple questions: the AI algorithm can be used to teach basic information that a new student might need. It can be presented as a smart chatbot that understands and responds to conversational text messages and questions from students. AI applications are not actually sentient and do not think, decide or understand; they apply logical rules to accomplish tasks that approximate these cognitive tasks. In building AI into e-learning is going to remain a hot topic in L&D; for a while, using AI in the actual e-learning content is not the only way to apply AI to improving e-learning. AI algorithms, and especially those smarter ML technologies, can help developers create better e-learning.

One way that AI can aid in e-learning development is by improving the classification of elements of content. As digital learners increasingly expect content to be offered in multiple formats and on a variety of platforms, many L&D teams might find themselves repurposing content and implementing plus-one design. A piece of information might be presented an infographic, the text file containing the video transcript, and a chat-based quiz that offers feedback.

AI in e-learning helps the registration and completion to be in an easy way and safe time. Students can register an e-learning course by using a computer anywhere anytime. AI will analyze academic record and decide that students have enough knowledge and quality to enroll for a course. Chatbots are a variant of the chat-driven method. Their primary function is to provide consistent answers through programming. The potential to assist build chatbots as a new form of contact. The AI level used in chatbots can differ. The current demand for chatbots is to be AI-based; the expectation is that they can begin to understand the feelings of the people they communicate with and then take appropriate action, such as offering extended service. The most successful chatbots use NLP, which is a human-driven AI training tool. A chatbot would be programmed to understand the question, phrase it in a number of ways and give a helpful answer. There are still enormous opportunities where AI can be incorporated into e-learning activities in the future.

5.18   Expectations of participant in artificial intelligence in e-learning

In today's world, we do expect to see major changes in how education institutes use AI in the growth of the institution, especially for e-learning. AI has shown the potential to make our work and life much easier; it is not only used in e-learning but also in our homes, business and our daily lives. It makes processes easier. It is used in e-learning, computer games, and participants are asked to make intelligent choices. In today's world, we do expect to see major changes in how education institutes use AI in the growth of the institution, especially for e-learning. AI has shown the potential to make our work and life much easier. It is not only used in e-learning but also in our homes, business and our daily lives. It makes processes easier. It is used in e-learning, and computer games and participants are asked to make intelligent choices for online learning that increase the thinking power of the students. Education can get a great benefit by means of the technology tools used. Availability and affordability, speed, effectiveness and personalization are a small part of the profits expected from the deployment of AI into the studying process. A variety of studies show the issue of personalizing the program in various ways, without having to rely on a single LMS. For example, [30] shows that by observing the output of students, three different techniques are possible to automatically identify and accurately change the learning styles of the students. A new approach [31] suggests using student-based web services such as initial knowledge, objectives, preferences, and addressing the automatic selection and integration of appropriate learning materials for students. More broadly, [32] suggests a paradigm for the integrated delivery of digital elements by streaming to students, taking into account their unique needs. This helps teachers build interactive course materials without being experts in multimedia programming and web technology.

The expectations of participants in AI in e-learning are increasing. AI coaching software can perceive areas in the content materials where the students are not faring well. From the supply material, the advanced versions can generate new questions. ML will be geared toward meaningful lessons. AI systems can identify individual student's learning needs based on the IQ level and suggest models that focus on method and reason. Personalized learning is another expectation of users in AI. AI will deliver individualized schooling. Thus, similarly to Netflix that uses ML to enhance the pointers listing because of the users' choices, AI can customize the revel in for college students as well. Therefore, the tech will permit monitoring interactions of newcomers for the duration of the path. That will supply the e-mastering the possibility to leverage the personalization, endorse specific and targeted content as per the aspirations of each online pupil. The device will be able to offer a more complete path for students with a lack of simple information and skip some modules for extra skilled and advanced students. AI can also be used for creating new content materials like easy articles for better understanding of students. Thus, the augmented studying asset can be produced and tailored to channel mechanically. AI in e-learning is dramatically shaping the e-learning industry. The benefits of implementing the technologies into the studying process are quite obvious so the future of AI can change where and how the participants can benefit from e-learning by staying on track and studying at the most convenient time and all that at a lower cost and more efficiently.

5.19 Future of AI in e-learning

AI now has evolved and has changed the phase of the teaching and online learning industry. From boring lectures to creative and more efficient ways of teaching (as shown in Figure 5.3), AI has brought in techniques and methods that are more productive and could be learned in the most efficient way by both teachers and students. With better visual and audio, there is a better understanding of the subject that results in better and longer retention of the information. Google and other chatbots have opened knowledge to flow in multidimensional that makes the moment of information simpler and much easier to understand. iPhone application of AI is evident in the form of app "Siri" that became part of everyday experiences. Earlier when there were any assignments or project students used to go to cyber cafes to get information regarding the topic, but now it is made easy to access the online portals from any remote location and acquire the information.

Personalized teaching or 1:1 tutoring is a simulation near reality using "ITS."

These systems determine the path which the student can take to learn effectively. If there is the individual attention given to each student, there is better

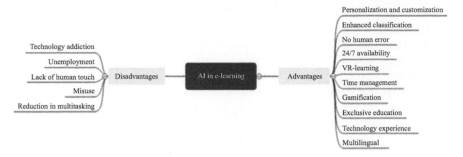

Figure 5.3   Advantages and disadvantages of AI in e-learning

knowledge shared between the receiver and the sender. In the past, there were huge groups that were thought by a single teacher who was not that much effective like that of today's scenario. In the future, there would be better improvements that would enhance the teaching process even better than now.

AI breaks complex subjects to simpler facts and figures, which helps in better grasping of knowledge and retention power. The lack of technology in the past had led to more head-breaking and made teaching a difficult process. For undergoing higher education, the need for AI is very much required as the complexity of topics increases from one degree to the other. AI opens a new horizon of possibilities for teaching and learning in higher education. The interface devices have reached a remarkable accuracy in assessing when the student is fully focused—brain–computer interface (BCI) is one such device.

In the past when there were exams, referring to older question papers was an exceedingly difficult task as the majority of the papers were stored as physical storage and not on the cloud. But due to recent developments, there are years of papers being uploaded on the cloud where students can refer to and have easy access to them with minimal effort. We must ensure that our education and training are tuned as per the new demands of the workplace and society [33].

The AI will continue to have a positive impact on the industry in education. Educational institutions need to deliver information effectively, helping students learn the way they are best suited. With time, more students are expected to receive personalized feedback and guidance from educational providers, and that is exactly what AI can help.

AI is enabling learning and is being able to get information from a global perspective and thus the knowledge. Noninvasive BCIs are challenging the role of the teachers so far; it also has the capability of aiding teachers with robots—virtual "Teacherbots" [34]. Helping teachers with teacher bots would ensure a better learning process through human–robot interaction. AI has its own advantages when it comes to e-learning. We should utilize the resources of AI to its maximum and yield more and better works [35,36].

5.20   Conclusion

This current research chapter focuses on the different areas of e-learning where AI can be implemented to make e-learning a better experience. E-learning is a 24/7 platform where learners can gain knowledge at the convenience of their home and timeframe. AI can help such learners with different adaptive technologies in clarifying the doubt, identifying the problem area of the learner and providing them a customized learning solution. Adaptive learning suggested that the learning pace is different for different learners. It must be made sure that the educational supplies and amenities provided must fit the requirement of each learner; else, it will lose its essence. There are different AI features to enhance the learning experience of e-learning. The providers must keep this in mind that the acquired information about learners must be wisely used while implementing the AI technology to e-learning mode so that the blended model can provide an enriching experience to the end-user. Cognitive learning can be a key to constructive, collaborative and contextualized execution of AI-enabled learning processes [37]. Maximization of AI effectiveness as a tool of e-learning can be brought only when it is implemented to overall program pedagogy and is monitored for continuous improvement.

References

[1]   Nkambou R, Bourdeau J, and Mizoguchi R. Introduction: what are intelligent tutoring systems, and why this book? In: Advances in Intelligent Tutoring Systems 2010 (pp. 1–12). Springer, Berlin, Heidelberg.

[2]   Ruiz JG, Mintzer MJ, and Leipzig RM. The impact of e-learning in medical education. Academic Medicine. 2006;81(3):207–12.

[3]   Trelease RB. Essential e-learning and m-learning methods for teaching anatomy. In: Teaching Anatomy 2015 (pp. 247–58). Springer, Cham.

[4]   Van Nuland S and Rogers K. E-learning: effective or defective? The impact of commercial E-learning tools on learner cognitive load and anatomy instruction. The FASEB Journal. 2015;29(1_supplement):550–77.

[5]   Wang TS. Design and assessment of joyful mobile navigation systems based on TAM and integrating learning models applied on ecological teaching activity. Eurasia Journal of Mathematics, Science and Technology Education. 2013;9(2):201–12.

[6]   Wilson S, Liber O, Johnson M, Beauvoir P, Sharples P, and Milligan C. Personal learning environments: challenging the dominant design of educational systems. Journal of E-learning and Knowledge Society. 2007;3(2):27–38.

[7]   Yoo SJ and Huang WD. Can e-learning system enhance learning culture in the workplace? A comparison among companies in South Korea. British Journal of Educational Technology. 2016;47(4):575–91.

[8]   Monahan T, McArdle G, and Bertolotto M. Virtual reality for collaborative e-learning. Computers & Education. 2008;50(4):1339–53.

[9]   Potode A and Manjare M. E-learning using artificial intelligence. International Journal of Computer Science and Information Technology Research. 2015;3(1):78–82.

[10]   Yousif JH, Saini DK, and Uraibi HS. Artificial intelligence in e-learning-pedagogical and cognitive aspects. InProc. of the World Congress on Engineering 2011 (Vol. 2, p. 452).

[11]   Teo T and Huang F. Investigating the influence of individually espoused cultural values on teachers' intentions to use educational technologies in Chinese universities. Interactive Learning Environments. 2019;27 (5–6):813–29.

[12]   Popenici SA and Kerr S. Exploring the impact of artificial intelligence on teaching and learning in higher education. Research and Practice in Technology Enhanced Learning. 2017;12(1):22.

[13]   Sarah S. The Future of Artificial Intelligence In eLearning Systems: eLearning Industry. April 23, 2016: 01-07. Available from https://elearningindustry.com/future-artificial-intelligence-in-elearning-systems. 2016.

[14]   Katrina H. E-Learning and Your Big Data – Effective Analysis: inside Bigdata. https://insidebigdata.com/2019/03/10/e-learning-and-your-big-data-effective-analysis/. 2019.

[15]   Zhang D and Nunamaker JF. Powering e-learning in the new millennium: an overview of e-learning and enabling technology. Information Systems Frontiers. 2003;5(2):207–18.

[16]   Castro F, Vellido A, Nebot A, and Mugica F. Applying data mining techniques to e-learning problems. In: Evolution of Teaching and Learning Paradigms in Intelligent Environment 2007 (pp. 183–221). Springer, Berlin, Heidelberg.

[17]   Jethro OO, Grace AM, and Thomas AK. E-learning and its effects on teaching and learning in a global age. International Journal of Academic Research in Business and Social Sciences. 2012;2(1):203.

[18]   Haber P, Herber E, and Mayr M. Curriculum Development, Implementation and Evaluation of Project Integrated Online Training. Cases on Technology Enhanced Learning Through Collaborative Opportunities. http://www.eportfolio.eu/resources/contributions/research/curriculum-development-implementation-and-evaluation-project. 2010.

[19]   Nwana HS. Intelligent tutoring systems: an overview. Artificial Intelligence Review. 1990;4(4):251–77.

[20]   De Freitas S, Rebolledo-Mendez G, Liarokapis F, Magoulas G, and Poulovassilis A. Learning as immersive experiences: using the four-dimensional framework for designing and evaluating immersive learning experiences in a virtual world. British Journal of Educational Technology. 2010;41 (1):69–85.

[21]   Chawla M. Bringing Learning to Life Through Immersive Experiences: Cognizant Education Practice. https://www.cognizant.com/whitepapers/bringing-learning-to-life-through-immersive-experiences-codex3774.pdf. 2018.

[22] Saadé R and Bahli B. The impact of cognitive absorption on perceived usefulness and perceived ease of use in on-line learning: an extension of the technology acceptance model. Information & Management. 2005;42(2):317–27.

[23] Alice B. Immersive Experiences in Education New Places and Spaces for Learning: Microsoft Education. https://techtrends.tech/tech-trends/report-immersive-experiences-in-education/. 2019.

[24] Song B and Yan X. Intelligent tutoring system of primary mathematics based on EGL and Web 2.0. Software Engineering. 2016;4(2):34.

[25] Liñán LC and Pérez ÁA. Educational data mining and learning analytics: differences, similarities, and time evolution. International Journal of Educational Technology in Higher Education. 2015;12(3):98–112.

[26] Aparicio M, Bacao F, and Oliveira T. An e-learning theoretical framework. An e-Learning Theoretical Framework. 2016 (1):292–307.

[27] Jordan K. MOOC Completion Rates: The Data. 2013. http://www.katy-jordan.com/MOOCproject.html. 2014.

[28] Mohanasundaram K. Curriculum design and development. Journal of Applied and Advanced Research. 2018;3(S1):4–6.

[29] Tsai CW and Shen PD. Applying web-enabled self-regulated learning and problem-based learning with initiation to involve low-achieving students in learning. Computers in Human Behavior. 2009;25(6):1189–94.

[30] Dorça FA, Lima LV, Fernandes MA, and Lopes CR. Comparing strategies for modeling students learning styles through reinforcement learning in adaptive and intelligent educational systems: an experimental analysis. Expert Systems with Applications. 2013;40(6):2092–101.

[31] Thyagharajan KK and Nayak R. Adaptive content creation for personalized e-learning using web services. Journal of Applied Sciences Research. 2007;3 (9):828–36.

[32] Thyagharajan KK and Anbumani B. An enhanced authoring and context-aware presentation model for web-based education. International Journal of Computer Science, Systems Engineering and Information Technology. 2009;2(2):191–5.

[33] Frey CB and Osborne MA. The future of employment: how susceptible are jobs to computerisation? Technological Forecasting and Social Change. 2017;114:254–80.

[34] Bayne S. Teacherbot: interventions in automated teaching. Teaching in Higher Education. 2015;20(4):455–67.

[35] Kurdi G, Leo J, Parsia B, Sattler U, and Al-Emari S. A systematic review of automatic question generation for educational purposes. International Journal of Artificial Intelligence in Education. 2020;30(1):121–204.

[36] Lin YT and Lin YC. Effects of mental process integrated nursing training using mobile device on students' cognitive load, learning attitudes, acceptance, and achievements. Computers in Human Behavior. 2016;55:1213–21.

[37] Shi B and Weninger T. ProjE: embedding projection for knowledge graph completion. In: Thirty-First AAAI Conference on Artificial Intelligence 2017 Feb 12.

Chapter 6

Mobile learning as the future of e-learning

Muruganantham Ganesan[1], Vivek Kumar Singh[1] and Subhojeet Biswas[1]

E-learning plays a crucial role in modern-day education. In traditional learning, a successful teacher can teach at one location in a given time. E-learning complements modern learning and an effective tool for the individual's intellectual development and helps one to create is an intelligent society. Among the various new trends in e-learning, mobile learning (m-learning) is the revolutionary measure and has lots of scopes and potential to transform India's educational system. Millennial generation heavily depends on the smartphone for its entertainment and educational needs. Changing technological advancement also provides an opportunity for higher education institutions to explore the various online educational methods to engage a large number of students. This chapter aims to provide the significant importance of m-learning, its opportunities, and challenges in the Indian higher education system.

6.1 Introduction

E-learning activities are essential to any country's growth. Student's fulfillment rates increment with e-learning contrasted with conventional learning, alongside usability and access, route, intuitiveness, and easy-to-use interface plan are observed [1]. E-learning can be achieved using a range of tools or software. This is intended to promote the transfer of information and the communication to the individual. It does not mean replacing the current classroom environment; rather it enriches and serves as an alternative at the right time as required. In e-learning, educational content can be accessed by the learner according to their needs and learning style.

In the present twenty-first century, a modern world has been experiencing a vital renovation to an information society. This kind of dynamic change promises the essential variations in all the aspects of individuals' lives, including a new form of social interaction, sharing knowledge, and entertainment [2]. There is a need to

[1]Management Studies, NIT, Tiruchirappalli, India

leverage m-learning techniques for the convenience and availability of tools and apps on smartphones. The higher education landscape is changing due to techno-logical revolution. The government of India is taking a lot of initiatives to reach to the maximum number of learners through formal, and hybrid educational mode, by leveraging various e-learning technologies.

6.2   E-learning

E-learning is an additional integral asset for upgrading instructive comprehen-siveness in our nation. In India, the level of educated people in the total population has expanded from 65% in 2001 to 74% in 2011 [3]. E-learning can be useful in reducing illiteracy rate. Technological advancement and Internet connectivity have made e-learning more accessible to educational institutions. India has a vast market for e-learning. Usage of the Internet via smartphones has increased in recent times, which serves as the customized personalized platform of e-learning in the compe-titive world [4].

E-learning is multifaceted, covering a range of methods. Research indicates that there are lots of scopes for e-learning method in India since many faculties in higher education institutions have started using it as blended learning approach. Educational institutions are using different modes of e-learning such as online mode, hybrid mode [5]. E-learning is a tool for the student, faculty, institute, and society. It provides maximum benefits to anyone with anytime usage. The aca-demic community benefits a lot by saving time, access to many students, and avoiding manual repetitive classes. E-learning facilitates the learners to learn according to their convenience and speed [6].

6.3   Mobile learning

"Mobile learning (M-learning) is a new way of accessing mobile devices for aca-demic learning purposes." Nowadays, higher and higher educational institutions have started using mobile-based teaching/learning process through various apps and other e-learning devices with different types of contents such as videos, audio files, and images along with suitable text contents. The m-learning process makes learning lively and more interesting with social interaction.

In the early 1970s, Alan Kay who was working in "Xerox" developed "Dynabook," a portable personal computer. It provided an opportunity for the kids to access and explore the digital world [7]. M-learning provides a kind of twenty-first century learning experience to the learner that includes flexibility, indepen-dence, ownership of their progress, and time management of their studies.

According to the author [8] who is a professor and expert in computer-based education, m-learning was defined "as the intersection between mobile computing (the application of small, portable and wireless computing and communication devices) and e-learning (learning facilitated and supported through the use of information and communications technology)."

6.3.1   Smartphone penetration in India

Cisco's 13th annual Visual Networking Index report [9] highlights that by "2022 there will be 829 million Smartphone users in India alone, comprising 60 percent of the population." According to the joint report by ASSOCHAM-PwC, the total number of smartphone users in India is projected at 859 million by 2022 [10]. These statistics suggest a trend toward harnessing smartphones' ability as an electronic tool to allow anyone to learn anytime, anywhere, and while on move.

When an Indian youth spends an average of 3 h a day on a smartphone, it is hard to ignore this device's potential to become a powerful driver of e-learning. Kantar IMRB reports 2018 on Internet penetration and digital adoption and use patterns reveal that the "internet users in India is estimated at 566 million and 97 percent of consumers are using cell phones as one of the tools for internet access" [11].

6.4   Need for mobile learning

Deloitte's global mobile consumer trends 2017 report highlights that smartphone has become increasingly pervasive and indispensable, with users all over the world over accepting its true potential [12]. As per the report from Pew Research Centre, "54 percent of adults in 21 developing countries are already using the internet. In developed countries, 87 percent of adults are internet users and 68 percent are already having smartphones" [13].

The Internet and Mobile Association of India report highlights that "77 percent of urban users and 92 percent of rural users are having access to the internet through smartphones." [14]. In India, mobile subscribers are crossing 800 million with more penetration in the rural market. M-learning is emerging as the next big revolutionary step in the Indian higher education system. It enables individual participants to communicate and interact, and through their position as always-on, always-available, versatile personal communication tools.

Technological advancement, affordability of smartphones, and Internet connectivity had encouraged the students in higher education to use a smartphone for educational content learning. These portable devices with the latest technology and high-speed Internet provide enhanced learning opportunities for students in the fast-changing learning environment and job market [15]. The traditional teaching–learning method consists of blackboard, books, instructors, and students in a classroom. The teacher is responsible for all the tasks for students inside the classroom. The latest research indicates that e-learning is more effective than the traditional method of learning. In the present knowledge-based society, there is an ever-increasing demand for innovative methods of delivering education and engaging the students to acquire new skills [16].

Although there are many notable features of m-learning, the added convenience for m-learning is one that tops all the others. However, m-learning facilitates the immediate capturing and sharing of content. It also provides instant feedback about the course, content, and methodologies. From a learning point of view, earlier studies show that m-learning is much more successful than the traditional learning process. It is largely due to comfort, peace of mind, and input provided to the learners. In today's world, every college student is using digital tools to read and learn, rather than reading paper books. Digital learning provides the opportunity to ask questions and get feedback immediately. For engagement of large-scale students, digital learning is cheaper than traditional classroom learning.

Smartphone devices were available to the learner all the time. In the technological revolution, like smartphones, no other devices generated much excitement, personal relationship, and bonding with humans. "Mobile phones are very close to the heart and wallet of the consumer at large" [17].

6.5   Mobile learning in higher education

M-learning is having enormous potential and scale to support all modes of education. Indian higher education is a more suitable platform for learning because of the availability of smartphones among college students, speed, and connectivity of Internet. Already, universities in the West, such as Stanford University, the University of Washington, are very successful in m-learning [18], but at the same time "implementing of m-learning in higher education is a challenging task because of organizational, social, cultural factors" [19].

Researchers [20] had used "the unified theory of acceptance and use of Technology" and found that factors like "performance expectancy, effort expectancy, social influence, perceived playfulness, and self-management of learning were important while adopting m-learning among college students in Taiwan." The "technology acceptance model" used in earlier research studies was focused on the perception of student users toward mobile technology's "functionality and characteristics" [21], but the latest m-learning apps provide a new approach and convenience to the learning process. M-learning helps the higher education institutions to receive attendance, assignments, and feedback from students and faculty immediately.

Khan Academy provides "free, world-class education for everyone, anytime and reaches more than one million teachers and ten million students" [22]. The lessons provided to students with video-based lectures. Due to growing disposal income, a younger population is having the smartphone and/or e-reader. Nowadays, all the text and reference book publishers are having e-book edition and prompting heavily to students, faculty members through the institute library. Online databases having research journals such as IEEE for engineering, PROQUEST, EMERALD, EBSCO for management discipline are available in electronic format.

Scholars and students are downloading research articles from their institutes' E-resources and reading through their smartphones and laptops. Through the usage of smartphone, an E-reader reduces the printing and photocopying charges heavily which in turn result in a green and clean environment. According to [23] the "next 100 years is the era of 'digitalism' and its disruption will be seen in an increasing number of usage in smart devices" for multiple purposes. Shri Suresh Narayanan,

Managing Director, Nestle India Ltd. pointed "Digitalism is a new religion." Students must be familiar with newer technologies like the Internet of Things coming and other latest technologies that are relevant to the job market.

Researchers [24] conducted a study among the University of Central American State graduates about the possible use and obstacles of m-learning. Study findings reveal that students want a lot of educational-friendly apps and additional resources to incorporate mobile technology into learning-related activities.

Many websites offer free educational videos and study resources from major universities. "Apple's iTunes U and Google's YouTube Edu" are popular among students. "iTunes offers open access to content from world-class institutions and universities such as Harvard, MIT, Cambridge, Oxford, Stanford, Yale, Princeton, Columbia, United Kingdom's Open University" [25].

There was a study on the use of smartphones among Ruaha Catholic University students in Tanzania for academic purposes. The findings revealed that the level of m-learning in the university is very poor [26]. "Teachers in higher education need to be trained on digital and mobile technology to facilitate their online classroom by generating an environment of interaction, cooperation, and collaboration" [27].

6.5.1   Intelligent technologies

Wireless, infrared, General Packet Radio Services, and Bluetooth communication systems are used in mobile devices. Augmented reality also helps one to improve smartphone apps and their performance. Augmented reality is user centered, helps one to visualize the processes, and offers immediate feedback [28]. Smartphones use cloud computing technology for processing and sharing the data. M-learning technology assists the interaction between teachers and learners [29].

6.6   Benefits of smartphone in academic learning

Mobile technology provides a variety of enriching educational contents, which invents a new method of learning, be it in the classroom or at home. M-learning facilitates easier access to the material of the course, better contact with other students and instructors, more information on the subjects learned [30]. Many educational institutions in India banned the usage of smartphones in the academic zone/inside the classroom. Students are not allowed to use the smartphones inside or during the classroom. In Indian higher education institutions, one can see the poster that "mobile phones are banned in the academic region." Smartphones and tablets are vital for students' e-learning purposes [31].

Smartphone and apps often control students' daily lives by providing information that is important, timely, and accessible [32]. A smartphone's ability to access, process, store, and distribute contents as and when it is produced, which provides an opportunity to explore the same for education purposes [33]. The increasing popularity among young college students to live and store videos, e-books can potentially revolutionize the way they learn. The Editor of Digital Trends, Scott Steinberg, said, "a smartphone is essentially a computer in our pocket. It is a cellular phone that does more than just make calls to the point that it can serve as a functional laptop or desktop replacement" [25].

Virtual education provides an alternative approach to conventional education. Technology is being used to promote active and interactive learning to address the requirements and aspirations of learners from learning styles [34]. E-learning helps students to improve their performance in terms of understanding of subjects with a blended approach [35]. It helps the students to grasp and improve the quality of education. Compared to traditional learning, course design, the motivation of the learner, and quality of time spent are convenient to the learner's e-learning technologies. E-learning is quite beneficial for providing extensive knowledge for the students. There is still a need to remove the hindrances and barriers for implementation, particularly in rural colleges of higher education with infrastructural development, trained staff, counseling, and motivation of students [36].

In academia and organizations, it seems that numerous lecturers and leaders are still pleased with utilizing traditional lecturing techniques. Promoting the usage of the e-learning method requires an appropriate understanding of the difference between e-learning and traditional learning. Graphical lessons that attain the e-learning technique would have a considerable impact on the excessive acceptance of the learning methods. "E-learning provides more benefits to students, because of its convenience, unlimited access to lecture, and availability of the variety of the resources" [37].

A student may use his/her smartphone to carry the softcopies of the class notes and carry out assignments and chat with the group for problems and discussion related activities. Smartphones support a range of functions that are only accessible on computers, including fast Internet access, and are now a convenient means of communication or interaction that conventional mobile phones do not have [38].

"Smartphones with useful apps capable of providing simulated visual and digital contents of the learning materials can be much more effective than the traditional classes" [39]. Smartphones become essential for a student's academic life. It provides relevant, timely, and accessible information [31]. M-learning facilitates "any location, any time learning" for the students [40]. Differences between traditional and e-learning are highlighted in Table 6.1.

6.7   Different types of e-learning

There are various kinds of e-learning activities being used in the education system at various levels of education in different regions. M-learning, artificial intelligence, and the Internet of Things have gained popularity in recent years.

6.7.1   Learning management system

"A Learning Management System a software application to monitor, record, track, report, and distributes instructional, training, or learning and development programs." "Blogs and social media have a significant influence on e-learning" [41]. Learning management system (LMS) helps students to fulfill simple online

Table 6.1   Difference between traditional and e-learning

Traditional learning	M-learning/E-learning
Students have to stay in the class	Student can learn from any place
Direct face-to-face contact with students	No direct contact with students
Fixed class timing	Learner manages his/her own
Lecture and lecture notes support the learning	Digital resources support learning
The teacher is the authority in the class	Most important factor is the learner
Internet technology is not required	Electronic devices and the Internet are needed
Teacher centric	Learner centric
Learning is common to all students	Learning is private
Periodical assessment for courses	Continuous tracking through online mode
Maximum reach to participants of a class	Having potential to reach mass

courseware resource management requirements, by tracking students' test results and completing content, and ensuring materials' quality and availability.

6.7.2   Blended learning

According to [42], "blended learning blends face-to-face instruction with computer-mediated learning and training, and provides benefits of enhanced pedagogy, increased access and versatility." "American Society for Training and Development identified blended learning as one of the top ten trends to emerge in the knowledge delivery industry" [43]. Blended learning provides more benefits than the "non-blended learning environment" for the learner [44].

6.7.3   Artificial intelligence

Artificial intelligence has "evolutionary algorithms, fuzzy logic, and computational neural networks" [45]. "Education and Artificial Intelligence are two sides of the same coin, education lets learners learn and expand the cumulative wisdom of a culture, and artificial intelligence offers resources for understanding simple thought processes and intelligent behaviour." Educational institutions are commonly utilizing "artificial intelligence-assisted e-learning scenarios to provide effective teaching" [46].

6.7.4   Internet of Things

"Internet of Things" is a "kind of network that connects everything to the Internet-based on specified protocols, through information-sensing equipment that exchanges and communicates information to provide intelligent identification, positioning, monitoring, and management." "Internet of things ensures that things are connected to anything, any place, any person, any network, and any service in an ideal way." A smart classroom and its application can be facilitated by the Internet of Things [47].

6.7.5   Flipped classrooms

Flipped classroom uses a "hybrid of face-to-face content delivery and offline learning" approach. In flipped classroom students have the facility to see the videos, lectures, and experiments well in advance to regular interactive class. "Massive Open Online Course (MOOC) is an open-source platform to offer high-quality online learning content/courses to anyone at no cost, with no clear constraints on attendance, age, geography in India" [48].

6.7.5.1   M-learning and government

Few governments are using the platform of m-learning for effective governance and communication of various policies, circulars, and training programs. A successful m-learning approach can be of assistance to the government in several aspects. A government can bring accountability in governance through m-learning by meaningful education among the people. It can also be done effectively to create social knowledge among residents to provide information about taxation and laws.

6.8   M-learning challenges

Lack of trust is the main barrier to the use of mobile apps, according to a Mobile Ecosystem Forum 2017 survey report. Smartphone users trust themselves to manage their data more than any single institution.

Service providers need to offer more consumer-friendly policies. In India, a number of professional course teachers find it difficult while using any e-learning platforms due to various problems [3]. In smartphones [49], these platforms prove to be inconvenient due to "mobile characteristics such as screen size, screen orientation, mobile storage and memory, and network bandwidth, instructional designers need to develop effective e-learning courses."

Technical challenges are major aspects while applying and incorporating mobile for academic learning. "Small screen size; insufficient memory; limited battery; network reliability; excessive screen brightness, safety and privacy" are the major limitations to the user while adopting m-learning [50]. In mobiles, learning is more contextual and heuristic. The content is different and smaller in size. This becomes more difficult as mobile learners do not remain static most of the time. Developing content for m-learning is different than that for traditional learning. Mobile apps offer a unique degree of versatility that has not been seen or experienced before; thus learners are more than happy to accept mobiles as a medium for learning delivery. The first and foremost request from millennial generation learners is to allow learning through smartphones inside and outside the classroom.

6.8.1   Cons of mobile learning

Any mobile devices in the classroom may lead to unethical behavior by students or diversion. Mobile apps can also jeopardize a student's physical health and privacy [51]. Most teachers and parents view mobile phones as a nuisance in school. There is no established learning theory for mobile technology that is universally accepted. Mobile devices are complex and this creates a huge obstacle for teachers. Certain mobile devices have weak designs and restrictions of use, which can adversely affect learning.

6.9   Education 4.0

"Education 4.0" is the emerging concept to respond to the requirements of "Industry 4.0" in which "man and machine align to enable new possibilities by harnesses the potential of digital technologies, personalized data, open-sourced content, and the new humanity of this globally-connected, technology-fuelled world." "Education 4.0 provides a framework for continuous lifelong learning" [52].

To meet the requirements of Education 4.0, that are evolving because of Industry 4.0, policymakers, educational content providers, teachers, and students are in a position to equip themselves for new kinds of teaching–learning experience. Universities must integrate their teaching–learning method with the aid of technical innovations to prepare potential students for the job. Social media, blogs, YouTube, etc. help one to develop a large amount of user-generated content. Smartphones and digital devices help one to access many online user-generated contents free of cost.

6.10   Conclusion

The present world is mobile. In the industrial age, we used to go to school, whereas now, schools' curriculum comes to us. Mobile technology is powerful, which can be used in several great ways for teaching and learning of students. Faculty, institute, universities, and students should jointly plan how to use smartphones smartly for effective academic learning. With flipped and blended classrooms, m-learning in Indian higher educational institutions is poised to provide a better experience to the millennial generation. The smartphone is an unavoidable electronic device in the hands of college students. By creating effective strategies, smartphone usage habits can be directed more for academic learning.

6.11   Future scope

To strengthen the cycle of m-learning, educational institutions and faculty need to develop an encouraging culture to use mobile phones. For a successful e-learning program, the content must be succinct, effective, and easily understandable. Opportunities to individualize tracking and tailor learning experiences to each student's success are the most significant advantages provided by m-learning [30]. In the future, wireless convergence and technological advancement may further facilitate "anytime and anywhere learning" in rural and urban areas [52].

This new challenge in teaching and learning is to provide a live classroom experience to students when learning experiences may vary according to the nature of subjects [53]. Latest novel coronavirus disease that requires social distancing for human beings has forced the educational institutions and government to explore the various virtual learning opportunities for schools, colleges, and higher educational institutions, all over the world. Educational institutions are opening a portal to upload the audio–video lectures, study materials by the course teacher, which can be accessed by students from their smartphones or other devices. Regular classes are conducted through online mode. Due to the coronavirus issue, m-learning becomes an essential and easy learning method.

Soon, penetration into m-learning will be pervasive. Country-and subject-specific learning apps and LMS will be developed to fulfill the needs of the students. Higher educational institutions shall use various digital tools to transfer knowledge from faculty to students and create a smooth teaching–learning process.

Case Study: SWAYAM—India's online education

SWAYAM is a Hindi acronym that "stands for Study Webs of Active Learning for Young Aspiring Minds." It is a free online educational platform created by the "Ministry of Human Resource Development," an e-learning government of India with Microsoft's support. It is the largest MOOC gateway in the world and is an initiative from the Government of India. Microsoft and WizIQ have collaborated to establish a network that will carry online education to remote locations in India. The government's dream for the platform was to help at least 30 million learners across India for the network. This initiative helps one to alleviate the crisis in education in the country where the number of teachers in colleges and schools is limited.

SWAYAM system aimed at achieving the "three basic principles of education policy: access, equality, and efficiency." SWAYAM offers more than 2,150 courses taught by approximately 1,300 instructors from more than 135 universities in India. More than 10 million learners have taken courses on SWAYAM ever since the platform was launched in 2017. All the lessons taught in classrooms from the ninth to the postgraduate classes are to be accessed at anytime, anywhere. Classes include engineering, science, humanities, management, language, math, arts and recreation, commerce, general, library, and education. "All SWAYAM courses are interactive, taught by the country's best teachers and available at no charge to Indian residents."

SWAYAM courses "consists of video lecture, reading materials specially prepared that can be downloaded/printed, self-assessment, assessments via exams and quizzes, and an online discussion forum to clear up doubts." The SWAYAM portal will be "one of the largest paperless education networks in the world, which will provide free education for everyone. SWAYAM will enable students to learn from their location, rather than to travel wide distances to study." The Android SWAYAM application is built to allow students to access all SWAYAM contents anywhere. Innovation in ICT aims to help the majority of the rural population to enroll for higher education.

Source for the case:

https://swayam.gov.in/about, https://www.wiziq.com/, https://vikaspedia.in/education/interactive-resources/swayam-learning-portal.

References

[1]   Harden RM and Hart IR. An international virtual medical school (IVIMEDS): The future for medical education?. Medical Teacher. 2002;24 (3):261–7.

[2]   Li F, Qi J, Wang G, and Wang X. Traditional classroom vs e-learning in higher education: Difference between students' behavioral engagement. International Journal of Emerging Technologies in Learning. 2014;9(2).

[3]   Arun G and Vrishali SR. E-learning in India: Wheel of change. International Journal of e-Education, e-Business, e-Management and e-Learning. 2004;6 (1):40–6.

[4]   Naresh B and BhanuSree Reddy D. E-learning in Indian higher education and future prospects. International Journal of Pure and Applied Mathematics. 2018;118(18):4301–8.

[5]   Jaiswal V. Current status of e-learning in Indian higher education: A case study of UP. SSRN Electronic Journal. 2013. Available at SSRN 2231910.

[6]   Vivekananda M and Satish R. Emerging trends of e-learning in India. International Journal of Advances in Electronics and Computer Science. 2017;4(6):115–8.

[7]   Maxwell JW. *Tracing the Dynabook: A study of technocultural transformations* (Doctoral dissertation, University of British Columbia).

[8]   Clark Q. M-Learning: Mobile, Wireless, In-Your-Pocket Learning, LineZine. 2000. http://www.linezine.com/2.1/features/cqmmwiyp.htm [Accessed on March 21, 2020].

[9]   Cisco's 13th Annual Visual Networking Index Report, https://www.cisco.com/c/en/us/solutions/collateral/executive-perspectives/annual-internet-report/white-paper-c11-741490.html [Accessed on March 21, 2020].

[10] Data Usage in India, https://www.assocham.org/newsdetail.php?id=7075 [Accessed on March 21, 2020].

[11] Kantar. IMRB Report 2018, Internet in India. https://imrbint.com/images/common/Highlights.pdf [Accessed on March 22, 2020].

[12] Deloitte's Global Mobile Consumer Trends 2017. https://www2.deloitte.com/il/en/pages/technology-media-and-telecommunications/articles/global-mobile-consumer-survey.html [Accessed on March 22, 2020].

[13] Silver L. Smartphone Ownership is Growing Rapidly around the World, but Not Always Equally. Pew Research Center. 2019. https://www.pewresearch.

org/global/2019/02/05/smartphone-ownership-is-growing-rapidly-around-the-world-but-not-always-equally/ [Accessed on March 23, 2020].

[14] IMRB Mobile Internet Report 2017. https://m.economictimes.com/tech/internet/internet-users-in-india-to-reach-503-million-by-2017-iamai/article-show/48144802.cms [Accessed on March 23, 2020].

[15] Al-Mashhadani MA and Al-Rawe MF. The future role of mobile learning and smartphones applications in the Iraqi private universities. Smart Learning Environments. 2018;5(1):28.

[16] Titthasiri W. A comparison of e-learning and traditional learning: Experimental approach. In International Conference on Mobile Learning, E-Society and E-Learning Technology (ICMLEET) – Singapore on November 2013 Nov (pp. 6–7).

[17] Bijoor H. Marketing on the mobile phone. Brand Line, The Hindu Business Line. 2009; 16, July.

[18] Wang YS, Wu MC, and Wang HY. Investigating the determinants and age and gender differences in the acceptance of mobile learning. British Journal of Educational Technology. 2009;40(1):92–118.

[19] Liu Y, Li H, and Carlsson C. Factors driving the adoption of m-learning: An empirical study. Computers & Education. 2010;55(3):1211–9.

[20] Cavus N and Ibrahim D. m-Learning: An experiment in using SMS to support learning new English language words. British Journal of Educational Technology. 2009;40(1):78–91.

[21] Attewell J and Webster T. Engaging and supporting mobile learners. Mobile learning anytime everywhere: A book of papers from mLearn 2004. 2005:15–9.

[22] Kelly DP and Rutherford T. Khan academy as supplemental instruction. International Review of Research in Open and Distributed Learning. 2017;18:4.

[23] Bijoor H. Govt Entry into Retail Can Disrupt the Sector. 2017. https://www.thehindubusinessline.com/companies/govt-entry-into-retail-can-disrupt-the-sector/article9869089.ece# [Accessed on March 24, 2020].

[24] Chen B and Denoyelles A. Exploring students' mobile learning practices in higher education. Educause Review. 2013;7(1):36–43.

[25] Kumar M. Impact of the evolution of smart phones in education technology and its application in technical and professional studies: Indian perspective. International Journal of Managing Information Technology. 2011;3(3):39–49.

[26] Kibona L and Mgaya G. Smartphones' effects on academic performance of higher learning students. Journal of Multidisciplinary Engineering Science and Technology. 2015;2(4):777–84.

[27] Basinets AV, Naranjo ME, Gallegos MC, and Benítez NM. Mobile devices in the learning process of the faculty of education science and technology of the technical university of the north in Ecuador. Formación Universitaria. 2017;10:79–88.

[28] Chou TL and Chanlin LJ. Location-based learning through augmented reality. Journal of Educational Computing Research. 2014;51(3):355–68.

[29] Wang CY, Liu BJ, Chang KE, Horng JT, and Chen GD. Using mobile techniques in improving information awareness to promote learning performance. In Proceedings 3rd IEEE International Conference on Advanced Technologies 2003 Jul 9 (pp. 106–9). IEEE.

[30] François-X. Mobile Learning: The Growing Role of the Smartphone in Education. 2016. https://blog.gutenberg-technology.com/en/mobile-smartphone-in-education [Accessed on March 25, 2020].

[31] Al-Daihani SM. Smartphone use by students for information seeking. Global Knowledge, Memory and Communication. 2018;67.

[32] Hossain ME and Ahmed SZ. Academic use of smartphones by university students: A developing country perspective. The Electronic Library. 2016;34.

[33] Woodcock B, Middleton A, and Nortcliffe A. Considering the smartphone learner: An investigation into student interest in the use of personal technology to enhance their learning. Student Engagement and Experience Journal. 2012;1(1):1–5.

[34] Ilie V and Ecaterina S F. Traditional learning versus E-learning. In The European Proceedings of Social & Behavioural Sciences 2018.

[35] Elfaki NK, Abdulraheem I, and Abdulrahim MR. Impact of e-learning vs traditional learning on students' performance and attitude. International Journal of Medical Research and Health Sciences. 2019;8(10):76–82.

[36] Tariq HS and Rachna G. E-learning for higher education. A case study. Journal of Advanced Research in Dynamical and Control Systems. 2018;10 (4):1539–45.

[37] Odhaib MF. Does E-learning give a better result than traditional learning?. International Journal of Computer Science and Mobile Computing. 2018;7 (9):29–36.

[38] Yi YJ, You S, and Bae BJ. The influence of smartphones on academic performance. Library Hi Tech. 2016 Sep 19.

[39] Hasan M, Rahman M, Islam M, and Hasan M. Smartphone and our students: It being good for their study. Journal of Information Engineering and Applications. 2017;7(3):32–42.

[40] Hashemi M, Azizinezhad M, Najafi V, and Nesari AJ. RETRACTED: What is mobile learning? Challenges and capabilities. Procedia – Social and Behavioral Sciences. 2011;30:2477–81.

[41] Davis B, Carmean C, and Wagner ED. The evolution of the LMS: From management to learning. Santa Rosa, CA: e-Learning Guild. 2009.

[42] Graham CR. Blended learning systems. The handbook of blended learning: Global perspectives, local designs. Pfeiffer Publishing, San Francisco, 2006:3–21.

[43] Rooney JE. Blending learning opportunities to enhance educational programming and meetings [Tekst]. Association Management [Tekst]. 2003(55):5.

[44] Kenney J and Newcombe E. Adopting a blended learning approach: Challenges encountered and lessons learned in an action research study. Journal of Asynchronous Learning Networks. 2011;15(1):45–57.

[45]   Russell S and Norvig P. Artificial intelligence: A modern approach. Upper Saddle River, New Jersey: Prentice-Hall, Inc. and Pearson Education, Inc, 1995.

[46]   Ziaaddini M and Tahmasb A. Artificial intelligence handling through teaching and learning process and its effect on science-based economy. International Journal on Soft Computing, Artificial Intelligence and Applications (IJSCAI). 2014;3(1):1–7.

[47]   Dlodlo N, Foko TE, Mvelase P, and Mathaba S. The state of affairs in internet of things research. Academic Conferences International Ltd.

[48]   Chen Y, Wang Y, and Chen NS. Is FLIP enough? Or should we use the FLIPPED model instead?. Computers & Education. 2014;79:16–27.

[49]   Alhajri R and Ahmed AH. Integrating learning style in the design of educational interfaces. Advances in Computer Science: An International Journal. 2016;5(1):124–31.

[50]   Park Y. A pedagogical framework for mobile learning: Categorizing educational applications of mobile technologies into four types. International Review of Research in Open and Distributed Learning. 2011;12(2):78–102.

[51]   Aithal PS. The usage of mobile learning technologies in class room – 21st Century. Research in Higher Education, Learning and Administration. 2019;18:156–162.

[52]   Jacob SM and Issac B. The mobile devices and its mobile learning usage analysis. Proceedings of the International Multi Conference of Engineers and Computer Scientists. 2008;1:19–21.

[53]   Mark L. Students Are Using Mobile Even If You Aren't. 2019. https://www.insidehighered.com/digital-earning/article/2019/02/27/mobile-devices-transform-classroom-experiences [Accessed on March 27, 2020].

Chapter 7

Smart e-learning transition using big data: perspectives and opportunities

T. Lucia Agnes Beena[1], T. Poongodi[2] and P. Suresh[3]

E-learning is providing education through a computing platform that encourages the learners to learn from anywhere at anytime. Web 5.0 will be able to map the emotions of the people when they are interacting with computers. The users can interact with content with the help of a headphone. While interacting with the content, their emotions are captured by the facial recognition system to bring real classroom learning into the existing e-learning system. Any e-learning approach will lead to the explosion of different types of information such as text, videos, and images, results in different data types that are not used in traditional data management systems. Analytical operations cannot be applied directly to these data. The online learning platforms generate enormous learner behavioral data, and educational big data plays an important role in transforming the data obtained from online learning platforms into useful information for the improvement of academic activities. The teachers can develop the content for personalized learning analyzing the current knowledge level of the students. The students have the opportunity to learn at their own pace. The key issue here is the effective analysis and utilization of the data to improve the e-learning features. Big data technology provides the capability of analytics to enhance the e-learning process. This chapter presents the outline of the big data techniques such as prediction, clustering, relationship mining, structure discovery, and various tools used for big data analytics in e-learning.

7.1 Introduction

The emerging web technologies introduce openness, interoperability, and intelligence on the web. This leverages the capabilities of the web to a greater extent so that it is termed Semantic Web of Data. The technologies that support the web transform how the content is provided by the e-learning environment.

[1]Department of Information Technology, St. Joseph's College, Tiruchirappalli, India
[2]School of Computing Science and Engineering, Galgotias University, Greater Noida, India
[3]School of Mechanical Engineering, Galgotias University, Greater Noida, India

E-learning is providing education through a computing platform that encourages the learners to learn from anywhere at anytime. e-Learning 1.0 provided the learner with information access. e-Learning 2.0 in addition offered authoring and interacting capabilities to the learner. Moreover, e-Learning 3.0 promoted intelligently collaborative, rich 3D virtual learning environments that brought learners together for anytime, anywhere, anyhow learning experience, exploiting the semantic capabilities to parse the global databases of knowledge. The backbone behind this is web technologies. The emerging Web 5.0 provides the space for human–computer interaction to deal with people's emotions. The users can interact with content with the help of a headphone. Even the facial expressions and emotions can be traced to bring real classroom learning into the existing e-learning system. The significant features of e-learning are listed as follows:

- Learn faster
- Forum discussion
- Gain knowledge
- Immersive approach
- Avoid travel time
- Real-time feedback
- Easy to absorb
- Performance analysis
- Hold learner's attention
- Interactive learning practices

E-learning platforms involve various components of e-learning such as content preparation, tutoring, coaching, mentoring, and cooperative learning [1]. The learner can learn synchronously or asynchronously. Video and audio conference, live webcasting, application sharing, whiteboard, polling are some of the synchronous e-learning mechanisms. Tools like e-mail or discussion forums are asynchronous communication tools where the learner learns the course in self-paced mode. Any e-learning approach will lead to the explosion of different types of information such as text, videos, and images, results in different data types that are not used in traditional data management systems. Analytical operations cannot be applied directly to these data. These data are semi-structured or unstructured. The data do not naturally show any valuable knowledge. The online learning platforms generate enormous learner behavioral data and educational data. Big data plays an important role in transforming the data obtained from online learning platforms into useful information for the improvement of academic activities [2]. The teachers can develop the content for personalized learning analyzing the current knowledge level of the students. The students have the opportunity to learn at their own pace [3]. The key issue here is the effective analysis and utilization of the data to improve the e-learning features. Big data technology provides the capability of analytics to enhance the e-learning process. The researchers are interested in the following goals [4]:

- Students' knowledge, metacognition, motivation, and attitudes are utilized for predicting students' future learning behavior.
- The different varieties of pedagogical methods and their impact on effective learning.
- Evolving the relationship between learner, learning, domain, and the software pedagogy.

Section 7.2 of this chapter has dealt with applications such as social network analysis (SNA), visual data analysis techniques, and semantic. The big data methods such as relationship mining, prediction, clustering, and structure discovery are discussed in Section 7.3. Section 7.4 elaborates on various tools used for big data analytics in e-learning. The rest of this chapter presents the outline of the recent research perspectives.

7.2   Big data applications in e-learning

Recent learning methods such as flipped classroom significantly depend on online activities. Several online learning management systems (LMSs) are proposed to enhance the learning experience. The entry of open source projects in mobile computing has made students to use smartphones to access learning content. These learning environments exploit the use of big data. The educational data mining (EDM) and learning analytics [5] are two main areas where big data makes a revolution. EDM utilizes procedures from data mining, machine learning (ML), and statistics to scrutinize data obtained in the teaching–learning process. Learning analytics apply approaches from psychology, information science, sociology, data mining, statistics, and ML to investigate data collected during the teaching–learning process. Big data [6] helps the teachers in the following aspects:

- To understand the way in which the learners are grasping the information and the most demanded e-learning method.
- To modify the modules of the e-learning course.
- To analyze the most visited e-learning modules in social learning.
- To predict the difficulty faced by the learners and the areas where learners put the leasing effort for learning.

In other words, big data lends a hand in targeted course recommendation, courseware construction, students' skill estimation, the performance of teachers and learners, and post-education activities. This section discussed these aspects of big data in e-learning that is portrayed in Figure 7.1.

7.2.1   Performance prediction

E-learning is blended online learning. Many analyses are using this concept and the area of implementation has still been increasing in a larger way on different websites. The main objective is to offer better education to its students. The learner-centric approach and adaptive e-learning system are adopted to have a positive

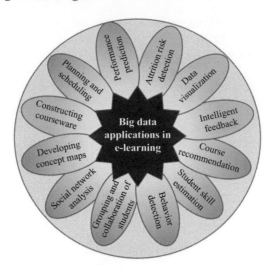

Figure 7.1 Big data applications in e-learning

impact on the learning process. Hussain *et al.* [7] made a study on the course of Open University (OU), the largest university in the United Kingdom. The study is to find out the students who have low curiosity in social science. OU delivers more than 1,000 online courses and offers online degrees. To assess the effect of commitment on student's performance, ML algorithms are used. The students' education level, course results, assessment score, the website access patterns of the student, link visitation, and pages visited by the students were taken as the input variables. The student's commitment to website access was rated.

To find out the less curious students, ML algorithms were applied. The training set was constructed using the ML algorithms, and its kappa values, accuracy, were compared. The observation showed that the JRIP, J48, gradient-boosted classifiers, and decision tree performed better compared to the testing set. Especially, the J48 model found out the students who were less curious about social science during the study. The researcher developed a dashboard to reveal the following:

- To inform about the reason for a student's less curiosity to the instructors.
- The instructor observes the student's behavior through graphs in real time and advises them for better interaction with the course activities.
- The feedback of teaching practices of the teaching staff is also depicted in the dashboard.
- The instructor can gain an assessment of the course material.
- Individual students in each valuation are identified by the instructor and the remedial materials can be forwarded to the student for better performance in the next valuation.
- The instructor can increase students' engagement by their contributions to the discussion forum.

Hence the application of big data techniques helped the instructors to find the key activities of the students and motivate them to be involved in those activities to accomplish high scores on course assessments.

7.2.2   Attrition risk detection

The current issues faced by the most of the higher education institutions around the world are the retention and success of students in their studies. To meet the increasing competition among higher educational institutes, most of them are interested in increasing students' retention rates. Also, student attenuation imposes a wrong notion among the students, the parents, and the institutions [8,9]. Students' dropouts lead to monetary losses as well as gave low ratings for the course at the society [10]. Hence, educationists are striving hard to reduce the student dropout rate. They have to take actions based on the following criteria [11]:

- Students at risk identification
- Evaluation of students and student support
- Availability of self-adjusting and dynamic system

Hence, higher educational institutions are concerned about the students' interest and try to assist students in getting their graduation.

A study was made by Abdulsalami [12] to build a risk model and to apply it for first-year students of Ahmadu Bello University, Zaria, to detect students at the risk of attrition. This study used structured query language for data collection and selection, python PL pandas library for data preprocessing, and python PL scikit-learn library for building classifiers. The confusion matrix was used as a performance evaluation metric of the classifiers. Also, a modified k nearest neighbor algorithm was proposed for better classification.

To face the challenges that are arising in the secondary schools, the government of Tanzania framed the Education Sector Development Plan and Education Training Policy [13]. The ensemble predictive model is presented by Mduma *et al.* [13] for an early prediction of student dropouts in Tanzania. Logistic regression and multilayer perceptron (MLP) are used in the ensemble classifier to form a prototype. The key features such as student's involvement in studies, parent contribution for student's progress used to detect the dropout were selected by the researchers. The prototype also has the visual module to aid the teachers to view the ML results. Through this prototype, the school can detect the student dropout rate and handle it with necessary action. These case studies proved that big data made it possible in identifying the attrition risk detection rate.

7.2.3   Data visualization

Analytics represents deriving inference and perceptions from a huge quantity of data. The perceptions are represented by various visual techniques for end-users who are operating the application platform [14]. Some of the used cases where big data visualization is applied are listed in Table 7.1.

Table 7.1   Data visualization techniques and their applications

Technique	Application
Connectivity chart [15]	The insights obtained in machine learning models can be represented through *connectivity charts*. It shows the connectivity between various events and their consequences
Word cloud [15]	The words depicted in different sizes in collection or cluster is called *word cloud*. The more often mentioned words within a given text appear bigger and bolder to represent its importance that may quantify the text-based insights into measurable analytics. A word cloud can be used to analyze customer feedback (the most liked and least liked) about the business. It is also easy to identify the pain point (wait time, price, or convenience)
Heat map [15]	Heat maps represent data by applying colors. A heat map is used to represent the regular student with green and irregular students with red
Network diagrams [16]	Network diagrams can be used to find the relationship between student groups, peer learning, and teamwork in social media
Correlation matrices [16]	A correlation matrix is used to find the relationship between the features in the dataset. Different colors are used to represent a strong correlation or a weak relationship. For example, students' attendance and their performance can be correlated
Augment geo maps [17]	Augment geo maps can be used for location analytics. For example, the influence of student locality in studies can be detected
Gauge [18]	A gauge is typically used to visualize metrics having a single value. Gauges are applied to represent students' enrollment, dropouts, pass percentage, etc. It is also used to show the allowable/not allowable range in different colors. It can be shown vertically or horizontally or in a grid layout. The subject-wise pass percentage can be displayed using the gauges
Line chart [15]	A line chart exhibits the change of data over a continuous time interval or time. The student's progress during study can be observed through this chart
Pie chart [15]	Pie chart is used to compare the components of the whole. Teachers can use this chart to find out the students' enrollment in various courses. The most demanding/least demanding courses can be viewed
Bar chart [15]	A bar chart is used to compare the performance of the students in various activities they are involved in completing a course
Gantt chart [18]	The Gantt chart visually depicts the timing of the project, the actual progress, and the comparison with the requirements. Hence, the managers can easily understand the progress of a project
Radar chart [19]	Multiple quantitative variables can be compared using radar charts. This describes the variables with similar values and any outliers amongst each variable. Radar charts also represent variables that are scoring high or low within a dataset. Specifically, improving the quality of performance metrics in any ongoing program
Rectangular treemaps [20]	Hierarchical data can be displayed by treemaps. They are made of a series of nested rectangles of sizes relative to the corresponding data value. A large rectangle corresponds to a branch of a data tree, and it is partitioned into smaller rectangles that represent the size of each

(Continues)

Table 7.1   (Continued)

Technique	Application
	node within that branch. Quick perception of sales data can be visualized using treemaps. Underperforming or over-performing items are indicated in different colors

7.2.4   Intelligent feedback

Education through e-learning is developing rapidly. Coursera statistics data [21] state that only 7%–9% of learners completed MOOCs (massive open online courses), though the enrollment for the course is high. Hence, it is necessary to enhance the teaching strategies to improve the course completion percentage. By understanding the student profile, personalized guidance can be given from the student's perspective. From the perspective of faculty, intelligent feedback encourages them to design effective e-content [22]. A study was carried out by Liang *et al.* [21] to analyze the features of learners using the attribute reduction method for data cleaning. Jaccard coefficient algorithm was applied to classify the students based on their behavior. This type of categorization helped the students to overcome their learning difficulties and to motivate them to complete the course. The research made by Al-Fraihat *et al.* [23] shows the importance of continuous reviews to ensure students' participation and course completion. The online platform must provide the features for interaction, valuation, and feedback for the continuous monitoring of the student activities throughout the course. Based on the students' feedback, the materials are to be updated regularly. All these activities are to be performed in a user-friendly manner for the ease of use by the students.

7.2.5   Course recommendation

With the introduction of MOOCs, an enormous amount of data is generated from the students' enrollment to the online courses. It will be easier for the students if a recommender system is available for them to choose the appropriate course. Hou *et al.* [24] suggest a recommender system based on the learning pattern of the students. Hierarchical bandits-based online learning algorithm was employed for this purpose. A high score is allotted by the system that it recommends for the students. The feedback from the user is also recorded for further improvement. A MOOC course recommender system [25] collected data by importing students' course enrollment information into Hadoop Distributed File System (HDFS) through Sqoop and preprocessed the data on Hadoop, storing it in the simplified format. Apriori algorithm in Spark was utilized to find out the best combination of courses in e-learning. After filtering and exporting the data to the relational database the course was recommended to the student. The course recommender system is depicted in Figure 7.2.

Dahdouh *et al.* [26] proposed a recommender system that applied association rules method to recommend appropriate learning materials based on

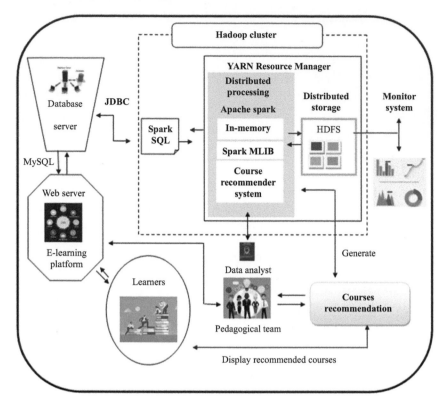

Figure 7.2   Overview of course recommender system [26]

student's activities. Using the log data they found out the key rules. These key rules are determined using frequent itemsets. The key rules can assist the user to choose their course applying their preferences. The recommender system utilized the Hadoop ecosystem and Spark Framework with a parallel FP-growth algorithm.

7.2.6   Student skill estimation

Online courses that are dealt with Internet-based learning frameworks [27] have lots of student information. They can be used to identify the cognitive activity of the students. The different measurements such as students' participation time on the web, recorded changes in the classroom, participation, lateness, and a student's course completion form the major points in predicting their learning experience. Bearing in mind a student's level of learning, his/her interaction with the framework, and sanctioned test scores, the student's skill level can be estimated. Yang and Li [28] analyzed student progress and performance. Matrix representation is used to show the student's progress and the attributes that determine the performance are also portrayed well.

The student attribute matrix scientifically models student's achievement- and nonachievement-related features. It applied Bloom's Taxonomy. Felder–Silverman's model was used to identify whether the student's comprehension improved in individual learning or collaborative learning. Back propagation neural network (BP-NN) was used to evaluate the student's performance. A student's ability development and its improvement can be identified through the progress of potential descriptors based on BP-NN. The student's score was considered as a performance metric. The factors that affect the student's performance were also brought to the notice. Thus, the students can be familiar with the factors that limit their performance or their abilities. The different groups of students, their progress, and development are known through student's progress indicators.

The results of the study proved to be precise with respect to all attributes. The classification of students with respect to the performance was accurate, and the students were able to determine the important issues that lead to low performance.

7.2.7   Behavior detection

The educators can retrieve the information from higher educational institutions for decision-making. Using association rules and classifiers, e-learners' behavior can be classified to decide their learning abilities and skills. Al Fanah and Ansari [29] used the logistic regressions, random forests, and Bayesian networks as classifiers with four variables (raised hands, discussion, view announcement, and visiting IT resources) and classified the e-learners into three classes (high, medium, and low). The Bayesian network revealed the student's behavior and their performance with more accuracy. Through this study, the teachers can recognize the behavior of the students and can take efforts to help the low performing students. The universities may redesign their curriculum, student policies, and decision-making.

The research made by Amo Filvá *et al.* [30] exploited click-stream data generated by e-learners during their browsing for behavior detection. The interpretation and valuable insights were generated through Hadoop. Tools such as Google Analytics, Piwik, FeedBurner, Google Webmaster, and Bing Webmaster [31] can be employed for click-stream analysis. The students' behavior in programming practice was investigated to give in time and quality feedback to the teachers. Based on the individuality, each student performs the programming activity differently and explores the various possibility of providing various solutions. Thus, the teacher has to analyze each of the possible solutions delivered. This process can be automated to ease the job of the teacher by automation using the Scratch tool. The Scratch tool captures the student clicks that are displayed in the visual programming environment. A web service app was developed to store the collected clicks in an MySQL database. Python was used for predictive analysis, and the results were displayed in the visual environment.

Based on the students' behavior in click collection, they were classified as blocked developer, normal developer, and rapid developer. A statistical approximation was used to analytically detect the three types of behavior (blocked, normal, and rapid). The statistical test proved that the result is significant ($p < 0.05$). It shows that the students who tried various possibilities and debugged the program many times produced better answers than the students who made the program in a simpler way.

This valuable information is exploited by the teacher to know the student's current status in relation to the assigned activities and the possibility in suspending the assigned activity. Hence, the teacher can provide better support to the students through enhance tutoring and adapting new activities.

7.2.8   Collaboration and social network analysis

In recent years, there is a wide usage of electronic devices both by the teachers and the learners. School students as well as university students use mobile phones, tablets, and computers for learning [32]. Big data analytics are used to analyze the huge volume of data generated during the learning process over a large network. Through this analysis, the researcher can identify the learners' likes and dislikes. There are varieties of tools used for prediction in e-learning. These tools are organized into four categories. They are collaboration, communication, storage, and assessment [33]. The most commonly used tools are related to collaboration and storage. The collaboration tool includes forum, glossary, Wiki, and social network.

Collaboration requires students to mutually and academically organize their efforts to interreliantly solve a problem, execute a task, or work collectively on a project. Collaborative learning shares a common learning objective and it is performed in groups. It is often characterized by extensive dialog and debate. Successful collaborative learning requires five vital elements such as accountability, good interaction, positive connectedness, effective application of social skills, and group dynamics [34]. The benefits of efficient collaborative learning make the students psychologically, socially, and academically sound. Four main methods are frequently used for the analysis of collaborative learning. They are interaction analysis, content analysis, EDM, and SNA.

Through interaction analysis statistics regarding forum activities, the contributions of students such as the frequency of posts by a student, participation statistics, and the number of replies in a discussion can be tracked. The statistical analysis informs the level of activity in a forum. Content analysis is related to the qualitative analysis of transcripts that reveal the process of knowledge construction and the social dynamics of interactions. Big data tools such as Apache Flink, Support Vector Machine, and Weka can be used for automatic analysis.

SNA [35] may be frequently useful for the analysis of the detailed tracing of relations and interactions. Responsibility is bestowed on the learners for constructing their knowledge. Teachers act as facilitators who stimulate learners' curious exploration, motivate them to reflect, raise questions, investigate answers, justify their perspectives, and debate with others. The SNA ranked the students using centrality measures to identify influencing, eminent students and to discover irregular students. The results of SNA also revealed the students' group formation. Communing mining approach was used to identify the students who made active interaction in the group. By applying dynamic analysis of networks, the researchers identified the students involved in message passing within/outside the groups.

Through dynamic analysis, patterns related to student's transition between groups, new group formation can be detected. This helps in regulating students' behavior in the group, and the teacher could recommend the remaining groups to invite the detached students for healthy discussions.

Rabbany *et al.* [35] designed a tool that visualizes the learners' interaction in the forum, the eminent/irregular learners, and the categories of groups over a time span. The instructor can view the summary of topics discussed online. The instructor can also evaluate the learners' participation.

7.2.9   Developing concept maps

Students should be able to connect principles, theories, and ideas of different subject areas and everyday life. Concept mapping is a valuable tool for evaluating inter-disciplinary understanding and analyzing levels of students pursuing their learning through the e-learning environment. In a personalized environment, the concept maps are designed automatically to help the learners to understand the subject clearly. But in a collaborative environment, the learners have to create the concept maps in discussion with their team members to learn the subject [36]. While using the web learning system, the learners' problems cannot be solved due to lack of immediate feedback. In the literature, EDM techniques such as Apriori, pathfinder network analysis, sequential probability ratio test, fuzzy set theory, direct hashing, and pruning were used. These techniques aid in improving learning performance, self-efficacy, identifying learning barriers, forming optimal learning sequences, understanding missing concepts, and defects in a concept map and detect common learner misunderstandings.

A novel method associating knowledge map to detect learners' cognitive and metacognitive strategy in the question-solving circumstances was proposed by Tian *et al.* [37]. In particular, to automatically map the cognitive approach to a meta-cognitive approach with raising thought level, a graph-based mining algorithm is designed. To make this process viewable and to understand the way a learner thinks while solving a question, a reverse engineering concept was applied. This system records the learning style and the behavior of the learners. A question-solving task, such as "compare array and pointer" for "The C Programming Language" course, and "compare packet switching and circuit switching" for the "Computer Network Principle" course, was assigned to the postgraduate and undergraduate students, and the observations were recorded. The experiment analyzed the metacognitive approaches such as "description–comparison–description," "comparison–description–description," and "description–description–comparison." Learners who take on the "description–comparison–description" model answer the questions sequentially in a step-by-step manner. But the learner using the other models answers the questions generally. Hence the models show the thinking process of the learners during the question-answering exercise.

7.2.10   Constructing courseware

Big data thinking has also realized the relevance in the curriculum construction of colleges and universities. Online teaching carriers are arising because of the big data environment. Therefore, the multimedia mode of teaching must be included in the college/university curriculum [38]. The students' thinking and imagination ability are improved through the adoption of pictures, audio, and video in teaching methods. Moreover, e-learning platforms that comprise multimedia, big data, and communication networks have become the medium of communication between teachers and students. Students can clarify their doubts in learning on these platforms and teachers can also respond to them. In the course construction of colleges and universities, scientific research analysis method, group cooperation inquiry method, scenario simulation method, practice training method, etc. can be applied as teaching methods. This kindles the enthusiasm of students to explore the curriculum. Hence the students actively solve problems, organize, and coordinate research activities by their initiative and truly take part in the course study.

The use of smartphones and laptops for self-learning and guided learning enables a barrier-free communication between instructors and learners. The use of big data establishes information-based teaching service platforms that actively gather relevant data on the market to do a vibrant market analysis of the assessment of the course being taught and provide data regulation for the curriculum development in colleges and universities. The course's construction in the curriculum must pay attention to the analysis report and regularly update its course content, enabling the students to be employable in the current market scenario.

Li *et al.* [39] discussed the ongoing developments in the curriculum reform at the Hunan University of Finance and Economics. The application of big data in syllabi modifications and curriculum were discussed. It stresses the need for data scientists and technical support in the institutes. The national level curriculum reform required in China was also discussed.

7.2.11   Planning and scheduling

The universities have course registration details, student details, student login particulars, curriculum details, students' access to the library, teachers' details, and other human resource details in their LMSs. The region-wise needs and issues can be settled with the help of the LMS data. The irregular students are identified and given guidance to avoid dropouts. Taking proper actions at the appropriate time advances the performance of the students, thereby developing outcome-based funding.

Segooa and Kalema [40] proposed a model that applied big data techniques to university data to enhance university performance. The analysis helped in decision-making and reporting. The reports emphasize strengths and weaknesses. The reports also recommend the issues that may arise and the solution appropriate to them. If the universities take necessary actions, improved performance will be observed in outcome-based funding.

The analysis of the LMS [41] by the combination of different learning analytical techniques with the big data will facilitate relevant information to the educational authorities and teachers to transform and to enhance the current methods. The involvement of various collaborative tools in the teaching–learning process can be accessed for student participation, motivation, and satisfaction in using the tools. This will encourage the teachers to develop new strategies for the improvement of the students' performance.

7.3   Big data techniques for e-learning

Classroom learning is based on cognitive, behavioral, and constructive models. The cognitive model is based on the active involvement of teaching and learning with the teacher's guidance. The behavioral model is highly dependent on observing the changes in the attitude of the student to assess the outcome. In a constructive model, knowledge can be acquired by the student, with the available knowledge on their own. Several innovative pedagogical methodologies have been introduced to enhance the learning experience in the online LMS without the direct interference of an instructor. E-learning brought the educational experience in a new realm with an effective and efficient teaching–learning process. It is commonly known as "e-teaching" or "web-based education" where a novel framework of education is introduced for a seamless teaching–learning interaction ubiquitously. Big data pays special attention in modeling techniques by focusing on large, complex, and heterogeneous database.

Generally, big data handles an immense amount of unstructured data and how the data is being managed, applied to predictive modeling for the better utilization of dataset. Nowadays, the education sector has become technology-oriented and enormous tools are available to understand the quality of students. Social Networks Adapting Pedagogical Practice (SNAPP) is exploited by the instructor to understand students' blogs [42]. It assists in visualizing the interaction among students and it can be concluded the level of interest of students in the particular course. SNAPP can also be united with any of the LMSs (modular object-oriented dynamic learning environment (Moodle)). The following types of data analysis are accomplished:

• Relationship mining
• Structure discovery
• Prediction

In the context of relationship mining, casual data, sequential pattern, correlation, and association rule mining are preferable. Factor analysis, network analysis, structure discovery, and clustering are recommended in structure discovery. Knowledge estimation, regression, and classification are preferred in prediction.

7.3.1   Classification in e-learning

In classification, the existing relationship among multivariate data items and its outcome is considered as class-membership labels. Some of the techniques that can be applied for e-learning are described later, which include fuzzy logic, artificial neural network (ANN), evolutionary computation, and association rules.

7.3.1.1   Fuzzy logic

Intelligent tutoring system (ITS) is introduced as a neuro-fuzzy model to evaluate students and particularly, a fuzzy theory is followed to find out the interaction among students and the system ITS in a linguistic form [43]. ANN is trained to identify the fuzzy relationship with minimum–maximum composition. Estimation is made to learn the association between a student characteristic and an observed response. A fuzzy approach is presented in the EWSE system for evaluating the educational websites exclusively by the domain experts [44]. A fuzzy rule-based approach is introduced to elucidate and integrate the knowledge in the intelligent LMS by persistently tracking web servers. Furthermore, the system is intelligent to predict and handle failures occurred in web servers, improves reliability and stability. Also, it promotes the self-assessment process of the student by providing suggestions using fuzzy reasoning. An algorithm known as the Apriori association rule mining algorithm along with a fuzzy set is presented to search out the information by the teachers to refine or reorganize the teaching material and assessment process. An inductive learning algorithm is presented to search out the missing concept at the time of learning. As a result, the learning path could be refined or reorganized to strengthen the teaching–learning process [45].

7.3.1.2   ANN and evolutionary computation

In ANN, an MLP is particularly approached to locate the suitable navigation strategies [46]. The knowledge acquired by learning the neural network is considered and the impact of navigation strategy is evaluated and validated. An evolutionary computational process is preferred to examine the learning behavior of students. In the web-based educational system, the classification and prediction about the grade of students are done by extracting the features from logged data [47]. The accuracy of classification and prediction could be improved by computing the weightage of data features using a genetic algorithm.

7.3.1.3   Association rule

Association rules such as Apriori and Predictive Apriori algorithms can be employed in e-learning to identify certain correlation patterns among data attributes. It assists in evaluating the performance such as accuracy, time consumption, and rules generation. It supports in generalizing the behavior of students from the set of enrolled students in the e-learning courses for further improvement. The association rule is determined by minimum support, confidence, and the rules that are generated. The frequent itemsets are being identified by an algorithm and the association rules could be generated from the existing itemsets. Support (S) refers

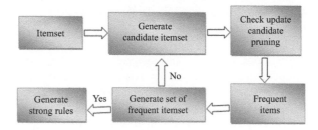

Figure 7.3   Apriori mechanism

to the number of records which includes XUY, the total number of records available in the dataset:

$$\text{Support } (X, Y) : \frac{P(XUY)}{n}$$

In addition, confidence (C) is a measure used to classify the possibility of rule, for instance, if an association rule $X \rightarrow Y$ results in 0.9 confidence then it concludes 90% of occurrences contain X also have Y in the dataset:

$$\text{Confidence } (X \rightarrow Y) : \frac{P(XUY)}{P(X)}$$

In [48], a study is being conducted to mine the rare rules exploiting association rule in e-learning. The main objective is to identify rare rules using RARC (rare association rule curating); hence the mentor/instructor can identify unusual learning patterns among students. A systematic course recommender system is demonstrated for e-learning to predict the best correlated subjects focusing on student's interest [49]. The statistical measures considered in Apriori and Predictive Apriori algorithms are standard deviation, mean, range, and predictive accuracy for evaluating the performance. The exploration of algorithms assists in comparing the students' performance and supports certain predictions by employing Apriori and Predictive Apriori algorithms. Both resulted in yielding accurate results and predicting best rules with regards in terms of time complexity. Consistent study attitude is considered as the key success in the educational domain and hard work in doing quizzes, and spending time in learning assignments would support to score well. The algorithm is designed to identify all frequent items and examine the outcome with the frequent itemsets. The process of generating association rules is shown in Figure 7.3.

7.4   Big data tools

Big data extract a massive amount of meaningful information and creates great opportunities for several organizations in order to serve customers in the market nowadays. The technologies include Hadoop, MapReduce, NoSQL, Hive, and PIG available for handling big data. NoSQL database lays the foundation for many systems. It is also opted for its operational, real-time data store, and offline capabilities. In traditional systems, different technologies and infrastructure are required to acquire, store, maintain, and analyze data. NoSQL is a database that becomes very popular amongst currently existing web companies. It improves scalability and performance when compared to traditional databases. It is robust in storing and managing "unstructured data" and it includes other products such as MongoDB and Redis. It encompasses a huge variety of heterogeneous database technologies in response to the amount of data stored, frequency of data access, performance, and processing requirement.

E-learning platform improves the coordination among students and teachers as well as enhances the interaction among students. Moodle is an efficient online educational platform that facilitates customized learning with the following features:

- Additional materials such as exercises, tasks, examples, and case studies can be created and published although these are visible only for a certain group of students.
- Reports submitted by the students regarding some doubts, problems, and propositions/solutions would help teachers to understand the flow and acquire knowledge about the process to enrich the course.
- Answers or solutions for certain tasks are provided in a request–response manner within a stipulated amount of time can be observed that too could be commented and corrected.
- Students' results are obtained and presented; opportunities are available to verify, compare the content such as data, code, indirect results, and solutions with the remaining team members for discussion.
- Own materials can be prepared and shared with the other students and teachers.

The primary purpose of teachers is accomplished well in this platform, and opportunities are available especially for the students to extend their knowledge in the course of their interest.

7.4.1   Hadoop platform for e-learning

Hadoop is an open-source platform that assists in managing huge amounts of data, and it is considered as a highly performing powerful platform to acquire, organize, and analyze big data. It controls the cost by integrating hardware and software components in a single big data framework. In general, the followings are the three main components of Hadoop:

- HDFS is maintained for distributed storage.
- Map reduce is considered for parallel processing.
- YARN is a framework meant for resource management and job scheduling.

Initially, the tools available to process big data are entirely based on Linux. Hence, the solution is the virtualization platform; a separate machine is executed using Oracle VirtualBox. The following points describe the process to create a Hadoop cluster for big data and the hardware resources required in forming a cluster:

- NameNode is a computer device with a 64 GB RAM that acts as a monitor and it coordinates the operation performed in a cluster.
- DataNode is a device store and processes files in it.
- Computer devices that are considered as virtual machines (VMs) are being allocated with four core processors each.

A block in HDFS is maintained at least in three machines and for storing 1 MB of data 3 MB of disk space is required; additional space is required for processing data. For data partitioning, four machines are required in the HDFS system. Hence the cluster is based on Linux; two versions of machines are required, namely, NameNode and DataNode. For preparing Hadoop cluster from binaries, it is required to edit the configuration files manually. The simplest approach is to use an integrated distribution such as Ambari or Cloudera, which has integrated tools also. Cloudera is chosen for installation, and the binaries are downloaded and stored in the NameNode machine and a web browser could be launched with the machine address along with a specific port. Furthermore, the DataNode can be chosen with the help of the browser with the desired set of tools.

- To exploit big data tools with VMs: Cloudera QuickStart, Oracle BigData Lite, Hortonworks Sandbox.
- IBM Cloud (Open source) Ambari consists of DataNode (3×64 GB RAM) and NameNode (1×256 GB RAM).
- Commercial clouds include Microsoft Azure, Amazon Web Services.

In Hadoop environment, every unit of data is maintained as several copies on different cluster nodes. Data can be processed locally and they are stored on the same cluster node that automatically reduces the network traffic. A fault-tolerant system is also embedded in HDFS and it is capable of surviving at the time of failure of significant units in the storage infrastructure. Hadoop constructs clusters of systems and the tasks are distributed and coordinated among them. It can even operate continuously without interruption or any loss of data by shifting the computational process to other systems in the same cluster. Hadoop is a scalable platform that stores an unlimited amount of data and it could be processed in a distributed environment. In particular, scaling hardware incurs additional costs and it is relatively easier to scale up as a software. As depicted in Figure 7.4, the complete process is made clear with the collected structured and unstructured data that are stored and maintained to assist the developer to create new applications.

7.4.1.1   Apache Hadoop

It is a popular open-source platform that promotes storing, maintaining, and processing of big data. MapReduce is a simplified processing model that is designed for distributed processing especially on huge clusters and it could be deployed over commodity hardware [50]. Moreover, it is designed to resolve the limitations and

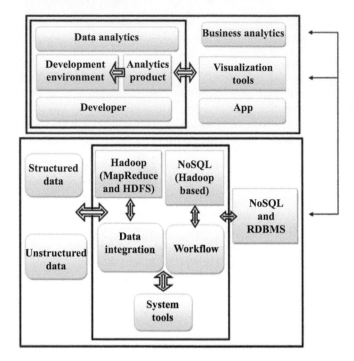

Figure 7.4   Hadoop framework for the educational sector

challenges met in the traditional approaches while analyzing the huge volume of data generated by different organizations. The three different modes are supported, namely, fully distributed, pseudo-distributed, and standalone mode. Hadoop ecosystem deals with several problems such as analysis (Spark), loading (Flume and Sqoop), querying (Pig), and computation (Storm). Hadoop technology is widely exploited in the different cloud providers such as Microsoft Azure, Amazon Web Services, Yahoo, and Facebook.

7.4.1.2   Hadoop Distributed File System

It is a widely used file system to manage data obtained from different clusters implemented in master–slave architecture [51]. Initially, the development of HDFS was encouraged by GFS (Google File System). The system was highly fault-tolerant and could be positioned even with the primitive hardware facilities. Moreover, it facilitates high-speed data access and particularly it is appropriate for the application that possesses larger datasets. It provides an abstract view of disk resources to manage the physical storage spaces of different nodes as if the complete nodes are working less than one hard disk. Furthermore, the data from various clusters in HDFS architecture are managed in the form of the block file structure. The namespace of files and its directories along with its location is maintained in NameNode.

7.4.1.3   MapReduce

MapReduce is a framework designed for parallel processing in a Hadoop environment using various tools and methodologies [52]. The two modes of operation are described in the following points:

- In map operation, key-value pairs should be computed for every record and the pairs with the same key are collectively in the same group. For example, if weather data is processed by considering year and temperature as a pair, then the observations for the same year would be maintained in the same group.
- In reducing operation, some features are extracted from the aggregated value in each group. For example, a maximum temperature can be determined for the same year–temperature pair in weather data.

7.4.1.4   YARN

YARN [53] is a framework designed for resource management and job scheduling and it segregates the resource management process from the computational process. It supports many distributed processing paradigms such as Storm, Giraph, and Spark. It comprises master and slave machines, namely ResourceManager (RM) and NodeManager (NM) to manage applications in a distributed way. The main responsibility of RM is to track, share resources among applications, and optimize the cluster utilization efficiently. NM's responsibility lies in task execution and monitors the utilization of resources by the slave node. The architecture of Hadoop cluster is depicted in Figure 7.5.

7.4.2   Spark

Apache Spark is a popular unified framework designated for efficient big data processing and it is capable of performing calculations in-memory that is a 100 times faster than MapReduce. It could be positioned in Hadoop YARN, standalone mode, Kubernetes, or Mesos. Moreover, it supports different commonly used data management systems such as Hive, HBase, HDFS, Amazon S3, Cassandra, and some database management systems such as Oracle, MySQL. Spark API facilitates standard libraries that support different use-cases. Some of the components in Spark are streaming (real-time data processing) and Spark SQL (processing structured data), SparkR, GraphX, and MLlib. It supports several programming languages including Java, Python, Scala, and R-programming. Spark task comprises different transformations and it constructs directed acyclic graph that refers to the set of operations. During task execution, the spark runs the graph by splitting into several stages. The set of tasks in each stage would be executed in parallel across many clusters.

7.4.3   Orange

Orange is software that can be chosen for processing and analyzing the data [54]. It is an open-source platform and it facilitates the mining and visualization process. It is compatible with different data formats such as excel sheets, CSV files, SQL

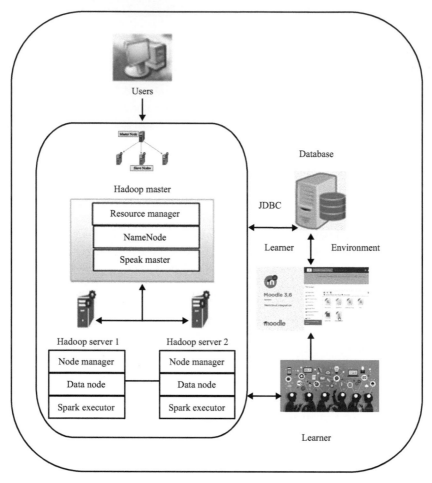

Figure 7.5　Architecture of Hadoop cluster

tables, and URL data. In the context, the student data can be loaded using instrument *File*. The examination details can be made using *Data Table* and the graphical representation is projected using the *Scatter Plot*. Data is filtered using *Select Rows* and it assists in identifying columns for continuing further analysis. The values that differ from others can be verified using *Outliers*.

7.5　Recent research perspectives and future direction

At 19.6% of the compound annual growth rate, the size of LMS market is predicted to reach USD 22.4 billion by 2023, which is depicted in Figure 7.6. The rapid growth drives the academic setup toward digital learning that increases the big data usage in e-learning. About 30% of learning and development professionals are

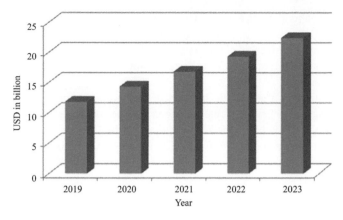

Figure 7.6   Learning management system (LMS) and e-learning market

planning to incorporate simulations and games in the e-learning program this year 2020.

The recent advancement in LMS technology reaches today's learners of adopting digital learning technology that enables learning at anytime. The main benefit of LMS technology lies in providing unlimited access to e-learning content to the learners. By comparing classroom and online teaching, 85% of students believe that learning via online platforms is better than classroom teaching. In this modern era, 94% prefer online learning because of some significant features mentioned in the table.

The revolution of big data in education throws up numerous challenges. They are systemic changes, modeling knowledge structures, technological infra-structures, and economic and ethical considerations [55]. As the e-learning systems involve the frequent use of computer-based systems, the collection of numerous data could encourage the reversal of learning systems and the retraining of teachers in the application of such systems. In modeling knowledge structure, the big data algorithms should know the structure of the subject and should suggest the topic to be learned by the students before other topics. This challenge can be solved with artificial intelligence, which deals with knowledge modeling and representation and assists in developing "smart" decision-making processes based on it. Lack of technological infrastructures and standardization of big data technologies would make the data processing difficult.

Another important challenge is in finding applicable economic models for the big data revolution in education. A set of clear and valid rules must be laid for the appropriate usage of technology and methodology to ascertain that the data collected are used appropriately and serves only for the betterment of education and learning. To overcome this ethical issue, the Internet of Things and data security methods should be applied in LMSs.

With the fast progress in e-learning, many new concepts such as artificial intelligence, virtual reality, big data, blended learning, gamification, mobile learning [56], and the Internet of Things help in creating innovations in the e-learning environment. With virtual reality, a real classroom effect can be created so that students chat with their classmates in real time. This facilitates better student participation and motivates them to concentrate on the learning process to attain learning objectives.

Gamification is a technique used to design tutorials for academic purposes. Through games, the students are engaged in the learning process. In mobile learning, simplified mobile apps are developed in the form of learning materials to aid the students to learn easily through their mobile devices. Internet of Things can be used to have intelligent control over the e-learners and their environment. E-learning ecosystem also helps one to perform resource management, data security, and student identity administration. These new e-learning trends with different features will rule the education institutions in the future.

7.5.1   *Future direction*

Several proposals are suggested to enhance the research in the arena of e-learning. Some of them are listed in the following points [57,58]:

- Finding the relationship between family poverty and student academic performance.
- Uncovering the relationship among social practice experiences, certification, and career development.
- Discovering the relationship among the length of stay in the library, book lending, and borrowing with the academic performance.
- Acquiring the relationship among sleeping behavior, diet, and grade points.
- Getting important insights to form the assessment processes by using data science techniques.
- Proper assessment of e-learning extended to other domains such as company learning and tourism-related learning must be encouraged.
- E-learning assessment in a scenario of ubiquitous education can be dealt with blockchain technology.
- More research should be done in the multidisciplinary areas such as SNA, gamification strategies, or prior knowledge evaluation with respect to e-learning.

7.6   Conclusion

The traditional e-learning architecture is superseded by the novel big data applications and cloud computing technologies in the e-learning process. These emerging technologies offer an opportunity to promote the interaction among teachers and students, by permitting them to track the individual requirement and performance of e-learners. Professionals can easily understand how learners are consuming information and their learning requirements. E-learning professionals can easily identify the part that requires to be fine-tuned in any specific module or a course. In social learning, e-learning links or modules that are being shared with other learners can be discovered for further improvement. In other words, big data lends a hand in targeted course offerings, behavioral processes, curriculum development, personalized learning, instructor performance, learning outcomes, enhanced research, and employment opportunities in the education domain. Factor analysis, network analysis, structure discovery, and clustering are recommended in structure discovery. Knowledge estimation, regression, and classification are preferred in prediction. The challenges faced in big data processing are accomplished using various tools. The wide tools such as Hadoop, MongoDB, MapReduce, and Orange are discussed in this chapter. Still, there are few open challenges related to assess and teach students with more strength. Creating interest and motivation for interaction in the class with effective communication in subject materials, e-mail content, assigning homework, and scheduling work hours for discussion and recording grades are few open issues. Another important issue is security, and e-learning tools do not afford complete protection to teachers' and learners' resources. Educational institutes should take responsibility to protect their systems using appropriate security tools. Finally, additional research work is required to examine the long-term effects on e-learning methodology and tools. The research effort has to be focused on investigating the impact of learners' self-perception on the course that highly concerns the academic development, creativity level, and collaborative knowledge construction with respect to the scope of the particular course in the academic surrounding.

References

[1] Epignosis LL. E-Learning Concepts, Trends, Applications. 2014.
[2] Student PG and Kumbharde MV. Technology and utilities of e-learning for knowledge based data mining. Technology. 2019;3(4).
[3] Logica B and Magdalena R. Using big data in the academic environment. Procedia Economics and Finance. 2015;33:277–86.
[4] Prakash BR, Hanumanthappa M, and Kavitha V. Big data in educational data mining and learning analytics. International Journal of Innovative Research in Computer and Communication Engineering. 2014;2(12):7515–20.
[5] Mining TE. Enhancing teaching and learning through educational data mining and learning analytics: An issue brief. In Proceedings of Conference on Advanced Technology for Education 2012 Oct (pp. 1–64).
[6] Christopher P. Big Data in eLearning: The Future of eLearning Industry – eLearning Industry, https://elearningindustry.com/big-data-in-elearning-future-of-elearning-industry, Accessed on January 14, 2020.
[7] Hussain M, Zhu W, Zhang W, and Abidi SM. Student engagement predictions in an e-learning system and their impact on student course assessment scores. Computational Intelligence and Neuroscience. 2018;2018.
[8] Bound J, Lovenheim MF, and Turner S. Why have college completion rates declined? An analysis of changing student preparation and collegiate

resources. American Economic Journal: Applied Economics. 2010;2 (3):129–57.

[9]   Bowen WG, Chingos MM, and McPherson MS. Crossing the finish line: Completing College at America's public universities. USA: Princeton University Press; 2009.

[10] Larsen MS, Kornbeck KP, Kristensen RM, Larsen MR, and Sommersel HB. Dropout phenomena at universities: What is dropout? Why does. Education. 2012;45:1111–20.

[11] Berens J, Schneider K, Görtz S, Oster S, and Burghoff J. Early detection of students at risk – predicting student dropouts using administrative student data and machine learning methods.

[12] Abdulsalami AO. Detection of students at risk of attrition using data mining approach. Thesis, 2016.

[13] Mduma N, Kalegele K, and Machuve D. An ensemble predictive model based prototype for student drop-out in secondary schools. Journal of Information Systems Engineering and Management. 2019;4(3):em0094.

[14] Hirve S and Reddy CP. A survey on visualization techniques used for big data analytics. In Advances in Computer Communication and Computational Sciences 2019 (pp. 447–59). Springer, Singapore.

[15] Alex B. Big Data Visualization: Value It Brings and Techniques It Requires, https://www.scnsoft.com/blog/big-data-visualization-techniques, Accessed on January 20, 2020.

[16] Choy J, Chawla V, and Whitman L. Data visualization techniques: From basics to Big Data with SAS visual analytics. SAS: White Paper. 2013.

[17] SAS Visual Analytics, https://www.sas.com/en_in/software/visual-analytics.html, Accessed on January 20, 2020.

[18] Lewis C. 16 Types of Charts: Finereport, https://www.finereport.com/en/data-visualization/top-16-types-of-chart-in-data-visualization.html, Accessed on January 20, 2020.

[19] Radar chart, https://en.wikipedia.org/wiki/Radar_chart, Accessed on January 20, 2020.

[20] Page L. Treemaps: Data Visualization of Complex Hierarchies, https://www.nngroup.com/articles/treemaps/, Accessed on January 22, 2020.

[21] Liang K, Zhang Y, He Y, Zhou Y, Tan W, and Li X. Online behavior analysis-based student profile for intelligent E-learning. Journal of Electrical and Computer Engineering. 2017;2017.

[22] Research on the Effectiveness of Online Learning a Compilation of Research on Online Learning, The Future of Universities, 2011, https://www.immagic.com/elibrary/archives/general/acptr_us/a110923f.pdf, Accessed on January 22, 2020.

[23] Al-Fraihat D, Joy M, and Sinclair J. Evaluating E-learning systems success: An empirical study. Computers in Human Behavior. 2020;102:67–86.

[24] Hou Y, Zhou P, Xu J, and Wu DO. Course recommendation of MOOC with big data support: A contextual online learning approach. In IEEE INFOCOM

2018—IEEE Conference on Computer Communications Workshops (INFOCOM WKSHPS) 2018 Apr 15 (pp. 106–11). IEEE.

[25]   Zhang H, Huang T, Lv Z, Liu S, and Zhou Z. MCRS: A course recommendation system for MOOCs. Multimedia Tools and Applications. 2018;77 (6):7051–69.

[26]   Dahdouh K, Dakkak A, Oughdir L, and Ibriz A. Large-scale e-learning recommender system based on Spark and Hadoop. Journal of Big Data. 2019;6(1):2.

[27]   Farhan M, Jabbar S, Aslam M, *et al.* IoT-based students interaction framework using attention-scoring assessment in eLearning. Future Generation Computer Systems. 2018;79:909–19.

[28]   Yang F and Li FW. Study on student performance estimation, student progress analysis, and student potential prediction based on data mining. Computers & Education. 2018;123:97–108.

[29]   Al Fanah M and Ansari MA. Understanding E-learners' behaviour using data mining techniques. In Proceedings of the 2019 International Conference on Big Data and Education 2019 Mar 30 (pp. 59–65).

[30]   Amo Filvá D, Alier Forment M, García Peñalvo FJ, Fonseca Escudero D, and Casany Guerrero MJ. Learning analytics to assess students' behavior with scratch through clickstream. In Proceedings of the Learning Analytics Summer Institute Spain 2018: León, Spain, June 18–19, 2018 2018 (pp. 74–82). CEUR-WS.org.

[31]   Web Analytics Tools, https://leadmarketinginfluencer.com/top-5-web-analytic-tools/, Accessed on February 02, 2020.

[32]   Ray S and Saeed M. Applications of educational data mining and learning analytics tools in handling big data in higher education. In Applications of Big Data Analytics 2018 (pp. 135–60). Springer, Cham.

[33]   García OA and Secades VA. Big data & learning analytics: A potential way to optimize elearning technological tools. International Association for Development of the Information Society. 2013.

[34]   Saqr M. Using learning analytics to understand and support collaborative learning. Doctoral dissertation, Department of Computer and Systems Sciences, Stockholm University. 2018.

[35]   Rabbany R, Elatia S, Takaffoli M, and Zaïane OR. Collaborative learning of students in online discussion forums: A social network analysis perspective. In Educational Data Mining 2014 (pp. 441–66). Springer, Cham.

[36]   Acharya A and Sinha D. An educational data mining approach to concept map construction for web based learning. Informatica Economica. 2017;21(4).

[37]   Tian F, Yue J, Chao KM, *et al.* Modeling e-Learners' Cognitive and Metacognitive Strategy in Comparative Question Solving. arXiv, pp.arXiv-1906. 2019.

[38]   Zhang D. Analysis on the Application of Big Data in Classroom Teaching. 2018 International Conference on Education, Psychology, and Management Science (ICEPMS 2018), Francis Academic Press, UK, 762. DOI: 10.25236/icepms.2018.165.

[39]   Li X, Fan X, Qu X, *et al.* Curriculum reform in big data education at applied technical colleges and universities in China. IEEE Access. 2019;7:125511–21.

[40]   Segooa MA and Kalema BM. The Big potential of Big Data towards universities outcome based funding. In 2019 IEEE 9th Annual Computing and Communication Workshop and Conference (CCWC) 2019 Jan 7 (pp. 0574–8). IEEE.

[41]   Secades VA and Arranz O. Big data & eLearning: A binomial to the future of the knowledge society. IJIMAI. 2016;3(6):29–33.

[42]   Ray S. Big Data in Education, Gravity, the Great Lakes Magazine. 2013;20:8–10.

[43]   Stathacopoulou R, Magoulas GD, and Grigoriadou M. Neural network-based fuzzy modeling of the student in intelligent tutoring systems. In IJCNN'99. International Joint Conference on Neural Networks. Proceedings (Cat. No. 99CH36339) 1999 Jul 10 (Vol. 5, pp. 3517–21). IEEE.

[44]   Hwang GJ, Huang TC, and Tseng JC. A group-decision approach for evaluating educational web sites. Computers & Education. 2004;42(1):65–86.

[45]   Tsai CJ, Tseng SS, and Lin CY. A two-phase fuzzy mining and learning algorithm for adaptive learning environment. In International Conference on Computational Science 2001 May 28 (pp. 429–38). Springer, Berlin, Heidelberg.

[46]   Minaei-Bidgoli B and Punch WF. Using genetic algorithms for data mining optimization in an educational web-based system. In Genetic and Evolutionary Computation Conference 2003 Jul 12 (pp. 2252–63). Springer, Berlin, Heidelberg.

[47]   Mizue K and Toshio O. N3: Neural network navigation support-knowledge-navigation in hyperspace: The sub-symbolic approach. Journal of Educational Multimedia and Hypermedia. 2001;10(1):85–103.

[48]   Romero C, Romero JR, Luna JM, and Ventura S. Mining rare association rules from e-learning data. In Educational Data Mining 2010 2010 Jun 11.

[49]   Aher SB and Lobo LM. Course recommender system in e-learning. International Journal of Computer Science and Communication. 2012;3 (1):159–64.

[50]   Apache Hadoop, http://hadoop.apache.org/, Accessed on February 14, 2020.

[51]   Dhruba B. The Hadoop Distributed File System (HDFS), https://hadoop. apache.org/docs/r3.1.1/hadoop-project-dist/hadoop-hdfs/Hdfs Design.html, Accessed on February 14, 2020.

[52]   Dean J and Ghemawat S. MapReduce: Simplified data processing on large clusters. Communications of the ACM. 51:107, 2008.

[53]   Apache Hadoop YARN, https://hadoop.apach e.org/docs/r3.1.1/hadoo p-yarn/hadoo p-yarn-site/YARN.html, Accessed on October 14, 2018.

[54]   Orange,   https://orange.biolab.si/training/introduction-to-data-mining/, Accessed on February 14, 2020.

[55]   Hershkovitz A and Alexandron G. Understanding the potential and challenges of Big Data in schools and education. Tendencias Pedagógicas. 2020;35:7–17.

[56]   Baz FÇ. New trends in e-learning. In Trends in E-learning. http://dx.doi.org/ 10.5772/intechopen.75623.

[57]   Lara JA, Aljawarneh S, and Pamplona S. Special issue on the current trends in E-learning assessment. Journal of Computing in Higher Education. 2020;32(1):1–8.

[58]   Zhong C and Cao Z. Study on student growth tracking system based on educational big data. In 3rd International Conference on Mechatronics Engineering and Information Technology (ICMEIT 2019) 2019 Apr. Atlantis Press.

Chapter 8

E-learning using big data and cloud computing

Dhanalekshmi Gopinathan[1] and Archana Purwar[1]

E-learning is a learning system in which educational content and technologies are combined to facilitate the learner. The unprecedented increase in the number of students and educational contents and services provided makes the e-learning method grow at an exponential rate. Many challenges such as optimized resource utilization, storage necessities along with management of dynamic parallel requests concurrently necessitate the use of a platform that demands cost control to be satisfied by the environment of cloud computing. Cloud-based e-learning architecture provides an enriched learning experience, including interactive features to challenge the user's depth of understanding and level of preservation. Big data, in the context of e-learning, is the data that are gathered from learners during the learning process from many platforms such as the progress of the learners, evaluation results, discussion forums, messages, feedback, collaborations with the learner communities, teaching interactions and any other data generated related to the learning process. The data collected by these mediums are still large and difficult to manage. Hence big data in e-learning helps in a better analysis and management of these data. Using big data technologies, the enormous amount of data generated by e-learning can be processed, analyzed, organized, filtered, which can be visualized efficiently in less time. The useful information can be extracted from a large volume of data that help one to take better, smarter, and fast decisions. Hence, it is better to make use of big data for a better quality of e-learning systems. This chapter provides insight into the drawbacks of the conventional e-learning model, e-learning using the technology of cloud computing and big data. It also shows how big data and cloud computing are integrated to provide e-learning support. Moreover, it uncovers some of the case studies in e-learning industries and concludes with challenges.

8.1 Introduction

E-learning is a virtualized distance learning method that extends the learning using the Internet to plan, implement, accomplish, and improve the efficiency of the

[1]Department of CSE/IT, Jaypee Institute of Information Technology, Noida, India

education. Ubiquitous learning environments must be constructed on a strong IT infrastructure that supports current pedagogical methods as well as a range of heterogeneous learning materials within the courses. Learning environments will be more effective if it is integrated with an existing e-learning environment under a learning management system (LMS). Cloud computing provides a powerful architecture for large and complex computations. It provides an easy way to access big data analytics. E-learning using cloud computing and big data helps the e-learning professionals to understand the behavior of their learners, the contents, assessment outcomes, etc. This successively can lead them to develop more relevant policies, increase the satisfaction of learners, advance training resources, lower prices, thereby providing improved LMS services. The learner's feedback also enables online learning professionals to design more customized online courses, track the learner patterns as they interact with a course. In addition to this, big data offers benefits to the learners in terms of storage and processing also. Most of the online learning systems use multimedia contents such as videos, audios, images. Big data offers better storage options to these large volumes of data. It can be viewed as a three-layered structure. The bottom layer could be the cloud layer that offers the resources. The middle layer is the big data, where the data analytics are done. The various big data frameworks such as Hadoop, Storm, and Spark allow distributed processing. These techniques allow learning professionals to assess the learning strategies effectively in real time to identify each learner's needs to provide customized educational resources. In addition, the learners also improve their skills by engaging in online courses, taking part in online tests and quizzes, gaining valuable feedback from the teachers, and sending online courses and projects to their instructors. Finally, the top-level will be the e-learning module. This chapter introduces concepts of issues in the conventional e-learning issues, cloud computing environment, e-learning on the cloud architecture and big data, the integration of cloud and big data for e-learning and open research ideas. The key contribution of this chapter includes the following:

1. issue of conventional e-learning systems,
2. characteristics of cloud in e-learning,
3. integration of big data and cloud computing in e-learning, and
4. discussion of some case studies in e-learning.

8.2   Conventional e-learning system and its issues

E-learning will have a lot of advantages. There is no space or time limitation as the source of learning is shared, and learners can learn at any time online. The learning materials can be reused. Contents can be understood by the help of multimedia. Moreover, it is based on individual teaching and learning. An instructor will assess every learning circumstance to support the learner and to improve the learner's learning interest as well.

Compared to conventional classroom-based learning, the web-based learning offers several advantages. The most important one is the reduced cost that a learner can learn anywhere at any time at his/her convenience. There is no limitation on the number of students as in the case of physical classroom. To facilitate better understanding, the learning material can be prepared by using multimedia contents. It also helps teachers to compare and evaluate their materials and utilize the common areas of knowledge [1].

However, there exist some drawbacks as well. The key challenge in e-learning is the efficient utilization of computing resources. Today, the courses supported by e-learning provide higher impact on the educative framework compared to classroom learning. As it is possible for a large number of users attempting to have access to the e-learning content, different issues need to be addressed efficiently.

In the traditional e-learning, the learning system and maintenance are located in universities or enterprises. E-learning requires numerous amounts of hardware and software resources, which may result in large investment and processing power. There are educational institutions that could not afford such large investment or processing power. The different issues affecting the conventional e-learning can be (i) the conventional web server that sometimes may fail to provide the infrastructure demand of concurrent access for the huge amount of students, (ii) high demand on the teaching resources, superior infrastructure, and charges only for resources that are used.

Could computing provides a solution to all these issues? Cloud computing [2,3] reduces the computational cost and provides increased flexibility and reliability of the systems. It offers various services to the users who do not even need to be aware of the underlying architecture and provides higher transparent scalability.

8.3   E-learning on cloud computing

E-learning is a paradigm shift in teaching and learning. It is a shift from top-down lecturing and passive students to a more collaborative, cooperative approach where the learning process is cocreated by students and instructors. The motto behind e-learning is to learn anywhere at any time. This satisfies the needs of an increasing growth of learners who cannot attend traditional classroom lessons for various reasons, such as those who cannot find a specific class at their chosen college, who resides in remote areas, who work long hours, and who can only learn at or after work and those who simply choose to learn independently. E-learning makes it possible with the help of access to a computer and the Internet. E-learning provides a tremendous method of delivery of courses unbound by time or location that allows access to instruction from anywhere at any time.

E-learning generates massive amounts of data such as registration, interaction among student–platform–teachers, and learning resources. The large databases generated from e-learning require different platforms to be applied on the datasets for easy access. Cloud platform provides an easy implementation of these techniques to work on the distributed scenario. The key concept behind cloud computing is virtualization that is achieved by partitioning the physical server into multiple logical servers. Each logical server behaves like the actual physical server and can run independently. Cloud computing that offers different services has different advantages such as scalability and reliability which is an application that meets demand with peak resources due to an increase in learners count or growth of the data as well as releases resources at the fall of demand. The cloud computing architecture is loosely coupled, highly interoperable and may have several interfaces that separate service from implementation and application.

There are two models of cloud computing: the **deployment model** and **service model** (Figure 8.1). The deployment models describe the location and purpose of the cloud. There are three kinds of deployment models. First, public cloud that is externally owned (as provided by Google, Amazon, and Azure) offers access to external users on pay-as-use basis. Second, private cloud is built within enterprises and operated for the exclusive use of enterprises, and users within its enterprise can access without any charge. Third, hybrid cloud combines multiple clouds that can be private and public.

The service model tells about the types of services that a service provider offers. Service providers can provide services as (i) software as a service (SaaS), that provides an application to the client through web interfaces. It provides a complete operating environment for the user. Some well-known software services are Google Apps such as Gmail, Google Docs; Oracle On Demand and SQL Azure. (ii) Platform as a service (PaaS) provides platforms as virtual machines, operating systems, deployment frameworks, and control structures. Some significant PaaS providers are Google App Engine, GoGrid Cloud Center, Amazon Web Services, Force.com, Microsoft Azure, Heroku, and OpenShift (from Red Hat). (iii) Infrastructure as a service (IaaS) provides infrastructure services such as hardware, storage, network technology, and virtual machines [3]. IaaS provides hardware of the computer along with an operating system that handles the management of the hardware resources, thereby facilitating access to them efficiently. Instead of buying and installing the computing resources on the local computer, the clients can rent the resources. The services are billed according to the use, which is an added advantage for clients. The main significant IaaS providers are Amazon with

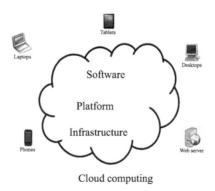

Figure 8.1   *Cloud computing*

Elastic Computer Cloud, Eucalyptus, GoGrid, FlexiScale, Linode, Google compute Engine, Windows Azure, and RackSpace.

8.4 Characteristics of cloud in e-learning

The characteristics of cloud computing are shown in Figure 8.2.

Resources pooling: Cloud provider servicers pull the computing resources and provide them to multiple customers in the multitenant model. Depending on the demand of customers, different physical and virtual resources are allocated or deallocated to the customers. The resources can then be modified according to the customer's demand.

On-demand self-service: The consumers will be able to use computing services as and when they need without the service provider requiring any human contact. The resources can include storage space, instances of virtual machines, databases, and so on. This helps users take better decisions on their needs and control.

Easy maintenance: Service providers help servers to regulate downtime that should be very less. It comes up with updates that make services better. It is compatible with the devices which make them perform faster.

Large network access: Another characteristic of cloud computing is large network access. Users can download to upload their data from cloud anywhere at any time with the help of computer/mobile connected to Internet.

Availability: Cloud computing automatically analyzes the data needed to support customers with an availability of resources as and when they need it. It also analyzes the storage space used by customers and allows buying extra storage space with at very low price if required.

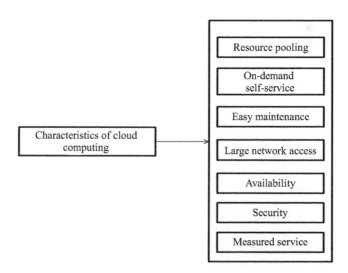

Figure 8.2 Characteristics of cloud computing

Security: Security is one of the important features of cloud computing. As the data stored in the cloud are spread on various servers and are out of customer control, there should be robust and efficient methods to provide security. It creates a snapshot of stored data to ensure security, so that data do not get lost even if one of the servers gets damaged. The data are stored inside the storage devices which nobody else can hack and use. The storage is swift and reliable.

Measured service: Resources used are getting monitored, measured, and reported to service providers. Users need to pay only for the resources they have utilized.

8.5   Cloud-based e-learning architecture

In the sense of e-learning, cloud computing architecture allows educators to access powerful computing resources that are delivered as a service for hosting and operating e-learning systems with minimal infrastructure and human resources investment. In addition to this, it is easy to keep an update of learning materials by teachers and can also provide multimedia content for a better understanding of concepts. They can develop e-learning contents using animations and simulations that are available on the cloud instead of purchasing and installing on a local computer. For example, they can make use of tools such as MySQL server, Tomcat, Apache.

E-learning system has been drawing people's attention at an exponential rate, with unparalleled increase in student numbers, educational materials, programs that can be provided, and opportunities made available by it. The major challenges it needs to tackle are handling dynamic concurrency requests, storage and communication requirements, and optimized resource computations.

Phankokkruad [4] proposed a cloud-based e-learning architecture with three layers, namely, hardware, platform, and application. The hardware layer includes upper level computation and storage capacity. This uses virtualization software technology that guarantees infrastructure's security and reliability. The middle layer that is server is web service. It offers training resources. The last layer is the application layer that provides the provision for an interface for students. E-learning systems can use benefit from cloud computing using (i) infrastructure layer in which infrastructures such as physical servers, storage, power supply and network components are provided; (ii) PaaS; and (iii) software as a service (SaaS) as shown in Figure 8.3.

Figure 8.3 illustrates the most common e-learning approaches on cloud. The bottom layer shows the cloud services provided by the cloud environment. It consists of IaaS that provides necessary computing resources, storage services, networks that manage the distribution of load among the virtual machines. The second layer is the e-learning approach that consists of learning contents, teaching methodologies, e-learning technologies, and evaluation strategies. The first layer shows the users that can be learners, instructors, or administrators who interact with the

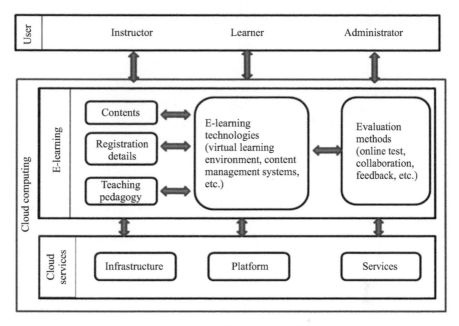

Figure 8.3   E-learning on cloud

cloud. Most of educational institutions are now willing to work in cloud archi-tecture as potential benefits are higher.

E-learning using big data on cloud computing is a new perception for higher education. However, according to [5] its employment involves different stages such as ensuring an incredible infrastructure, consisting of the software and hardware computing resources needed for e-learning activities, seeking a unique solution for the representation of training materials, given that most universities have their own LMS, privately cloud-based implementation, but it is a distinct one-foot solution, accessing tutorial content, and making full use of collaborative tools for university scholars and teachers involved in e-learning cloud project, and creating open-source cluster architectures for collecting and processing unstructured data. The volume of data may not always be the reason for the implementation of big data in education, rather the main challenge may be its complexity, with much of the available data unstructured, avoiding the use of traditional relational databases. Consequently, IT world launched a new wave of technology capable of solving the problem, such as the Hadoop and Spark applications.

Prominent cloud services such as Amazon Web Services, Google, Microsoft, Rackspace, and IBM have cloud-based big data stages for Hadoop and NoSQL databases [6]. The services running on these platforms get benefit of reduced costs, and enhanced flexibility prefers big data on cloud computing as a prime choice for many business organizations. The motivation to use cloud can get benefit of an abundance of access to knowledge and information shared between learners and teachers, which helps one to empower the scientific research.

8.6   Cloud computing service-oriented architecture for e-learning

Service-oriented architecture (SOA) emerges as a very agile and productive alternative to promote the creation and maintenance of learning platforms, regardless of technical changes and evolutions.

An e-learning platform based on service has the advantage that its parts can be produced in different languages and distributed on different servers. Thus, multiple platforms can use each component revealed as a service. Such an approach would save a lot of effort, cost, and implementation time. Using SOA in e-learning has many advantages. The services can be dynamically coupled, which makes adding or removing services simple. Systems communicate with simple common protocols and specifications. Also, service-based systems can be easily extendable. Mobile learning that focuses on the cloud will further increase stakeholders that include cloud service developers, developers of mobile learning applications, organizations of learners.

Web services can implement SOA. Web service is a software application which is defined by a URI that uses XML to define and discover its interface. Then Web Services Definition Languages encapsulates the Service Interface. It is subsequently published in the Universal Discovery Description Integration known as Broker or Registry. The service can then be transferred by forwarding the HTTP message [7]. The SOA handles three roles such as service provider who provides access to services. The second is the service registry which contains service descriptions provided by service providers, and finally service requesters who seek for the service and retrieve it using binding service descriptions from the registry.

In SOA-based e-learning, the service course developer or teacher plays the role of service provider. They deploy and publish the description of services to the service registry by hosting and controlling access to them. The service requester is the user or student who uses an e-learning platform. They work with service registry to find the optimal services that meet their specifications. The service registry is the repository that looks for the services requested by a service requester and sends them if available.

8.7   Big data in e-learning

8.7.1   *The need for big data in e-learning*

Big data is a major trend among various industries. In the e-learning area, these are the data collected from learner's activities while undertaking various courses on e-learning platforms. In these e-learning environments, users can interact and get knowledge from online groups such as online chats, instant messaging clients, discussion groups, and many LMSs like Adobe Captivate Prime, Moodle. Currently, learning ways such as Flipped Classroom [8] are majorly dependent on users' online things. Various frameworks [9] and designs have been developed for web-based LMSs to enhance the learning. Data generated from all of these activities can be used for analytic tasks, which, based on that analytics of the data, can help you improve learning materials, activities and even create a personalized e-learning experience. Due to the entry of low-cost devices in the smartphone industry, these smartphones have made learning content readily available everywhere with the help of Internet connection. Students can access their courses any time and continue their learning activities. A great deal of data is produced via student activities through LMSs that may be used in implementing these platforms, helping these students in tracking their progress, and generating insights to help them perform better.

Besides the data generated from student tasks, those are also generated by educational organizations. Big data generated from these educational institutions can assist enhancing students' results and performance. Also, it will facilitate a reduction in quitting rates at schools and colleges. Technical as well as non-technical organizations can employ predictive methods on all the data that are collected to know the outcomes of student activities in the future. Moreover, various organizations conduct different training programs. When an employee completes a module on some topic, additional data generated are also considered to be "big data." Big data is a concept that propounds a huge volume of data. Big data does not depict the giant volume of data being gathered through various resources merely. Also, it is characterized mainly by three Vs, namely, volume, variety, and value. From these web-based learning frameworks, big data is generated from various sources that are the LMS, discussion forums, questionnaire findings, social media polling, video lectures, etc.

The quantity of data generated from the earlier mentioned sources is so huge that traditional systems are not suitable to extract information from them. Because of the constraints of traditional techniques and the volume of data generated, these academic organizations have carried out research on "big data" [10,11] innovations to tackle the data. The data generated from all of these sources can be analyzed and organized in a way to help these institutions and e-learning professionals. When these data are harvested effectively, this information can bring many new possibilities for e-learning platforms, and further managing your data effectively can streamline your instructional strategies. The available information will enhance and empower online training, which also provides metrics to help improve the platforms. These analytics can give points on learning styles, preferences, and any areas where learners are getting stuck at and when and why they are getting stuck, by enabling them to provide their personalized experience to users. The latest data analysis systems will be able to track the user experience in a sense that we are not just tracking the answers marked by users but also can track where they might have gotten stuck and the amount of time they spent on a particular module. To analyze, such kind of behavior through the data generated by the user is used to study the behavior patterns as well as the trends of the industry by applying logical association within the dataset. In this way, both big data and analytics play a vital role that directly impacts these e-learning platforms.

8.8   Review on big data-based e-learning systems

The advent of big data technologies in e-learning systems has increased the decision making capability automatically by analyzing structured as well as unstructured data and hence no interference of human beings is needed by making use of machine learning algorithms. The research work in [27] incorporated the big data concepts into e-learning systems by devising a framework that ensures high-quality service education to online learners. The framework proposed by this paper used the advanced analytical and management approaches to get the maximum benefit. This framework is composed of three tiers, namely, e-learning, big data, and data visualization. E-learning tier makes use of learning management software, study materials and learner's profile, choices, etc. A big data layer provides the storage as well as analytical approaches for such voluminous data. Finally, results drawn from these data are envisaged in the third tier.

Another research study by [7] demonstrates the use of big data technologies that help us to deal with the problems faced by the distance learning education and improve the efficiency and of e-learning platforms. They devised a system that integrates big data concepts and tools in LMSs, namely, computing environment for human learning. Their system has four stages, namely, identification of e-learning sources, extracting useful data gathered from various identified sources, processing of this big data, and analyzing and interpreting the results.

A research study done by [12] has surveyed the 143 papers on e-learning using big data between 2010 and 2018. They have analyzed the papers along with three major categories, namely, institutional goals, problems faced in teaching and learning, and big data techniques used. The outcome found four major types of e-learning objectives that have an obvious prevalence of quality assurance. Further, four major educational problems such as learner's behavior modeling, wastage of resources, inapt course syllabus, teaching methodologies, and ethical issues were also highlighted. Many big data e-learning frameworks are facilitated with machine learning techniques that help one to enhance the value of education and also reduce the wastage of resources.

Recently, [10] suggested an integration of big data with cloud technology in e-learning systems to harness the computing power of big data technology and services provided by the cloud providers. It improves the quality of education delivered to e-learners all over the world. They also tackled how they deploy distributed e-learning systems by employing big data tools and their strategy to decentralize the data as well as parallelized computation in a cluster of nodes. Further, they designed and implemented a course recommendation system using machine learning approaches along with big data solutions using Moodle. The work was made possible by the ESTenLigne platform and Spark Framework.

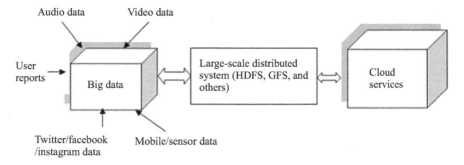

Figure 8.4   Association of big data and cloud computing

8.9   Association of big data and cloud computing

Big data contends with a bulky amount of data categorized as structured, semi-structured, or unstructured data. These data can be described in terms of its variety, velocity, value, variability, veracity, visual, or virtual. This big data can be stored using extract–transform–load tools such as Alooma in any chosen big data framework and analyzed for making useful decisions. Cloud computing on big data offers various kinds of benefits to e-professionals on a payment-basis according to the chosen model [16].

8.9.1   Infrastructure as a service (IaaS) in the public cloud

IaaS is a cheaper way to avail of services provided by the cloud. By utilizing this cloud service, people can access limitless storage and computational power for their applications. It is a very economical option for organizations in which cloud providers accept all the expenses involved in providing hardware-related requirements.

8.9.2   Platform as a service (PaaS) private cloud

PaaS companies integrate big data technologies with their services. It removes the necessity for tackling the complications while managing single software and hardware elements. Hence, this service provides the solution for terabytes of data which is a major concern.

8.9.3   Software as a service (SaaS) in a hybrid cloud

SaaS companies provide an excellent platform for conducting the analysis from the data obtained from social networking websites as well as e-newspapers, which is a very critical factor these days for companies in the analysis of their business. Association of big data and cloud computing is depicted using Figure 8.4.

Cloud computing in the previous picture is facilitated by the "as-a-service" pattern [11]. It does so by hiding various issues and complexities by making use of a scalable and flexible self-service application. Big data investigation is a vast and demanding strenuous task on infrastructure as the data are available in huge sizes with different speeds and different natures that current systems are not able to tackle. Subsequently, cloud computing innovation provides a flexible framework, which can be extended as per the requirements at that point. It additionally helps us to coordinate data from various sources and oversee remaining burdens. Big data together with the use of cloud gives an advantage to organizations by reducing ownership. Apache has decreased authorizing charges of big data that are needed to build and buy. With the use of the cloud, clients are allowed for big data preparing with less big data resources. Consequently, big data along with cloud is lowering the cost for large-scale business. Besides, the application that is deployed on a cloud, due to its availability and client control security, poses a challenging problem. Moreover, due to its open-source availability, big data frameworks such as Hadoop, Spark make the use of external control. Hence, these days private cloud solution is used, which is elastic and scalable.

Moreover, virtualization innovation is suitable for big data. Virtualized big data applications such as Hadoop have different advantages that are not open on physical infrastructure; however, it disentangles big data management. Big data and cloud processing point to the combination of various changes in the business that makes IT infrastructure and related applications increasingly unique, progressively extra, and progressively measured. Consequently, big data and cloud computing ventures depend vigorously on virtualization. Top cloud specialist coops are Amazon Web Service, Microsoft Azure, and Google Cloud Platform.

8.10   Use of big data and cloud technology for e-learning

Generally, the structure of e-learning frameworks is a multidisciplinary procedure grasping the teaching method, instructional plan, psychology, and numerous fields of engineering. The advancement of an e-learning framework requires characterizing three components in any event [17]. The first part is service architecture that oversees instructive materials, students, instructors, and guides. It is additionally answerable for the ceaseless evaluation of the whole learning process. Conceivable architectural models are LMSs or massive open online courses (MOOC). The second part is learning objects that speak to the instructive resources and intensely impact the structure of the whole equipment/programing framework. For example, multimedia-sound MOOCs may have severe data-transfer capacity and continuous requirements, hence requiring versatility properties. The last part is a strategy that it characterizes the connection between different kinds of users such as understudies and instructors and the stage. The philosophy drives the decision of the learning approach, and the most famous flavors are computer-supported collaborative learning, collaborative knowledge building, or learning using smart devices. These segments regularly make use of multimedia data such as recordings, pictures, sound to manage this assortment of gigantic data. Big data can keep the storage of these enormous quantities of an assortment of data. It permits presenting databases to save assorted data, for example, student profile, learning procedure, instructive assets, and log document. Consequently, big data technologies such as Hadoop and Spark (talked about in the past segment) permit the processing of data in a distributed fashion.

Utilizing progressed hugely parallel big data methods, web-based learning experts can right now evaluate continuously the viability of learning systems and recognize the requirements of every student to offer customized educational assets adjusted to each learning circumstance. It helps e-learning experts to identify topics, maybe, that ought to be calibrated inside the Internet adapting subject or topic. For instance, if numerous students are consuming an extensive effort to complete a specific module, it likely implies that the module should be amended to get it increasingly appropriate to the students. Students additionally get more benefitted from web-based learning websites/portals using new data technology as they can improve their aptitudes by enrolling on the web courses, going to online tests, following criticism from educators and can mail assignments as well as projects and ventures using websites to their instructors. Besides, it is additionally helpful for instructors as they can plan online tests for understudies, association and better assets for understudies through evaluation tests, content management, assignments, quizzes, and projects embraced by learners, likes/dislikes, and correspondence through the discussion on the web.

Albeit enormous information innovation had colossal advantages for e-learning experts, it needs more ways to an internal data warehouse or channels additional servers to consider the fast-growing analytics requirements. Even with the increase in technological advancements, it will be unable to keep up in the long run. Thus, cloud innovation comes into the picture image. Distributed computing has become another option and alluring model for delivering information and communication technology services with which most different advances might want to be joined with. Right now, "look into" has directed toward applications using cloud computing and its potential outcomes. Cloud computing is leading technologies of enthusiasm for e-learning due to different reasons. Educational organizations are utilizing e-learning frameworks where the utilization of PCs is progressively escalated for labs, computer centers, and servers. It gives free or minimal effort options in contrast to costly and selective tools. It also has advanced the development of online teaching with its "spend more as you use services." With this service, clients can utilize PC assets at any place, whenever, just on request and pay for the use thereof. This model is adjusted to different sizes of spending plans and necessities of clients. In this manner, by creating an utilization of Internet and PC systems, cloud computing was presented as a truly outstanding and conservative choice to the necessities of educational organizations. E-learning-based instructive foundations require complex assets for the cost of the colossal speculations of which they cannot bear. By utilizing cloud computing, the cloud framework is brought together to consuming organizations [18] that need to spend just for used assets. Subsequently, it lowers upkeep cost, equipment necessities, software, and hardware costs [19,20]. It permits one to educational organizations to expand their services as per their interest, offers boundless capacity limit with respect to the information and different applications, and gives information access from any place at any time to simply get to and check information. It results in bringing down the expense and a fewer data innovation representative for instructive foundations just as different associations. In addition, the idea of virtualization permits a quick substitution of an undermined cloud located server without significant expenses or harms. It is conceivable to incorporate another replica of a virtual machine; hence, the cloud downtime is required to be decreased generously. Additionally, it is amazingly hard for a programmer to recognize the location of the PC that stores needed information such as students' profiles, students' notes, results, and documents. Also, it is not easy to discover the PC one needs to damage to get information. Likewise, the information in the cloud is naturally copied to many locations, the crashing of PC in the cloud does not decimate the information, which will in any case be accessible from different PCs in the cloud. This kind of computing can consequently identify the hub crash and reject it without influencing the ordinary activity of the e-learning framework [21]. As the cloud speaks to an extraordinary section point for every scholarly client, the security amendments can be effectively examined and developed [22]. Big data together with cloud technology can be viewed as three-tier architecture as shown in Figure 8.5 [17,29].

The first-tier is a "framework" which is the lowest tier of the proposed approach. The framework tier is developed using the concept of virtualization, storage, and various resources of the network. This tier provides an abstraction for hardware sources, which is intended to give the adaptability requested by clients. Inside, the virtualization understands the computerized provisioning of various sources and improves the management of the framework. The second tier of this methodology is the "big data" tier. This tier comprises various technologies that provide the way for storing, processing, analyzing, and optimizing the data. These technologies include Hadoop, Apache Spark, Apache Kafka, cloud databases, distributed file system, and Hbase. This tier gives numerous tools and techniques supported by innovative technologies to learners to improve the productivity and unwavering quality of the e-learning platform. "E-learning" is the third tier that

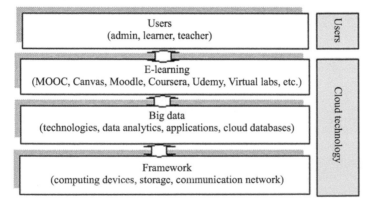

Figure 8.5   Use of big data and cloud technology in e-learning

likewise comprises a platform for instructing as well as learning and technologies for education. Data from this tier combines different data coming from the course/module content, professional's profile, feedback, course registrations, etc. These pieces of information facilitate to update course content to meet the requirement of the e-learning community and provide a more flexible educational environment globally. Lastly, the fourth tier is the "user" of this architecture. This tier can have three sorts of users as admin, learner, or teacher.

By and large, web-based applications for learning purpose are made up of software, hardware as well as a person. The hardware incorporates devices for communication and processing. E-learning is a form of software products such as LMS and MOOC. The persons are doers who utilize the framework to convey, store, and process data.

8.11   Casestudies on e-learning

Various case studies on e-learning [23–27] are described in following section.

- **Hampden-Sydney College, United States**

    In the United States, the Hampden-Sydney University hired "Canvas" as LMS. While being smaller entities, they wanted to extend the classroom beyond the standard four walls. They began their online programs using Canvas to satisfy the needs of the Faculty of intricate graders. It has "like solid gold" drag and drops feature Contact with the student information system of the school, which provides immediate alerts for tests and assignments to be done outside the specified class period. Support and authentication teams from Canvas helped us migrate data, files, and quizzes and feed content from the information system for the students.

- **Nepal Open University, Nepal**

    The Nepal Open University is a public university sponsored by the Nepal government with the goal of making higher education open to all people, including those living in remote areas and unable to attend university on a regular basis. They created a virtual world using the Moodle LMS, which includes the possibility of attending live lectures, sending assignments and taking assessments, offering both in-class and remote learners high-quality education. Through this learning environment, NOU offers about 40 online classes daily, representing over 80% of all university teaching.

- **Royal College of Art, London, UK**

    The Royal Art College, a specialized and research-intensive postgraduate university located in the heart of London, hires about 1,000 professionals from around the world—including teachers, academics, art and design practitioners, consultants and guest lecturers—to teach and cultivate students in about 30 academic programs. To meet the increased usability criteria and the demand for more visual systems, Moodle had to make the device update process smoother.

- **Jiffy Lube in Houston, TX, United States**

  It is a leading oil change company with a national network of more than 2,000 franchise-owned 100% locations and more than 20 million customers per year. It needed to train employees efficiently to provide quality customer service while reducing the expense of doing so across a fragmented regional franchise network. It created a virtual instructor-led training version of an online course using Blackboard's (LMS) partnership offerings, encouraging employees to help consumers understand specialty motor oil choices based on vehicle and driving trends. It also developed virtual training courses for almost 5,000 participants, using Blackboard Collaborate to promote virtual training and training.

- **"Ayandeh" in Iran**

  The application of Armangarayan company is to deliver e-learning materials to "Ayandeh" bank using the SaaS model through cloud computing. They reached a total cost reduction of 65%, and the cost of IT personnel and development teams dropped to 66% as they moved from conventional e-learning to e-learning cloud.

- **MOOCs: ALISON (Advanced Learning Interactive Systems Online) platform**

  MOOC are also very famous in the e-learning world. Higher-level technical institutions are presently offering online courses that can be chosen by students of the different institutions. It is getting very popular as MOOC courses are free. Students can register and attend virtual classrooms from the comfort of their homes or office and earn course completion certificates from reputed institutions. With time, a large number of MOOCs platforms have been designed either independently or in association with reputed organizations such as SWAYAM, Udacity, Coursera, WizIQ, and Edx. As of March 1, 2019, Alison has partners with 69 publishers giving many courses.

8.12   Case study of a cloud and big data-based Evaluation and Feedback Management System (EFMS) in e-learning

This case study belongs to an institute of higher education that uses Evaluation and Feedback Management System (EFMS) where an instructor places various quizzes, class tests, Lab evaluations for the e-learning system on the Google cloud. It provides flexibility for students and instructors to do things from anywhere at any time. The course outcome is evaluated through feedback form placed on the Google cloud, free cloud storage by Google which allows us to store up to 15-GB data free. This will help us to reduce the time for evaluating the forms, interaction time with students during activities like an evaluation of learning outcomes. Also using Google classrooms created by the instructors, students can easily upload their assignments, codes, class tests, etc. Hence e-learning is much more easily using Google cloud that is storing large amounts of data in various forms. The head of the institution/department as an admin also can view the statistics simply by enabling sharing on. For an institution with graduate and undergraduate engineering students with too many courses, these kinds of e-learning evaluations on Google cloud will improve the latency and storage as compared to manual evaluations.

In EFMS, the feedback evaluation for five courses was carried out as shown in Figure 8.6. The number of students who registered for the course and the number of students who have filled the feedback forms to evaluate the course outcomes of each course are shown in the Y-axis. The X-axis shows the course name (Figure 8.7).

The time taken to access the feedback evaluation form for each course is depicted in Figure 8.8. The Y-axis shows the feedback access time of each course in seconds and the X-axis denotes the course name. On average, the access time takes approximately 1.1 s which is much lesser than manual evaluation. Thus, by making use of cloud technology along with big data such as Google cloud in e-learning, organizations will substantially reduce the effort, time, and infrastructure cost.

8.13   Open research challenges

In spite of the fact that utilization of big data and cloud gives a few advantages in the e-learning framework, there are a few burdens that must be tended to before integrating e-learning into the academic system. Many resources in e-learning frameworks can be set up and relegated only for explicit errands with the goal that, while accepting high outstanding workload, the framework is necessary to include and arrange innovative sources of a similar sort, creating expense and management

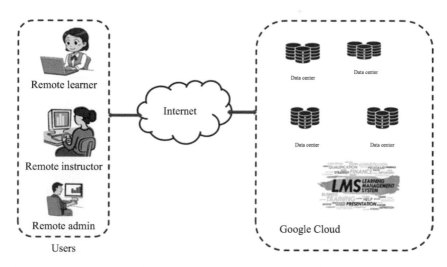

Figure 8.6   Framework for the cloud-based Evaluation and Feedback Management System (EFMS)

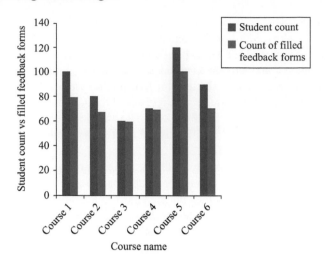

Figure 8.7   Student strength vs count of filled feedback form

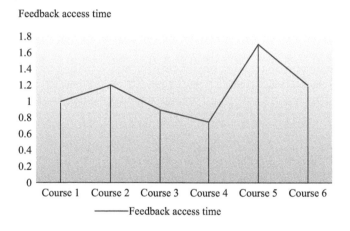

Figure 8.8   Feedback access time

of resources very costly [22]. This key issue is likewise identified with the proficient use of these resources. For instance, in an educational institution, computer
laboratories and servers are not fully utilized during the night. These systems are
also not used when the students go on vacations at the time of the semester/year.
Furthermore, such sources are on levels of popularity mostly toward the finish of a
semester, observing a powerful standard of utilization. Computers are held even if
they are doing any job. It leads to wastage of resources. Lastly, we should com-
prehend that it involves a cost incurred with computers or infrastructure upkeep, yet
that educational organizations must give the compensation for the site permitting,
deployment, and technical services [28]. At present, cloud specialist coops are

receiving proprietary APIs to develop their applications. Currently, cloud organizations, namely Amazon web services, Microsoft Azure, and Google cloud, are agreeing to proprietary APIs to develop various applications. As a result, sit is quite difficult and time-consuming if one wants to switch from one service provider to another. Some more challenges faced by e-learning community in moving big data to the cloud are as follows.

8.13.1   Limited control over security and privacy

Big data often contains valuable and personal details such as person's locations, debit/credit card information, account number, Aadhaar, permanent account number details. Cloud providers ensure that personal information is maintained secured and is of principal worth because data theft means severe punishment under various guidelines and a mottled organization name. As a result, these providers would lose customers as well as revenue. In fact, cloud providers have straight away power to manipulate your data, which can be a big organizational change and might create inconveniences for moving educational big data to the cloud. To tackle this problem, e-learning systems designers must ensure that they have checked the security protocols carefully. They must have also a clear understanding of the shared responsibility model of the cloud service providers so that roles and obligations are clear between two parties.

8.13.2   Limited control over compliance

Another important challenge is compliance. Although every Content Security Policy has to follow a definite line of agreement with different regulatory bodies such as HIPAA and PCI, full control is no longer with you on data's compliance requirements. Hence, one should be very much vigilant on cloud service providers whether it has robust compliance policies or not. We must go for service-level agreements for agreement to ensure compliance policies.

8.13.3   Limited control over institutional data

By adapting the e-learning system using cloud and big data, an institute is able to centralize the data that can be accessed any time anywhere. However, it also makes overdependence on cloud providers. For example, an organization might have integrated into an intricate network of services that can be shut down overnight in the case of any failure or whose costs can rise dramatically with no further notice. It leads to a very critical situation and should be dealt with necessarily.

8.13.4   Network dependency issues

Though cloud provides easy access to the data by different cloud service providers such as AWS and AZURE, yet data available to users are heavily dependent on network communication. These dependencies on the Internet connection make the system prone to service to service interruptions.

8.13.5   Latency problem

Although big data technologies along with cloud have facilitated traditional teaching and learning to online mode, cloud systems as well as big data approaches in e-learning still have the problem of latency faced by the e-learning community. Further, these systems still suffer from the problem of noise in the case of audio and video lectures in the cloud and big data-based e-learning systems.

Therefore, more research works are required to be carried out to design a variety of big data and cloud-based e-learning solutions, in improved revolutionary and proficient modes. Moreover, most of the recent big data and cloud-based e-learning systems are focusing only on posting and sharing more and more study kinds of stuff and teaching tasks, sooner than building and offering a built-in solution based on big data and cloud-based technology for e-learning industries.

8.14   Conclusion

The chief aim of the chapter is to give insights for innovative learning environments using big data as well as cloud technology for e-learning systems. The innovation of cloud and big data together builds to visualize novel and outcome-based learning methods, which maximizes the contentment of students to their requirements and circumstances. The e-learning system with big data provides huge learning content from the home itself, thus allowing reducing extra training or learning time and decreasing students' mental overload. It comprises the modified and flexible study materials as these learning systems take into account the different educational resources from various experts from all over the world. Moreover, cloud computing is facilitating the e-learning system with big data at affordable prices without acquiring much hardware as well as software. Finally, it uncovers the case studies using different e-learning software and also poses the challenges for the e-learning community.

8.15   Future work

In the future, researchers should focus on building solutions that have minimum latency, less costly, and dealing with privacy and security. Moreover, optimized intelligent techniques can be employed to deal with a vast amount of data over the cloud.

References

[1]   Jolliffe A, Ritter J, and Stevens D. The online learning handbook: Developing and using web-based learning. Routledge; 2012.
[2]   Mell P and Grance T. The NIST definition of cloud computing; 2011.
[3]   Judith SH. Cloud computing for dummies. John Wiley & Sons; 2019.

[4]   Phankokkruad M. Implement of cloud computing for e-learning system. In: 2012 International Conference on Computer & Information Science (ICCIS) 2012 Jun 12 (Vol. 1, pp. 7–11). IEEE. Tucker B. The Flipped Classroom-Education Next: Education Next.

[5]   https://media.featuredcustomers.com/CustomerCaseStudy.document/Hampden-Sydney_College.pdf.

[6]   https://moodle.com/news/category/case-studies/.

[7]   Birjali M, Beni-Hssane A, and Erritali M. Learning with big data technology: The future of education. In: International Afro-European Conference for Industrial Advancement 2016 Nov 21 (pp. 209–217). Springer, Cham.

[8]   Raghunathan S and Kaur A. Assessment of online interaction pattern using the Q-4R framework. In: The International Lifelong Learning Conference 2011.

[9]   Ray S. Big data in education. Gravity, the Great Lakes Magazine. 2013:8–10.

[10]   Dahdouh K, Dakkak A, Oughdir L, and Ibriz A. Improving online education using big data technologies. In: The Role of Technology in Education 2020 Mar 11. IntechOpen.

[11]   Verma A. Big data and cloud computing – A perfect combination, 2019, July 21 https://www.whizlabs.com/blog/big-data-and-cloud-computing/.

[12]   Quadir B, Chen NS, and Isaias P. Analyzing the educational goals, problems and techniques used in educational big data research from 2010 to 2018. Interactive Learning Environments. 2020;29:1–7.

[13]   Dahdouh K, Dakkak A, Oughdir L, and Ibriz A. Improving online education using big data technologies. In: The Role of Technology in Education 2020 Mar 11. IntechOpen.

[14]   Goyal M, Yadav D, and Choubey A. E-learning: Current state of art and future prospects. International Journal of Computer Science Issues (IJCSI). 2012;9(3):490.

[15]   Goyal M, Krishnamurthi R, Gupta G, and Sharma A. Intelligent techniques for prediction of engineering colleges after XII. International Journal of Swarm Intelligence Research (IJSIR). 2020;11(1):24–43.

[16]   Masud MA and Huang X. ESaaS: A new education software model in E-learning systems. In: International Conference on Information and Management Engineering 2011 Sep 17 (pp. 468–475). Springer, Berlin, Heidelberg.

[17]   Vaughan J. Big data and cloud computing look for bigger foothold in enterprises, 2014 http://searchdatamanagement.techtarget.com//Big-dataand-cloud-computing-look-for-bigger-foothold-in-enterprises.

[18]   Masud MA and Huang X. An e-learning system architecture based on cloud computing. System. 2012;10(11):255–259.

[19]   Ouf S and Nasr M. Business intelligence in the cloud. In: 2011 IEEE 3rd International Conference on Communication Software and Networks 2011 May 27 (pp. 650–655). IEEE.

[20]   Benta D, Bologa G, and Dzitac I. E-learning platforms in higher education. Case study. In: ITQM 2014 Jan 1 (pp. 1170–1176).

[21] Wheeler B and Waggener S. Above-campus services: Shaping the promise of cloud computing for higher education. EDUCAUSE Review. 2009;44 (6):52–67.

[22] Riahi G. E-learning systems based on cloud computing: A review. In: SCSE 2015 Sep (pp. 352–359).

[23] https://media.featuredcustomers.com/CustomerCaseStudy.document/blackboard_ jiffy-lube_210959.pdf.

[24] Roveicy MR and Bidgoli AM. Migrating from conventional E-learning to cloud-based E-learning: A case study of Armangarayan Co. In: Computer Science On-line Conference 2017 Apr 26 (pp. 62–67). Springer, Cham.

[25] ur Rehman I, Bano S, and Mehraj M. MOOCS: A case study of ALISON platform. Library Philosophy and Practice. 2019;1–8.

[26] Brown A, Johnston S, and Kelly K. Using service-oriented architecture and component-based development to build web service applications. Rational Software Corporation. 2002;6:1–6.

[27] Udupi PK, Malali P, and Noronha H. Big data integration for transition from e-learning to smart learning framework. In: 2016 3rd MEC International Conference on Big Data and Smart City (ICBDSC) 2016 Mar 15 (pp. 1–4). IEEE.

[28] Masud MA and Huang X. An e-learning system architecture based on cloud computing. System. 2012;10(11):255–259.

[29] Dahdouh K, Dakkak A, Oughdir L, and Messaoudi F. Big data for online learning systems. Education and Information Technologies. 2018;23 (6):2783–2800.

[30] Velte AT, Velte TJ, Elsenpeter RC, and Elsenpeter RC. Cloud computing: A practical approach. New York: McGraw-Hill; 2010.

Chapter 9

E-learning through virtual laboratory environment: developing of IoT workshop course based on Node-RED

*Rajalakshmi Krishnamurthi[1] and
Dhanalekshmi Gopinathan[1]*

At present, there are tremendous growth and opportunities in the field of the "Internet of Things" (IoT). Further, various application systems, such as smart city, smart grid, smart healthcare system, smart transportation, require the adaptation of IoT within it to enhance the smartness of such systems. In addition, several industrial organizations are focusing on the generation of revenues out of these IoT-based services. Hence, in this perspective, there is an extensive demand for human knowledge power on IoT technologies. There exists an increase in demand for professionals in IoT technology. Need for preparing engineering graduates to face this demand of IoT technology is the key focuses of educational institutions. In the revised course curriculums, IoT specialized courses remain the main focuses to be framed and offered to students. This chapter discusses one such course named IoT workshop, which was offered to the sixth semester students of undergraduate engineering. This chapter presents the requirements of offering IoT course, Node-RED as programming environment, course contents delivered, learning outcomes, course assessments, projects, and results achieved through this course by students.

9.1 Introduction

According to Gartner's report, it can be envisaged that more than 26 billion individual things will be connected by 2020 through Internet [1]. Further, based on the concept IoT, a huge amount of data are generating from these things. In 2017, Capgemini Asia Pacific Wealth Report predicted that particularly Asia Pacific countries would contribute more toward the IoT growth with the compound annual growth rate of around 33.3%, expected by 2020 [2]. This report alarms the requirement for preparing future brainpower toward the increasing demand for IoT

[1]Department of Computing Science and Engineering, Jaypee Institute of Information Technology, Noida, India

professionals. Hence, in this regard, the department of computer science and engineering at Jaypee Institute of Information Technology (JIIT) has introduced several new courses based on IoT concepts in its graduate and undergraduate engineering curriculums. JIIT always provides a platform to be ahead and meets the futuristic demand in the computer science and engineering field. Further, the students are provided with opportunities and equipped with the current state of technologies to set their career growth and prepared for industrial jobs.

There are four basic building blocks of IoT, namely, edge systems, connecting systems, storage systems, and service systems. At the department of computer science education (CSE), students are exposed to certain-level basic concepts of IoT. The courses, namely, computer organization, computer networks, embedded systems, database systems, and web technology, already target several basic IoT concepts. Hence, the curriculum is providing support to introduce new IoT technology-based courses for engineering graduates. As IoT is an emerging field, only a limited number of literature are available about IoT-based curriculum and courses at the university level. This chapter provides insight into how IoT-based course was carried out at JIIT.

Authors [3,4] discussed the IoT course based on the SenseBoard hardware platform. The course involves SENSE visual programming language as support for developing IoT-based applications. The teaching mode of this course incorporates video lectures for elaborating basic IoT practical exercises. Further, the students are exposed to hands-on practice using wireless sensors, actuators, and different computing devices. The offline mode of teacher–student interaction offers students outside classroom assistance. In research papers [5,6], the IoT course was opened as elective for undergraduate engineering students of Computer Science during the eighth semester. The course content, activities involved throughout the learning process, and various levels of IoT course delivery and knowledge delivery mechanism are discussed by the authors in detail. Authors [7,8] discussed the impact of introducing IoT coursed for liberal arts students. The basic goal of the course is to allow students to explore the IoT opportunities, identify real-life problems, and synthesize solutions through IoT technology. The course objectives, course contents, and teaching methodology are elaborated in detail. In [9–11], the authors discussed the project ideas generated by undergraduate students through IoT project-based course. The students are evaluated on the basis of the prototype developed for IoT projects, a methodology adopted, the performance achieved, and cost-effectiveness.

The key contributions of this chapter are as follows:

1. Identify and address the need for IoT course at the engineering undergraduate level.
2. Propose visual programming language, Node-RED, based learning methodology for IoT workshop.
3. Design course syllabus for IoT workshop for undergraduate students.
4. Discuss the teaching methodology, assessment techniques for IoT workshop.
5. Discuss learning outcomes for IoT workshop after course work completion.

The remainder of the chapter has the following sections. Section 9.2 discusses the importance of e-learning through virtual programming and laboratory. Section 9.3 addresses the building blocks of IoT; Section 9.4 discusses the visual programming language tool, Node-RED. Section 9.5 discusses the IoT workshop course information, contact hours, student details, foundation courses, and assessment criteria. Section 9.6 discusses the teaching methodology of the IoT workshop course. Section 9.7 discusses the course content, learning outcomes, sample laboratory exercises, project ideas, and the feedback for the course.

9.2 Virtual laboratory

E-learning engineering courses need to focus on two important aspects. The first one is that whether hands-on laboratory sessions are achieved using an online platform, and the second is how to ensure whether the online program equips the graduate students with the desired skill to begin professional practice to enter the industry. Hence, engineering courses should satisfy certain requirements like how best they can provide practical knowledge through laboratory exercises when those are offered as distance mode [12,13].

A virtual laboratory in engineering courses offers students easy access to the applications at any time and from any computing setting. This interactive learning stimulates deeper thinking by providing content with demonstrations, simulations, and hands-on exercises to make active learning. According to the Ministry of Human Resource Development, India [14], the objective of the virtual labs must include the following: (i) provide remote access to labs in interdisciplinary courses in computer science and engineering for undergraduate level, graduate level, and research scholars; (ii) invoke the enthusiasm and curiosity in students to conduct the experiments that help them to learn the concepts from basic to advanced level through the remote experimentation; (iii) use the learning management system (LMS) to incorporate the virtual labs where students should be able to gain access to various tools for learning in addition to web resources, video lectures, and simulations; (iv) share expensive equipment and services; otherwise, it would be accessible to a small number of users due to time limitations and geographic distances.

Virtual labs allow students to participate and engage in interaction-based classes where they can conduct and evaluate their own experiments, learn using virtual objects and apparatuses. Using virtual labs offers students the ability to learn critical thinking, creative skills, and teamwork skills, all of which are highly regarded in today's job market. Various organizations and large-scale international projects have developed various virtual laboratories, and several of these are available as open-source applications.

Virtual laboratories use an easy-to-use graphical user interface (GUI) to provide access to a real device with all or most of its operating characteristics. The use of distant access to educational services has been explored in distance education [15,16].

It has advantages from the faculty and student point of view. From faculty viewpoint, a virtual or remote laboratory provides the possibility of getting away from the physical constraints of a conventional laboratory and making the experiments accessible to a broader student audience. Since both of these laboratories include information and communication technology, the students' activity can be monitored and statistics collected that can be used to obtain valuable feedback on the efficacy of a given virtual or remote laboratory, which can be used to identify problems with given content. The most enticing advantage from the students' viewpoint is the freedom to perform the experiment in a self-paced way, and that the lab is accessible from anywhere at any time. Many organizations, universities, and even industry leaders have established their own virtual laboratories, covering a very wide range of disciplines [17–19].

While setting up a virtual laboratory environment (VLE), the preliminary requirement to design a VLE is the GUI at front-end. The main user interface must be consistent and intuitive, including the teacher administration interface and the student–user interface. During the experiment, the second necessity, which comes from the cognitive perspective, is to reduce the required context changes, i.e., to display all relevant and related materials on a single interface. Nowadays, most students use smartphones and tablets primarily to gain access to online services instead of desktop and laptop computers, and these devices need to be supported. At the backend, VLE should have a Lab manager (LM) and Lab repository (LR). The LM provides a web server service and authenticates the clients. It is also responsible to deploy, manage, and monitor the virtual lab instances. The LR is the repository that stores all the contents, descriptions, source code or sample files of the simulation, and the virtual lab templates.

The key issue is whether the use of a virtual laboratory helps students. That is, do students learn something by using the virtual lab (as opposed to learning from lectures only)? To evaluate this, there should be some assessment methodology that distinguishes between lecturing and learning in the laboratory. It should quantify student learning in lectures and labs. The knowledge achieved by the students is assessed by participating in the process of acquiring and adding information, including critical thought, and connecting their current knowledge to the new collection of knowledge they expect to learn. The knowledge acquisition by the students is validated from the perspective of the students after it is produced and captured. The use of these virtual laboratories allows students to participate in higher-order thought and helps teach and transfer qualitative information, internal/external mechanisms/processes, working methods and procedures, and engineering equipment information.

CSE is a field where special effort is needed to prepare the appropriate virtual laboratory for it. Here, the theoretical component deals with the theory and knowledge required for the courses and practical part that concerns the experience acquired by the learner through practical sessions. This part requires virtual lab support and can use computer applications (e.g., language compiler programming, UML drawing, UNIX environment). Hence, the virtual lab must include the development tools into the LMS framework using different integration approaches.

These strategies can provide the students from anywhere and at any time with the accessibility facility of the LMS devices. The two integration approaches generally followed to prepare virtual labs are web-based and service-oriented architecture (SOA) approaches. The web-based approach uses a cloud-based application platform to prepare software. It creates the application software and provides it to LMS as a web application. SOA supports the integration of software applications by reusing existing platforms and languages that utilize and adopt an existing legacy systems [20]. Like web applications, several LMSs are usually implemented following the client/server approach [21].

Currently, Moodle is the most popular open-source LMS. It is a learning management system that stands for the dynamic learning environment of modular object-oriented learning. Under General Public Licenses (GNU), it is an open-source program. The advantages of being an open-source are to promote its production and maintenance according to the needs of the customers. Moodle includes hundreds of general plugins that are created by many developers to enhance Moodle's functionality. Such resources include web, talk, quiz software, wiki, and much more. One of the plugins related to CSE is the Virtual Programming Lab [22]. It is a compiler that helps the students to compile and apply the assignments through different programming languages. This software plugin tool forms part of the activity module and is built with the same Moodle programming language. The key advantages for students of virtual laboratories are listed as follows:

- Students who are absent during regular college hours will make up learning from their home. Virtual laboratories provide access from home to the web-based resource and perform remote practical and experimentations with realistic features.
- Students have the opportunity to repeat experiments several times to improve the effectiveness and deeper comprehension. In addition, step-by-step wizards assist the students to easily conduct experiments.
- Modern looking components offer a true laboratory feel to the learners.
- By modifying various variables or parameters, the students can understand more comprehensive experiments.
- The design and development of new solutions using a virtual laboratory can easily solve a wide range of complex problems.
- Available 24×7, students can do their own laboratory work as planned.
- Learners are able to achieve end-user satisfaction by using the VLE.

9.3 Building blocks of IoT

The objective of IoT is to interconnect several autonomous heterogeneous things among each other independent of platform used, communication, and connecting environment [23]. These factors are essential to provide smart communication and efficient computing between real-world things and digital computing devices. IoT-based course is approached in three levels, namely, edge level, connectivity level, and service level, as depicted in Figure 9.1.

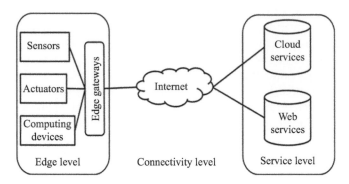

Figure 9.1   Basic architecture of IoT

9.3.1   Edge level

1. Sensors: The objective of sensors is to measure the surrounding environment based on standard metrics such as performance, energy consumption, and applications. The sensors are biological or no hardware-based sensors. Some examples for sensors are proximity sensors, light sensors, smoke detectors, pressure sensors, and touch sensors. The physical features that are sensed include light intensity, pressure movement, acceleration, position, proximity, and humidity. For example, location-based services use the location sensors, like a global positioning system to obtain the position of the object. Further, the vital signals of the body or biological signals can be sensed through sensors such as blood pressure monitor, heart rate monitor, muscle tension, neural activity monitors.

2. Computing devices: The sensed data from the physical world are raw electrical signals that are converted into some counts based on metrics. The gathered raw data from different sensors are needed to be analyzed and processed to obtain the intended services of the applications. Some of the computing devices are autonomous and have the capability to perform computations. Such devices are embedded systems, microprocessor boards, microcontrollers, and external interface devices. Further, the raw data need to be aggregated, validated and free from the data replications, data outliers, and missing data. Moreover, the relevance of the data also is estimated by these computing devices. Several critical factors lead to concern about computing devices. Basically, these computing devices are limited in resources such as memory, processor, and battery power [24].

9.3.2   Connectivity level

1. API: Application program interface (API) consists of several functionalities that offer services to application users. Further, the APIs involved in data interrogation and validation, obtained through different sensors and hardware. Then, the APIs forward these data to the higher-level functioning modules of software for further data-processing according to the requirements.

2. Edge gateway: The edge gateway incorporates technology such as Wi-Fi or 4G to get connected to the resource-rich remote servers through the Internet. Edge gateways involve routers, gateways, switches, and access points. These edge gateways connect the end systems such as sensors, computing devices with service modules through Internet networking.

9.3.3 Communications level

1. Wired and wireless communication: In this communication layer, the different IoT end devices are connected to the remote cloud server through networking using wired or wireless transmission medium. For example, in a personal area network, IoT devices are connected through serial communication, USB for connection to the computing devices, and low-range wireless frequencies. The most popular method of connecting IoT devices with remote servers is through Wi-Fi or LTE/4G networks.
2. Networking protocols and standards: IoT ecosystem consists of a hetero-geneous set of network standards and protocols. Particularly, to operate at the personal area network level, the communicating protocol includes Bluetooth, ZigBee, and 6LoWPAN. The applications layer protocols such as Message Queuing Telemetry Transport (MQTT), CoAP, and REST are also needed to address resource-constrained computing devices. IoT protocol stack includes a physical layer, medium access layer, network layer, session layer, application layer, security, and management layer [25].

9.3.4 Service level

1. Cloud services: IoT devices are resource constraints in terms of energy, sto-rage, memory, and computing capacity. To overcome resource constraints, these resources are obtained through remote cloud systems. The connectivity to the remote cloud servers and utilizing the cloud resources are carried out at the service level. The cloud provides three types of services, namely, platform, infrastructure, and software.
2. Data analytics: The data gathered from the sensors are then stored at the remote cloud server. The data on the cloud system are further processed to meet the requirements of the IoT applications. Some of the methods are mining, ana-lyzing, and then processing data. Particularly, specialized software is used for performing these functions. Artificial intelligence and machine learning tech-niques are used to bring out the required context as output.

9.4 Node-RED tool

Node-RED was developed by IBM based on visual programming language. It provides a GUI for programming platforms to develop a variety of IoT-based applications. Several hardware developer boards can be an interface to the Node-RED through a plug and play method. Arduino, Raspberry Pi, Beagle

Bone are a few examples of popular developer boards that can be interfaced with the Node-RED. It also supports a wide collection of internal APIs, namely, graphical user APIs, Storage APIs, Shell Prompt APIs, and runtime APIs. The platform also supports a wide range of external APIs and can be imported through inbuilt dashboard features. Further, the Node-RED software supports different data-handling formats such as XML, EXI, JavaScript, JSON, HTTP, and CSV. The various patches, IoT applications, and developer contributions are available through the GitHub Repository available at http://github/node-red/node-red.

9.4.1   Why Node-RED?

In [4], the author has elaborated 13 different visual programming language based IoT tools. According to this report, the Node-RED software is outperforming and providing a convenient way of understanding and visualizing the IoT modules.

The major advantages of using Node-RED:

1. Using flows to represent the logic programming, easy for the beginners to visualize the application basic logics.
2. Users can visualize the interaction among various logical nodes used in IoT applications.
3. Users need not worry about syntax error, as logical modules already available in the form of nodes.
4. Ease of code portability into hardware components through simple USB, or interfacing connectivity.
5. Reduces the programming time to develop IoT application.
6. Internet-based connectivity protocol, remote cloud services, and web service can be easily integrated with Node-RED.
7. Advanced APIs such as RESTFUL, MQTT, Web socket, XML, and JSON are readily available through a Node-RED platform.

9.4.2   Installation of Node-RED

The Node-RED is installed on top of the Node JS platform. JavaScript is used as programming languages in Node-RED. The Node-RED consists of two basic building components, namely, nodes and flow, as depicted in Figure 9.2. Nodes are prebuilt APIs available through the dashboard that can be installed or upgrade through third party API providers. The web socket client for Node-RED is provided at http://localhost:1880. The various application layer protocols such as MQTT, REST, CoAP, and Web sockets can also be performed using a Node-RED platform. Here, the data processing can be done through various functional nodes. The user has to simply drag and drop off these function nodes into the flow interface. The user-defined functions can also be created using JavaScript and integrated with existing flows. Also, JavaScript supports various data representations such as CSV, JSON, and XML. The Node-RED allows the user flow to be imported and exported through manage palette interface.

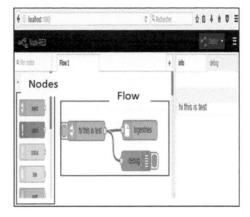

Figure 9.2   Graphical user interface of Node-RED and its components

9.5   IoT workshop

1. Course information: The IoT workshop is a laboratory and project-based course of two credits. This course offers no lecture and tutorial contact hours. But a practical laboratory has four contact hours. The contact hours per week are 4 for students. The faculty–student ratio is maintained at 1:15. Every individual student is provided with a desktop computer with NodeJS, Node-RED, and Internet to perform their laboratory exercises. There are two practical classes per week. Each class is for 2 h. Total 4 contact hours are provided for the students to meet with instructors.

2. Students: IoT workshop was offered to students in the sixth semester of undergraduate engineering degree. The course was offered as elective to students of three different departments, namely, computer science, information technology, and electronics and communication departments. The total number of students registered for this course is 64. Out of that CSE students are of 23 and ECE students are of 38 in number, and IT are of 3 students.

3. Foundation courses: IoT workshop is an introductory course, where the main objective is to provide students with hands-on experience about IoT technology. Therefore, there was no strict prerequisite required for opting for this course. However, some of the core compulsory courses such as computer networks, operating systems, database systems, and computer organizations are assumed to be completed by the students before opting for the IoT workshop course.

4. Assessment criteria: The assessment criteria for IoT workshop consist of three parts. The first criteria are based on lab tests conducted during lab hours. Each test is 20% of the total marks. The lab tests target to assess the programming skill of the students based on IoT exercises with a stipulated period. The second assessment is continuous evaluation throughout the semester. The

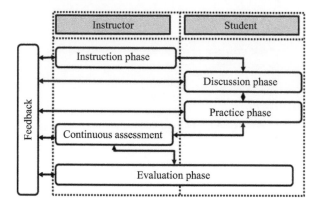

Figure 9.3　Methodology for teaching in IoT workshop course

continuous assessment is conducted by 35% of total marks. The third assessment is based on the everyday performance of registered students in IoT workshop course. This is based on the attendance records of individual students, student's attentiveness, and interactions with the instructor during the laboratory. The day-to-day (D2D) assessment is assigned for 25% of total marks.

9.6　Teaching methodology

The teaching methodology of IoT workshop course is divided into five phases: instruction phase, discussion, practice, continuous assessment, and evaluation phase (Figure 9.3). The main objective of teaching methodology is to kindle and evaluate the critical thinking ability of students [12,26].

Instruction phase: Through this instruction phase, the course instructor will describe and elaborate on IoT topics planned for that week. The topics are discussed using a blackboard, and a practical demo of the IoT experiments is given. Most of this phase is a one-way lecture of the instructor to the students. Every week, a new set of assignments is posted for teaching to the students.

Discussion phase: The objective of this discussion phase is to perform group interaction between instructor of IoT workshop and students. Some of the activities are mentoring students and doubt clearing, and clarification of solution approaches for given problems to solve. In this, mentors (final year students) actively participate to guide these students. Mostly, the instruction phase and discussion phase are interleaved and more interactive.

Practice phase: The students are provided with a set of practical exercises to be carried out based on the practice demo of the topic discussed earlier in the instruction phase. Then, in the practice phase, students have to exhibit more creativity. The problem-solving and thinking ability of students are harnessed during this phase.

Continuous assessment: The objectives of the continuous assessment are to evaluate the student level of IoT concept understanding, creativity in developing a solution for IoT problems, the capacity of problem-solving, and critical, lateral thinking ability of students. The assessment is carried out at the end of each laboratory session of the IoT workshop.

Evaluation phase: The objective of the evaluation phase is to analyze the student's performance within a confined test duration to solve the given practical IoT problem beyond laboratory exercises. The evaluation phase has defined the time frame for solving the posed questions. The question will be based on the syllabus covered so far until the evaluation phase. Consequently, two such evaluations were conducted during a semester, namely, Lab Test 1 and Lab Test 2. The time duration for these tests is typically 45 min. Within this duration, students must understand and program the solution.

9.7   Course details

1. Course outline: The laboratory-based IoT workshop course focuses on three levels of IoT systems, namely, edge systems, connectivity and communication systems, and service systems. Accordingly, the following five components constitute the IoT workshop course as discussed in detail:
    (i)   Formulate and deploy Java scripts suing inbuilt functional nodes on Node-RED: The first part focuses on introducing the IoT stack and hand-on experience for using Node-RED. The students are encouraged to write basic JavaScript on Node-RED platforms using existing functional nodes. Also, flow-based programming is introduced.
    (ii) Creation of user-defined functional nodes: Next, students are taught to create user-defined functional nodes and produce API node.js customization. This part enhances the students toward programming skills on JavaScript and for IoT application development.
    (iii) Flow generation using Node-RED and FRED: This part focuses on connectivity to the cloud through Internet communication. The students are explained about using cloud-based utilities such as platform, infrastructure, and software services. In this sense, the students learn about data gathering from IoT sensor devices, data streaming into the cloud system, and finally data analysis for the decision-making based on stored data in cloud.
    (iv) Hands-on experiment for using dashboard-based user interfaces and tool kit for data analysis: In the fourth part, the various data analysis methods and the data visualization support of Node-RED are explored. The data analysis techniques such as statistical methods (average, standard deviance, variance, covariance, and regression) and convenience methods (sequential, reciprocation, summation, and product, minimum, and maximum). Also, a random number functionalities such as exponential distribution, normal distribution, and uniform distribution are covered.

Further, the string-handling functions (concatenate, split, palindrome, reverse, letter case, string matching, size, and clear) are also introduced. Various visualization nodes are explored using interactive dashboard widgets such as gauge, graph plot, accelerometer, sliders, charts, and text.

(v)   Publish/subscribe in MQTT protocol using MQTT: In this part, the MQTT protocol is introduced. Sending multiple inputs and multiple outputs to the various IoT devices are explained. Hive-based MQTT web socket client is used for the creation of MQTT broker http://www. hivemq.com/demos/websocket-client/.

(vi)   Traffic flow analysis using HTTP, TCP, and UDP protocol for IoT applications: Internet application protocols such as HTTP (request and response), web socket, RESTful APIs, twitter API, and SMTP are introduced to the students. The laboratory exercises are developed in storing and extracting the data from remote servers using these application layer protocols. Further, file formats such as JSON, XML, and CSV are introduced.

Further, the students of IoT workshop course are encouraged to do IoT projects as their minor project course of five credits. This IoT project is to develop a prototype of any IoT system applied in the real world, by them based on skills gained in IoT workshop course.

2. Learning outcomes: Upon the completion of the course, the students will be able to

(i)   set up and install Node.js and Node-RED as an IDE platform for IoT application development;

(ii)   demonstrate I/O nodes, flows, third party palettes, import/export of flows in Node-RED, and interconnection with IoT boards such as Raspberry Pi, Arduino;

(iii) develop java scripts for user-defined functional nodes and deploy it in Node-Red flows;

(iv)   design and develop UI modules for peripheral sensors and devices that can be controlled through smartphones and web pages;

(v)   implement MQTT brokers for publish/subscribe between IoT sensors and computing devices;

(vi)   design and develop HTTP, TCP, and UDP traffic flow, web sockets for IoT applications.

3. Sample exercises: Create Node-RED Flow to check when the temperature is (i) greater than 35 then send "VERY HOT TEMP" message into your tweet account; (ii) less than 12 then send "COLD TEMP" message into your tweet account; (iii) temperature between 12 and 25 then send "PLEASANT TEMP" message into your tweet account.

Solution approach to sample problem in Node-RED:

Step 1: Creating a flow of project using Node-RED

Step 2: Deploying JavaScript-based Node-RED flow

Step 3: Debugging the project flow

Step 4: Connecting twitter API
Step 5: Performing data analysis based on data stream fetched from sensors
Step 6: View output results in twitter API.

4. Feedback process: The feedback about the delivery and outcomes of the IoT workshop course is obtained from registered students during the last week of the semester. The feedback rubric is designed on 10 components.

9.8 Experiment and result discussion

1. Analysis of attendance maintained by students: The attendance is marked by the instructor on the web kiosk for every contact hour. That is taken twice in every week, corresponding to two laboratory classes per week. Table 9.1 shows the statistic of attendance for a total of 64 registered students in IoT workshop course. The average attendance recorded was 82% for the entire semester. The breakup of student attendance at various levels is set at 60%, 70%, 80%, and 90%.
2. Analysis of marks obtained by students out of evaluation: For the evaluation purpose, six components are considered, namely, Test 1, Test 2, evaluation (Eval) 1, Eval 2, D2D marks, and marks for attendance. The statistic of performance based on various components is depicted in Table 9.2. It is observed that the average score of the IoT workshop course is obtained as ~56%. Also, students performed well in Test 2 conducted in the later part of the semester. Also, the score for attendance is estimated at 10.8 out of 15 depicts the good interest of students within the IoT course.
3. Analysis of grades obtained by IoT workshop students: The components for analyzing the grades obtained by the students for IoT workshop courses are depicted in Table 9.3. The components are upper boundary value, lower boundary value, eligible grade, and a number of students obtained that particular grade.

    The normal distribution between grades and the number of students is plotted in Figure 9.4. The standard deviation was achieved as 15.7 and average as 56.94, and maximum scored at 91, the minimum score obtained as 32.
4. Analysis of feedback: Total 10 items are considered for student feedback analysis as follows:

Table 9.1   Attendance analysis of IoT workshop course

Boundary value for attendance	No. of students (out of 64 total students)
Less than 60%	0
Less than 70%	3
Less than 80%	6
Less than 90%	11

Table 9.2   *Performance of students*

Components	Average marks	Maximum marks
Test 1	7.4	20
Test 2	12.63	20
Eval 1	7.3	15
Eval 2	9	15
D2D	8.81	15
Attendance	10.8	15
Total	*55.94*	*100*

Table 9.3   *Grades obtained by IoT workshop students*

Upper boundary values	Lower boundary values	Grade	No. of students
100	80	A+	4
79	70	A	7
69	60	B+	12
59	50	B	20
49	43	C+	13
42	37	C	5
36	30	D	3
29	0	F	0

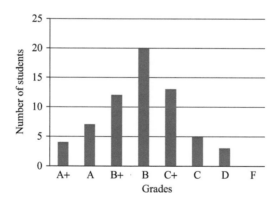

Figure 9.4   *Bar chart of grade distribution*

(i)   time management and regularity;
(ii)   outside laboratory work to support and guidance;
(iii) awareness of safety and risk among students;
(iv)   delivery of contents about laboratory exercises;
(v)   support to ask questions and opinions by students;

Table 9.4   Number of responses for each metrics

Metrics	Count
Excellent	391
Very good	142
Good	65
Satisfactory	35
Unsatisfactory	7

   (vi)   contribution of the laboratory work on conceptual understanding;
  (vii)   gratitude to students for showcasing good and novel work;
 (viii)   creating curiosity and interest by innovative practical approach of students;
  (ix)   student-oriented concerns and extended help outside the laboratory hours;
   (x)   classroom and discipline management.

Let j represents the total number of registered students registered for the IoT workshop course and i represents the total number of responses to fill the feedback form. M represents a set of metrics and W represents the weighted count of the items. Further, W_i represents the weight of each corresponding metric. Let C_{ij} represents the matrix of the total number of respondents for each item. The first step estimates the item rating (I_r) in (9.1). The overall average rating is obtained by using (9.2) in the following:

$$Item\ rating(I_r) = \frac{\sum C_{ij} \times W_{ij}}{\sum C_{ij}} \tag{9.1}$$

$$Overall\ average\ rating(OVR) = \frac{\sum I_r}{I} \tag{9.2}$$

In our study, the metrics consist of a set of five parameters, namely, $M = \{$Excellent, Very good, Good, Satisfactory, and Unsatisfactory$\}$. Next, the values of weightage (W_i) are assigned as $\{10, 8, 7, 5, 3\}$ for each corresponding metrics. The total number of respondents for various metrics is presented in Table 9.4.

The overall rating achieved for IoT workshop course is 8.9 out of 10. It is obvious from the ratings that the IoT workshop was a popular course among the prefinal year undergraduate engineering students of JIIT.

9.9   Conclusion

In recent decades, the IoT has a huge scope of job opportunities, economic growth, and career growth. It is essential for educational institutes to harness the skill of their students toward IoT through innovating curriculum and courses. This chapter discusses one such course, namely, practical-based IoT workshop, offered at JIIT, for undergraduate engineering students. The IoT workshop was conducted through a visual programming tool named Node-RED. Further, the chapter discusses the aspects such as course content, learning outcomes, teaching methodology, assessment criteria, and evaluation methodology. Further, from an analysis point of view, the feedback mechanism and performance of students registered for the IoT workshop are also elaborated. The IoT workshop engages students in such a way that they can gain good fundamental concepts of IoT architecture, protocols, and data analytics involved to meet out the requirements of particular IoT application areas.

References

[1]   https://www.gartner.com/technology/research/internet-of-things/report/ [Accessed on July 24, 2020].

[2]   https://www.capgemini.com/news/capgeminis-asia-pacific-wealth-report-2017-asia-pacific-continues-to-dominate-high-net-worth-individual-population-and-wealth/ [Accessed on July 24, 2020].

[3]   Kortuem, G., Bandara, A.K., Smith, N., Richards, M., and Petre, M.: 'Educating the internet-of-things generation' *Computer (Long Beach. Calif.)*, 2013. 46(2), pp. 53–61.

[4]   Fambon, O., Fleury, E., Harter, G., Pissard-Gibollet, R., and Saint-Marcel, F.: 'FIT IoT-LAB tutorial: Hands-on practice with a very large scale testbed tool for the Internet of Things' *UbiMob2014*, 2014. pp. 1–5.

[5]   Raikar, M.M., Desai, P., and Naragund, J.G.: 'Active learning explored in open elective course: Internet of Things (IoT)', in 'Proceedings – IEEE 8th International Conference on Technology for Education, T4E 2016' (2017). pp. 15–18.

[6]   Ali, F.: 'Teaching the internet of things concepts', in '2015 Workshop on Embedded and Cyber-Physical Systems Education, WESE 2015 – Proceedings' (2015).

[7]   Giang, N.K., Blackstock, M., Lea, and R., Leung, V.C.M.: 'Developing IoT applications in the fog: A distributed dataflow approach', in 'Proceedings – 2015 5th International Conference on the Internet of Things, IoT 2015' (2015). pp. 155–162.

[8]   Majeed, A. and Ali, M.: 'How Internet-of-Things (IoT) making the university campuses smart? QA higher education (QAHE) perspective', in '2018 IEEE 8th Annual Computing and Communication Workshop and Conference, CCWC 2018' (2018). pp. 646–648.

[9]   Bagheri, M. and Movahed, S.H.: 'The effect of the Internet of Things (IoT) on education business model', in 'Proceedings – 12th International Conference on Signal Image Technology and Internet-Based Systems, SITIS 2016' (2017). pp. 435–441.

[10] Akiyama, K., Ishihara, M., Ohe, N., and Inoue, M.: 'An education curriculum of IoT prototype construction system', in '2017 IEEE 6th Global Conference on Consumer Electronics, GCCE 2017' (2017). pp. 1–5.

[11] Maenpaa, H., Varjonen, S., Hellas, A., Tarkoma, S., and Mannisto, T.: 'Assessing IOT projects in university education – A framework for problem-based learning', in 'Proceedings – 2017 IEEE/ACM 39th International Conference on Software Engineering: Software Engineering and Education Track, ICSE-SEET 2017' (2017), pp. 37–46.

[12] Kovatsch, M., Duquennoy, S., and Dunkels, A.: 'A low-power CoAP for Contiki', in 'Proceedings – 8th IEEE International Conference on Mobile Ad-hoc and Sensor Systems, MASS 2011' (2011). pp. 855–860.

[13] Rodríguez, J.C., Rubio, E., and Hernández, Z.J.: 'VPL: Laboratorio virtual de programación para Moodle', in 'XVI Jornadas Enseñanza Univ. la Informática' (2010). pp. 429–435.

[14] http://www.vlab.co.in/ [Accessed on July 24, 2020].

[15] Aktan, B., Bohus, C.A., Crowl, L.A., and Shor, M.H.: 'Distance learning applied to control engineering laboratories' *IEEE Trans. Educ.*, 1996. 39(3), pp. 320–326.

[16] Bagnasco, A., Buschiazzo, P., Ponta, D., and Scapolla, M.: 'A learning resources centre for simulation and remote experimentation in electronics', in '1st International Conference on Pervasive Technologies Related to Assistive Environments, PETRA 2008' (2008).

[17] Peidró, A., Reinoso, O., Gil, A., Marín, J.M., and Payá, L.: 'A virtual laboratory to simulate the control of parallel robots' *IFAC-PapersOnLine*, 2015. 48(29), pp. 19–24.

[18] Valdez, M.T., Ferreira, C.M., and Barbosa, F.P.M.: '3D virtual laboratory for teaching circuit theory – A virtual learning environment (VLE)', in 'Proceedings – 2016 51st International Universities Power Engineering Conference, UPEC 2016' (2016). pp. 3–6.

[19] Booth, C., Cheluvappa, R., Bellinson, Z., *et al.*: 'Empirical evaluation of a virtual laboratory approach to teach lactate dehydrogenase enzyme kinetics' *Ann. Med. Surg.*, 2016. pp. 6–13.

[20] Al-Ajlan, A. and Zedan, H.: 'E-learning (MOODLE) based on service oriented architecture', in 'Proceeding of the EADTU's 20th Anniversary Conference' (2007).

[21] Vossen, G. and Westerkamp, P.: 'Towards the next generation of E-learning standards: SCORM for service-oriented environments', in 'Proceedings – Sixth International Conference on Advanced Learning Technologies, ICALT 2006' (2006). pp. 1031–1035.

[22] Cardoso, M., Marques, R., de Castro, A.V., and Rocha, Á.: 'Using Virtual Programming Lab to improve learning programming: The case of Algorithms and Programming', in 'Expert Systems' (2020).

[23] Kozak, S., Ruzicky, E., Stefanovic, J., and Schindler, F.: 'Research and education for industry 4.0: Present development', in 'Proceedings of the 29th International Conference on Cybernetics and Informatics, K and I 2018' (2018). pp. 1–8.

[24]   Iborra, A., Sanchez, P., Pastor, J.A., Alonso, D., and Suarez, T.: 'Beyond traditional entrepreneurship education in engineering promoting IoT start-ups from universities', in 'IEEE International Symposium on Industrial Electronics' (2017). pp. 1575–1580.

[25]   Mooney, A., Bergin, S., and Hegarty Kelly, E.: 'Incorporating the Virtual Programming Lab into a First Year Computer Science Module' *Technol. Feed. Approaches First-Year Y1Feedback Case Stud. Pract.*, 2017.

[26]   Casado, L. and Tsigas, P.: 'ContikiSec: A secure network layer for wireless sensor networks under the Contiki Operating System', in 'Lecture Notes in Computer Science (including subseries Lecture Notes in Artificial Intelligence and Lecture Notes in Bioinformatics)' (2009). pp. 133–147.

Chapter 10

Mnemonics in e-learning using augmented reality

Dinesh Kumar Saini[1], Arun Kumar Yadav[2] and Kartik Sharma[3]

10.1 Introduction

Retaining information for a longer time in learners' mind is a big challenging task, instructional designers propose mnemonics for enhancing learners retention of critical information and knowledge. Augmented reality (AR) and virtual reality (VR) devices enhance the learner's capabilities. Mnemonics with VR and AR will help learners a large piece of information such as algorithms, flowcharts, steps, parts and stages of process and procedures.

Today, AR applications are required to be adopted in education so that students can learn actively and motivates students to learn effectively. AR applications within an electronic learning (e-learning) environment have been accepted by the primary educators [1]. It also combined the aspect of ubiquitous computing, tangible computing and social computing. Development of AR technology allows researchers to create visual stories in such a manner that the student can connect and remember in a better way. AR is considered as a potential field for research for specially abled children [2].

Mnemonic is one of the techniques that have been used in teaching and learning to avoid knowledge loss. Method of loci (MOL) is one of the techniques that have been practised in different domains of real-world applications [3]. MOL technique is also used with the combination of head-mounted display (HMD) [4,5]. Pictures and their translations have also been using in learning to improve long-term retention [6]. It is also used with e-learning and M-learning [7].

[1]Department of Computer and Communication Engineering, Manipal University Jaipur, Jaipur, Rajasthan, India
[2]Department of Computer Science and Engineering, NIT, Hamirpur, India
[3]Department of Computer Science, JIIT, Noida, India

10.2   Literature survey

10.2.1   E-learning

Because of the unprecedented prevalence of information technologies in recent years, e-learning has become much popular in academics and corporate sectors [8]. E-learning provides exposer for studying not only the traditional subjects but also helps one to increase the quality of self-learning as well as to prune the professional knowledge in limited time and space constraints [6]. Learning and teaching is always an art of growth of individuals as well as society. As compared to e-learning, traditional teaching/learning knowledge loss increased by up to 60 per cent [2]. Traditional teaching and learning are effective for some types of audience, but due to diversity in mass, knowledge gap and lack of personal attention, it increases knowledge loss. In the paper [9], authors explained that e-learning can be the need as electronics-supported learning and teaching for overall development with reference to individual experience, including computer-based training and online education. The author concluded that e-learning is an effective tool for the learning process, which gives an opportunity for learners without any physical boundaries. E-learning is classified into formal and informal learning [10]. One-to-one individual interaction in education enables them to access a unique and attractive learning experience based upon their individual needs, rather than traditional learning procedure [11]. According to authors in the paper [12], students and their requirements are in top priority and their queries are in the form of how, what, when and where they learn. It is much efficiently possible by using individual interaction with modern e-learning technologies. One more issue is raised by authors in the paper [13] that today students lack memory power and they need arithmetic tools even for simple calculations. To resolve issues noticed in the paper [13], researchers have carried out a tool called 'mnemonic' [14]. The objective of mnemonic strategies is to develop an application to encode information, so that mnemonic-enabled devices can be attended as improved learning strategies [3]. Its main role is to connect students, who are already locked in long-term memory, to stay with active memory for a long time. Over the decade, a lot of research has been carried out with a rapid evolution of technology to develop learning applications. In the continuation of the research, AR is also considered as an educational medium that uses for K-12 and higher education [15].

10.2.2   Augmented reality (tools and techniques)

Objects are tracked in the physical world in real time with the help of AR. AR is classified into two categories: (a) an image-based AR that includes marker-based and marker-less solutions and uses image recognition techniques to track an object and its position and (b) a location-based AR that uses position data to identify an object and its position.

In advances in recent technologies, AR plays an important role in things more realistic and familiar with real objects. Due to this inherent property and low-cost hardware development, nowadays it becomes a very popular research topic in computer science and engineering. In general, it is a combination of a real environment and a virtual environment. In a single sentence, we can say that it is a mixed reality environment. This is the place where the real world and virtual world objects are available on a single display. Although AR is a new technology, it has 3D view characteristics and benefits to support e-learning. Due to its acceptance of 3D objects, it also provides a 3D view of learning content [16]. According to [17], AR environments could boost student's motivation and interest, which helps them for a better understanding of contents. According to [15], AR is a totally different technology from VR (users work in a virtual environment) in which computer-generated imaginary environment is created from real object in real time. AR is a computerized 3D imaginary view of real objects in real time. Ronald Azuma defines three characteristics to summarize the strength of AR [4]: (a) combines imaginary and real object; (b) remains interactive in real time; (c) gets registered in 3D real-time interaction in a 3D environment. It is a combination of a mixture of real and virtual objects on a single platform. There are three-dimensional display techniques used in AR applications. The idea is to present a perspective image to the user when he moves or changes the display. The three major techniques used for AR applications: HMDs, handheld displays and spatial displays.

10.2.2.1 Display techniques

Head-mounted display

It is a head-worn display device with a helmet on head with a small display optic in front of both the eyes. It can be video/optical see-through and can be seen in one/both eye display optics.

Handheld display

Handheld displays consist of small computing devices that make them portable to use them and allow them to be held it in their hands. These devices are video see-through specific and very useful to overlay graphics onto real environments. They use sensors to detect the degree of freedom. Currently, they are used for smartphones, PDAs and tablets. Android-based smartphone and iPhone are very popular and useful nowadays. They can be used in a better way for the learning and implementation of AR.

Spatial display

Spatial augmented reality (SAR) is very useful to augment real-world objects and scenes if there are limited devices such as monitors, HMDs or handheld devices. It uses a digital projector to display graphical information. Besides connecting a one-to-one user, SAR groups users based on their location and displays the real objects group wise. It is called a spatially aligned display. The paper [18] proposed this variation as technological variation SAR. They suggest that this technology is very useful and prominent in many areas to reduce the error rate and to increase display accuracy.

10.2.2.2   Tracking techniques

The tracking method is based on the types of environment and AR-implemented system. There are different tracking systems available based on indoor, outdoor or any other typical locations. Tracking devices include optical sensors, GPS, and camera. According to [19], the following types of tracking techniques are available.

Sensor-based tracking techniques

Sensor-based tracking techniques are magnetic, acoustic, inertial, and optical sensors. Each type has its respective advantages and disadvantages. Zhou *et al.* [19] provide a detailed review of different sensor-based trackings. According to them, some of the most common tracking techniques today are acoustic tracking, inertial tracking, mechanical tracking and optical tracking.

Vision-based tracking techniques

Vision-based tracking techniques use image-processing and feature-/model-based methods to find 2D images and convert them into 3D images. It also helps one to set the position of the camera with respect to the real object with minimal error dynamically.

Hybrid tracking techniques

Due to the limitation of providing a robust tracking system in a previous tracking system, hybrid methods have been developed by combining several sensing technologies [20]. In the vision tracking system, there is low jitter and no drift, but in a hybrid tracking system, it is fast and robust and can be used for motion prediction.

10.2.3   *Method of loci*

The structure of the memory frame is called mnemonics, which is classified as MOL. Earlier, this method was used only in the medical field in neuroscientists and psychologists. In e-learning, the MOL is used to place the learning content in an appropriate environment. The proposed research tests the user's mental factors to optimize the virtual memory place [21]. These strategies are based on remembering a certain learning content by creating mental associations with other, easy-to-remember entities. The first level of learning of MOL was used in 2002 and 2011 in the papers [22,23]. The idea of using mnemonics had been implemented in complex botanical and hierarchical relationships in the paper [24]. Later on, the paper [21] stated that mnemonics are not integrated into the teaching community yet. In the next year, the paper [25] announced the possibility of supporting the application of the MOL in virtual worlds. The basic idea of training using the MOL is to give a virtual template for her/his memory place. The method is a promising way to improve student's careers to increase their memory capacity and learning power. This can work as a training device to learn and improve their memory in the long run. It also supports huge information in a very precise and systematic way. To facilitate an emphasized way of e-learning, this chapter suggests a novel paradigm using the MOL. These strategies are based on tracking imaginary and phonetic similarity. In this chapter, the MOL is implemented in combination with HMD. The decision of using HMD is based on a high level of acceptance to apply the MOL than a casual desktop display.

10.3   Related work

As we know, education plays an important role in the overall development of all human beings in society. The world is going in the twenty-first century, but most of the areas of the world are lagging from basic education. In totality, due to these lagging, it is creating resistance to the overall development of society. The other concern is to provide quality education at minimal cost to the last person of society with zero knowledge loss. Historically, there are three types of learning systems, i.e. speech learning, paper learning and e-learning. All three learning systems help each other for how to deliver knowledge and how quality learning should be given. In the era 1990s, e-learning had become very popular and useful as a third learning system. Technology can play an important role in the growth of the individual in society in terms of providing quality education. Computers, mobile phones and other electronic devices are used for traditional education as well as providing a new ways of learning [2]. Technology gives the opportunity to students to select learning options related to their interest. It provides multiple learning options, such as multimedia that are new ways to engage students and virtual learning environments. One of them is virtual manipulative, which is an 'interactive, web-based visual representation of a dynamic object that presents opportunities for constructing mathematical knowledge' [26]. In recent years, new technologies are developing with the potential such as interactive games, AR, robotics technology and mobile computing and communication [27]. The users of AR can enhance their perception as well as thought process by using virtual information of a real object in the real world. This process will motivate e-learning users to AR-based e-learning system. This system also effectively performs for uninteresting books to get high interactive digital experience [28]. In the paper [9], the authors explain some projects developed by exploring different techniques for applying AR in education. They received very positive feedback to implement it in the education system. In the paper [29], the authors introduced a framework for the development of handheld AR. In the same year in the paper [30], the faculty of MIT developed an AR-based game for their students to understand the real objects in an imaginary environment. In 2009, Arvanitis *et al.* developed a project names CONNECT that used a mobile AR system for students learning in formal and informal learning environments. The evaluation of the project had been done by conducting a study with learners with physical disabilities [1]. In the paper [31], the authors presented a mobile AR game to increase awareness regarding the importance of recycling and its process. The evaluation was done based on the recycling of knowledge gained by the children, easy usability and their level of engagement. Results showed that instead of any significant difference between the two games, 69.4 per cent of the children preferred the AR-based games. In the paper [7], the authors developed a tangible and AR model to teach graphics courses to engineering students which helped them to understand 3D objects and their projections.

This chapter discusses e-learning with AR. An MOL is used with a mnemonic technique to explain the concept. AR enhances information and communication technology more effectively in terms of learning of students with fun and without knowledge loss during the teaching-learning process. This chapter also explains the advantages of using proposed techniques such as improving memory quality, enhancing imaginary quality and retrieving important information. It also concludes with a brief discussion of possible future research directions.

10.4   Theory and research approach

Modern technology has been involved in education and shown a positive impact on teaching and learning. As per the discussion in Section 10.2, education with the latest technologies increases the intensity of teaching/learning. In recent years, AR plays an important role to grow and improve the teaching/learning process [5]. With the use of AR with a method of an e-learning, a tool is developed that helps students to memorize complex things in a simpler way and also helps them to retain that concept for a very long period. Figure 10.1 explains the procedure of executing the AR-based e-learning.

>   Step 1: Create the memory place (using the MOL) and map with the concept of learner applied in the AR platform.
>   Step 2: Generate the links/QR codes for every created memory place of all topic sections.
>   Step 3: Write the concept that the user wants to learn above the links/ QR codes.
>   Step 4: Write the mapping of the memory place and the part of the concept in the memory place itself.
>   Step 5: Create the section for non-learners so that they can also add some content that will certainly benefit the learners. All these are explained in detail in Figure 10.1.

The proposed approach is used for subjects such as physics, chemistry for the K-12 students.

10.5   Implementation and results

To implement the MOL using the AR technology for an e-learner, a Metaverse Studio is used. It is markerless-based AR. To create the front end, HTML, CSS and JavaScript are used. MOL technique may help the student to learn the concept

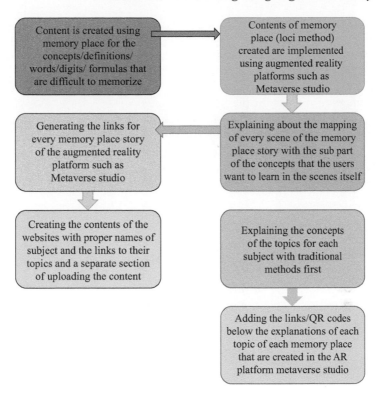

Figure 10.1   Architecture to implement augmented reality

easily and he may remember the concept for a longer time. Moreover, while learning the concept student may not feel lonely, bored rather feels motivated to learn more.

The aim is to create stories using the MOL, which are mapped with the concept for e-learners and then add it to the AR platform by using the given method in Section 10.3. The following sections show some of the concepts created in the Metaverse Studio.

10.5.1   Concept-1

Let the students want to remember the speed of light which is equal to 299,792,458 m/s, which is difficult to be remembered. A story is created, which explains that you are going home by using bike of 2 wheels after attending the college. Here 2 is the first digit of the speed of light. The second scene of the story relates the nine while returning home and your wristwatch shows exactly 9.00 p.m. After reaching your building, your flat is on the ninth floor, which reflects the number 9. Then you tried to open the door of your flat with the key, written a number 7 on the key chain. After opening, you were surprised to see your nine friends at your home. After that,

Figure 10.2   Concept of speed of light

you see a cake, written 24 on top, realized that it is your 24th birthday. After getting birthday wishes from all your friends, five of them give you five gifts. After that you checked your phone, you see eight missed calls from your mother, who also wanted to wish you a 'Happy Birthday'.

This is how a story is created by using the Metaverse application to remember the speed of light. One of the traits of the learner is that if he visualizes, he perceives the content in a better way. Thus, this story may help the learner to remember the speed of light. Figure 10.2 shows a snapshot of the story of the speed of light using AR.

10.5.2   Concept-2

AR using the method of link is designed to learn Avogadro's number which is 6.022×10^{23}. Figure 10.3 shows the scene to learn Avogadro's number. The concept relates the link to get up at 6.00 a.m. to get ready for school. The point is related to

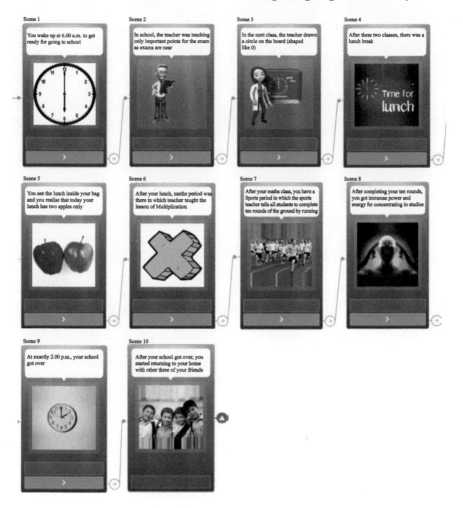

Figure 10.3   Avogadro's number

that teacher discusses some important points for exams. To represent the zero, a story is created as a teacher drawn a circle on the board.

Double 2 are represented as there is lunch break after two classes and for lunch, there are two apples. Scene 6 is explained as multiplication. Scene 7 represents the sport period and student takes ten rounds to gain power. Scene 8 represents to remember the value 2 as school got over, and the last scene is represented to remember 3 as you return home with three friends.

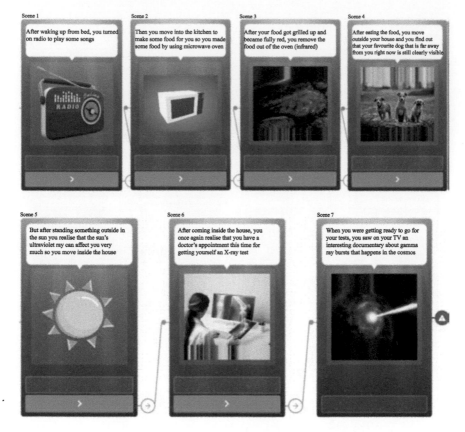

Figure 10.4   Electromagnetic spectrum radiations

10.5.3   Concept-3

Concept-3 explains the electromagnetic spectrum radiations order wise. An electromagnetic spectrum concept explains in a manner that you turned on the radio to play some songs (Figure 10.4).

Scene 2 represents that you are cooking some food using an oven. After food got grilled up in Scene 3, it flashes the red rays outside the oven. Likewise, other scenes have been depicted.

10.5.4   Concept-4

The next concept explains to remember the universal gravitational constant value that the learner wants to learn, that is 6.67×10^{-11}. It is difficult to remember such values. So the story is created in a manner that incident happening in your life accordingly. Most of us wake up in the morning at 6.00 a.m. So that scene can be depicted (Figure 10.5) as a clock wall showing 6.00 a.m.

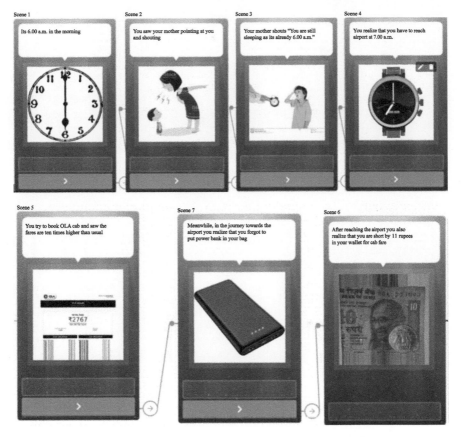

Figure 10.5 Universal gravitational constant value

To represent $10^\wedge$, Scene 5 is explained as that you booked an Ola cab and fares are ten times higher than usual. To explain the negative sign, Scene 6 represents that you forgot to put power bank in your bag. Likewise, a numerical value can be learned.

10.5.5 Concept-5

Concept-5 discusses the distance formula in mechanics (Figure 10.6). The details of the distance formula are $s = ut + 1/2$ at $^\wedge 2$ where s is distance, u is initial speed, v is final speed, a is acceleration, t is time.

The story can be created in that manner that addition is represented as the teacher teaches the addition in the class. While taking the class half of the class is present. AT square is depicted in Scenes 6 and 7.

Figure 10.6   Distance formula in mechanics

10.5.6   Concept-6

Concept-6 explains Newton's first law. The law states that an object will remain at rest or in uniform motion in a straight line unless acted upon by an external force. It may be seen as a statement about inertia (Figure 10.7).

10.5.7   Concept-7

Concept-7 describes Newton's second law. This law states that the rate of change of velocity of an object is directly proportional to the force applied on that object and inversely proportional to the mass of that object. In other words, $F = MA$ (Figure 10.8).

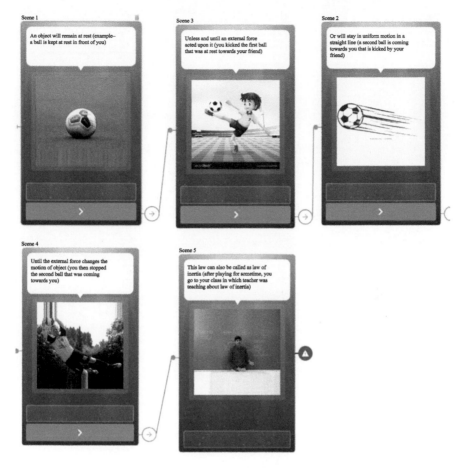

Figure 10.7   Newton's first law

10.5.8   Concept-8

Concept-8 describes Newton's third law. This law states that all forces between two objects exist in the equal magnitude and opposite direction: if one object A exerts a force F_A on a second object B, then B simultaneously exerts a force F_B on A, and the two forces are equal in magnitude and opposite in direction: $F_A = -F_B$ (Figure 10.9).

10.5.9   Concept-9

Concept-9 explains the gravitational force formula. The formula is $F = GMm/r^2$ (Figure 10.10):

10.5.10   Concept-10

The detail of the golden ratio value (phi) is equal to 1.618, shown in Figure 10.11.

Figure 10.8   Newton's second law

Earlier the examples of some of the concepts are cited, which student learn during the K-12 education. A test has been conducted among K-12 students to see the performance of the student without an AR tool and, after that, to deliver the content by using the app. It has been found that after learning using the AR tool, the student performance has increased by 30 per cent. Thus the AR technique helps a student to better understand the concept, long-term memory retention, less isolation and enhances motivation. Thus the MOL is an effective method to recall information with its use. Research shows that it is one of the best mnemonic techniques to improve the performance of the learners.

There are some challenges to implement AR in e-learning scenarios such as attention tunnelling. The students are unable to take part in teamwork. The other challenge is to use an AR system. The teacher dominates the classroom and student engagement during the learning phase is less than other modes.

Figure 10.9   *Newton's third law*

Figure 10.10   *Gravitational force formula*

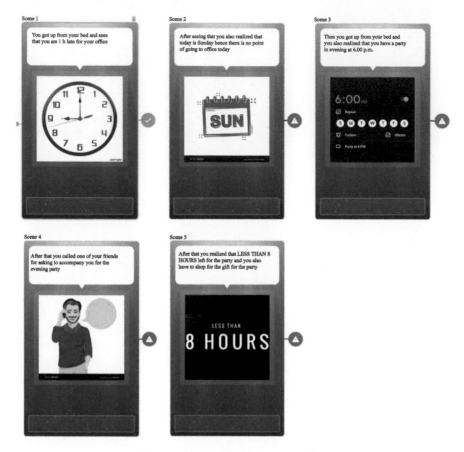

Figure 10.11   Golden ratio value

10.6   Conclusion

AR has great potential to affect the learning experience. Developments in AR technology have motivated the researchers to develop applications using hardware, software and the authoring of content. A summary of the main findings of this chapter are as follows: Published surveys show that AR in education has progressively increased year by year intensively and mainly in the last 8 years. AR has been mostly applied in professional education as well as higher education. Location-based AR along with marker-based AR is very widely used.

10.7 Future work

Some issues are to be covered in future research which are as follows:

1. The transition from a traditional approach to AR-based instruction in e-learning platforms.
2. AR instruction and teaching style alignment.
3. Collaborations.

There are two research directions: (a) understanding the learning effect of various design strategies and (b) investigating the generalization and maintenance of AR learning gains as well as the effectiveness of instruction with AR applications and similar computational systems.

References

[1] Arvanitis TN, Petrou A, Knight JF, *et al*. Human factors and qualitative pedagogical evaluation of a mobile augmented reality system for science education used by learners with physical disabilities. Personal and Ubiquitous Computing. 2009;13(3):243–50.

[2] Balaji DR, Ramniklal D, Balasupramanian N, and Malathi ER. Mnemonics for higher education using contemporary technologies. arXiv preprint arXiv:1305.2609. 2013 May 12.

[3] Bellezza FS. Mnemonic devices: Classification, characteristics, and criteria. Review of Educational Research. 1981;51(2):247–75.

[4] Billinghurst M, Clark A, and Lee G. A survey of augmented reality. Foundations and Trends in Human-Computer Interaction. 2014;8(2–3):73–272.

[5] Dierking LD. Lessons without limit: How free-choice learning is transforming science and technology education. História, Ciências, Saúde-Manguinhos. 2005;12:145–60.

[6] Chao RJ and Chen YH. Evaluation of the criteria and effectiveness of distance e-learning with consistent fuzzy preference relations. Expert Systems with Applications. 2009;36(7):10657–62.

[7] Chen YC, Chi HL, Hung WH, and Kang SC. Use of tangible and augmented reality models in engineering graphics courses. Journal of Professional Issues in Engineering Education & Practice. 2011;137(4):267–76.

[8] Zaíane OR. Building a recommender agent for e-learning systems. In International Conference on Computers in Education, 2002. Proceedings 2002 Dec 3 (pp. 55–59). IEEE.

[9] Woods E, Billinghurst M, Looser J, *et al*. Augmenting the science centre and museum experience. In Proceedings of the 2nd International Conference on Computer Graphics and Interactive Techniques in Australasia and South East Asia 2004 Jun 15 (pp. 230–236).

[10] Putnam AL. Mnemonics in education: Current research and applications. Translational Issues in Psychological Science. 2015;1(2):130.

[11] Dwivedi P and Bharadwaj KK. Effective trust-aware e-learning recommender system based on learning styles and knowledge levels. Journal of Educational Technology & Society. 2013;16(4):201–16.

[12] Tarng W and Ou KL. A study of campus butterfly ecology learning system based on augmented reality and mobile learning. In 2012 IEEE Seventh International Conference on Wireless, Mobile and Ubiquitous Technology in Education 2012 Mar 27 (pp. 62–66). IEEE.

[13] Moseley D, Higgins S, Bramald R, *et al*. Ways Forward with ICT: Effective Pedagogy Using Information and Communications Technology for Literacy and Numeracy in Primary Schools. 1999.

[14] Jurowski K, Jurowska A, Krzeczkowska M, and Własiuk P. Mnemonic methods as a sophisticated tool in learning the science subjects from Polish pupils point of view. 2014.

[15] Kamalika D. Augmented Reality for E-Learning. 2018;13–17. https://www. researchgate. net/.../304078112_Augmented_Reality_for _E-Learning.

[16] Chien CH, Chen CH, and Jeng TS. An interactive augmented reality system for learning anatomy structure. In Proceedings of the International Multiconference of Engineers and Computer Scientists 2010 Mar 17 (Vol. 1, pp. 17–19). Hong Kong, China: International Association of Engineers.

[17] Billinghurst M. Augmented reality in education. New Horizons for Learning. 2002;12(5):1–5.

[18] Bimber O and Raskar R. Spatial augmented reality: Merging real and virtual worlds. Wellesley, MA, USA: A. K. Peters; 2005.

[19] Zhou F, Duh HB, and Billinghurst M. Trends in augmented reality tracking, interaction and display: A review of ten years of ISMAR. In 2008 7th IEEE/ ACM International Symposium on Mixed and Augmented Reality 2008 Sep 15 (pp. 193–202). IEEE.

[20] Seichter H, Looser J, and Billinghurst M. ComposAR: An intuitive tool for authoring AR applications. In 2008 7th IEEE/ACM International Symposium on Mixed and Augmented Reality 2008 Sep 15 (pp. 177–178). IEEE.

[21] Putnam AL. Mnemonics in education: Current research and applications. Translational Issues in Psychological Science. 2015;1(2):130.

[22] Anderson LW and Bloom BS. A taxonomy for learning, teaching, and assessing: A revision of Bloom's taxonomy of educational objectives. New York, NY: Longman; 2001.

[23] McCabe J. Metacognitive awareness of learning strategies in undergraduates. Memory & Cognition. 2011;39(3):462–76.

[24] Levin ME and Levin JR. Scientific mnemonomies: Methods for maximizing more than memory. American Educational Research Journal. 1990;27 (2):301–21.

[25] Martín-Gutiérrez J, Mora CE, Añorbe-Díaz B, and González-Marrero A. Virtual technologies trends in education. EURASIA Journal of Mathematics, Science and Technology Education. 2017;13(2):469–86.

[26] Moyer PS, Bolyard JJ, and Spikell MA. What are virtual manipulatives? Teaching Children Mathematics. 2002;8(6):372–7.

[27] Nincarean D, Alia MB, Halim ND, and Rahman MH. Mobile augmented reality: The potential for education. Procedia—Social and Behavioral Sciences. 2013;103(0):657–64.

[28] Kerawalla L, Luckin R, Seljeflot S, and Woolard A. "Making it real": exploring the potential of augmented reality for teaching primary school science. Virtual reality. 2006;10(3–4):163–174.

[29] Schmalstieg D and Wagner D. Experiences with handheld augmented reality. In 2007 6th IEEE and ACM International Symposium on Mixed and Augmented Reality 2007 Nov 13 (pp. 3–18). IEEE.

[30] Squire K and Klopfer E. Augmented reality simulations on handheld computers. The Journal of the Learning Sciences. 2007;16(3):371–413.

[31] Juan M C, Furió D, Alem L, Ashworth P, and Cano J. ARGreenet and BasicGreenet: Two mobile games for learning how to recycle. In 19th International Conference in Central Europe on Computer Graphics, Visualization and Computer Vision, WSCG 2011 – In Co-operation with EUROGRAPHICS, Full Papers Proceedings Jan 2011 (pp. 25–32).

Chapter 11

E-learning tools and smart campus: boon or bane during COVID-19

Shikha Mehta[1] and Krishna Bihari Dubey[2]

The sudden spread of novel coronavirus COVID-19 across the world has been leading to the drastic changes in complete structural, organizational and social aspects of every sector, including the education system. The quick closure of universities and schools for public health safety during COVID-19 pandemic has become a catalyst for searching innovative solutions within a short span of time. In the context of this new and challenging situation, e-learning tools have become the new educational policy and practice for virtual classrooms. This chapter presents an analysis of various e-learning tools for synchronous and asynchronous learning. It also focuses on the various health issues arising due to the excessive exposure of everyone to screens with the growing adoption of online learning tools and technologies.

11.1 Introduction

Education is a right but quality education is the key to transforming lives by enduring various societal challenges [1]. Over the decades, the advancement of technologies has brought a paradigm shift in the teaching–learning process. Delivery of education is evolving from traditional classroom teaching to e-learning along with the advancement in technologies. Smart education has gained significant attention over the years. However, there was a dual opinion on full-fledged adoption due to the various challenges such as security, environmental issues and operating costs associated with technology-assisted learning. Nevertheless, the sudden outbreak of COVID-19 has changed the whole scenario. Due to COVID-19, schools across the world are shut. Billions of students are out of the classrooms [2].

It has closed all the options and brought everyone to one single platform of online learning. Educators are compelled to adapt their decades-old pedagogies according to the new market conditions. During this COVID-19 situation, the main concern of academicians is not about quality education but to handle the challenge

[1]Computer Science and Engineering, Jaypee Institute of Information Technology, Noida, India
[2]Department of Computer Science and Engineering, ABESIT, Ghaziabad, India

of adopting online learning on a large scale [3]. These tough times have generated an immediate need for scenario planning for academic institutions [4]. These are testing times for all sectors, including the educational sector, and resistance would not help. Success will be determined based on the ability to adapt to the education system with this "New Normal" condition along with maintaining the quality of delivery. There is no alternative to online teaching and learning amidst the crisis. Innovative solutions need to be designed by the academicians for survival in this pandemic [5]. Dramatic transformation of education delivery from physical classrooms to e-learning where teaching is carried out remotely using digital platforms is a must. It seems instructors delivering and interacting with students in big lecture theaters will become a thing of the past [6]. Although the adoption of online education was already growing pre COVID-19 with Global EdTech investments reaching US$18.66 billion in 2019 and post COVID-19, it is expected to reach $350 billion by 2025. COVID-19 has paved the opportunities for the growth of e-learning content and platforms and its swift adoption overcoming all obstacles such as budgetary constraints due to economic instability, lack of infrastructure and, most importantly, unavailability of e-learning content and trainers with remote training expertise [7]. According to Li Kang, Ai English Executive Director, "Online Learning is the future and if there was no virus, that realization would have taken another few years but this has accelerated the process." [8]. It is considered that online learning increases the retention of information and takes less time, so this transformation in the teaching–learning process is going to stay. There has been a significant increase in the demand and usage of mobile apps, virtual tutoring, video conferencing tools, virtual labs, digital ports, remote learning and online learning software since the outbreak of COVID-19. With online education, numerous options are available to the students to decide when, where and how to study as homework assignments, lectures, grades are all accessible through smartphones, laptops, etc. The Internet has become the lifeline of the education system across the world for both teaching and learning [9]. During this COVID-19 phase, the usage of e-learning tools has boosted drastically. This phase has brought new opportunities for the e-learning industry due to the transition of all schools and universities around the world from physical institutions to virtual institutions with the help of online learning tools. Nevertheless, the adoption of these online tools for delivery of education has led to the early exposure of kids to screens and hence affecting their physical and mental health. Thus, an important question needs to be answered: adoption of e-learning tools during COVID-19 is a boon or bane for humans? The rest of the chapter is organized as follows: Section 11.2 presents various types of e-learning techniques. The analysis of various online learning tools based on various parameters is discussed in Section 11.3. Section 11.4 presents the side effects of increased usage of screens followed by a conclusion in the last section.

11.2 E-learning

E-learning [10] is defined as "an information system that can integrate a wide variety of instructional materials (via audio, video, and text mediums) conveyed through email, live chat sessions, online discussions, forums, quizzes, and assignments." E-learning is an aggregation of all kinds of learning that use the computer as a medium to support the learning process. The main benefit of e-learning is the flexibility as it has no geographical boundaries, and learners across the globe can attend the same course and learning communities. The definition of e-learning has been updated from time to time with the evolution of the World Wide Web (WWW) from Web 1.0 to Web 4.0 [11]. In the 1990s, when WWW was in its early stages, e-learning was limited to web-based applications where anyone could just read content on the web. There was no user interaction or personalization of contents as per the need and learning level of the user. The next generation, i.e. Web 2.0, led to the revolution of social web that was totally driven by user interactions, personalization, collaborative virtual communities, etc. Subsequently Web 3.0 and Web 4.0 focused on understanding semantics and adding intelligence to the activities over the WWW. These advancements in the web applications also influenced e-learning tools, technologies, content and communities. Lately, e-learning is defined as the transfer of knowledge and skills through intelligently designed course materials with the help of an electronic media such as the Internet, Web 4.0, intranets and extranets [11]. Over the years, new terms have evolved such as online learning, open learning, web-based learning, computer-mediated learning, blended learning and m-learning, and all these offer a common medium to learn from anywhere, anytime, in any tempo, with any platform [12]. Mobile learning [13] refers to the learning that is delivered through mobile devices such as smartphones or tablets. Online learning is defined as a tool aimed to make the teaching–learning process more innovative, flexible and student oriented. Online learning moves what we know as face-to-face learning to a computer screen [13]. Various definitions have emerged based on varied perspectives; accordingly [14] online learning is defined as "learning experiences in synchronous or asynchronous environments using different devices with internet access. In these environments, students can be anywhere (independent) to learn and interact with instructors and other students." To offer flexibility and cater the varied needs of users with different learning styles and abilities, e-learning course strategies are divided into synchronous and asynchronous learning techniques (Figure 11.1).

11.2.1 Synchronous e-learning

With the advancement in technologies and Internet bandwidth capabilities, synchronous e-learning has gained immense popularity. Synchronous e-learning or real-time learning is a kind of remote classroom teaching where teachers take live lectures through electronic devices using the Internet and students can have real-time interactions with instructors and can share the feedback. It provides enough opportunities for face-to-face interaction during the live classes [15]. Teachers share learning resources with the students via virtual classroom, audio and video conferencing, chat, Webinar, application sharing, messaging instantly, etc. Students find online learning more appealing as it can be accessed by anyone from anywhere. Online learning is becoming far easier for both instructors and students with

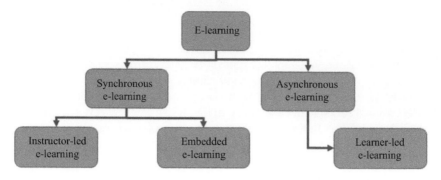

Figure 11.1   Types of e-learning

the availability of tools to create learning content, storage and distribution components, resources banks and overcoming the time and place constraints on instruction that are usually found in the traditional classrooms [15]. Active participation of students during class and discussion with peers, asking queries and getting solutions, is strenuously carried out in virtual classrooms. However, synchronous e-learning becomes difficult when students are scattered across different time zones, limited access to computers and unreliable Internet connections.

Amidst this deadly virus spread, that is COVID-19 pandemic, while maintaining social distancing, the only way left to continue teaching and learning is e-learning platforms whether synchronous or asynchronous learning as shown in Figure 11.2 [17]. Synchronous e-learning can be accomplished with online platforms providing various features such as video conferencing application with at least 30–100 students as class sizes vary in schools and colleges, student–teacher interaction to maintain the students' interest, good Internet connections, online platforms compatibility across devices, lecture recording facility, options to take instant feedback and share assignments [16].

11.2.2   Asynchronous e-learning

It is also known as learner-led learning or self-paced learning. Asynchronous learning is not mediated by any instructors; it is learner-led learning where learners can learn at their own pace. It also lacks interactions with the instructor and instant feedback [17]. In asynchronous learning environments, learning content may be available in different forms such as notes, recorded videos, online tutorials, and Massive Open Online Course (MOOC). In the last few years, the MOOC [18] has become a popular tool for online learning in the field of education. The features provided by MOOCs are mostly similar to e-learning, where the learning materials are delivered for a specified period [15]. In [19], it was emphasized that learning can become more interesting through MOOC. Users can considerably enhance their conceptual knowledge through the MOOCs at their own pace in any part of the world [20].

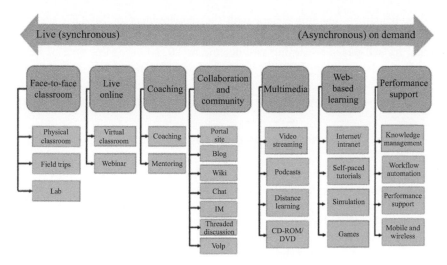

Figure 11.2   Relationship between synchronous and asynchronous learning

Asynchronous learning is also known as just-in-time learning as it is associated with sufficient study materials that can be used by learners in the time of need. It is very useful for working professionals, house makers, etc. as in this type of learning, learners have full flexibility to learn and follow the curriculum at their own pace without affecting their other commitments. It is considered to be a perfect option for self-motivated learners as they can explore and spend time on the curriculum topics as per their own interest preferences. Nevertheless, this option is not suitable for learners who require constant motivation for completing the tasks. Some learners also feel isolated and enjoy learning with interactions only. When the self-paced e-learning contents or videos, etc. are of 5–15 min as compared with traditional 30–45 min, it is known as microlearning. In large corporate organizations, these self-paced learning modules are available on learning management systems (LMS) [21]. These modules are very useful as they help in reducing the training along with increasing convenience and effectiveness. These self-paced modules are created using instructional design models. The two popular models used in the literature are the ADDIE (analysis, design, development, implementation and evaluation) model and the SAM (successive approximation model), which are widely used for creating self-paced e-learning modules [22]. The various tools used for asynchronous learning [23] are as follows:

- Discussion boards
- Web logs (blogs)
- Messaging (e-mail)
- Streaming audio/Streaming video
- Social media
- Website links
- WhatsApp chats

Asynchronous learning began with the development of MOOCs courses to provide maximum flexibility to the learners. However, it is estimated that the market for self-paced e-learning will decline by 2021 [24] as this type of learning though sounded good in theory, it is not found useful in real life. E-learning providers have experienced that the majority of the people do not complete their courses and are therefore exploring new methods to retain and engage the learners.

11.3   Tools for synchronous e-learning

The unusual dependency on technology begotten during COVID-19 lockdown has become a hot topic of research to continue the operations in every sector in the long run. To provide the different types of synchronous e-learning services, specialized software known as e-learning platforms or online learning tools are created. These e-learning platforms are popularly called as LMS. A broad range of services is provided by these e-learning platforms to support the instructors in the successful delivery of their lectures. Table 11.1 depicts the top 16 tools developed in various countries [25–28] and Table 11.2 shows the list tools for synchronous e-learning with Indian origin [31]. Analysis of these tools is done based on nine important features that are critical for the smooth running of online classes, online meetings, video conferences, etc.

11.4   Side effects of using online learning tools or e-learning

With the rapid spread of coronavirus (COVID-19) in major parts of the globe, online teaching and learning is no longer a choice but has become a necessity [30]. This new solution no doubt has been a savior for the whole world in these tough times and is expected to stay for long. However, this new solution is associated with a number of physical, mental and social health and technical challenges [31].

11.4.1   Technical challenges

According to the National Center for Education Statistics [32], 18% of people lying between the ages of 3 and 18 years have no Internet access at their homes nationwide. It was reported by the center that technology is increasingly becoming an integral part of the K-12 curriculum, and the current coronavirus pandemic has further catalyzed its adoption. There are numerous issues associated with technologies varying from buying to usage. Sometimes tools are paid, audio–video problems, downloading problems, installation problems, login problems, etc. Besides, there is a shortage of phones and laptops, erratic power supply and nonavailability of separate rooms for the child to attend undisturbed online classes. Students have less preparedness for e-learning contents and usage of LMS [33]. These problems are further escalated if the families of students are less affluent and digitally savvy. Also, to conduct smooth teaching–learning programs, a list of online etiquettes was

Table 11.1 Synchronous e-learning tools across the world

S. no.	Tool	Free/Paid	Allowed participants	Duration of meeting/class	Availability of recording facility?	Annotation	White board facility	Video conferencing	Instant chat/messaging	Country
1	Google Meet	Free, if you have a Gmail account	100	60 min /meeting NOTE: From September 30, 24-h meeting will be allowed	Yes You can record your meeting/call to rewatch or share with others	Does not have a direct annotation tool	No built-in whiteboard tool. But Google's Chrome Canvas and Google Jam board are two tools that can be used for whiteboard	Yes	Yes	California, USA
2	Zoom	Free	100 (can be extended to 500 in additional license)	40 min (in basic plan)	Yes You can record your meeting/call to rewatch or share with others	Yes It allows one to draw on shared screen	Yes We can start whiteboard session and invite others to view and annotate	Yes (up to 40 min)	Yes (supported)	American
3	Microsoft Teams	Free	10,000 Members may be in a team and there may be 100 owners per team	24 h	Yes Users can record their teams meeting and group calls	Yes We can access the annotation pens from bottom left corner	Yes It acts like a digital canvas where people can share their ideas and content	Yes	Yes	American
4	Skype	Free calling from anywhere in the world	50 People at once	100 h/month with no more than 10 h/day and 4 h per video call	Yes On a desktop, go to more option and click record	Yes. It opens automatically on everyone's screen during a call	Yes	Yes	Yes	Estonia (in Europe)

(Continues)

Table 11.1 (*Continued*)

S. no.	Tool	Free/Paid	Allowed participants	Duration of meeting/class	Availability of recording facility?	Annotation	White board facility	Video conferencing	Instant chat/messaging	Country
5	GoToMeeting	Free	26 People Use GoToWebinar which supports 1,000 participants	2 h (but no time limit if your attendees are in session)	Yes	Yes	Yes. You can use drawing tools for whiteboard presentation	Yes	Yes (by enabling it)	Germany
6	Free Conference. com	Free	100 People for 6 h	6 h	Only in paid plans	—	Yes	Yes (up to 1,000 participants)	Yes	California, USA
7	BlueJeans	Free in only on trial version	25 Attendees in basic plan	No time limit	Yes Just login and click on "Recordings"	Yes	Yes	Yes	Yes	California, USA
8	Cisco Webex	Free/Paid	25 (if all users have free accounts) 100 (if all users have free accounts)	24 h	Yes There are two options for recordings:1—Record on server2—Local recording	Not supported	Yes Go to Menu and select Whiteboard	Yes	Yes	California, USA
9	Intermedia Any Meeting	Free until 2021	4 Participants in free starter planPaid plan starts at $9.99 in 2021	12 h	Yes	Yes	Yes	Yes	Through a Chat Tab	Toronto, Canada
10	Join.me	Free only on trial versionPaid starts at $10 per user per month	250 People in Pro account	No time limits	Yes	Yes	Yes	Yes	Yes	

(Continues)

No.	Name	Cost	Participants	Duration	Built-in feature					Location
11	GoToWebinar	Free	Free (150) Paid (2,000)	5 h	Yes	Yes	Yes	Yes	Yes	California, USA
12	Adobe Connect	Free	1,000		Yes	Yes	Yes	Yes	Yes	San Jose, California, USA
13	Click Meeting	Paid service	25	By default: 5 min minimum 3 h maximum	Yes	Yes	Yes	Yes	Yes Through Chat Pod	
14	TANDBERG Video Conferencing	Free	10	24 h	Yes, built in feature	Not sure	Not sure	Yes	Yes	Norway
15	Talk Point Convey	Paid	Not known	Not known	Not sure	Not known	Not known	Yes	Yes	United States
16	Google Hangouts	Free version of Gmail	150 Participants	60 min	Only in paid subscription	No direct annotation tool	No built in whiteboard tool	Yes	Yes	California, USA

Table 11.2 Synchronous e-learning tools of Indian origin

S. no.	Tool	Free/ Paid	Allowed participants	Duration of meeting/class	Availability of recording facility?	Annotation	White board facility	Video conferencing	Instant chat/messaging	Country
1	Jio Meet by Reliance	Free	100	Unlimited	Yes	Yes	Yes	Yes	Through "Jio Chat"	India
2	FLOOR by 10 times	Free	Up to 1 million participants	10 h	Yes	Yes	Yes	Yes	Yes	Noida, India
3	SAY NA-MASTE, by In scripts	Free	50	Not known	Yes	Yes	Not sure	Yes	Yes	Mumbai, India
4	KL Meet by Knowl-edge Lens	Free	Not known	Not known	Yes	Yes	Yes	Yes	Yes	Bengaluru, India
5	AIRMEET	Free	Up to 1 million without any degrade in quality of communication	No limit	Automatic meeting re-cording	Yes	Not sure	Yes	Yes	Bengaluru, India

shared with students, and proper instructions for attending classes were given to them [34].

11.4.2   Health issues

Online learning has turned up as a remedy during this COVID-19 pandemic but is associated with additional physical and mental health risks. The time spent by students on digital devices has increased due to virtual learning. According to research, there is a positive relationship between attaining a degree and long-term health of a college student. Therefore, the time spent on computers should not have a negative effect on the completion of their degree [35]. Nevertheless, due to unavoidable excessive screen time of toddlers to youngsters, all are facing multiple health risks. Screen time is mainly associated with an increased sedentary lifestyle [35]. Thus, via online learning, institutions are able to follow the social distancing norms and provide easy access to education but at the cost of health. Inexorable screen time is becoming the cause of diseases related to sedentary lifestyles such as cardiovascular disease, premature death, stroke, some types of cancer, type 2 diabetes, osteoporosis and depression [36–39]. Therefore, in this pandemic situation, it is important to watch the functional health requirements of the kids attending online classes [40].

11.4.3   Social and economic challenges

According to [43], 40% of the population across the globe are offline due to obvious reasons. As per UNESCO, half of the total number of learners (826 million) are out of the classroom due to the COVID-19 pandemic as they have limited or no access to household computers or the Internet. Students of less-developed economies are left behind either due to the cost of devices or nonavailability of personal devices and data plans. The situation may become worse as most of these students will not be able to appear in the online exams. The income gap is seen everywhere across the countries as well as within the countries. The gap between education quality and socioeconomic equality may escalate further unless the technology access costs are controlled and the quality of access improves for all economies. The digital divide may escalate further if educational access would be governed by ingress to the latest technologies [41]. These are real-world issues that impede the adoption of online learning. According to the United Nations Children's Fund (UNICEF), as millions of children go online, there is an increased risk of harm to their lives based on humanitarian grounds [42]. As the life of children is just shrunk to their homes and screens, their all-round development is also at stake.

The rebooting of lives due to COVID-19 has brought numerous challenges as well as opportunities for everyone. The field of education is no escape as getting quality education is the fundamental right. With the compulsory adoption of virtual schooling, people with low income, low literacy, residing in rural areas are worst affected. This opens the door for corporates to develop and provide low-cost user-friendly solutions so that no one is deprived of education. The educational institutions are not only facing the problem of finding and adapting to new technologies but also to reinvent education for everyone seeking guidance for digital literacy. The government needs to interfere and take steps in this direction to overcome the various social, economic, technical and health challenges posed due to the transformation of the complete education system online.

11.5   Future of education: e-learning + smart campus

The crisis due to COVID-19 has taught a lesson that the future of educational institutions lies in hybrid learning approaches. The current pandemic has revealed the ill-preparedness of the majority of the institutions for remote learning capabilities. Educationalists need to redesign the policies for blended teaching and learning which would include a combination of both physical classroom teaching and virtual classroom teaching. Teachers must be trained for both types of learning in the future. This also drives the need for smart campuses to handle problems such as COVID-19 and others in the future. Now, students also expect online connectivity in their learning and social environments. Therefore, the idea of digitalizing traditional campuses would now be favored by most of the academicians. Everyone tries to mitigate security and environmental issues and also focused to find out new ways to improving the experience of students both socially and academically. With the help of Wi-Fi, IoT technologies and other advanced technologies, colleges and universities across the world would now be able to transform themselves into digital campuses which provide benefits to the learners, faculties and societies.

Such modern digital campuses provide enhanced learning and quality life to their students and adapt the teachers to virtual learning environments. Some other benefits are lower operating costs, greater safety and security, etc.

11.5.1   Smart campus

A campus is a place that is used for educating students, for enhancing the development of any individual or society. Campuses are digitalized by embedding information technology in the field of education and become a smart campus. Therefore, it can be said that smart campuses are the advanced level of digital campuses [43].

Smart campuses have the capability to sharply change the education system by providing high-quality services to its members. It can provide an interactive environment for faculty and students.

Features of smart campus:

1.   The smart campus uses IoT-based services to promote energy management, water management, etc. For example, by using various sensors in the campus, lights and fans can be turned on or off according to the movement inside the room. Smart grid, by using smart meter, smart appliances and energy-efficient resources, decides when and how much electricity is required to use them and at what price.

2. By using various sensors on the devices, its maintenance can be done automatically using an expert computer system that reduces the response time for the maintenance.
3. Campus surveillance and real-time incident warning can be done on smart campuses by using IoT. Open doors and windows can also be detected, which prevents any intruders.
4. By using sensing technologies in parking areas and driveways, students, faculties and staff members can find the nearest available car parking in their daily life, and it saves a lot of time, decreases the pollution level and reduces the traffic jam.
5. In a smart campus, automated attendance tracking for students can save a lot of time and reduce human errors in recording student attendance. It is a very time-consuming process to take attendance in a class with a large number of students.
6. In smart campuses, navigation of students, faculties and staff members can be made easy by providing a map of campus to them. In this way, they can find their classrooms, examination halls, available lab slots, available library seats, nearest canteens, etc.

11.5.2   Smart classroom

The smart classroom is a setup that is the integration of different technologies such as voice recognition, computer vision, real-time multimedia communication software, tele-education software, SmartBoard device and wireless microphones. By using various natural modalities, a teacher can interact with remote students and feels the same response of these students as he feels with local students in a real classroom. Similarly, the remote students also get the same feeling as they can get in real classrooms [44]. Figure 11.3 gives an overview of a smart classroom.

Teachers of smart classrooms can teach remote students as well as local students by walking freely using conventional methods of teaching because they are in a real classroom environment. This simultaneous teaching method for both the local and remote students does not need any larger workforce, and it also facilitates students with recorded lectures as hypermedia courseware that can be viewed many times by students after their class [44].

A text-to-speech module is also required to notify the teacher about any event. For example, if any remote student raises hand in the client program because they

Figure 11.3   Smart classroom

have queries regarding the topic taught, the system alerts the teacher about the same [45].

Smart classroom devices can be divided into two categories: infrastructure and mobile.

- The infrastructure devices are stationary. These devices exist in the class-rooms, and mobile devices get the necessary information from them, e.g. locations of mobile devices with respect to the infrastructure devices and the intensity of light in the classroom.
- Mobile devices usually belong to the learning students and their instructors and used to provide an active interaction among them in a classroom [46].

A biometrics-based login is required to identify a lecturer before authorizing facilities of the classroom. In the smart classroom, face-recognition and speaker-verification technologies are combined to automatically identify a teacher [47,48].

Thus, a smart classroom helps in e-learning in a collaborative way among students. Students in such an e-learning environment can form small groups and solve any specific problem or develop a group project with the help of various facilities.

11.5.3   Importance of smart classrooms in e-learning application

- Admin can easily share teacher's notes with their learners outside the class-room with the help of smart e-learning applications.
- Collaborative learning environments can be created where students with dif-ferent classrooms and different areas can be clubbed in one place.
- Learners get the opportunity to attend lectures of excellent professors in their fields.
- Learners can test their knowledge by competing with other performing students.
- Communication of teachers with their students is enhanced through IoT devices.

11.5.4   What turns an ordinary classroom into a smart classroom that is required for e-learning?

- Modern communication techniques SmartBoard with IoT.
- Monitoring of class activities and its synchronization with e-learning systems.
- An amalgamation of smart boards from different locations to create colla-borative classroom teaching.
- Low-energy consumption through IoT devices.
- Easy sharing of digital notes among students, which is collected from various smart boards.
- Use of excellent congestion algorithms to avoid data congestion that is a cri-tical part of IoT.

Through smart classrooms, students can achieve academic excellence by getting quality education through understanding the concepts in a better way, improving their reading and comprehension skills.

A smart campus and smart classroom is an innovative concept for students and teachers.

11.6 Conclusion

Studying from home has become a new way of life during COVID-19. Educationalists were compelled to think and act beyond their old stigma overnight as all schools were closed during the lockdown. There was a time when no one could imagine studying from home, but online learning tools have proved that everything is possible. Synchronous learning tools have turned out beneficial for virtual face-to-face classes with most of the facilities available in the offline classroom. However, the complete adoption of online schooling is leading to excessive screen time leading to various physical and mental health problems. In the current scenario, the main focus of online teaching is on academics, no option for cocurricular and extracurricular activities. So online schooling may not lead to all-round development of future leaders, and educational institutions would adopt blended learning pedagogies with smart campuses and classrooms and prepare themselves for COVID-19 like the crisis in the future.

11.7 Future work

IoTs can provide an effective learning method for school and college students. Various researches and analyses have reported that the IoT technology will drive the e-learning in the future. Thus, future work can include the energy-efficient classroom facilities provided using IoT for smart campus. In the future, smart classroom notes can be upgraded by adding short audio and video clips to the notes. A live chat session can also be facilitated during accessing the notes.

References

[1]   https://en.unesco.org/themes/education [Accessed on May 20, 2020].
[2]   https://www.weforum.org/agenda/2020/04/coronavirus-education-global-covid19-online-digital-learning/ [Accessed on May 20, 2020].
[3]   Carey K. Everybody ready for the big migration to online college? Actually, no. The New York Times. 2020, https://www.nytimes.com [Accessed on May 25, 2020].
[4]   Rieley JB. Corona virus and its impact on higher education. Research Gate. 2020. [Accessed on June 5, 2020].
[5]   Liguori E and Winkler C. From offline to online: Challenges and opportunities for entrepreneurship education following the COVID-19 pandemic.

Entrepreneurship Education and Pedagogy. https://doi.org/10.1177/2515127420916738 [Accessed on June 5, 2020].

[6]   https://spaces4learning.com/Articles/2019/03/01/Smart-Campuses.aspx?Page=2#.

[7]   https://elearningindustry.com/covid-19-disrupting-online-learning.

[8]   https://www.ft.com/content/879ba44b-fa16-4a9d-afa4-f7f4e149edec. 2019.

[9]   https://theprint.in/india/education/why-online-classes-may-not-be-such-a-good-idea-after-all-especially-for-kids/406979/ [Accessed on June 5, 2020].

[10]   Lee YH, Hsieh YC, and Hsu CN. Adding innovation diffusion theory to the technology acceptance model: Supporting employees' intentions to use e-learning systems. Journal of Educational Technology & Society. 2011;14 (4):124–37.

[11]   Choudhury S and Pattnaik S. Emerging themes in e-learning: A review from the stakeholders' perspective. Computers & Education. 2020;144:103657.

[12]   Cojocariu VM, Lazar I, Nedeff V, and Lazar G. SWOT analysis of e-learning educational services from the perspective of their beneficiaries. Procedia—Social and Behavioral Sciences. 2014;116(0):1999–2003.

[13]   Xu D and Jaggars SS. Adaptability to online learning: Differences across types of students and academic subject areas. 2013. CCRC Working Paper No. 54. New York: Columbia University.

[14]   Singh V and Thurman A. How many ways can we define online learning? A systematic literature review of definitions of online learning (1988-2018). American Journal of Distance Education. 2019;33(4):289–306.

[15]   Bates R and Khasawneh S. Self-efficacy and college students' perceptions and use of online learning systems. Computers in Human Behavior. 2007;23:175–91.

[16]   McBrien JL, Cheng R, and Jones P. Virtual spaces: Employing a synchronous online classroom to facilitate student engagement in online learning. The International Review of Research in Open and Distributed Learning. 2009;10(3):1–17.

[17]   Basilaia G, Dgebuadze M, Kantaria M, and Chokhonelidze G. Replacing the classic learning form at universities as an immediate response to the COVID-19 virus infection in Georgia. International Journal for Research in Applied Science & Engineering Technology. 2020;8(III).

[18]   Purnomo W. Penerapan Massive Open Online Course (MOOC) Berbasis Moodle Sebagai Learning Management System (LMS). Simposium Nasional Pengembang Teknologi Pembelajaran, 2016.

[19]   http://cyprusinternetmarketingservices.com/e-learning. [Accessed on June 6, 2020].

[20]   Littlefield J. The difference between synchronous and asynchronous distance learning. 2018, https://www.thoughtco.com/synchronous-distance-learning-asynchronous-distance-learning-1097959.

[21]   Ismail ME, Utami P, Ismail IM, Hamzah N, and Harun H. Development of massive open online course (MOOC) based on ADDIE model for catering courses. Jurnal Pendidikan Vokasi. 2018;8(2):184–92.

[22] Sarah C. What is an LMS?. 2020, https://www.docebo.com/blog/what-is-learning-management-system/.

[23] Zulkifli N, Hamzah MI, and Bashah NH. Challenges to teaching and learning using MOOC. Creative Education. 2020;11(3):197–205.

[24] Basics of eLearning and its implementation in corporates. 2020, https://www.commlabindia.com/elearning.

[25] Andy C. Synchronous and Asynchronous Tools. 2020, https://canvas.vt.edu/courses/12378/pages/synchronous-and-asynchronous-tools.

[26] Global Industry analysts Inc., E-learning – global market trajectory and analytics. 2020, https://www.strategyr.com/market-report-e-learning-forecasts-global-industry-analysts-inc.asp.

[27] Drake N and Turner B. Best video conferencing software in 2020. 2020, https://www.techradar.com/in/best/best-video-conferencing-software.

[28] Adobe. Adobe connect mobile. Adobe. Retrieved 18 September 2015.

[29] https://blog.zoom.us/wordpress/2020/04/27/its-here-5-things-to-know-about-zoom-5-0/. 2020.

[30] Ahamed S and Siddiqui MZ. Disparity in access to quality education and the digital divide, https://www.ideasforindia.in/topics/macroeconomics/disparity-in-access-to-quality-education-and-the-digital-divide.html [Accessed on June 8, 2020].

[31] Comparison of web conferencing software. 2020, https://en.wikipedia.org/wiki/Comparison_of_web_conferencing_software.

[32] Priyadarshini P. Indian video conferencing apps to use instead of zoom. June 2020, https://www.entrepreneur.com/article/352911.

[33] Halupa C. Risks: The Impact of Online Learning and Technology on Student Physical, Mental, Emotional, and Social Health. 2016, pp. 6305–14. 10.21125/iceri.2016.0044.

[34] Rachel O. For thousands of students without home internet access, remote learning is an extra challenge. 2020, https://www.pressherald.com/2020/04/05/for-thousands-of-maine-students-without-home-internet-access-remote-learning-is-an-extra-challenge/.

[35] Saxena K. Coronavirus accelerates pace of digital education in India. EDII Institutional Repository. 2020.

[36] Wang L, Luo J, Gao W, and Kong J. The effect of Internet use on adolescents' lifestyles: A national survey. Computers in Human Behavior. 2012;28 (6):2007–2013. https://doi.org/10.1016/j.chb.2012.04.007

[37] University of Minnesota. Report on health and habits of college students released. Minnesota: University of Minnesota. 2007. Retrieved from https://www.sciencedaily.com/releases/2007/11/071115125827.htm#.V7Kbc-De_S0.email.

[38] Fishman EI, Steeves JA, Zipunnikov V. *et al.* Association between objectively measured physical activity and mortality in NHANES. Medicine and Science in Sports and Exercise. 2016;48(7):1303–1311. https://doi.org/10.1249/MSS.0000000000000885.

[39]   Katzmarzyk PT. Studies of sedentary behavior, activity, and mortality: Duplication or replication?. Medicine & Science in Sports & Exercise: Official Journal of the American College of Sports Medicine. 2016;48(7):1302.

[40]   Schmid D, Ricci C, Baumeister S, and Leitzmann M. Replacing sedentary time with physical activity in relation to mortality. Medicine & Science in Sports & Exercise. 2016;48(7):1312–9.

[41]   Mangis J. Online learning and the effects on functional health: A pilot study, https://dc.ewu.edu/theses/386.

[42]   Kemp S. Digital trends 2019: Every single stat you need to know about the internet. The Next Web. 2019, https://thenextweb.com/growth-quarters/2020/01/30/digital-trends-2020-every-single-stat-you-need-to-know-about-the-internet/.

[43]   Dhawan S. Online learning: A panacea in the time of COVID-19 crisis. Journal of Educational Technology Systems. 2020;49(1):5–22.

[44]   Bao W. COVID-19 and online teaching in higher education: A case study of Peking University. Human Behavior and Emerging Technologies. 2020;2(2):113–5.

[45]   Huang R, Zhang J, Hu Y, and Yang J. Smart campus: The developing trends of digital campus. Open Education Research. 2012;4(004).

[46]   Shi Y, Xie W, Xu G, Shi R, Chen E, Mao Y, and Liu F. The smart classroom: Merging technologies for seamless tele-education. IEEE Pervasive Computing. 2003;2:47–55. [Accessed on June 5, 2020].

[47]   Tao JH and Cai LH. A Neural Network Based Prosodic Model of Mandarin TTS System-2. Proc. Int'l Conf. Spoken Language Processing (ICSLP 2000), China Military Friendship Publish, vol. II, 2000, pp. 75–8.

[48]   Yau SS, Gupta SK, Karim F, Ahamed SI, Wang Y, and Wang B. Smart Classroom: Enhancing Collaborative Learning Using Pervasive Computing Technology. Proceedings of 2nd ASEE International Colloquium on Engineering Education (ASEE2003), 2003 Jun, pp. 1–10.

[49]   https://www.ft.com/content/879ba44b-fa16-4a9d-afa4-f7f4e149edec.

[50]   Raju PR. E-Learning Boon or Bane. An HRD Perspective. Retrieve on. 2019 Jan;24.

[51]   Parkes M, Stein S, and Reading C. Student preparedness for university e-learning environments. The Internet and Higher Education. 2015;25:1–10, https://doi.org/10.1016/j.iheduc.2014.10.002.

[52]   U.S. Department of Health and Human Services. 2008 physical activity guidelines for Americans. 2008. Retrieved from https://health.gov/paguide-lines/pdf/paguide.pdf.

[53]   Xie F, Xu GY, and Hundt E. A Face Verification Algorithm Integrating Geometrical and Template Features. Proc. 2nd IEEE Pacific-Rim Conf. Multimedia (PCM2001), Springer, 2001, pp. 253–60.

[54]   He ZY and Hu QX. A Speaker Identification System With Verification Method Based on Speaker Relative Threshold and HMM. Proc. 6th Int'l Conf. Signal (ICSP 2002), People's Posts and Telecomm. Publishing House, 2002, pp. 488–91.

Part III

Case studies

Chapter 12

Bioinformatics algorithms: course, teaching pedagogy and assessment

Suma Dawn[1] and Prantik Biswas[1]

This chapter is a case study for presenting various modes of in-class lecture delivery, student–instructor interaction, and topic discussion. The aim of using numerous forms of teaching–learning pedagogy is for justifying and achieving the learning outcomes of the course. We have tried to incorporate and change strategies of having instructor-led training (ILT) materials to student-centric learning. It explores various learning styles and dimensions so that the course content may be delivered to its fullest. Adaptation of different types of learning styles is implemented to promote flexibility with the instructor and help the students perceive a topic in various flavours. The chapter also puts forth topic-wise teaching–learning pedagogy availed, students' motivations, as justified from their informal feedbacks, recommended actions that have a positive influence in topic delivery and understanding and usage in exploring the subject in relation to other domain studies. Blooms' cognitive level is also mentioned to give a concise idea of the topic depth that would be followed in this particular course delivery.

The chapter also discusses the concept development and exploration, course-related material design and development, and evaluation and analysis. The measurement framework is developed on the basis of the following criteria of intuitive capability levels, in-class response, topic understanding (based on student's informal and formal feedback), and marks-based evaluations. This inherently incorporates certain evaluation practices followed in this course. Having a high cohesion with bioinformatics, the course helps in offering computational solutions to sustainability-related issues. Further, based on NBA requirements, the course outcomes are also measured as per their given directives.

Based on student's interactions, the course was found to be popular and useful to students. The computer science and engineering and information technology (CSE and IT) students could easily relate the understanding of data structures and algorithms captured in the interdisciplinary course, whereas the biotechnology students could relate their core knowledge in bioinformatics, genes, genetics, protein, and other domain knowledge to the various algorithms that can help in

[1]Department of CSE & IT, Jaypee Institute of Information Technology, Noida, India

addressing solutions. The subject presents a win–win situation for students as they get to work in a domain with a vast dataset and that can have a huge impact on the human lifestyle and lifespan understanding.

Key contributions: The key contributions of the study are as follows:

- Present the course content and related outcomes to understand the students' performance in the elective course of bioinformatics algorithms.
- Extrapolate students' experience with an interdisciplinary course so that they can incline the way computational solutions may be useful in different fields, especially in bioinformatics.
- Detail the course syllabus by giving a comprehensive description of the course content. Certain algorithms and examples are also presented.
- Discern various strategies used while teaching the course and the motivations for doing well in the course.
- Perceive the various forms of assessment techniques that were found to be relevant while course delivery.

12.1   Introduction

Bioinformatics is a versatile and collaborative domain of science that combines notions from biology, computer science concepts, information engineering abstractions, postulations from mathematics and statistics to examine, evaluate, and interpret data from the biological field. Bioinformatics is used in the study of many fields such as study of cancer, genetics, medicine and drug discovery, the application of computers in protein-sequence analysis and tracing protein evolution, and other applications.

With the intention of organizing and handling numerous bioinformatics' requirements, diverse programmes have been transcribed by utilizing various available computing grammar and expressions. The concluding objective of bioinformatics is to ascertain fresh and unprecedented biological perceptions through the interpretation of biological data. Exhaustive and highly intensive data used and present in this domain can be addressed from a computational perspective. Though it is not a new field, it has gained a lot of importance.

The course of bioinformatics algorithms focuses on the study of known methods and data structures for problems in the analysis of biomedical mass data. It can also help in the development of novel algorithms. It introduces algorithmic techniques for solving bioinformatics problems [1–5]. For each topic, the existing methods, their examples, probable solution approach, the relationship between the algorithms, and the biological problems have been discussed [6–11,28–30].

Bioinformatics algorithms is a subject that is currently being offered as an elective to Odd Semester Final-year B.Tech students, i.e., for VII semester students. Initially, it was offered to only CSE and IT students. This year, the course was opened to Electronics and Communication Engineering (ECE) and to Biotechnology (Biotech) students. For the previous two consecutive years, this elective course was offered to students belonging to the department of CSE and IT.

For this elective course, there were no prerequisites; however, a basic understanding of biology and some intent on algorithms and programming language were thought to be helpful. This course tries to bridge a gap between various algorithms that students may have studied in their previous semester and the field of bioinformatics leading to an interdisciplinary field that can be explored more as a course as well as a research domain.

Teaching such a reach-oriented course can be done both during in-class teaching and using certain enhanced forms such as e-learning technologies [12–16]. A bioinformatics algorithm deals with applications of informatics on biological systems. This allows for using computational methods. Most explored topics in this domain include sequencing technologies, molecular sequence analysis, computational genomics, genome assembly, transcriptomics, metagenomics, immunogenomics, and others.

The various sections of the present study are as follows: course content's creation and access, and course outcomes are detailed in Section 12.2. In Section 12.3, various strategies for lecture delivery are discussed. Various related in-class activities are also particularized therein. Section 12.4 details the topics of the course. In-class assessment approaches are showcased in Section 12.5. Discussions and feedback aggregation are showcased in Section 12.6. Section 12.7 concludes this study along with presenting a few pointers as a future scope.

12.2 Course content: creation and access, course outcomes

The course should have content that would impress and excite students to programme and apply computational methods. Also, since the field is biological, there would be huge volume of data that would need to be mined and analysed to present useful derivation. This should also help students understand the various manners, in which various algorithms with different parameter sets may be applied for real-life situations. The topics covered should have an application of general algorithmic techniques, tools for analysis, understanding various issues and situations for thought-provoking discussions, analysis, and various modifications of the approaches. In this course, the aim is to give a walkthrough of the major aspects related to bioinformatics such as the usage of databases, computationally derived control structures, consuetude various hypotheses, algorithms, computer-aided drug design, and protein–protein interactome design. This course is designed to nurture the skills and knowledge required for students aspiring to work in the field of bioinformatics. The content of the course was prepared after going through the content uploaded at multiple websites and by considering the various books and notes available for similar courses.

The initial introductory topics included discussions about biological algorithms versus computer algorithms and comparative analysis of various classes of algorithms. Then molecular biology was introduced.

Computational algorithms related to searching, sequencing, motif finding, string-related problems, trees, graphs, and other such methods are exhaustively used. Applications of various algorithms were tested with data from BLAST and

FASTA databases. These include comparing a sequence against a database, gene expression analysis, understanding corrupted cliques, discerning small and large parsimony, and other such problems. These topics were delved with respect to the analysis of genetic variations and requirements.

12.2.1   Access of course content

The content can be accessed from the repository provided by the institute. Every student has his/her own login account through which they can log in to the institute server. The instructors can upload the content. This does not follow any structured procedure.

The course description, evaluation criteria, course-specific outcomes, text and reference books, tutorials, lecture notes, and other such details are uploaded in the institutional repository for the course. Each course content can be accessed in their corresponding departmental semester-wise aggregated folders. The students may also be given external URLs wherein specific course-related content may be present. These are used as additional materials.

The course of bioinformatics algorithms is run as an elective for the final-year, VII semester students. These students are considered to have cognitive maturity in understanding various subject-related contents. Hence, apart from regular book-based content, students are also encouraged to explore research papers related to various topics.

For easy delivery of the content, certain learning objects may be designed, which can help in creating small self-contained modules. In the course of the bioinformatics algorithms, these learning objects are related to certain biological concepts and revision of some algorithmic concepts. These relate to the various course outcomes. These are sometimes presented as reading materials to supplement the topic being taught [17]. The relationship between various stakeholders, namely, the instructor, students, course, and learning objects are depicted in Figure 12.1.

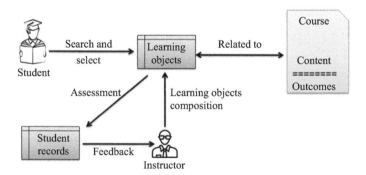

Figure 12.1   Relationship between instructor, student, learning objects, and course

The instructor must (i) determine the course outcomes related to specific learning objects, (ii) establish the sequence of introducing the learning objects to the students, (iii) determine the assessment activities for evaluating student's performance, and (iv) take feedback about these learning objects and their usefulness.

12.2.2 Course outcomes

Outcome 1. Relate to different computational challenges in computational molecular biology. The various topics had interpreting materials such as explanation or summarization. This outcome is related to 'comprehension', cognitive level two.

Outcome 2. Examine proper algorithmic concepts to solve a computational problem. With the usage and modification of various algorithms and techniques, the students should be able to compartmentalize and modularize structures and use various principles in different forms of applications. This outcome is related to 'analysis', cognitive level four.

Outcome 3. Determine the importance of traditional to contemporary approaches for solving biological problems. Students should be able to aggregate different algorithms and principles to present solutions. This outcome is related to 'synthesis', cognitive level five.

Outcome 4. Design strategy to resolve real-world biological challenges. Understanding a new situation and presenting probable solution was required. This outcome is related to 'evaluation', cognitive level six.

Outcome 5. Identify appropriate algorithmic technique to solve a given bioinformatics-related task. The aim is to use the discussed topics in new and concrete situations. This outcome is related to 'application', cognitive level three.

Outcome 6. Develop an optimized solution model for computational biology problems. The algorithms must be optimized so that the huge datasets and parameters may be aggregated and used. This outcome is related to 'evaluation', cognitive level six.

Outcome 7. Formulate prediction tools and estimate the solutions for biological problems. Given a solution to some events, students should be able to evaluate the proposed solutions. This outcome is related to 'evaluation', cognitive level six.

12.2.3 Course content

It is assumed that in a semester, there are approximately 14 weeks of teaching with 3 teaching hours per week. Assuming that a lecture is equivalent to each teaching hour, then there are 42 lecture hours. The content presented later is divided into 42 lecture hours with each topic consisting of a few of these.

1. *Algorithms and complexity:* Introduction, Biological Algorithms versus Computer Algorithms, the Change Problem, Comparative Analysis of Various Classes of Algorithms. (2 Lecture hours)
2. *Molecular biology:* Introduction, Structure of Genetic Materials, Structural Formation of Proteins, Information Passage between Deoxyribose Nucleic Acid (DNA) and Proteins, Evaluation of Bioinformatics. (3 Lecture hours)
3. *Exhaustive search:* Restriction Mapping, Practical Restriction Mapping Algorithm, Regulatory Motifs in DNA Sequences, Profiles, Search Trees, Finding Motifs, Finding a Median String. (4 Lecture hours)

4. *Greedy algorithms:* Genome Rearrangements, Sorting by Reversals, Approximation Algorithms, Breakpoints – A Different Face of Greed, A Greedy Approach to Motif Finding. (3 Lecture hours)

5. *Dynamic programming algorithms:* Classical Problems: DNA Sequence Comparison, The Manhattan Tourist Problem, etc., Edit Distance and Alignments, Global Sequence Alignment, Scoring Alignments, Local Sequence Alignment, Alignment with Gap Penalties, Multiple Alignment, Gene Prediction, Statistical Approaches to Gene Prediction, Similarity-Based Approaches to Gene Prediction, Spliced Alignment. (7 Lecture hours)

6. *Divide-and-conquer algorithms:* Divide-and-Conquer Approach to Sorting, Space-Efficient Sequence Alignment, Block Alignment and the Four Russians Speedup, Constructing Alignments in Sub-quadratic Time. (4 Lecture hours)

7. *Graph algorithms:* Graphs and Genetics, DNA Sequencing, Shortest Superstring Problem, DNA Arrays as an Alternative Sequencing Technique, Sequencing by Hybridization, SBH as a Hamiltonian Path Problem, SBH as an Eulerian Path Problem, Fragment Assembly in DNA Sequencing, Protein Sequencing and Identification, The Peptide Sequencing Problem, Spectrum Graphs, Protein Identification via Database Search, Spectral Convolution, Spectral Alignment. (8 Lecture hours)

8. *Combinatorial pattern matching:* Repeat Finding, Hash Tables, Exact Pattern Matching, Keyword Trees, Suffix Trees, Heuristic Similarity Search Algorithms, Approximate Pattern Matching. (4 Lecture hours)

9. *Clustering and trees:* Hierarchical Clustering, *k*-Means Clustering, Evolutionary Trees, Distance-Based Tree Reconstruction, Reconstructing Trees from Additive Matrices, Evolutionary Trees and Hierarchical Clustering, Character-Based Tree Reconstruction. (3 Lecture hours)

10. *Applications:* BLAST-Comparing a Sequence against a Database; The Motif Finding Problem, Gene Expression Analysis, Clustering and Corrupted Cliques, Small and Large Parsimony Problem, Hidden Markov Models, Randomized Algorithms. (4 Lecture hours)

12.3   Strategies of lecture delivery

Various strategies for in-class lecture delivery and discussion were used. These are canvased and stated in this section. Some of these include the following:

1. Visualization aspects: The usual lecture delivery pattern of having ILT materials such as PowerPoint, or facilitator guides or student handouts can be converted to the following:
    (i)   A mixture of short-duration requirement description lecture with visually appealing content. This can help in effective and engaging delivery.
    (ii) Different formats so that students can download and/or view content on different platforms, including note-sharing, blogs, and discussion threads.

2. Having infographics, the addition of code executables, YouTube or course links, etc.
3. Clear and precise presentation of the context and requirements so that the students can understand this interdisciplinary field.
4. Research papers related to various topics are discussed. This basically follows a discussion-based and/or problem-based teaching–learning framework.

The numerous related activities and teaching–learning methods [18] that may be employed during lecture delivery are enumerated in Table 12.1. Students' feedback was presented, and the percentage of students who have marked it higher (i.e., greater than 3 on a Likert scale of 1–5) is also presented.

Reading, critically comprehending and interacting with texts are central to graduate and undergraduate education. Spelman (assessing classroom quality) defined reciprocal teaching with fab four: predicting, clarifying, questioning, and comprehension/summarization in their own words. Student's performance can be measured at various levels. Though the most common form is to evaluate their performance during the semester written exams, evaluations may be done during lecture classes as well. The interactions with students serve as indicators for assessing classroom quality. These interactions are mostly related to the process of arriving at a problems' solution conferred during lecture sessions and usually demonstrate a candidate's view of the activity. While these views may be classified as incomplete, performed, and managed, they help the instructor in forming an informal cognitive standing of the students.

12.4   Details of the topics discussed

12.4.1   Topic 1: algorithms and complexity

Bioinformatics is a truly interdisciplinary field of computational and biological sciences. It is not only a very interesting domain for exploration but, given the current world scenario, also its usefulness is without any doubt. It is also a very rapidly evolving field with a major impact on human life. Many challenges in the postgenomic biomedical sciences find solutions with algorithmic techniques. The fundamental mechanisms in genome evolutions, protein-interaction network structures, and other such works have been improved using an algorithm basis. Such interesting problems that have a life-changing impact in biology, pharmacy, and other related fields present stimulating challenges to students to strive and present the solution(s). Though the thought-provoking ideas are very welcome during class discussions, it is a difficult call to make to first teach algorithms to the students or teach biological-science-related concepts.

In the initial part of the first lecture, the students are introduced to the subject, the faculties involved, the course outcomes, curriculum, evaluation strategies, and a general introduction to the topics. Then a few algorithms and data structures are also discussed.

Table 12.1 Various activities and teaching–learning methods used during lecture delivery

In-class teaching and activities conducted	Type	Percentage of students who rated high (>3)	Topics
Solving algorithms manually	Whiteboard	97.59	All basic algorithms
Depiction of algorithm solution via animation or using other forms of ICT	Use of ICT	58.77	Greedy algorithms, dynamic programming algorithms, divide-and-conquer algorithms, graph algorithms
Assignment of small warm-up exercises transmitted to students prior to starting the lecture class	Just-in-time-teaching	62.98	Structure of genetic materials, structural formation of proteins, information passage between DNA and proteins, evaluation of bioinformatics
Interactive lecture	Just-in-time-teaching	96.15	Space-efficient sequence alignment, block alignment and constructing alignments; Hamiltonian path problem, Eulerian path problem
Collaborative recitation involving small groups to show problem-solving on a whiteboard with the help of instructors input as and when needed	Just-in-time-teaching	94.71	Clustering techniques; testing data using BLAST and FASTA databases; understanding corrupted cliques; motif finding
Division of class in small group to present a research paper with each member of the group presenting a particular aspect	Peer-reviewed research assignments/ group projects	87.98	Gene expression analysis; testing of data using BLAST and FASTA databases
Creation of a visual representation of models to depict an idea	Concept mapping	98.08	Character-based tree reconstruction; clustering techniques; tools for genome and sequence analysis
Discussion of case studies related to particular topics or current trends	Problem-based learning/case studies	86.06	Distance and alignments, global sequence alignment, scoring alignments, local sequence alignment, alignment with gap penalties, multiple alignment, gene prediction, statistical approaches to gene prediction
Discussion of smaller algorithms	Think/pair/share	85.09	Tools for genome and sequence analysis; block alignment and constructing alignments

The student-crowd is a mix of scholars from the streams of Computer Science and Engineering, Electronics and Communication Engineering, and Biotechnology. These scholars have undertaken an initial course in data structures and algorithms. Keeping this in mind, not only the class curriculum had been designed to present both – a compendium of computational protocols, statistical approaches, and algorithmic techniques, as well as be useful for the development of various methods for biological requirements.

Biological applications many-a-time use tools such as BLAST or FASTA (database search tools) but students are not acquainted with their working and usage. This can hinder the search parameter set. Knowledge about the tool are not critical for the course, but understanding these would help in verification of results and acquisition of new data sets. Hence, the course presentation is done in such a manner that it holds students' interest and introduces algorithms as well as biology concepts without compromising on the knowledge aspects. The algorithm is nothing but a sequence of instructions to be performed to solve a problem. To list the steps, pseudocoding is used. These pseudocodes are easy to understand and can be converted to any programming language as and when needed. Though a pseudocode writing does not have a specific standard, it is found that the pseudocodes do not use the natural language-like structure but very much near it. An example is shown later.

Let us say that the algorithm is to be designed to find the smallest number from a given list of numbers:

===

Algorithm 12.1 Find smallest ()

Input: List of number, A
Output: smallest number in the list A.

Read A;   //read all numbers in the list A
Let small=$A[0]$
//Assume that the variable 'small' contains the first number of // list A and it is assumed that this is currently the smallest // number.
// Now check if the variable 'small' contains the smallest
// number of all the numbers in the given list A.
Examine $A[1]$ to $A[n]$ // checking all the elements of A except $A[0]$
if $A[i]$ is smallest,
      return small=$A[i]$;
else check $A[i+1]$;
      return small;   //returning the smallest number of the list A

As described earlier, the algorithm has a name that may be assumed to be the name of the function. Also present are the inputs given to the algorithm and the expected output. Further, it uses data to perform manipulations. Hence, along with the knowledge, the know-how of data, its type and its storage, i.e., the data structure knowledge is also very important. Linear data structures such as arrays, strings, stacks, queues, and non-linear data structures trees and graphs are very useful in solving various types of problems. These will be discussed later in much detail, as and when required. An example of how biological problems may be mapped to an algorithm is the problem of DNA replication which takes a single strand of DNA and returns its replica. This can be simplified as a text copy problem, in which the elements of the text are nothing but the protein symbols of A, T, G, and C.

Considering that there may be multiple ways, in which a particular problem can be solved, in computational sciences, we should be able to understand the time and resource requirements of the various algorithms for solving a particular problem. This analysis helps one to understand the complexity of the algorithms, thereby making it suitable in various situations depending on the need and available resources. Computer science students know them as the complexity analysis with various notations of Big-O asymptotic notation giving the worst-case scenario giving the upper bound of the function. Big-Ω denotes the asymptotic lower bound, while Big-Θ denotes the asymptotic tight bound notations and is useful for many other analyses.

In most analyses, usually, the O-notation is considered as it presents the upper limit of the execution time, i.e., the execution time in the worst case. Tools like 'Profilers' are available that measure the running time of the programme (in milliseconds) and help in an understanding bottleneck and optimization of the codes. Though very useful, such tools are not very relevant for figuring out the complexity of the algorithms. The algorithm's complexity is found by comparing the algorithm at an abstract level. It ignores the implementation details of the programming language, the hardware, or the instruction set of the given CPU. Hence, complexity analysis is used to measure how fast a programme is, while performing computations. It also explains the behaviour of the algorithm and the programme when the input grows. This aspect of the complexity analysis is very important as most biological data are not only large (storage size of each element), but also, large in number (count of such elements). The asymptotic behaviour helps in assimilating the behaviour of the factors that grow larger in correspondence to the input size.

In the introductory class, the discourse happens on what algorithms are, what are the various data structures and their techniques. The complexity of the algorithms is also discussed. Understanding the relationship between the biological sciences and computations using the models and algorithms is very important, which is shown in Figure 12.2. It is also a huge challenge in proposing a model for solving a biological problem. Sometimes the solutions are straightforward, while in many cases multiple models need to be tested to present a good solution.

Finding solutions for many biological problems is complemented with the use of the proper computational model. Understanding, if the problem can be formalized as a computational model, is an important aspect of it. The analysis would have to be done to predict if such a model is an accurate depiction of the biological problem in hand. The model then needs to be implemented using an appropriate algorithm. The algorithm draws inputs, i.e., data from the problem domain itself. It should satisfy data quality, quantity, size, etc. Further, the algorithm needs to be

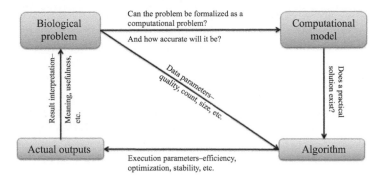

Figure 12.2 Challenge in forming a computation model from a given biological problem and the usage of algorithms within the framework

tested not only for its correctness but also for parameters such as efficiency, robustness, optimization, convergence, energy function, and others. The actual output given by the algorithm must be useful by presenting interpretable data. During these sessions, concepts of iteration, recursion, greedy approaches, dynamic programming, and divide-and-conquer are also presented. Some introduction to random algorithms, machine learning concepts, and other such new techniques are also offered.

12.4.2 Topic 2: molecular biology

All the functionalities in our bodies or any living organism are performed by organs made up of tissues, which, in turn, are built from cells. These cells are the smallest living units. Though the cells have a high water content of almost 70%, the rest is made up of micromolecules (almost 23%) and macromolecules (remaining). There are certain common functionalities and some specific functions. These specifications allow these cells to form tissues and organs to help one to perform body tasks. However, there are two basic functions that each cell must perform: (i) perform chemical reactions required to maintain life and (ii) reproduction to pass the information for maintaining life actions, to the next generation. For performing these actions, the cell actors consist of (i) protein to help one to perform various chemical reactions; (ii) DNA to store and pass information for various functions, including reproduction; and (iii) RNA (ribose nucleic acid) to act as intermediary requirement between DNA and proteins.

The lecture sessions include discussion about a brief history of molecular biology; genetic content, and molecular codes for genes; the structure of DNA, protein, and the information transfer between them. Another lecture session included the analysis of DNA such as copying DNA, cutting and pasting DNA, measurement of the length of the DNA strand. Also discussed during these sessions, was how species differ due to molecular evolution, or genomic rearrangements, etc.

Molecular biology was given a big push by Robert Hooke who had made the great discovery that organisms are made of cells. The study of cells was extended by scientists such as Scheide, Schwann, while heredity was studied to a larger extent by Gregor Mendel who is also called the Father of Genetics. DNA was discovered by Friedrich. In 20 years starting from 1881 to 1900, more discoveries such as understanding the chemical structures of all the 20 amino acids were done.

In the first decade of the twentieth century, other famous discoveries of facts about RNA and the fact that chromosomes are the units of heredity were put forth. Famous scientists – George Beadle and Edward Tatum – recognized that genes were made up of proteins. The prominent helical structure of DNA was established by James Watson and Francis Crick. The Watson–Crick rules help in understanding the bonds between the complementary bases of (i) A with T (two hydrogen-bonds); and (ii) C with G (three hydrogen-bonds). These helped one to understand the stability of the double-helix model of the DNA.

A DNA strand is engendered by binding together nucleotides. The DNA has a phosphate–sugar backbone. Its orientation has directed from 5' to 3' because DNA always extends from 3' end. The 5' to 3' is called upstream, while the 3' to 5' forms the downstream orientation. The two strands are antiparallel with one being the reverse complement of the other. Though the DNA usually has a linear form, in simple organisms like *Escherichia Coli*, they exist in circular form.

A protein called histone helps the DNA wind tightly to form a chromosome. The aggregate information warehoused by all chromosomes together constitutes a genome. A DNA sequence is called a gene. This gene helps in the encoding of a protein or an RNA molecule. The RNA is known to have both the properties of DNA and proteins. They are similar to DNA, in the terms that they can accumulate and transfer information. They are similar to proteins, in the terms that they can form a complex three-dimensional structure and perform some functions.

Other important discoveries such as ribosomes, isolation of tRNA, gene cloning, the 5' splice junctions, automated sequencing mechanism, sequencing the bacterial genomes, and sequencing the first human chromosome were done in the twentieth century. The twenty-first century saw more growth in this field of the sequencing of genomes, including projects such as 'Human Genome Project' (Figure 12.10). These great discoveries shape the way microbiology has moved forward and is being used.

Proteins contained in the cells are what drive all living things. These cells may be categorized as prokaryotes or eukaryotes though they evolve from the same primitive cell. The structure of the cells is very complex. The cell cycle involves replication, synthesis, and division among other stages. The chemical composition of a cell is 70% water and rest 30% being micro- and macromolecules. These can result in biochemical reactions and metabolic pathways. These pathways also give rise to the translation of mRNA to proteins. The class discussions also encompass understanding-related terminologies such as gene, genome, genotype, nucleic acid, and protein strands.

Discussions on genes and genetic materials included topics about Mendel's experiments, mutations, chromosomes, linked-genes, genetic maps, meiosis and mitosis forms of reproductions, and other subtopics. Analysis of DNA incorporates techniques for copying, cutting, pasting, measuring, and probing DNA. Copying of

DNA, though not interesting from the computational point of view, is very useful in wet-lab experiments. Methods such as polymerase chain reaction, or PCR, and cloning are used for copying DNA. Cutting and pasting genes is a common way of analysing the gene. A particular enzyme called the restriction enzyme is used as a molecular scissor to cut DNA. The DNA is cut at every instance of a particular string. Such problems can use the computational method of string find. Pasting of genes uses processes such as hybridization and ligation. These involve mimicking the complementary base-paring. Measuring DNA length uses a process like gel electrophoresis, while probing DNA essentially uses hybridization. Probing tests whether a given DNA segment is a part of the DNA solution or not. This problem finds similarity with the string existence problem. These discussions formed the basis of study and some small experimentation during the course.

12.4.3 Topic 3: exhaustive search-mapping, searching

Exhaustive search methods fall under the domain of brute-force search techniques. Though they are simple to design, many-a-time, they have huge resource and time requirements which may not be as per our requirements. DNA restriction mapping and regulatory motif finding are known problem domains where such brute-force techniques may not give very good results.

In molecular biology, restriction maps are used for narrowing the locations of particular genetic markers. Gel electrophoresis is used in wet-labs to find the distance between two separate restriction sites. This illustrates the branch-and-bound techniques. Biologists may experiment to get complete or partial digest. Restriction mapping involves convalescing locations of points when only pairwise distances between those points are known. Certain concepts such as multiset and pairwise distance are needed to understand the concept of digests. A multiset is a set that allows duplicate elements. Let the set of n points, in increasing order, be denoted by X, such that $= \{x_1, x_2, \ldots, x_n\}$. The distance pair denoted by ΔX is defined as $\Delta X = \{x_j - x_i : 1 \leq i \leq j \leq \} n$.

Example 12.1 Complete digest and partial digest

Let $X = \{4, 8, 17, 30\}$. The complete and partial digest calculations are shown later. The complete digest finds the distance between two consecutive restriction sites shown in Figure 12.3.

Partial digest problem (PDP) yields distance between any two restriction sites. The ΔX for partial digest finds the fragments between all the restriction sites which are then presented in increasing order. For the given example as shown in Example 12.1, $\Delta X = \{4, 4, 8, 9, 13, 13, 17, 22, 26, 30\}$ for partial digest in increasing order is shown earlier. This can be calculated as shown in Table 12.2.

The turnpike problem solution is very similar to the PDP solution. While comparing different multisets, it is possible to have two different multisets that are *homometric*, while their original sets are not the same. An interesting problem for biologists is finding

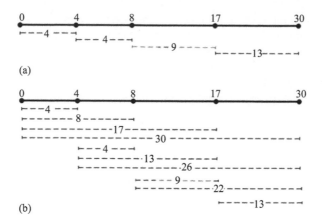

Figure 12.3   Types of digest generation in DNA molecule: (a) depicts the complete digest and (b) depicts the partial digest

Table 12.2   *Partial digest representation of ΔX for Example 12.1*

	0	**4**	**8**	**17**	**30**
0		4	8	17	30
4			4	13	26
8				9	22
17					13
30					

all the homometric sets which can be performed using the brute-force technique. However, for practical implementations, such usage of brute-force is not useful.

A method proposed by Skiena [19] uses *backtracking* for optimized search. Given the size of ΔX, the number of points (n) in the solution may be given by $n(n-1)/2$.

In the Example 12.1, discussed earlier, $n=5$, with the first element $x_1 = 0$; therefore, $X = \{0, x_2, \ldots, x_5\}$. Now take the largest distance, i.e., 30, and put it as $x_5 = 30$. Now intermediary $X = \{0, 30\}$, while removing it from the ΔX. Hence, currently, $X = \{0, 30\}$, and $\Delta X = \{4, 4, 8, 9, 13, 13, 17, 22, 26\}$.

The remaining largest distance is 26, with two choices of $x_4 = 26$ or $x_2 = 4$. Since these are mirror images, $x_2 = 4$ may be assumed with loss of generality. Now removing the distances of $x_5 - x_2 = 26$ and $x_2 - x_1 = 4$ from ΔX, the following are obtained: $X = \{0, 4, 30\}$, and $\Delta X = \{4, 8, 9, 13, 13, 17, 22\}$.

Next, the remaining largest distance is 22, with two choices of $x_4 = 22$ or $x_3 = 8$. Now removing the distances of $x_5 - x_4 = 8$ and $x_4 - x_2 =$ from ΔX, the following are obtained after removing the distances, $X = \{0, 4, 8, 30\}$, and $\Delta X = \{4, 9, 13, 17\}$.

Similarly, in the next step, we get, $X = \{0, 4, 8, 17, 30\}$.
All these stages may be aggregated as Algorithm 12.2 [20].

Algorithm 12.2 Partial digest problem (ΔX)

Input: ΔX
Output: Placement of elements within X.

Length=Maximum number of element in L
DELETE (Length, ΔX)
$X \leftarrow \{0, \text{Length}\}$
PLACE($\Delta X, X$)

The sub-module of 'PLACE' is given in the following.

Algorithm 12.2_1 PLACE($\Delta X, X$)

---

if ΔX is empty
      output X
return
$y \leftarrow$ Maximum element in ΔX
If $\Delta(y, X) \subseteq \Delta X$
Add y to X and remove lengths $\Delta(\text{lynx})$ from ΔX
PLACE($\Delta X, X$)
Remove y from X and add lengths $\Delta(y, X)$ to ΔX
if $\Delta(\text{Length} - y, X) \subseteq \Delta X$
      Add Length $- y$ to X and remove lengths $\Delta(\text{Length} - y, X)$ from ΔX
PLACE ($\Delta X, X$)
Remove Length $- y$ from X and add lengths $\Delta(\text{Length} - y, X)$ to ΔX
return

An interesting problem is finding *regulatory motifs*. These are responsible for turning on immunity. Motif finding is therefore another interesting problem that is solved using alignment, profile, and consensus score. The *motif finding* problem can be reframed as finding a *median string* that inherently uses *Hamming distance*. Concepts involving Search Trees inherently use Tree traversal techniques such as post- or pre-order. Knowledge of these concepts helps students implement and understand relevant requirements.

12.4.4   *Topic 4: greedy algorithms*

It is a well-known fact that there have been similarities between genes of various mammals. Though the genes are present, their positions may differ. So for many fragments, rearrangements of genes can happen. Evolution is demonstrated as the departure in the gene order. Analysing the rearrangement history of mammalian genomes is a challenging problem. Rearrangement actions can be moulded by a sequence of reversals that transmute one genome into another. The simplest form of sorting by reversal method is presented in Algorithm 12.3 [20]. A numerical example is depicted in Example 12.2.

Example 12.2 Consider that the list of elements
(Curtsey: www.bioalgorithms.info):
π=3 4 2 1 5 6 7 10 9 8
π=4 3 2 1 5 6 7 10 9 8
π=4 3 2 1 5 6 7 8 9 10
π=1 2 3 4 5 6 7 8 9 10
Therefore, a minimum count of transformation=3

===

Algorithm 12.3 Sorting by reversals

Input: Permutation π
Output: A series of reversals ρ transforming the given permutation into the identity permutation such that into the identity permutation such that the series of transformation is minimum

---

for i=1 to $n - 1$
    j←position of element i in π (i.e., π_j=i)
if $j \neq i$
$\pi \leftarrow \pi \cdot \rho(i, j)$
output π
if π is the identity permutation
return

Considering the various types of polynomial algorithms, the solution may exist from various approximation techniques. These approximation algorithms are used to present a worst case scenario about maximum throughput of the algorithm, wherein the reasoning is distinct from the ideal algorithm. If the objective function of a problem is not defined as in PDP, approximation algorithms may not be successful in such cases. A pair of neighbouring elements π_i and π_{i+1} for $0 \leq i \leq n$, is called *adjacent* if they form consecutive numbers; otherwise, the pair forms a *breakpoint*. This forms the basis of the breakpoint-based reversal sorting algorithm. This version of the algorithm steadily reduces the number of steps. Example 12.3 showcases this.

Example 12.3 Consider the following list of elements [20]:

(0 8 2 7 6 5 1 4 3 9) $b(\pi)=6$
→← →← -- →← - →
(0 2 8 7 6 5 1 4 3 9) $b(\pi)=5$
→← ← - - - →← - →
(0 2 3 4 1 5 6 7 8 9) $b(\pi)=3$
→ ← -- → - -- →
(0 4 3 2 1 5 6 7 8 9) $b(\pi)=2$
→ ← - - - ---- →
(0 1 2 3 4 5 6 7 8 9) $b(\pi)=0$
- - - - - - - - - - →

There exist many algorithms for greedy motif finding too.

12.4.5 Topic 5: dynamic programming algorithms

Understanding the functionality of a new gene is a challenging problem. Biologists use an approach very similar to reverse engineering. They try to find similarities between the gene sequences with known genes and their associated functions. In 1984, Russell Doolittle and his colleagues established resemblances between cancer-causing and normal growth factor genes. Another example of this was the understanding of cystic fibrosis gene. Finding sequence similarities with genes of known function is a common approach to infer afresh-sequenced gene's function. The similarity score can lead to known inferences to biologists. Dynamic programming techniques help in finding such similarity. In this topic, students were acquainted with various algorithms that helped biologist divulge the resemblance between different DNA sequences.

The various functionalities of the genes may be considered as parameters such as coin denominations (in association with 'the change problem'), or with various destinations (in association with 'The Manhattan Tourist Problem'). The process of travelling from source to destination or sink, while making sure to visit each of the required places, is presented in Algorithm 12.4. It helps one to find the longest path in a weighted grid [20].

Consider the following symbols for Algorithm 12.4: let $s_{i,j}$ be the score in a single sweep of the grid; $w \downarrow$ represents a 2D array in the grid's edges that go from north to south; $\vec{w}$ represents the weights of the grid's edge that go from west to east;

$\vec{w}_{i,j}$ is the weight of the edge between $(i, j-1)$ and (i, j); and $w \downarrow_{i,j}$ is the weight of the edge between $(i, j-1)$ and (i, j).

===

Algorithm 12.4 Manhattan tourist problem

Input: A weighted grid G with two mandatory vertices – source and sink.
Output: The longest path in G from source to sink.

$s_{0,0} \leftarrow 0$

for $i \leftarrow 1$ to n

$\quad s_{i,0} \leftarrow s_{i-1,\,0} + w \downarrow_{i,0}$

for $j \leftarrow 1$ to m

$\quad s_{0,j-1} \leftarrow s_{0,j-1} + \overrightarrow{w_{0,\,j}}$

for $i \leftarrow 1$ to n
$\quad$ for $j \leftarrow 1$ to m

$\quad s_{i,j} \leftarrow \max \left\{ \begin{array}{c} s_{i-1,j} + w \downarrow_{i,j} \\ s_{i,j-1} + \overrightarrow{w_{i,j}} \end{array} \right\}$

return $s_{n,m}$

Distance concepts are very vague in this domain. Though Hamming distance has been used, it may not be useful always. Vladimir Levenshtein [21] in 1966 established the notion of 'Edit Distance'. This distance finds the distance between two strings (or gene proteins) as the minimum number of editing operations for transformation from one string to another. Editing operations may consist of insertion of a symbol, deletion of a symbol, or substitution of one symbol for another. An example [20] is shown in Figure 12.4.

Another common problem is finding the longest common substring or subsequence. It awards a score of 1 for any matches but does not penalize indels. This scoring may be generalized for having particular values for matches, mismatches, and indels. Such an algorithm can solve for global alignment problems, where the task is to find the maximal among all possible alignments between two strings as shown in Figure 12.4. Global alignment helps one to understand the similarity between two strings which, in turn, may be interpreted as the similarity between functions of a gene or a particular gene sequence. It is seen that in many applications, the alignment score between two substrings might be larger than their entirety alignment score. In such cases, the target is to maximize the alignment score over all possible substrings. This is called the local alignment problem as it is limited to substrings rather than the entire strings.

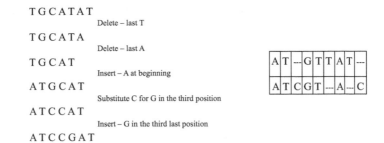

TGCATAT

Delete – last T

TGCATA

Delete – last A

TGCAT

Insert – A at beginning

ATGCAT

Substitute C for G in the third position

ATCCAT

Insert – G in the third last position

ATCCGAT

Figure 12.4   Five edit operations can take TGCATAT into ATCCGAT [20]

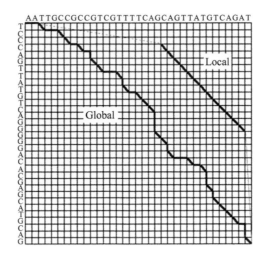

Figure 12.5   Global versus local alignment [20]

While DNA is replicating, there might occur errors. Such errors, insertion, deletion, changes in a substring or a single nucleotide, lead to mutations. If there exists a contiguous sequence of spaces in a row, it is considered as a gap in the alignment. A penalty called 'affine gap penalty' is a linearly weighted score for larger gaps in the gene. It is depicted in Figure 12.5. Finding structural or functional similarities between proteins is the aim of comparison of protein sequences and is presented in Figure 12.6.

12.4.6   Topic 6: divide-and-conquer algorithms

Divide-and-conquer approach to sorting, space-efficient sequence alignment, block alignment, constructing alignments in sub-quadratic time.

The design parameter of divide-and-conquer involves two phases of divide and conquer. Sometimes it is said that the said algorithm has three steps of the divide, conquer, and combine. Dividing the problem involves the same into smaller but

```
--T --C C --C --A G T ---T A T G T --C A G G G G A C A C G ---A --G C A T G C A G A --G A C
   |    | |         | |   |   |   |   | | |        | |   |     |   |   |   | | | |      |
A A T T G C C G C C --G T C G T --T --T T C A G ------C A --G T T A T G --T --C A G A T --C
| | | | |   |         x | | | |   |              | |   x x x | | |   | | | |   |   |
--A T T G C --G ---A T T C G T A T --------G G G A C A --T G G A T G C A T G C A G --T G A C
```

Figure 12.6   Example of a multiple-alignment problem [20]

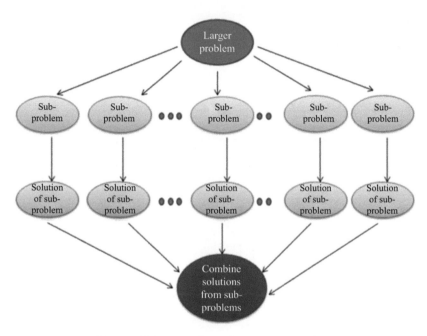

Figure 12.7   Divide-and-conquer paradigm

non-overlapping problems. Conquer comprises solving the smaller sub-problems recursively. And the final state uses these solutions to combine and present the final solution (Figure 12.7).

It is known that the space complexity of the algorithms usually used for edit distance calculations is large and based on the number of vertices in the edit graph.

The block alignment problem uses two strings or sequences and partitions them into blocks of a specified size. The output gives the maximum score (Figure 12.8). The lookup table is constructed using the Four-Russians Speedup.

12.4.7   Topic 7: graph algorithms

Graph theory concepts may be used in finding solutions to bioinformatics. The various moves by chess-pieces on the chessboard, depiction of such moves and others use graphs. A graph (G) may be described as a set of vertices (V) and edges (E) and may be represented as G: (V, E).

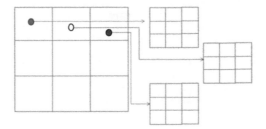

Figure 12.8   Block-pair representation

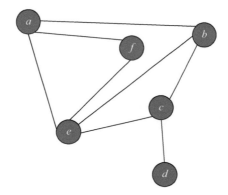

Figure 12.9   Example of a graph

Example 12.4 For the graph shown in Figure 12.9

$V = \{a, b, c, d, e\}$
$E = \{(a,b), (a,e), (a,f), (b,c), (b,e), (c,d), (c,e), (e,f)\}$

The diagram of a graph is irrelevant as a graph may be represented in different ways. An example is shown in Figure 12.10. An example of graph algorithms used is Knight's Tour. Another example is the Bridge Obsession problem or Eulerian cycle problem or the Hamiltonian cycle problem or the shortest path problem. Graphs are also used in the depiction of chemical bonds. Seymour Benzer, in the 1950s, applied graph theory to present a near-linear structure of genes. Mutation of a gene sequence can be commenced using graph theory. Hybridization of a target DNA uses a problem like *l-mer composition*.

Sequencing by hybridization problem can use the Hamiltonian path solution. An example is shown in Figure 12.11 wherein a sequence from ATG can be changed to

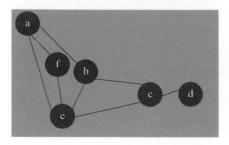 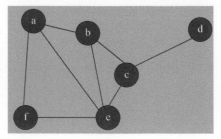

Figure 12.10   Two equivalent representations

S={ATG   AGG   TGC   TCC   GTC   GGT   GCA   CAG}

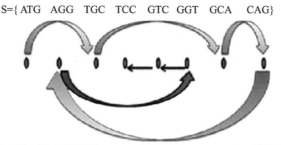

Path visiting ALL VERTICES corresponds to sequence reconstruction ATGCAGGTCC

Figure 12.11   Traversing from ATG to TCC using sequencing by hybridization approximated by the Hamiltonian path solution [20]

TCC using the following sequence: ATG→TGC→GCA→CAG→AGG→GGT→ GTC→TCC. Numerous paths too may be found in Figure 12.11. The numerous paths are depicted in Figure 12.12.

The superstring finding problem is several of these mentioned graph algorithms.

12.4.8   Topic 8: combinatorial pattern matching

Several genetic ailments have been linked with removals, duplications, and reshuffles of longer chains of chromosomal expanses. Such studied actions affect the large-scale genomic designs and might encompass numerous of nucleotides. Repeat Finding is an interesting problem. It involves finding all the repeat sequences in the protein chains. A hash table is an interesting concept. Hash Tables are usually used for indexing, especially hierarchical indexing. In bioinformatics, it has several applications, including sequence alignment, genome and transcriptome assembly, RNA-sequence expression quantification, *k-mer* counting and error correction [22]. In DNA/protein sequence search, hashing constructs a list capable of determining where in a sequence given query *k-mer* is located.

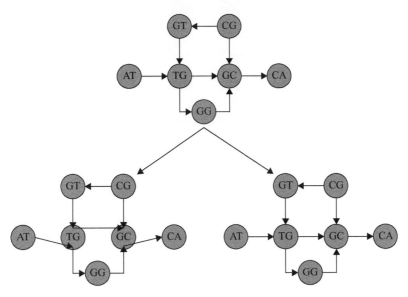

Figure 12.12 Various paths depicted for visiting all possible edges resembling the sequence reconstructions [20]

A familiar issue in bioinformatics is to search a database(s) of arrangements for a known sequence. The pattern matching problem is depicted in Algorithm 12.5.

==

Algorithm 12.5 Pattern matching problem

Input: Pattern $p = p_1, p_2, \ldots p_n$, and string $s = s_1, s_2, \ldots s_m$.
Output: Find all positions $1 \leq i \leq m-n+1$ occurrences of the string pattern, such that the *n-mer* substring of s starting at i overlap with the pattern p.

$n \leftarrow$ length of pattern p
$m \leftarrow$ length of text t
for $i \leftarrow 1$ to $m-n+1$ if $si=p$
return i

Keyword tree, suffix tree, and such algorithm can be applied to genome strings. An algorithm is shown in Figure 12.13.

Usage of Heuristic Similarity Search Algorithms is used in querying databases especially searches in molecular biology. Approximation Pattern-Matching-based solutions to strings in molecular biology are valuable. Finding mismatches and querying for matching too are very motivating problems. Approximation query

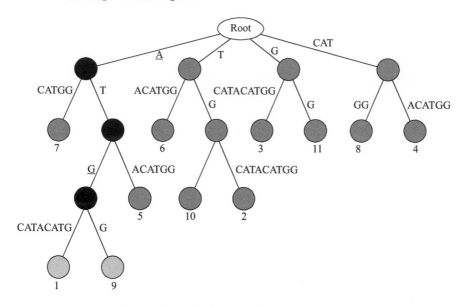

Figure 12.13   An example of tree usage

matching using filtration algorithms uses the following two stages – (i) selection of positions, (ii) verification of potential positions.

12.4.9   Topic 9: clustering and trees

Gene expression analysis uses a sequence comparison. Procedures such as clustering and tree formations help partition or cluster data points in such a manner that it may represent similar features. Conditions such as homogeneity and separation are aspects that have to be implemented for clustering. Homogeneity implies that the genes within a single cluster should have certain similarity parameters. Also, between different clusters, there must be a specific separation criterion. An example is shown in Figure 12.14.

Numerous clustering algorithms are studied by computer science students. They can be used for finding similarities between features and parameters of the gene's biological problems under consideration. Clustering using clique graphs can also be used. A distance matrix can be used for clustering. Evolutionary trees are used for the study of the phylogeny trees. Parsimony tree also finds solutions in these requirements.

12.4.10   Topic 10: applications

BLAST is a very prominent database search tool used in molecular biology. FAST (A) is also another such querying technique. These are discussed in detail in class along with various implantations.

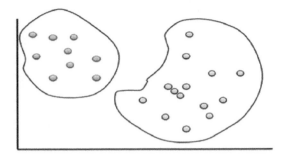

Figure 12.14   Two different clusters (light pink and light blue). These have a clear separation between one another and similarity within the cluster itself

12.5   In-class assessment approaches

The instructor and evaluator are the same in many cases, especially during in-class teaching assessment. The observed behaviour of the students may be compartmentalized as (i) monitoring the answers and class-interactions; (ii) detecting incongruities/anomalies while critiquing case studies; (iii) self-correction depending on the topic being considered. For example, a problem may be solved in multiple ways, but the most optimized method would need to be understood and used by students; (iv) planning and goal-setting of modules for implementing assignment solutions, i.e., designing the various modules/functions that would lead to a probable solution; (v) reflecting on the solution proposed and another probable manner of solving the questions. Other common practices that are being followed in this course include the following: evaluation practices that may be used for short answers, in-class quizzes, research-paper reading and presentation, group-based domain-specific topic-wise presentation, and evaluation of certain tutorials.

The manner in which the students react to the instructor during lecture delivery includes some metacognitive and non-metacognitive aspects [23–26]. These are shown in Table 12.3. These were considered from the feedback given by students.

These are also affected by academic and non-academic aspects. Figure 12.15 depicts this relationship.

12.5.1   Self-assessment by students

Students were also encouraged to engage in self-assessment by observing their own performance while they worked out solutions during class-activities and/or for assignments. These may depend on academic as well as non-academic contexts that derive a student to perform self-assessment.

Students may evaluate themselves using some of the understated essential, but not limited to, (i) approximate time required to arrive at a particular solution; (ii) did they feel that they had improved upon their skills while they solved similar problems in a given domain? (iii) able to summarize a concept/algorithm

Table 12.3   Some metacognitive and non-metacognitive aspects related to teaching–learning styles feedback taken from students

Aspect	Aspect type
Instructor charisma	Traditional non-metacognitive
Teaching environment	Traditional non-metacognitive
Classroom communication	Traditional non-metacognitive
Teacher friendliness	Traditional non-metacognitive
Student interest	Traditional non-metacognitive
Sequence of the topics considered	Metacognitive
Assessment techniques	Metacognitive
Choice of instruction techniques	Metacognitive
Interconnectedness between the topics being taught and the assignments discussed	Metacognitive

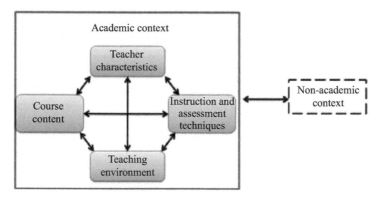

Figure 12.15   Relationship between various academic contextual requirements

adequately; (iv) were they able to switch on to an alternate solution(s) if the current approach did not seem to give correct/quick solution? (v) for a given question, were they able to present a time-bounded solution? (vi) for a similar type of questions, were they able to predict the type of bugs/bottlenecks? (vii) are they able to formulate questions/problems related to various cognitive levels (remember, understand, apply, analyse, evaluate, and create)?

Such assessment helped them understand their weakness and reach out to the instructor for doubt-solving [24,25]. These aspects and their feedback are depicted in Table 12.4.

Based on student–instructor interactions, it was found that many students were intrinsically motivated if the topic was as follows: (i) easy to understand; (ii) the basic algorithm understanding may be wrapped in around 50–75 min; (iii) the algorithm can be easily solved using simple examples; (iv) the

Table 12.4   Parameters of student self-assessment aspects used in this course

Aspect	Student assessment	Rating by faculty
Able to arrive at a solution within certain time-bound?	Mostly True	Mostly True
Confident that they would be able to arrive at a solution independently?	Yes	Yes
Summarize a concept	Yes	Yes
Able to present multiple / different types of procedures to arrive at a solution.	Usually True	Usually True
Are they able to formulate relevant questions / problems themselves?	Yes	Usually True

application of the algorithms is relevant to the topic under discussion. Related extrinsic motivations include gaining marks during their exams and not being penalized for not completing a given tutorial or assignment. As per ARCS model (ARCS abbreviated from attention, relevance, confidence, and satisfaction attributes), students may be motivated using attractive, satisfying, and stimulating learning material [27].

12.6   Discussion

The course was run in the 3L+1T – 3 lectures and 1 tutorial mode. In aggregate, the course was conducted for 42 lectures and 14 tutorial hours. Coding assignments were usually given in the tutorial sessions. It was found that all students responded favourably to understanding basic concepts of the topic as well they appreciated the interdisciplinary aspects related to the topic. There was reluctance in implementing codes for performing various algorithms. However, they were able to propose solutions as a group and as individuals for queries and assignments.

Several metrics were used to evaluate the efficacy of our teaching methods. Course grades measured student progress towards course objectives. Class students were asked to give web-based feedback about the course offered to them. These deal with the evaluation of course efficacy and the overall course experience. Certain feedback criteria are depicted in Table 12.5. These feedbacks were aggregated as ratings based on a frequency scale or a Likert scale.

Students from all disciplines appreciated the interdisciplinary nature of the course as well as the vastness of the usage of various algorithms in various domains. They felt stimulated in tackling real-life problems. They also felt invigorated with their ability to work in groups for small discussions as well as assignments. Due to the limitation of time for submission of assignments, they felt that they could do much better if they were given more time or had better hold over their programming skills, especially the students of ECE and BT.

Table 12.5   Summarized feedback from students who have taken this course and the percentage of students who have rated it more than 50%

Feedback	Percentage of students who have rated more than 50%
Understanding of topic	100
Can answer higher-order thinking related to the topic	74.51
Is interested in coding the algorithms undertaken in the topic	61.5
Is able to critique codes already available as implementation for various algorithms	69.23
Is able to propose solutions individually	91.34
Is able to contribute fruitfully in a group-based learning module	75
Is able to appreciate the interdisciplinary concepts in the topic	100

12.7   Conclusions and future scope

The goals, as proposed, for the study were met and are presented in this paper. 'Algorithmic bioinformatics' is a very dynamic course that can help students explore a various dimensions of usage. This interdisciplinary course also boasted the confidence of the instructors that such a course will be accepted by not only the students of CSE and IT but also by the students belonging to other streams such as ECE and Biotech. Reactions and feedback from students were helpful in constructing and understanding various aspects of teaching–learning.

This chapter discusses the course content of algorithmic bioinformatics. Student access to various course-related teaching–learning materials is presented. The relationship between the various stakeholders of the instructor, students, course, and course-learning objects is also depicted. The various outcomes that a student should be proficient with are also listed. Various strategies for lecture delivery and in-class teaching approaches were presented. Assessments done by the instructors as well as self-assessment by students themselves were also discussed. Various academic contextual requirements for the successful delivery of a course were also portrayed.

Further experimentation may be done by presenting a collaborative course that may be taught in an interdisciplinary manner. Additional improvements may include the following: (i) students may work on live data from government-sponsored projects; (ii) different programming platforms may be explored for implementing algorithms and querying databases; (iii) statistical results and conclusions for large assignments and projects may be considered. These would help in enriching the course to a larger extent.

References

[1] Schmidt B, editor. Bioinformatics: High performance parallel computer architectures. Boca Raton, FL: CRC Press; 2010.

[2] Das S, Abraham A, and Konar A. Swarm intelligence algorithms in bioinformatics. In Computational Intelligence in Bioinformatics 2008 (pp. 113–47). Springer, Berlin, Heidelberg.

[3] Sung WK. Algorithms in bioinformatics: A practical introduction. Boca Raton, FL: CRC Press; 2009.

[4] Armañanzas R, Inza I, Santana R, *et al.* A review of estimation of distribution algorithms in bioinformatics. BioData Mining. 2008;1(1):1–2.

[5] Fourment M and Gillings MR. A comparison of common programming languages used in bioinformatics. BMC Bioinformatics. 2008;9(1):82.

[6] Parida L. Pattern discovery in bioinformatics: Theory & algorithms. Boca Raton, FL: CRC Press; 2007.

[7] Frank E, Hall M, Trigg L, Holmes G, and Witten IH. Data mining in bioinformatics using Weka. Bioinformatics. 2004;20(15):2479–81.

[8] Mitra S and Acharya T. Data mining: Concepts and algorithms from multimedia to bioinformatics. Hoboken, NJ: John Wiley & Sons, Inc.; 2003.

[9] Cohen J. Bioinformatics—An introduction for computer scientists. ACM Computing Surveys (CSUR). 2004;36(2):122–58.

[10] Gautham N. Bioinformatics: Databases and algorithms. Alpha Science Int'l Ltd.; 2006.

[11] Jin B and Zhang YQ. Evolutionary granular kernel trees for protein subcellular location prediction. Machine Learning in Bioinformatics. 2009;4:229.

[12] Marriott RD and Torres PL. Handbook of research on e-learning methodologies for language acquisition. Information Science Reference; 2009.

[13] Oye ND, Salleh M, and Iahad NA. E-learning methodologies and tools. International Journal of Advanced Computer Science and Applications (IJACSA). 2012;3(2).

[14] Arunachalam AR. Bringing out the effective learning process by analyzing of e-learning methodologies. Indian Journal of Science and Technology. 2014;7:41.

[15] Nath J. E-learning methodologies and its trends in modern information technology. Journal of Global Research in Computer Science. 2012;3(4):48–52.

[16] Penalvo FJ. Advances in E-learning: Experiences and methodologies. Hershey, PA: Information Science Reference; 2008.

[17] De Marcos L, Pages C, Martínez JJ, and Gutiérrez JA. Reflections on e-learning lifecycle and learning objects lifecycle. In International Technology, Education and Development Conference INTED2007. Valencia, Spain, March 2007 (pp. 7–9).

[18] Tewksbury BJ, and Heather RM. Designing Effective and Innovative Courses. 2012. https://serc.carleton.edu/NAGTWorkshops/coursedesign/tutorial/index.html.

[19] Skiena SS. The algorithm design manual: Text. Springer Science & Business Media; 1998.

[20] Jones NC, Pevzner PA, and Pevzner P. An introduction to bioinformatics algorithms. MIT Press; 2004.

[21] Compeau P and Pevzner PA. Bioinformatics algorithms: An active learning approach. La Jolla, CA: Active Learning Publishers; 2018.

[22] Mohamadi H, Chu J, Vandervalk BP, and Birol I. ntHash: Recursive nucleotide hashing. Bioinformatics. 2016;32(22):3492–4.

[23] Hartman HJ. Teaching metacognitively. In Metacognition in Learning and Instruction 2001 (pp. 149–72). Springer, Dordrecht.

[24] Hiver P and Whitehead GE. Teaching metacognitively: Adaptive inside-out thinking in the language classroom. In Metacognition in Language Learning and Teaching (Open Access) 2018 (pp. 243–62). Routledge.

[25] O'Hara S, Pritchard R, and Pitta D. Teaching with and for metacognition in disciplinary discussions. In Metacognition in Learning 2019. IntechOpen.

[26] Hartman HJ, editor. Metacognition in learning and instruction: Theory, research and practice. Springer Science & Business Media; 2001.

[27] Gopalan V, Bakar JA, Zulkifli AN, Alwi A, and Mat RC. A review of the motivation theories in learning. In AIP Conference Proceedings 2017 Oct 3 (Vol. 1891, No. 1, p. 020043). AIP Publishing LLC.

[28] Sedgewick R and Flajolet P. An introduction to the analysis of algorithms. Pearson Education India; 2013.

[29] Mandoiu I and Zelikovsky A. Bioinformatics algorithms: Techniques and applications. John Wiley & Sons; 2008.

[30] Della GV and Dondi R. A library of efficient bioinformatics algorithms. Applied Bioinformatics. 2003;2(2):117–21.

Chapter 13

Active learning in E-learning: a case study to teach elliptic curve cryptosystem, its fast computational algorithms and authentication protocols for resource constraint RFID-sensor integrated mobile devices

Adarsh Kumar[1], Alok Aggarwal[1], Kriti Sharma[1,2] and Mukta Goyal[3]

Elliptic curve cryptosystem (ECC) is a public key-based cryptosystem. All algorithms in ECC are based on point addition and point doubling arithmetic operations. This explains the active learning process and its usages in teaching elliptic curve cryptography-based contents to undergraduate and graduate students. Here, the emphasis is given to mathematical contents that make the cryptography concepts easy to understand. Mathematical concepts mainly include point addition and doubling with examples. Further, technical observations are made while teaching these contents. For example, to reduce computation cost, there is a need for fast computations method in point addition and doubling operations. Thus, the fast computational algorithms are important to understand with examples for reducing the cost in ECC arithmetic operations. These algorithms reduce the number of steps required to perform cryptography operations by reducing compute addition and doubling operations. Group authentication is one of the major application domains of ECC. This work presents the ECC-based authentication protocols that provide authentication using encryption/decryption, digital signature, and other cryptography primitives. In observations, it is found that the proposed approach is much better quantitatively and quantitatively compared to traditional teaching.

[1]Department of Systemics, School of Computer Science, University of Petroleum and Energy Studies, Dehradun, India
[2]Department of Computer Science Engineering and Information Technology, K.R. Mangalam University, Gurgaon, India
[3]Department of Computer Science Engineering and Information Technology, Jaypee Institute of Information Technology, Noida, India

13.1   Introduction

The active learning process involves students to approach their preferred way of learning rather than a passive classroom teaching–learning methodology. Almost every good university is considering such practices into consideration for improving student performance and teacher active involvement. A similar but innovative process is followed in the University of Petroleum and Energy Studies (UPES), Dehradun, India. In this instructional and evidence-based active learning process, teachers were trained in pre-teaching boot camp to give active learning practices to students. In this chapter, active learning processes followed to train teachers and students are discussed in a case study. These active learning practices are applied to teach the network security course with elliptic curve cryptography as major content that summarizes the point addition and doubling mathematical operations required in the ECC [1–5]. All possibilities in point addition and doubling are presented in detail with examples. Further, fast computational algorithms are discussed with examples to reduce the cost of elliptic curve cryptography operations. Finally, ECC-based protocols are presented to provide authentication using encryption/decryption, digital signature, and other cryptography primitives [6–9]. After discussing the proposed active learning process and elliptic curve cryptography contents, it has been observed that the proposed approach is much better quantitatively and quantitatively as compared to traditional teaching. Thus, it is suggested to every teacher–participant in this study to adopt the proposed approach in their courses and classrooms and prepare a detailed report [10–14].

This chapter is summarized as follows: Section 13.2 discusses the related work in active learning for E-learning. Section 13.3 introduces UPES management efforts in designing and developing an active learning process for increasing student performance for the online system. This active learning process is applied for teaching the elliptic curve cryptography course, and results are analyzed to estimate the improvement in student performance. Section 13.4 introduces the basics of elliptic curve cryptography course and explains the elliptic curve cryptography operations (point addition and point doubling). It also presents how the elliptic curve cryptography multiplication operation can be computed faster with various algorithms. Section 13.5 introduces the fixed-base doubling and additional method used and applied in the elliptic curve cryptography course with binary operations. Section 13.6 presents the elliptic curve cryptography approach applied in authentication using authentication protocols. Section 13.7 presents the discussions over teaching elliptic curve cryptography courses to undergraduate and graduate students with both traditional and active learning approaches. A comparative analysis of student performance is also drawn in this section. Finally, the conclusion is discussed.

13.2   Related work

Learning is expected to be meaningful. It should produce problem solver, skillful, and competent graduates. The performance of the E-learner should be increased. It should be possible when the teacher explores the different pedagogies in an E-learning environment. In the teaching–learning system, when the learner has exposed the material according to his learning capability, the learner gets motivated to learn that may increase the performance of the learner.

Active learning is one of the techniques which can be used to enhance the performance of the learner. The methods such as collaborative learning, group-discussion, cases, and brainstorming, role play, simulation-based games with imaginary conditions, challenging problem-based teaching/learning, projects (individual or group), peer learning/teaching, and debates are active learning methods that increase the learner performance. These learning strategies enhance students to think critically and creatively manner. These strategies also explore personal attitudes and values, and students can share their ideas through writing [10].

This chapter suggests that active learning strategies such as small to medium scale groups, guided-inquiry learning, specific targeting teacher–student engagement having identified topics/curriculum are proposed for the paramedicine bioscience units. The result shows that active learning helps the student to improve the student grades if used in a classroom with positive student perception [11].

Quire based on the min–max approach is used to view the active learning, combines the informativeness and representativeness unlabeled instances. This work can be enhanced for multiclass learning [12]. The mechanism of the online learning method provides students to get engaged to gain knowledge and skill at that time. This increases the effectiveness of education [13]. The success of teaching and learning depends on student engagement. Various strategies have been proposed to design an online course to explore student engagement with the help of tools and intelligent techniques. The motive of the instructor is to engage the student in the course by using multiple pedagogies in such a manner so that students can participate actively. Active learning pedagogy is one of the techniques that facilitate student engagement is more during learning [13]. Apart from the engagement, it also requires the learner to gain the confidence to be more creative and experimental [14].

Since active learning develops knowledge, skills, and attitudes, authors have promoted various teaching active-learning teaching strategies associated with nature and society. The findings suggest that active learning stimulates the environment at the beginning of education, but it requires creating a learning community at later levels of education [15]. Active learning is an instructional technique applied in a traditional environment that can be applied in an online environment [16]. This chapter suggests that active learning should supersede the instruction technique "learning from examples." The authors discuss the concept of learning a binary in the absence of noise [15]. Frame and framing technique is used to understand the nature of activity in anthropology and sociolinguistics. The learner understands the nature of the activity effects of accessing knowledge and how she thinks to act with the concept of the frame [15].

Traditional pedagogy for medical students did not help much in their performance that results in reducing the motivation to learn. Some of the researchers suggest that online open-book quizzes with multiple attempts may increase the learning outcome. While students were attempting the test, learners were free to refer to their books or materials in the allotted time. Findings concluded that the response was very enthusiastic and learners avail maximum marks in the course [10]. Authors discuss the cognitive models that make help learners to learn the material [11].

13.3   The methodology of active learning process

UPES started a student–teacher freehand teaching–learning-based active and interactive learning process for the online system. After experimenting over two semesters, it has been observed that the proposed one is beneficial to both teachers and students. It is good for a teacher because it self-motivates the teacher to have a higher quality of teaching with his/her learning, and it provides the student's way to learn a subject. Here, the student has the provision to give his/her constant feedback and request to change the strategy as per his/her convenience. Figure 13.1 shows the architecture of active learning for the E-learning system. Figure 13.2 shows the role of a teacher in the E-learning system.

The method proposes for an interactive small to medium scale group-wise to teach elliptic curve cryptography theoretical, mathematical, and simulation aspects. It is assumed that the teachers are trained by an industry expert via hands-on experience over the majority topic of a course. There were peer–teacher group discussions to have self-motivated learning experiences and implement health teaching practices. The teachers' training program could be attended with a maximum strength of 30 faculty members with an exception to certain basic courses. Figure 13.1 shows that students learn the course through an online medium. Here the students register for subjects floated by the department. Teachers collect their interests and way to learn a course. The teacher prepares an interactive active learning strategy and shares it with students. The student gives feedback and class starts. If there are multiple opinions, then teacher construct groups. Students are

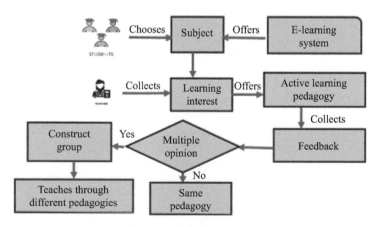

Figure 13.1   Teacher–student relationship

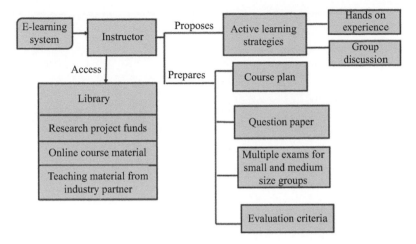

Figure 13.2   Role of a teacher in an E-learning system

divided into groups to have multiple sessions and multiple ways to implement different teaching–learning strategies.

Figure 13.2 shows the role of a teacher in an E-learning system. Each teacher is given a fixed research and teaching fund to implement his/her own interactive active learning process with the concrete result of improving the student contribution and performances. The teacher uses UPES provided resources (library, industry partner visits, research project funds, online course material, teaching material from an industry partner, etc.) and teaches students. The teacher applies the UPES management proposed active learning architecture and regularly measures his/her teaching quality quantitatively and qualitatively. The teacher prepares a course plan and revises it in regular intervals after discussions with the peers.

The teacher is assigned a responsibility to prepare question paper and conduct mid-semester and end-semester examinations. A teacher constructs small to medium size groups and prepare multiple exams and assign one to each group. Each teacher prepares his/her evaluation criteria but maximum marks for evaluation are fixed. A similar process is executed for the end-semester examination. A grade sheet is also prepared automatically by the system and is uploaded for its availability to students and parents. Every teacher prepares a course file and adds his/her observations in applying active learning practices during his/her teaching. This is a comprehensive report prepared qualitatively and quantitatively for examination.

The subsequent sections explain the detailed course contents of one computer science engineering course taken for analysis and discussions in this study.

13.4   Introduction to elliptic curve cryptography

ECC and its mathematical operational-variant were invented by Victor Miller and Neal Koblitz in 1985 and 1987 independently [12,17,18].

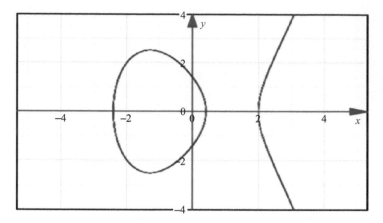

Figure 13.3 $Y^2 = X^3 - 2X + 1$ and $4A^3 + 27B^2 \neq 0$

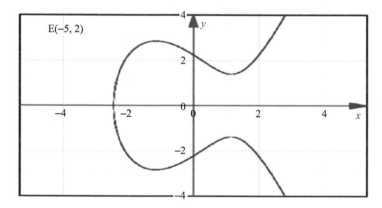

Figure 13.4 $Y^2 = X^3 - 5X + 2$ and $4A^3 + 27B^2 \neq 0$

The common form of the elliptic curve is the Weierstrass equation:

$$E(A, B):   Y^2 = X^3 + AX + B \tag{13.1}$$

where A and B are real numbers. It should satisfy $4A^3 + 27B^2 \neq 0$. This ensures that the elliptic curve does not intersect itself. Figures 13.3–13.5 show the examples of acceptable elliptic curves and satisfy (13.1). Figure 13.6 shows an example of an elliptic curve that intersects itself and cannot be used for a cryptosystem.

13.4.1   Elliptic curve operations

A straight line is drawn on an elliptic curve such that it intersects the curve at least on a single point. ECC uses the intersection point to encrypt or decrypt the data.

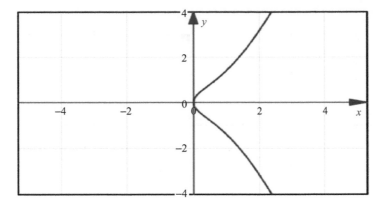

Figure 13.5 $Y^2 = X^3 + X$ *and* $4A^3 + 27B^2 \neq 0$

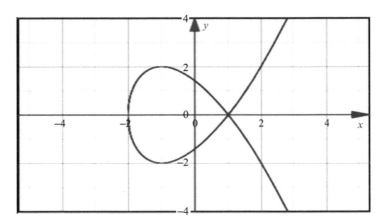

Figure 13.6 $Y^2 = X^3 - 3X + 2$ *and* $4A^3 + 27B^2 \neq 0$

Two operations are performed in cryptosystem using these intersection points: point addition and point doubling [19].

13.4.1.1 Point addition

Figure 13.7 shows an example of two-point addition: $P_1(x_1, y_1)$ and $P_2(x_2, y_2)$ over E $(-5,3)$. When a line $Y = 0.3X + 2$ is drawn and it intersects the $Y^2 = X^3 - 5X + 3$ on three points $P_1(x_1, y_1)$, $P_2(x_2, y_2)$ and $P'_3(x'_3, y'_3)$. Here, $P'_3(x'_3, y'_3) = -(P_1(x_1, y_1) + P_2(x_2, y_2))$ and $P_3(x_3, y_3) = -P'_3(x'_3, y'_3) = P_1(x_1, y_1) + P_2(x_2, y_2)$. In this case, $P_1(x_1, y_1) \neq P_2(x_2, y_2) \neq P'_3(x'_3, y'_3) \neq O(\infty, \infty)$, i.e. all points are distinct and lying on the elliptic curve. Here, $O(\infty, \infty)$ is defined as a point of infinity. Let the

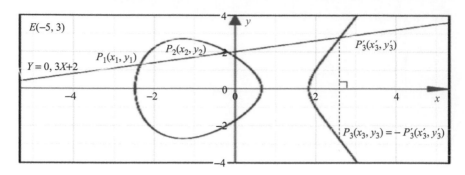

Figure 13.7   Point addition example using elliptic curve: $Y^2 = X^3 - 5X + 3$ and line: $Y = 0.3X + 2$

equation of the line passing through $P_1(x_1,y_1)$ and $P_2(x_2,y_2)$ with constants' and C be

$$Y = mX + C \tag{13.2}$$

Slope of line (m) passing through $P_1(x_1,y_1)$ and $P_2(x_2,y_2)$ is written as

$$m = \frac{y_2 - y_1}{x_2 - x_1} \tag{13.3}$$

Square (13.2) on both sides and compare it with the Weierstrass elliptic curve equation defined in (13.1).

$$(mX + c)^2 = m^2X^2 + c^2 + 2mcX = X^3 + AX + B$$
$$X^3 - m^2X^2 + (A - 2mC)X + (B - C^2) = 0 \tag{13.4}$$

Let x_1, x_2, and x_3 be the roots of (13.4) then

$$x_1 + x_2 + x_3 = m^2 \quad \text{and} \quad x_3 = m^2 - x_1 - x_2 \tag{13.5}$$

Now, the slope of the line passing through points $P_1(x_1,y_1)$ and $P_3'(x_3',y_3') = -P_3(x_3,y_3) = P_3(x_3, -y_3)$ is

$$m = (-(y_3) - y_1)/(x_3 - x_1)$$
$$y_3 = -y_1 - m(x_3 - x_1) \tag{13.6}$$

Hence, $P_3(x_3,y_3) = (m^2 - x_1 - x_2), (y_1 - m(x_3 - x_1))$ for $P_1(x_1,y_1) \neq P_2(x_2,y_2)$ $\neq P_3'(x_3',y_3') \neq O(\infty, \infty)$. When $P_1(x_1,y_1) \neq P_2(x_2,y_2)$ and $x_1 = x_2$ but $y_1 \neq y_2$ then P_3 $(x_3, y_3) = O(\infty, \infty)$ as shown in Figure 13.8. So, if a line is passing through two different points and lying parallel to the Y-axis then the point of addition is infinity.

13.4.1.2   Point doubling

Figure 13.9 shows an example of point doubling over $E(-5,3)$. When a line $Y = 0.2X + 3$ is drawn, it intersects the $Y^2 = X^3 - 5X + 3$ on two points

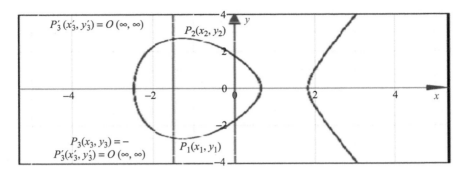

Figure 13.8   Point addition example using elliptic curve: $Y^2 = X^3 - 5X + 3$ and line: $Y = -1.5$

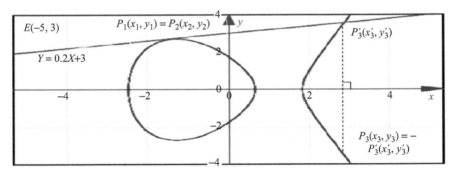

Figure 13.9   Point doubling example using elliptic curve: $Y^2 = X^3 - 5X + 3$ and line: $Y = 0.2X + 3$

$P_1(x_1,y_1) = P_2(x_2,y_2)$ and $P_3'\left(x_3',y_3'\right)$. Here, $P_3'\left(x_3',y_3'\right) = -2P_1(x_1,y_1) = -2P_2(x_2,y_2)$ and $P_3(x_3, y_3) = -P_3'\left(x_3',y_3'\right) = 2P_1(x_1,y_1) = 2P_2(x_2,y_2)$. In this case, $P_1(x_1,y_1) = P_2 (x_2,y_2) \neq P_3'\left(x_3',y_3'\right) \neq O(\infty, \infty)$, i.e. point of doubling is distinct from point of the tangent to curve. Now, differentiate the Weierstrass form of elliptic curve (13.1).

$$\frac{2ydy}{dx} = 3x^2 + A$$

Now, the slope of line (m) passing through $P_1(x_1,y_1)$ is calculated as

$$m = \frac{dy}{dx} = \frac{(3x_1^2 + A)}{2y_1} \tag{13.7}$$

if $x_1 = x_2$ then (13.5) is written as

$$x_3 = m^2 - 2x_1 = m^2 - 2x_2 \tag{13.8}$$

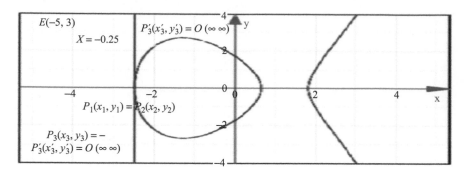

Figure 13.10   Point doubling example using elliptic curve: $Y^2 = X^3 - 5X + 3$ and line: $X = -0.25$. Here, $P_1(x_1,y_1) = P_2(x_2,y_2) \neq O(\infty, \infty)$

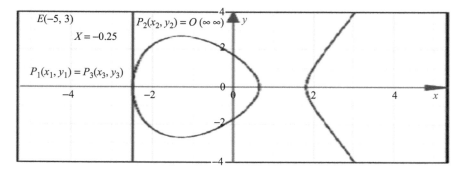

Figure 13.11   Point doubling example using elliptic curve: $Y^2 = X^3 - 5X + 3$ and line: $X = -0.25$. Here, $P_1(x_1,y_1) \neq P_2(x_2,y_2)$ and $P_2(x_2,y_2) = O(\infty, \infty)$

Similarly, y_3 for point doubling is calculated using (13.6). Further, when $P_1(x_1,y_1) = P_2(x_2,y_2)$ and the line passing through $P_1(x_1,y_1)$ is tangent to elliptic curve then $P_3(x_3,y_3) = -P'_3(x'_3,y'_3) = O(\infty, \infty)$ as shown in Figure 13.10. In another example, if $P_1(x_1,y_1) \neq P_2(x_2,y_2)$, $P_2(x_2,y_2) = O(\infty, \infty)$ and the line passing through $P_1(x_1,y_1)$ is tangent to elliptic curve then $P_3(x_3,y_3) = -P'_3(x'_3,y'_3) = P_1(x_1,y_1) + P_2(x_2,y_2) = P_1(x_1,y_1)$ as shown in Figure 13.11.

Finally, Table 13.1 summarizes mathematical calculations required to complete the elliptic curve operations.

13.4.2   Fast point multiplication algorithms

Various methods are discussed in the literature for performing the faster operations in the elliptic curve arithmetic [16,20–28]. Some of these methods are explored with examples in this work.

Table 13.1 Summarization of elliptic curve operations

Elliptic curve operation	$P_3(x_3, y_3)$	Conditions	Reference
Point addition	$x_3 = m^2 - x_1 - x_2$ $y_3 = -y_1 - m(x_3 - x_1)$ $m = (-(y_3) - y_1)/(x_3 - x_1)$	$P_1(x_1, y_1) \neq P_2(x_2, y_2) \neq P_3'(y_3', y_3') \neq$ $P_3(x_3, y_3) \neq O(\infty, \infty)$	Equations (13.5) and (13.6), Figure 13.5
Point doubling	$x_3 = m^2 - 2x_1 = m^2 - 2x_2$ $y_3 = -y_1 - m(x_3 - x_1)$ $m = (3x_1^2 + A)/2y_1$	$P_1(x_1, y_1) = P_2(x_2, y_2) \neq P_3'(x_3', y_3') \neq P_3(x_3, y_3) \neq O(\infty, \infty)$ and the line passing through $P_1(x_1, y_1)$ is tangent to elliptic curve	Equations (13.6), (13.7), and (13.8), Figure 13.7
Other cases	$O(\infty, \infty)$ $O(\infty, \infty)$ $P_1(x_1, y_1)$	$m = 0$ or $P_1(x_1, y_1) \neq P_2(x_2, y_2)$ and $x_1 = x_2$ but $y_1 \neq y_2$ $m = 0$ or line passing through $P_1(x_1, y_1)$ is parallel to the y-axis and tangent to elliptic curve, and $P_1(x_1, y_1) = P_2(x_2, y_2) \neq O(\infty, \infty)$ $P_1(x_1, y_1) \neq P_2(x_2, y_2)$, $P_2(x_2, y_2) = O(\infty, \infty)$ and the line passing through $P_1(x_1, y_1)$ is tangent to elliptic curve	Figure 13.6 Figure 13.8 Figure 13.9

13.4.2.1   Double and add algorithm

Algorithm 1 Double and add algorithm (left to right binary method)

Input: An elliptic curve E, a point on elliptic curve P and a scalar multiplier n. Let $b_{m-1}b_{m-2}\cdots b_0$ represent the binary bits of scalar multiplier n and m, the binary length of n.

Output: nP

Steps:

1. Initialization: $\text{Temp}_0 = P$
2. for $i = m - 1$ to 0 do:
3. $\text{Temp}_0: = \text{Temp}_0 + \text{Temp}_0 \bmod m$
4. If $b_i == 1$:
5. $\text{Temp}_0: = \text{Temp}_0 + P \bmod m$
6. end if
7. end for
8. return(Temp_0)

Exercise: Find the total number of addition and doubling steps required to compute $100P$ using double and add algorithm (left to right binary method).

Solution: $100P = (1100100)_2 P$, $m = 7$

Initialization: $\text{Temp}_0 = P$

Explanation: The number n is converted into a binary string. This binary string is processed from right to left as shown in Table 13.2. In this algorithm, doubling is performed at every step and addition is performed if the bit is required to be changed from 0 to 1. For example, $100P = (1100100)_2 P$, $b_6 = 1$ thus $P + P = 2P = (10)_2 P = (b_6, b_5)_2$, i.e. one doubling. Now, $b_5 = 0$ but in input string, this bit is required to be 1 thus one addition operation is performed, i.e. $2P + P = 3P = (11)_2 P$. This process continues until complete binary string is processed.

Thus, a total of six doubling and two additional operations are required to compute $100P$. Total computational cost = 8 operations.

Algorithm 2 (Method 1): Double and add algorithm (right to left binary method)

Input: An elliptic curve E, a point on elliptic curve P and a scalar multiplier n. Let $b_{m-1}b_{m-2}\cdots b_0$ represent the binary bits of scalar multiplier n and m, the binary length of n.

Output: nP

Steps:

1. Initialization: $\text{Temp}_0 = O$, $\text{Temp}_1 = P$
2. for $i = 0$ to $m - 1$ do:
3. if $b_i == 1$:
    a. $\text{Temp}_0: = \text{Temp}_0 + \text{Temp}_1$

4. $\text{Temp}_1: = 2\text{Temp}_1$
5. end for
6. return (Temp_0)

Solution: $100P = (1100100)_2 P$, $m = 7$

Initialization: $\text{Temp}_0 = O$, $\text{Temp}_1 = P$

Explanation: Table 13.3 shows the computational cost calculation of $100P$ using double and add algorithm (right to left binary method). In this algorithm, an input number is $n = 100$ is converted into its binary string form, i.e. $100P = (1100100)_2 P$. This binary string is processed from right to left. If the b_i bit of input string is 0 then $\text{Temp}_1: = 2\text{Temp}_1$ else $\text{Temp}_0: = \text{Temp}_0 + \text{Temp}_1$ and $\text{Temp}_1: = 2\text{Temp}_1$. For example, $b_0 = 0$ thus $\text{Temp}_1 = 2\text{Temp}_1 = 2P$. Further, $b_1 = 0$ thus $\text{Temp}_1 = 2\text{Temp}_1 = 4P$. Now, $b_2 = 1$ thus $\text{Temp}_0 = \text{Temp}_0 + \text{Temp}_1 = O + 4P = 4P$ and $\text{Temp}_1 = 2\text{Temp}_1 = 2(4P) = 8P$. This process continues until complete binary string is processed.

Thus, a total of seven doubling and three addition operations are required to compute $100P$. Total computational cost = 10 operations.

Table 13.2 Computational cost of 100P using double and add algorithm (left to right binary methods)

Step	i	Temp_0	b_i	Operation
1	6	$P + P = 2P = (10)_2 P$	1	Doubling
2	5	$2P + P = 3P = (11)_2 P$	1	Addition
3	4	$3P + 3P = 6P = (110)_2 P$	0	Doubling
4	3	$6P + 6P = 12P = (1100)_2 P$	0	Doubling
5	2	$12P + 12P = 24P = (11000)_2 P$	1	Doubling
		$24P + P = 25P = (11001)_2 P$		Addition
6	1	$25P + 25P = 50P = (110010)_2 P$	0	Doubling
7	0	$50P + 50P = 100P = (1100100)_2 P$	0	Doubling

Table 13.3 Computational cost of 100P using double and add algorithm (right to left binary methods)

Step	I	Temp_0	Temp_1	b_i	Operation
1	0		$2P$	0	Doubling
2	1		$2(2P) = 4P$	0	Doubling
3	2	$O + 4P = 4P$	$2(4P) = 8P$	1	Doubling + addition
4	3		$2(8P) = 16P$	0	Doubling
5	4		$2(16P) = 32P$	0	Doubling
6	5	$4P + 32P = 36P$	$2(32P) = 64P$	1	Doubling + addition
7	6	$36P + 64P = 100P$	$2(64P) = 128P$	1	Doubling + addition

Table 13.4   Computational cost of 100P using double and add algorithm (right to left binary methods)

Step	i	$Temp_0$	$Temp_1$	b_i	Operation
1	0	O	$2P$	0	Doubling
2	1	O	$2(2P) = 4P$	0	Doubling
3	2	$O + 4P = 4P$	$4P$	1	Addition
4	3	$4P$	$2(4P) + 4P = 12P$	0	Doubling + addition
5	4	$4P$	$2(12P) + 4P = 28P$	0	Doubling + addition
6	5	$2(4P) + 28P = 36P$	$28P$	1	Doubling + addition
7	6	$2(36P) + 28P = 100P$	$28P$	1	Doubling + addition

Algorithm 3 (Method 2): Joye double and add algorithm (right to left binary method)

Input: An elliptic curve E, a point on elliptic curve P and a scalar multiplier n. Let $b_{m-1}b_{m-2}\cdots b_0$ represent the binary bits of scalar multiplier n and m, the binary length of n.

Output: nP

Steps:
1. Initialization: $Temp_0 = O$, $Temp_1 = P$
2. for $i = 0$ to $m - 1$ do:
3. $Temp_{1-b_i} = 2Temp_{1-b_i} + Temp_{b_i}$
4. end for
5. return($Temp_0$)

Exercise: Find the total number of addition and doubling steps required to compute $100P$ using Joye double and add algorithm (right to left binary method).

Solution: $100P = (1100100)_2P$, $m = 7$

Initialization: $Temp_0 = O$, $Temp_1 = P$

Explanation: Table 13.4 shows the steps required to calculate the computational cost of $100P$ using the double and add algorithm (Algorithm 3, Method 2). In this method, n is converted into its binary form, i.e. $100P = (1100100)_2P$. The b_i bit of binary form is inserted in the equation: $Temp_{1-b_i} = 2Temp_{1-b_i} + Temp_{b_i}$ to calculate the values of $Temp_0$ and $Temp_1$. For example, in step 1, $b_1 = 0$ thus $Temp_1 = 2Temp_1 + Temp_0 = 2P + O = 2P$. Next, $b_1 = 0$, $Temp_1 = 2Temp_1 + Temp_0 = 4P + O = 4P$. In step 3, $b_1 = 1$, $Temp_0 = 2Temp_0 + Temp_1 = O + 4P = 4P$. This process continues until every b_i bit of input binary string is processed.

Thus, a total of six doubling and five addition operations are required to compute $100P$. Total computational cost = 11 operations.

Algorithm 4 (Method 3): Double and add algorithm (right to left method)

Input: An elliptic curve E, a point on elliptic curve P and a scalar multiplier n.
Output: nP
Steps:
1. Initialization: $Temp_0 = O$, $Temp_1 = P$
2. while $(n > 1)$ do:
3. If $(n\%2! = 0)$:
    a. $Temp_0 := Temp_0 + Temp_1$
4. $n := floor(n/2)$
5. $Temp_1 := 2Temp_1$
6. end while
7. $Temp_0 := Temp_0 + Temp_1$
8. Return $(Temp_0)$

Exercise: Find the total number of addition and doubling steps required to compute $100P$ using double and add algorithm (right to left method).

Solution:
Initialization: $Temp_0 = O$, $Temp_1 = P$

Explanation: In the double and add algorithm (right to left method), modulus 2 computations are performed over n. If the remainder is 1, then $Temp_0$ is changed, else $Temp_1$ is changed. Table 13.5 shows the computational cost analysis of $100P$ using this method. For example, step 1 starts with computation of $100\%2 = 0$ then $Temp_1 := 2\,Temp_1 = 2P$. This required a single doubling operation. Next, a new value of $n = floor\,(100/2) = 50$ is computed. The modulus operation $50\%2 = 0$; thus $4P$ is computed and this required one more doubling operation. In step 3, $25\% 2 = 1$; thus it changes the $Temp_0$ value, i.e. $Temp_0 := Temp_0 + Temp_1$ and $Temp_1 = 2Temp_1$. This process continues until $n > 1$. When $n == 1$ then $Temp_0 := Temp_0 + Temp_1 = 36P + 64P = 100P$.

Thus, a total of six doubling and two addition operations are required to compute $100P$. Total computational cost $= 8$ operations.

Table 13.5   Computational cost of 100P using double and add algorithm (right to left binary methods)

Step	N	n%2	Temp$_0$	Temp$_1$	Operation
1	100	0	O	$2P$	Doubling
2	50	0	O	$4P$	Doubling
3	25	1	$4P$	$2(4P) = 8P$	Doubling
4	12	0	$4P$	$2(8P) = 16P$	Doubling
5	6	0	$4P$	$2(16P) = 32P$	Doubling
6	3	1	$4P + 32P = 36P$	$2(32P) = 64P$	Doubling, addition
7	1		$36P + 64P = 100P$		Addition

13.4.2.2   *w*-**Windowed algorithm**

Algorithm 5 *w*-Windowed algorithm

Input: An elliptic curve E, a point on elliptic curve P and a scalar multiplier n. Let $b_{m-1}b_{m-2}\cdots b_0$ represent the binary representation of scalar multiplier n and m, the binary length of n. Suppose, w is the user input window size.

Output: nP

Steps:

1. *Pre-computation*

Compute all 2^w values of nP for $n = 0, 1, 2, \ldots, 2^w - 1$.

2. *Main algorithm*

(i)   *Initialization:* $\text{Temp}_0 \; := O$

(ii)   for $i = 0$ to m do:

(iii) $\text{Temp}_0: = 2^w\text{Temp}_0$

(iv)   If $b_i > 0$:

(v) $\text{Temp}_0: = \text{Temp}_0 + b_iP$

(vi)   return (temp_0)

Exercise: Find the total number of addition and doubling steps required to compute $100P$ using w-Windowed algorithm ($w = 3$).

Solution:

Initialization: $\text{Temp}_0 = O$, $\text{Temp}_1 = 2^wP$

1.   Pre-computation

$100_{10} = (001\ 100\ 100)_2$

$1P = 1P$

$1P + 1P = 2P = (10)_2P$ Doubling

$2P + P = 3P = (11)_2P$ Addition

$3P + P = 4P = (100)_2P$ Addition

$4P + P = 5P = (101)_2P$ Addition

$3P + 3P = 6P = (110)_2P$ Doubling

$6P + P = 7P = (111)_2P$ Addition

2.   Main algorithm

$(001)_2P = P$

$P + P = 2P = (001\ 0)_2$ Doubling

$2P + 2P = 4P = (001\ 00)_2P$ Doubling

$4P + 4P = 8P = (001\ 000)_2P$ Doubling

$8P + 4P = 12P = (001\ 100)_2P$ Addition

$12P + 12P = 24P = (001\ 100\ 0)_2P$ Doubling

$24P + 24P = 48P = (001\ 100\ 00)_2P$ Doubling

$48P + 48P = 96P = (001\ 100\ 000)_2P$ Doubling

$96P + 4P = 100P = (001\ 100\ 100)_2P$ Addition

Explanation: In this algorithm, n_{10} is converted to binary form and w-size arrays are formed from least significant bit (LSB) to most significant bit (MSB). In order to complete the window, zeros could be appended at MSB position. For example, 100_{10} is converted to $(001\ 100\ 100)_2$. Next, 2^w values are computed in pre-computational step. For example, if $w = 3$ then $P, 2P, \ldots, 7P$ are calculated in pre-computational step and require four additions and two doubling operations. The main algorithm starts with first most significant window, i.e. $Z = (001)_2 P$. Next, doubling operations are performed till next the window size is reached. For example, $2P, 4P$, and $8P$ are computed using doubling operation. Since $8P = (001\ 000)_2 P$ computation reached to the next window size, addition operation is required to meet the next window with the second most significant window of binary form of n. Since window is having 000_2 bits but required to be $100_2 P$, $4P = 100_2 P$ is picked from pre-computational stage and an additional operation is performed, i.e. $8P + 4P = 12P = (001\ 100)_2 P$. These operations continue until complete binary string is processed.

Thus, a total of eight doubling and six addition operations are required to compute $100P$. Total computational cost $= 14$ operations.

Algorithm 6 Sliding window algorithm

Input: A point on elliptic curve P with an integer $k = \sum_{j=0}^{m-1} k_j 2^j$, $k_j \in \{0,1\}$, where m is the length of binary string and r is the window size.
Output: kP
  1. Pre-computation
      a. $P_1 = P, P_2 = 2P$
      b. For $i = 1$ to $2^{r-1} - 1$:
          i. $P_{2i+1} = P_{2i-1} + P_2$
      c. $j = m - 1, Q = O$
  2. Main algorithm
      a. While $j \geq 0$:
          i. If $k_j == 0$:
              1. $Q = 2Q$
              2. $j = j - 1$
          ii. Else
              1. Choose t such that $j - t + 1 \leq r$ and $k_t = 1$
              2. $h_j = (k_j k_{j-1} \cdots k_t)_2$
              3. $Q = 2^{j-t+1} Q + P_{h_j}$
              4. $j = t - 1$
      b. return (Q)

Exercise: Let $k = 143{,}695$. Find the number of doubling and addition operations required to compute kP using sliding windowing method.
  Solution: $k = 143{,}695_{10} = (100011000101001111)_2$
  1. Pre-computation

$$P_1 = P$$
$$P_2 = P + P = 2P \qquad \qquad \text{Doubling}$$
$$P_3 = P_1 + P_2 = P + 2P = 3P \qquad \text{Doubling}$$

$$P_5 = P_3 + P_2 = 3P + 2P = 5P \qquad \text{Doubling}$$
$$P_7 = P_3 + P_2 = 5P + 2P = 7P \qquad \text{Doubling}$$
$$P_9 = P_5 + P_2 = 7P + 2P = 9P \qquad \text{Doubling}$$
$$P_{11} = P_9 + P_2 = 9P + 2P = 11P \qquad \text{Doubling}$$
$$P_{13} = P_{11} + P_2 = 11P + 2P = 13P \qquad \text{Doubling}$$
$$P_{15} = P_{13} + P_2 = 13P + 2P = 15P \qquad \text{Doubling}$$

2. Main algorithm

$$Q = (1)_2 P = P$$
$$Q = (1\ 000)_2 P = 8P \qquad\qquad\qquad 3D$$
$$Q = (1\ 000\ 11)_2 P = 4(8P) = 32P \quad Q = 32P + 3P = 35P$$
$$2D + 1A$$
$$Q = (1\ 000\ 11\ 000)_2 P = 8(35P) = 280P \qquad\qquad 3D$$
$$Q = (1\ 000\ 11\ 000\ 101)_2 P = 8(280P) = 2{,}240P$$
$$Q = 2{,}240P + 5P = 2{,}245P\ 3D + 1A$$
$$Q = (1\ 000\ 11\ 000\ 101\ 00)_2 P = 4(2{,}245P) = 8{,}980P \quad 2D$$
$$Q = (1\ 000\ 11\ 000\ 101\ 00\ 1111)_2 P = 16(8{,}980P) = 143{,}680P$$
$$Q = 143{,}680P + 15P = 143{,}695P \qquad\qquad 4D + 1A$$

Explanation: Sliding window algorithm for fast addition and doubling is having pre-computation and main algorithm execution. In pre-computation, r is the window size and P_i is calculated until $2^r - 1$. For example, let $k = 143{,}695$ and $r = 4$ thus P_1 to P_{15} are computed in the pre-computation step. In the main algorithm, k's binary string $(10001100010100111)_2$ is divided as $(1\ 000\ 11\ 000\ 101\ 00\ 1111)_2 P$. This algorithm process the string from left to right. It starts with $Q = P$ and for every bit, it doubles the value of Q. Here, for every consecutive value of 1s, it adds the window value. For example, the second window is 000 and corresponding $Q = (1\ 000)_2 P = 8P$, the next window is 11 and the corresponding $Q = (1\ 000\ 00)_2 P = 4(8P) = 32P$ and $Q = (1\ 000\ 11)_2 P = 32P + 3P = 35P$. This process continues to complete binary string until it is processed.

The pre-computational step requires eight doubling operations. The main algorithm requires 17 doubling and 3 addition operations. Thus, a total of 28 operations are required to calculate kP.

13.4.2.3 Fixed-base doubling and addition method

Algorithm 7 Fixed-base Euclidean method

Input: Let $\{a_0, a_1, \ldots, a_n\}$ be an integers set, where $n \geq 2$. Further, M and N are the integers in the interval $[0,n]$ such that $a_M \geq a_i$, $0 \leq i \leq n$, $N \neq M$. $r_N \geq r_i$ for all $0 \leq i \leq n$, $i \neq M$.

Output: rP
1. *Pre-computation*
   Compute all B^w values of nP for $n = 0, 1B, 2B, \ldots, (2^w - 1)B$.
2. *Main algorithm*
(i) For $i = 0$ to t:
   2.i.1. $P_i \leftarrow b_i P$
   2.i.2. $a_i \leftarrow r_i$
(ii) Determine M and N for $\{a_0, a_1, \ldots, a_n\}$.
(iii) While $a_N \neq 0$:
   2.iii.1. $Q \leftarrow \text{floor}(a_M/a_N)$, $P_N \leftarrow q(P_M) + P_N$, $a_M \leftarrow a_M \bmod a_N$.
   2.iii.2. Determine new values for M and N from $\{a_0, a_1, \ldots, a_n\}$.
(iv) Return (P_M)

Exercise: Find the total number of addition and doubling steps required to compute $965P$ using fixed-base doubling and addition method.

Solution: $r = 965$, $r = (3, 12, 5)_{16}$, $P_0 = 1P$, $P_1 = 16P$, $P_2 = 256P$
1. Pre-computation

$P + P = 2P$	Doubling
$2P + 2P = 4P$	Doubling
$4P + 4P = 8P$	Doubling
$8P + 8P = 16P$	Doubling
$16P + 16P = 32P$	Doubling
$32P + 32P = 64P$	Doubling
$64P + 64P = 128P$	Doubling
$128P + 128P = 256P$	Doubling

2. Main algorithm

Explanation: In main algorithm, $r = 965$ is converted into selected base form (hexadecimal in this example), for example, $r = (3, 12, 5)_{16}$. As shown in Table 13.6, step 1 initializes the values $\{a_0, a_1, a_2\} = \{3, 12, 5\}$. Since a_1 is having the highest value thus $M = 1$, and a_0 is having the second highest value thus $N = 0 \neq M$. Next, quotient $q = \text{floor}(12/5) = 2$, $P_0 = 2(P_1) + P_0 = 2$ $(16P) + P = 33P$, $P_1 = 16P$, and $P_2 = 256P$. This step requires one doubling (2 $(16P)$) and one addition operation $(32P + P)$. In step 2, new values for $\{a_0, a_1, a_2\}$ are selected as $a_M = a_M \bmod a_N \rightarrow a_1 = 12 \bmod 5 = 2$, $a_0 = 5$ and $a_2 = 3$. After finding the new values for $\{a_0, a_1, a_2\}$, new indices (M and N) are also evaluated as $M = 0$ (highest) and $N = 2$ (second highest). Now, $N = 2$ so P_2 will only change its value to $1(256)P + 33P = 289P$. This step requires one addition $(256P + 33P)$ operation only. This process will continue until $a_N \neq 0$. In step 6, $a_N = a_1 = 0$, hence P_M will be returned, i.e. $P_2 = 965P$.

The algorithm works in two sequential steps. In the initial step, the pre-computational step, it calculates B^w values of nP for $n = 0, 1B, 2B, \ldots, (2^w - 1)B$ and the second step runs the main algorithm. The pre-computation step for this example requires eight doubling operations and the main algorithm requires two doubling and five addition operations. Thus, a total of 10 doubling and 5 addition

Table 13.6   Computational cost calculations for 965P using fixed-base doubling and addition algorithm

Step	a_0	a_1	a_2	M	N	q	P_0	P_1	P_2	Operations
1	5	12	3	1	0	2	33P	16P	256P	Doubling + addition
2	5	2	3	0	2	1	33P	16P	289P	Addition
3	2	2	3	2	0	1	322P	16P	289P	Addition
4	2	2	1	0	1	1	322P	338P	289P	Addition
5	0	2	1	1	2	2	322P	338P	965P	Doubling + addition
6	0	0	1	2	1	–	322P	338P	965P	–

operations are required to compute 965P. Total computational cost = 15 operations.

Algorithm 8 An integer to nonadjacent form conversion

Input: $b \epsilon N$
Output: $\{b_n, b_{n-1}, \ldots, b_0\}$
(i) $i = 0$
(ii) while $b \neq 0$:
    a.   if $b\%2 == 0$:
       i. $b_i = 0$
    b.   else
       i. $b_i = b(\text{mods } 2^B)$
    c.   end if
    d. $b = (b - b_i)/2$
    e. $i = i + 1$
(iii) end while
(iv) return $\{b_n, b_{n-1}, \ldots, b_0\}$
Exercise: Let $k = 143{,}695$. Find the nonadjacent form of k, i.e. $NAF_3(k)$.
Explanation: An integer to nonadjacent form conversion is helpful in a fixed-base windowing method for calculating the number of doubling and addition operations required to compute the cost. Algorithm 8 shows the steps required to convert an integer to a nonadjacent form. Let $k = 143{,}695$ be an integer (Table 13.7). The process of nonadjacent form conversion starts with checking whether an integer is even or odd. If an integer is an even integer then b_i is considered to be zero (e.g. when $i = 0,2,4,5,7,8,9,10,11,13,14,15$, or 16 then b is an even integer and $b_i = 0$) else $b \bmod 2^B$ is calculated to find b_i (e.g. when $i = 0, 3, 6$, or 12 then b is an odd integer and $b_i = b \bmod 2^B$). Finally, nonadjacent form for integer $k == 143{,}695$ is $NAF_3(k) = 100003000005001007$.

Table 13.7   NAF₃(k) calculation for k = 143,695

i	b_i	b
0	143,695 mod 2^3 = 7	71,844
1	0	35,922
2	0	17,961
3	17,961 mod 2^3 = 1	8,980
4	0	4,490
5	0	2,245
6	2,245 mod 2^3 = 5	1,120
7	0	560
8	0	280
9	0	140
10	0	70
11	0	35
12	35 mod 2^3 = 3	16
13	0	8
14	0	4
15	0	2
16	0	1
17	1	–

Algorithm 9 Fixed-base windowing method for doubling and addition (Yao's algorithm) [29]

Input: $\{2^0P, 2^1P, \ldots, 2^wP\}$, h
Output: kP
  1. sum = 0
  2. For j from (h − 1) down to 1:
      a. For each i for which $b_i = j$:
          i. sum: = sum + $j \times 2^{i-1}P$
  3. return (sum)

Exercise: Let k = 143,695. Find the number of doubling and addition operations required to compute kP using fixed-base windowing method.

Solution:
  1. Pre-computation
  2. Main algorithm

Explanation: In the fixed-base windowing method, the first nonadjacent form of k is calculated as discussed in Algorithm 8. In the second step, doubling operations are performed as equivalent to a number of bits in nonadjacent form. For example, the nonadjacent form of k = 143,695 is having 18 bits thus requires 17 doubling operations as shown in Table 13.8. Further, Algorithm 9 operates to compute kP as shown in Table 13.9. Here, d(1) = 100000000000001000, d(3) = 000001000000000000, d(5) = 000000000001000000, and d(7) = 000000000000000007. In result $1 \times d$(1) + $3 \times d$(3) + $5 \times d$(5) + $7 \times d$(7) = 100003000005001007. Algorithm 9 starts with the calculation of $7 \times d$(7) = 7P. This operation requires two additions (4P + 2P + P).

Next, $5 \times d(5) = 320P$ is calculated. This operation requires one addition operation ($256P + 64P$). New sum $= 7P + 320P = 327P$ requires one more addition operation. Similarly, $3 \times d(3) = 12,288P$ requires one addition operation ($8,192P + 4,096P$) and one addition operation is required for sum $= 327P + 12,288P = 12,615P$. Finally, $1 \times d(1) = 131,080P$ requires one addition ($131,072P + 8P$) and one addition operation is required for sum $= 12,615P + 131,080P$. In total, 25 operations (17 doubling and 8 additions) are required to compute kP.

Algorithm 10 Fixed-base windowing method for doubling and addition (modified Yao's algorithm) (Meloni and Hasan, 2009)

    Input: $\{2^0P, 2^1P, \ldots, 2^wP\}, h$
    Output: kP
      1.   sum $= 0$
      2.   For j from (3^{b_n}) down to (3^{b_1}):
        a.   For each i for which $3^{b_n} = j$:
           i.   sum: $=$ sum $+ (3^{b_i} \times 2^{t_i})P$
      3.   return (sum)

Exercise: Let $k = 143,695$. Find the number of doubling and addition operations required to compute kP using fixed-base windowing method (modified Yao's algorithm).

    Solution:
    1.   Pre-computation
    2.   Main algorithm

Explanation: One of the representations of k in the double-base number system (DBNS) is: $2^{10}3^4 + 2^63^6 + 2^53^5 + 2^63^4 + 2^53^3 + 2^33^3 + 2^23^2 + 2^13^2 + 2^03^0$. Now, $d(0)P = P$, $d(2)P = (2^2P + 2P)$, $d(3)P = 2^5P + 2^3P$, $d(4)P = 2^{10}P + 2^6P$, $d(5)P = 2^5P$, and $d(6)P = 2^6P$. Further, $kP = 3^6d(6)P + 3^5d(5)P + 3^4d(4)P + 3^3d(3)P + 3^2d(2)P + d(0)P$. Modified Yao's algorithm uses DBNS form rather than NAF of k. Table 13.10 shows the pre-computation steps for $k = 143,695$ similar to Table 13.8 of Yao's algorithm. Table 13.11 shows the main algorithm steps using DBNS form (i.e. $3^{b_i} \times 2^{t_i}$) of k, i.e. $kP = 3^6d(6)P + 3^5d(5)P + 3^4d(4)P + 3^3d(3)P + 3^2d(2)P + d(0)P$. For $j = 3^6$, $3^6d(6)$ is calculated as $3^62^6P = 46,656P$. So, five additions ($2,768P + 8,192P + 4,096P + 1,024P + 512P + 64P$) are required to compute $46,656P$. A new value for $j = 3^5$ is selected to compute 3^52^5P. This is calculated as $7,776 = 4,096P + 2,048P + 1,024P + 512P + 64P + 32P$ and requires five additions. One more addition is required to compute $54,432P$ ($= 46,656P + 7,776P$). This process continues till $j = 3^0$ and 3^02^0P is computed. In total, 42 operations (17 doubling in pre-computation and 25 additions in main algorithm) are required to compute kP.

Table 13.8 *Doubling operation computations for k = 143,695*

Computation	Operation	Computation	Operation
$2^0P = P$		$2^9P = 512P = 256P + 256P$	Doubling9
$2^1P = 2P = P + P$	Doubling1	$2^{10}P = 1,024P = 512P + 512P$	Doubling10
$2^2P = 4P = 2P + 2P$	Doubling2	$2^{11}P = 2,048P = 1,024P + 1,024P$	Doubling11
$2^3P = 8P = 4P + 4P$	Doubling3	$2^{12}P = 4,096P = 2,048P + 2,048P$	Doubling12
$2^4P = 16P = 8P + 8P$	Doubling4	$2^{13}P = 8,192P = 4,096P + 4,096P$	Doubling13
$2^5P = 32P = 16P + 16P$	Doubling5	$2^{14}P = 16,384P = 8,192P + 8,192P$	Doubling14
$2^6P = 64P = 32P + 32P$	Doubling6	$2^{15}P = 32,768P = 16,384P + 16,384P$	Doubling15
$2^7P = 128P = 64P + 64P$	Doubling7	$2^{16}P = 65,536P = 32,768P + 32,768P$	Doubling16
$2^8P = 256P = 128P + 128P$	Doubling8	$2^{17}P = 131,072P = 65,536P + 65,536P$	Doubling17

Table 13.9 *Main algorithm run for computing the doubling and addition operations*

j	7	6	5	4	3	2	1
Sum	$7 \times 2^0 P = 7P$	—	$5 \times 2^6 P = 320P$	—	$3 \times 2^{12} P = 12{,}288P$	—	$1 \times (2^{17}P + 2^3 P) = 131{,}080P$
Computation	$7P$	$7P$	$7P + 320P = 327P$	$327P$	$327P + 12{,}288P = 12{,}615P$	—	$12{,}615P + 131{,}080P = 143{,}695P$
	$4P + 2P + P = 7P$	—	$7P + 256P + 64P = 327P$	—	$327P + 8{,}192P + 4{,}096P = 12{,}615P$	—	$12{,}615P + 131{,}072P + 8P = 143{,}695P$
Operation	2 Additions	—	2 Additions	—	2 Additions	—	2 Additions

Table 13.10 Doubling operation computations for k = 143,695

Computation	Operation	Computation	Operation
$2^0P = P$		$2^9P = 512P = 256P + 256P$	Doubling9
$2^1P = 2P = P + P$	Doubling1	$2^{10}P = 1,024P = 512P + 512P$	Doubling10
$2^2P = 4P = 2P + 2P$	Doubling2	$2^{11}P = 2,048P = 1,024P + 1,024P$	Doubling11
$2^3P = 8P = 4P + 4P$	Doubling3	$2^{12}P = 4,096P = 2,048P + 2,048P$	Doubling12
$2^4P = 16P = 8P + 8P$	Doubling4	$2^{13}P = 8,192P = 4,096P + 4,096P$	Doubling13
$2^5P = 32P = 16P + 16P$	Doubling5	$2^{14}P = 16,384P = 8,192P + 8,192P$	Doubling14
$2^6P = 64P = 32P + 32P$	Doubling6	$2^{15}P = 32,768P = 16,384P + 16,384P$	Doubling15
$2^7P = 128P = 64P + 64P$	Doubling7	$2^{16}P = 65,536P = 32,768P + 32,768P$	Doubling16
$2^8P = 256P = 128P + 128P$	Doubling8	$2^{17}P = 131,072P = 65,536P + 65,536P$	Doubling17

Table 13.11 Main algorithm run for computing the doubling and addition operations

j	Sum	Computation	Operation
$3^6 2^6 P = 46,656P$	$46,656P$	$2,768P + 8,192P + 4,096P + 1,024P + 512P + 64P$	5 Additions
$3^5 2^5 P = 7,776P$	$46,656P + 7,776P = 54,432P$	$46,656P + 4,096P + 2,048P + 1,024P + 512P + 64P + 32P$	6 Additions
$3^4(2^{10} + 2^6)P$	$54,432P + 88,128P = 142,560P$	$142,560P + 65,536P + 16,384P + 4,096P + 2,048P + 64P$	5 Additions
$3^3(2^5 + 2^3)P$	$142,560P + 1,080P = 143,640P$	$142,560P + 1,024P + 32P + 16P + 8P$	4 Additions
$3^2(2^2 + 2)P$	$143,640P + 54P = 143,694P$	$143,640P + 32P + 16P + 4P + 2P$	4 Additions
3^1	$143,694P$	–	
$3^0 2^0 P$	$143,694P + P = 143,695P$	$143,694P + P$	1 Addition

13.5 Elliptic curve cryptography (ECC)-based authentication protocols

Authentication can be achieved through the ECC for various applications. This is a preferable method of public-key cryptosystem used in resourceful as well as resource constraint networks. Various mechanisms are explored in the literature for providing authentication through ECC [1–4]. This work discusses some of the important ECC-based authentication mechanisms.

Protocol 1 ECC-based authentication with encryption/decryption

    Step 1: Reader sends a hash of a random number r_1 and applies encryption algorithm over the random number and tag's identification combination. Now, identification, hash, and ciphertext are sent to tag.

R : Pick $r_1 \epsilon Z_n$

        : Calculate (i) $H = h(r_1)$

             (ii) $C_R = E(r_1, ID_T)$

$R \rightarrow T$: C_R, ID_T, H

    Step 2: Tag receives the message, use the decrypted message and identification for generating message digest. This value is verified before sending a random response y to the reader.

T : $(y, ID_T) = D(C_R)$

        : If $h(y)$ equals H and d ID_T is valid, then move to the next step

$T \rightarrow R$: y

    Step 3: Now, it is the reader's turn to verify the response. If the received value and the randomly generated value are found to be the same then reader trusts the tag, i.e.

R: if $y == r_1$ then tag T is trustworthy and the user having this tag can be trusted.

Protocol 2 ECC-based signature generation scheme for authentication and user verification

    Step 1: Reader R has to send a random r_1 value to T.

$R \rightarrow T$: r_1

    Step 2: Tag receives the reader's random value and uses its random number (e_1) and reader's identification to sign a message that is usable to the reader for user verification

T : $y = $ Signature (r_1, e_1, ID_r)

$T \rightarrow R$: e_1, ID_r, y, $CERT_{TAG}$

    Step 3: Reader executes the matching of received certificate and self-generated certificate value. If both match, then the user is authentic.

R: Match $CERT_{TAG}$ and VERIFY y

        : if matches, then both tag and user are authentic.

Protocol 3 Schnorr identifier and the user authentication protocol

Step 1: Tag ask a query (Z) to the user having reader R

T: Generate query $Z = r_1P$

$T{\rightarrow}R$: Z

Step 2: Reader replies to the query with a random value, i.e.

$R{\rightarrow}T$: e_1

Step 3: Now, the tag uses constant a, another random value e_1 and received random value r_1 to generate a new query.

T : Generate query $y = ae_1 + r_1$

$T{\rightarrow}R$: y

Step 4: Reader solves the query with y, elliptic base point P, random value e_1 and tag's public key W. If queries are solved, then tag and the user are authentic, i.e.

R: if $yP + e_1W == Z$, then both tag and user are valid

13.6   Experimental results

This section discusses the impacts of the proposed active learning approach in one computer science and engineering department subject "Network Security." The sample size of data is 60 students. Initially, a detailed study of elliptic curve cryptography and network security is given to students. As elliptic curve cryptography content is a major part of the network security course. Thus, students were asked to cover the detail of each of this course from different resources apart from the contents discussed earlier. Here, the teacher has also given a large number of extra courses preparing material and teaching. The overall performance of the course is as shown in Figures 13.12–13.15. The x-axis in Figure 13.12 shows the concept of the course network axis, whereas the y-axis shows the mean of the student marks. The assessment of each concept as shown in Figure 13.12 reflects that student has performed well while learning through active learning as compared with traditional learning. Likewise, Figure 13.13 shows the performance of the learner in assessment methods. When active learning methods are being used, the performance of the learner is increased. Figure 13.14 shows the question-wise performance of the learner, whereas Figure 13.15 shows the performance of the internal assessment. It has been observed that the proposed approach is widely accepted by both teachers and students through qualitative and quantitative approaches. Table 13.12 is one such experimentation and outcome. Results show that the proposed active learning group outperforms traditional learning group because of interactive and innovative processes. To validate this claim, short- and long-term evaluations are conducted for this course. As shown in Table 13.12, short-term evaluation shows that unit-wise subject outcomes, mid-semester evaluations, end-semester evaluation, and internal evaluations. Almost, all of the evaluations are showing better student performance. Thus, the proposed active learning process is suggested to all university teachers in consultation with officials.

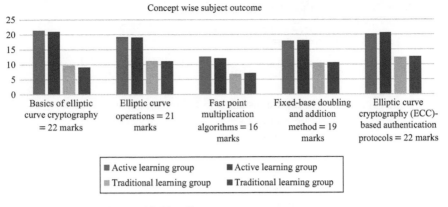

Figure 13.12   Concept-wise course outcome

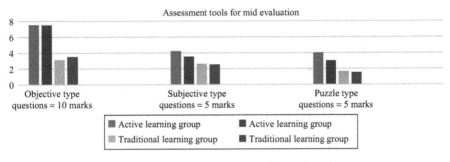

Figure 13.13   Assessment tools for mid evaluation

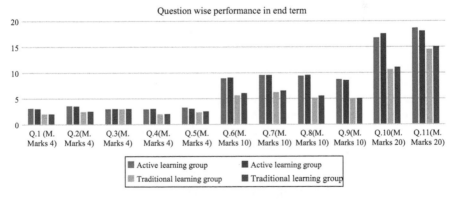

Figure 13.14   Question-wise performance in end term

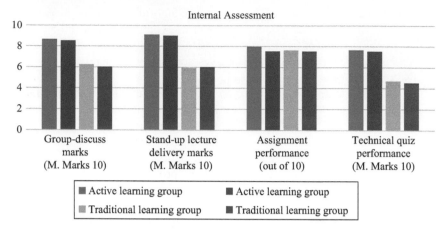

Figure 13.15   Internal assessment

Table 13.12   Statistical analysis using t-*test*

Teaching strategies	Concept-wise subject outcome		Assessment tool for mid evaluation		Question-wise performance in end term		Internal assessment	
	Mean	*P*-Value	Mean	*P*-Value	Mean	*P*-Value	Mean	*P*-Value
Active Learning Group	18.19	0.00054	5.24	0.04	7.9718	0.0005	8.335	0.0205
Traditional Learning Group	10.06		2.453		5.3336		6.108	

A statistical evaluation is done using *t*-test. Table 13.12 shows the *P*-value is less than (alpha = 0.05) 0.05, which rejects the null hypothesis that the mean value is equal to the traditional method with an active learning method. Likewise, the *P* values using the assessment tool for mid evaluation are also less than an alpha value for both the groups. Thus, Table 13.12 shows that unit-wise subject outcomes, mid-semester evaluations, end-semester evaluations, and internal evaluations reject the null hypothesis that means values are equal to both the strategies.

13.7   Conclusion

This work discusses the implementation of the interactive active learning processes in UPES. An interactive active learning process is applied to the network security course having an elliptic curve cryptography module in all of its units. Elliptic curve operations are explained in this chapter. Every possibility of point addition and doubling is discussed with examples. The complexity of mathematical operations is calculated using fast computational algorithms. These algorithms also reduce the number of steps required to perform cryptography operations by reducing the number of steps required to compute addition and doubling operations. Elliptic curve cryptography based primitives are used in authentication protocols. The use of primitives provides multiple solutions for providing authenticity and integrity. These multiple solutions have various applications in different domains. Light computational protocols are useful for resource constraint devices like RFID networks or sensor networks, whereas high computation-based protocols are meaningful for resourceful networks like computer networks. After applying the active learning process over teaching and evaluation of discussed contents, it has been observed that the proposed active learning process is much better than traditional learning and shows improvements in all evaluations. Both short- and long-term evaluations are performed to study the impact of the proposed active learning process. Results show that the proposed approach is comparatively much better in all scenarios. As future work, the strategies for active learning can be explored for various subjects in the E-learning system. Assessment strategies can be improved using active learning.

References

[1] Alagheband, M. R. and Aref, M. R. (2013). "Simulation-based traceability analysis of RFID authentication protocols", *Wireless Personnel Communication*, 77(2), pp. 1019–1038.

[2] Alario-Hoyos, C., Estevez-Ayres, I., Kloos, C. D., Muñoz-Merino, P. J., Llorente-Pérez, E. N. R. I. Q. U. E., and Villena-Roman, J. (2019). "Redesigning a freshman engineering course to promote active learning by flipping the classroom through the reuse of MOOCs", *International Journal of Engineering Education*, 35(1B), pp. 385–396.

[3] Boyd, C. and Mathuria, A. (2003). "Protocols for Authentication and Key Establishment", Information Security and Cryptography book series (ISC), Springer.

[4] Clarke, N. (2011). "Transparent User Authentication: Biometrics, RFID, and Behavioral Profiling", Management of Computing and Information Systems (Book Series), Springer.

[5] Deslauriers, L., McCarty, L. S., Miller, K., Callaghan, K. and Kestin, G. (2019). "Measuring actual learning versus the feeling of learning in response to being actively engaged in the classroom", *Proceedings of the National Academy of Sciences*, 116(39), pp. 19251–19257.

[6] Kumar, A. and Aggarwal, A. (2012). "Survey and taxonomy of key management protocols for wired and wireless networks", *International Journal of Network Security & Its Applications*, 4(3), pp. 21–40.

[7] Kumar, A., Gopal, K. and Aggarwal, A. (2013). "Outlier detection and treatment for lightweight mobile ad hoc networks", *In International*

Conference on Heterogeneous Networking for Quality, Reliability, Security and Robustness, Springer, Berlin, Heidelberg, pp. 750–763.

[8] Kumar, A., Gopal, K. and Aggarwal, A. (2017). "A novel lightweight key management scheme for RFID-sensor integrated hierarchical MANET based on internet of things", *International Journal of Advanced Intelligence Paradigms*, 9(2–3), pp. 220–245.

[9] Kumar, A., Aggarwal, A. and Gopal, K. (2018). "A novel and efficient reader-to-reader and tag-to-tag anti-collision protocol", *IETE Journal of Research*, pp. 1–12.

[10] Julià, C. and Antolí, J. Ò. (2019). "Impact of implementing a long-term STEM-based active learning course on students motivation", *International Journal of Technology and Design Education*, 29(2), pp. 303–327.

[11] Lugaresi, G., Lin, Z., Frigerio, N., Zhang, M. and Matta, A. (2019). "Active learning experience in simulation class using a LEGO®-based manufacturing system", *In 2019 Winter Simulation Conference (WSC)*, IEEE, pp. 3307–3318.

[12] Miller, V. (2004). "The Weil pairing and its efficient calculation", *Journal of Cryptology*, 17(4), pp. 235–161.

[13] Persano Adorno, D. and Bellomonte, L. (2019). "Active learning in a real-world bioengineering problem: A pilot-study on ophthalmologic data processing", *Computer Applications in Engineering Education*, 27(2), pp. 485–499.

[14] Shekhar, P., Prince, M., Finelli, C., Demonbrun, M. and Waters, C. (2019). "Integrating quantitative and qualitative research methods to examine student resistance to active learning", *European Journal of Engineering Education*, 44(1–2), pp. 6–18.

[15] Stoll, L. K., Lamont, L. B., Block, S. B. and Esselman, B. J. (2019). "Redesigned pre-service training for teaching assistants in high enrollment, active learning based general chemistry courses", *In Best Practices in Chemistry Teacher Education*, American Chemical Society (ACS) Publications, SA, pp. 97–117.

[16] Hankerson, D., Menezes, A. and Vanstone, S. (2004). "Guide to Elliptic Curve Cryptography", New York, NY, Springer Science & Business Media.

[17] Hankerson, D., Menezes, A. and Vanstone, S. (2003). "Guide to Elliptic Curve Cryptography", Cryptology (Book Series), Springer.

[18] Iijima, T., Momose, F. and Chao, J. (2013). "Classification of Elliptic/Hyperelliptic Curves With Weak Coverings Against the GHS Attack Under an Isogeny Condition", *IACR Cryptology ePrint Archive* 2013, pp. 487. https://eprint.iacr.org/2013/487.pdf.

[19] Ismail, A. M., Said, M. R. Md., Atan, K. A. M. and Rakhimov, I. S. (2010). "An algorithm to enhance elliptic curves scalar multiplication combining MBNR with point halving", *Applied Mathematical Sciences*, 4(26), 1259–1272.

[20] Daniel J. B., Mike, H. A. K. and Tanja, L. (2013). "Alligator: elliptic-curve points indistinguishable from uniform random strings", *In ACM Conference on Computer and Communications Security 2013* (pp. 967–980). Berlin, Germany.

[21]   Daniel, J. B. and Tanja, L. (2007). "Faster addition and doubling on elliptic curves", *In ASIACRYPT 2007* (pp. 29–50), Kuching, Malaysia.

[22]   Daniel, J. B. and Tanja, L. (2014). "Hyper-and-Elliptic-Curve Cryptography", *IACR Cryptology ePrint Archive* 2014, pp. 379. https://eprint.iacr.org/2014/379.pdf.

[23]   Kumar, A., Gopal, K. and Aggarwal, A. (2013). "Lightweight trust propagation scheme for resource constraint mobile ad-hoc networks (MANETs)", *In Sixth International Conference on Contemporary Computing (IC3-2013)*, (pp. 421–426), JIIT, Noida, India.

[24]   Kumar, A., Gopal, K. and Aggarwal, A. (2013). "Lightweight trust aggregation through lightweight vibrations for trust accumulation in resource constraint mobile ad-hoc networks (MANETs)", *In World Conference on Advances in Communication and Control Systems (CACCS-2013)*, (pp. 530–535), DIT University, Dehradun.

[25]   Kumar, A., Gopal, K. and Aggarwal, A. (2013). "Outlier detection and treatment for lightweight mobile ad hoc networks", *In Int. Conf. on Heterogeneous Networking for Quality, Reliability, Security and Robustness (QSHINE 2013)*, (pp. 750–763), Gautam Budh University, Greater Noida, India.

[26]   Kumar, A., Gopal, K. and Aggarwal, A. (2014). "Design and analysis of lightweight trust mechanism for accessing data in MANETs", *KSII Transactions on Internet and Information Systems*, 8(3), pp. 1119–1143.

[27]   Kumar, A., Sharma, K., Singh, H., Naugriya, S. G., Gill, S. S. and Buyya, R. (2020). "A Drone-Based Networked System and Methods for Combating Coronavirus Disease (COVID-19) Pandemic", *arXiv preprint arXiv:2006.06943*.

[28]   Kumar, A., Gopal, K. and Aggarwal, A. (2016). "Design and analysis of lightweight trust mechanism for secret data using lightweight cryptographic primitives in MANETs", *IJ Network Security*, 18(1), pp. 1–18.

[29]   Méloni, N. and Hasan, M.A., (2009). "Elliptic curve scalar multiplication combining Yao's algorithm and double bases", In *International Workshop on Cryptographic Hardware and Embedded Systems* (pp. 304–316), Springer, Berlin, Heidelberg.

Chapter 14

Conclusion

Mukta Goyal[1], Rajalakshmi Krishnamurthi[1] and Divakar Yadav[2]

This book is addressed to techniques, technologies, pedagogies, and issues in implementing an e-learning system. The sustainability of any system depends on the four-pillar model of sustainability such as human, social, economic, and technical. Human sustainability allows us to protect the individual need and support the system in such a way that it improves the quality of human life. The book explores the adaptive e-learning systems and accommodates an extensive range of learners with the varied background to fulfill their specific aims. Behavioral engagement in microlearning, one of the techniques that help the instructor to develop the e-learning applications. Artificial intelligence (AI) is another technique that supports a more personalized e-learning environment. AI injected e-learning platforms that can adapt from the previous learning pattern of the users and empower them with a customized pedagogy for better understanding. Personalized learning and recommender systems can help widely in mining the required information for the learner from the information overload. Use of AI in e-learning is gaining a lot of importance and is becoming a wide area of research to improve learning experience with advanced technology.

In online education, e-learning is also a mode of interaction among learners and between the learners and the instructors, i.e., through this online medium, learners and instructors can share their ideas, emotions, interests, and activities. In this way, they form an online social group. Compared with the traditional setting, e-learning requires more close collaboration between members. In the e-learning platform, the instructor is a facilitator rather than a messenger, and the learner is expected to be an active participant in the pursuit of knowledge rather than merely being the product of an education system. A good e-learning system engages the learner in a manner that he should have the ability to think, solve the problem, manage the time and self-discipline toward e-learning. The content should be displayed in a manner that learners should not feel isolated and demotivated toward learning.

[1]Department of Computer Science and Engineering, Jaypee Institute of Information Technology, Noida, India
[2]Department of Computer Science and Engineering, National Institute of Technology, Hamirpur, India

The usage of mobile learning provides a new direction in the education system. Mobile learning allows the learner to access the learning resources anywhere anytime. Emerging technologies such as big data applications and cloud computing promote interaction between teachers and students. E-teacher can track the individual requirement and performance of the students. These technologies efficiently promote collaborative learning. E-learners can share links or modules with other e-learners. Internet of Things (IoT) uses connectivity technologies such as Wi-Fi, Zigbee, NFC, RFID, and bluetooth to observe the teaching activity, and the required data is transferred to recording devices that share it on e-learning platforms. The IoT functions with cloud-based applications for interpreting and transmitting the data coming from sensors. Thus, e-learning system is evolving with changes in a fair means.

Augmented reality (AR) in e-learning has great potential to reduce the isolation of a learner. A learner connects himself with the system during the teaching–learning process and motivates himself to learn. The inclusion of AR/VR technology in the e-learning system motivates the researchers to develop the smart learning content for the learner. Development of learning content using AR technology allows researchers to develop the application embedded with cognitive psychology applications such as mnemonic techniques and theory of mind.

14.1 Future work

COVID-19 pandemic has changed the education sector in an online learning mode. Meanwhile, education has shifted to online learning, but the future will be blended learning, which includes smart campuses. In the current scenario, the traditional college campus does not have modern technologies that support e-learning. The IoT influences the field of education and will change the infrastructure of the campus very soon. By adopting IoT technologies, humans, devices, and systems can be intelligently connected and the campus can be converted to an i-campus that can effectively support e-learning.

Massive open online courses (MOOC) will also play a vital role in the future. The concept of MOOC through which course contents are shared online with each other is an Internet of Everything (IoE) enabled. The IoE refers to devices and consumer products connected to the Internet. Smart campus idea will allow students to complete their degree with some of the credit of MOOC courses. Hence e-learning system will be designed with an IoE-enabled education tool on a portal that connects users through video using Internet. "New technologies and IoT applications can be leveraged to further enhance e-learning platforms and improve completion, reduce costs, and improve learning outcomes for careers."

Future work will explore developing algorithms that support the mobility feature of e-learning. E-learning devices are mobile, but different networks have different settings and security parameters. As the number of learners increases, e-learning devices are increasing day by day. Therefore, designing an e-learning system that is equipped with very high security with a highly scalable capacity is a challenging task. Moreover, there are a variety of devices that can be used by the learner in an e-learning environment like personal computers, smartphones, tablets, and PDAs. Therefore, building a security plan to support all such devices is not an easy task. A blockchain network can be used for the secure transmission of data.

Index